D1383102

Liberalism and American Constitutional Law

Liberalism and American Constitutional Law

Rogers M. Smith

Harvard University Press
Cambridge, Massachusetts, and London, England

Copyright © 1985, 1990 by the President and Fellows of Harvard College
All rights reserved
Printed in the United States of America
10 9 8 7 6 5 4 3 2

Library of Congress Cataloging in Publication Data

Smith, Rogers M., 1953–
    Liberalism and American constitutional law.

    Includes index.
    1. United States—Constitutional law.   2.   Liberalism
—United States.   3.   Liberalism.   I.   Title.
KF4550.S55   1985   342.73′001   84-27879
ISBN 0-674-53015-2 (alk. paper) (cloth) 347.302001
ISBN 0-674-53016-0 (paper)

To Marian
in lasting friendship

· Preface to the 1990 Edition

Since *Liberalism and American Constitutional Law* appeared, the nation has acquired two new Supreme Court justices, a new chief justice, all conservatives, and a new President whose campaign countered his opponent's more liberal constitutional views. The "law and economics" school of jurisprudence, which advocates wealth maximization via law, has moved out of the academy onto the lower federal bench. The media have publicized controversies over the leftist Critical Legal Studies movement. Allan Bloom has decried current American political thought, including its legal theories, in his bestseller *The Closing of the American Mind* (New York: Simon & Schuster, 1988). One might conclude that liberalism is not faring too well in constitutional law. All this makes the chief arguments of my book even more pertinent today.

On the premise that ideas matter, I sketch here several deep patterns of evolution in American constitutional doctrines. Those patterns stem in part from weaknesses in the early liberal principles shared by the framers of the Constitution. Most important, American thinkers, including lawyers, courts, and scholars, have tried to shed the rationalistic natural law premises with which the nation began and to replace them with either consensual social values or commitments to fair, usually democratic, decision-making procedures, or both. Though it has precursors, such as nineteenth-century American romanticism, that effort began in earnest in the Progressive era. With the New Deal it came to prevail amongst the nation's political and intellectual elites, but not so much amongst the general public.

As Bloom bemoaned, these attempts to eschew reliance on natural standards have proven troubling. Modern liberals have found it hard to identify any persuasive, enduring sense of shared public principles. Instead, American governance has come to seem mere bargaining among selfish special interests seeking governmental largesse, or else incessant moralistic challenges to much of what the electorate cherishes. This climate helps explain the appeal of Ronald Reagan, who rhetorically reaffirmed certain traditional values. His chief justice's Court is similarly advancing a jurisprudence aimed at revivifying such traditional values — by bowing to certain state prerogatives, by permitting more governmental aid to religion, by weakening federal protection of racial minorities and women, and by restoring some old-time judicial solicitude for property rights. Most of these rulings have been defended as flowing from a "jurisprudence of original consent," though the property rulings also reflect "law and economics" defenses of less constrained markets.

These developments have gained impetus from the failure of modern democratic liberalism to provide uplifting alternatives to the old verities it has challenged. But the conservative responses strike me as stopgaps, not solutions, to that failing. I am agnostic on whether divine or natural moral imperatives exist; but I do not think any recent effort to establish them in order to vindicate a return to traditional values has successfully confronted the intellectual challenges the task poses.[1] By now most thoughtful observers also admit that a jurisprudence of original consent cannot be successfully executed on its own terms.[2] The "law and economics" school has produced much useful scholarship, but also much dubious legal history, narrow economics, and questionable normative guidance.[3]

Practical lawyers, suspicious of theorizing, often believe the country should simply muddle through its difficulties.[4] It can probably do so, but matters are not then likely to get better. Hence, like others, I think it wise to explore new directions in constitutional and political thought. Some advocate reviving a more strongly communitarian republicanism;[5] and if republicanism means deliberative popular self-governance, it is desirable on liberal grounds. Scholars who instead thought the Constitution's republicanism rested on values distinct from early liberalism have abandoned that claim; and insofar as republicanism *is* severed from liberal commitments, history suggests it often sanctions brutal tyrannies.[6] The Critical Legal Scholars find liberal constitutional traditions incoherent, yet their leading philosopher, Roberto M. Unger, defines freedom so one-sidedly, as "context-smashing," that he denigrates all enduring forms of life that comprise freedom for most people.[7]

In this book I lay out an alternative response: Despite its flaws, liberalism has elements that can form the core of a more sustaining public philosophy. The key is to recognize that liberalism at its best has been a vision of never-ending political *purpose.* Liberals have often sought to replace stifling political, economic, intellectual, and social institutions with ones better suited to protect and enhance everyone's cognitive and

material capacities for reflective self-governance, personally and collectively — that is, they have fought on many fronts to promote human
freedom. This quest can guide social criticism as we seek more generally
empowering arrangements. Yet it also supports protection of the institutions and ways of life that we judge to be the best now possible.

Able critics have read me as contending that this sense of political
purpose should be endorsed because liberalism is America's "dominant"
tradition.[8] That is not my argument. History does help us judge liberalism's strengths and weaknesses.[9] But my case rests on an account (in
Chapter 8) of what I take to be basic aspects of human consciousness
and the human condition. Those aspects suggest that a society dedicated to respecting and furthering human powers of reflective self-
determination is more likely to relieve fundamental human uneasiness,
foster more successful pursuits of happiness, support a firmer sense of
human moral dignity, and provide standards that can better moderate
conflicts than any other yet found.[10]

Without speculating on whether one can prove this is so, I simply
offer reasons for thinking it is. If they are persuasive, the American
constitutional order should be seen as establishing much democratic
self-governance, but self-governance that is compatible with personal
freedom, understood as deliberative self-direction. Despite its generality
and despite postmodernist doubts, that standard is meaningful, because
experience suggests our wealth of perspectives and shared circumstances
do enable us to reach corrigible but useful judgments on what measures
can advance such liberty. My account here can mislead, because I use
judicial protection of individual freedoms as my window on the problems
of American public philosophy. Hence I may seem to portray deliberative
self-governance largely as an internal, psychological matter, to be protected mostly by courts enforcing individual rights. Instead I mean to
urge not only protection but expansions of liberty, via achievement of
better social and political institutions that give more people more resources, abilities, and opportunities to lead lives of reflective freedom.
That work cannot be done chiefly by courts, which limit collective self-
governance in some ways even when they assist them in others; nor simply
by asserting legal rights, for rights are not "trumps" but tools, social
creations to be adopted only when they seem the best means to accomplish
liberal goals. Sometimes they are. But generally the unfinished task of
finding shared forms of life that enhance freedom for all must be done
democratically, by elected officials and by citizens.

This work reflects the influence of many people. The dedicated teachers
at James Madison College, Michigan State University, especially Richard
Zinman, first persuaded me it was worthwhile to reflect on political

principles at a time when I doubted that and much else. Harvey Mansfield, Jr., and Michael Walzer taught me much at Harvard University about the weaknesses of liberalism, and Professor Walzer gave helpful advice on the manuscript. My students at Harvard and Yale have been a chief source of energy and enthusiasm. My greatest debt is to Judith Shklar, who has been an inspiring model of liberal education and governance, as well as a source of continual and incalculable assistance.

Others who read the manuscript at some stage and offered highly appreciated comments include Bruce Ackerman, Peter Hall, Gary Handwerk, Sanford Levinson, Jerry Mashaw, Grant Mindle, Walter Murphy, Ian Shapiro, and Bernard Yack. Aida Donald and Virginia LaPlante of Harvard University Press helped make the final book more readable. Virginia Smith, who began life roughly when the book did, made everything else more enjoyable.

1. Rogers M. Smith, "The New Institutionalism and Normative Theory: Reply to Professor Barber," *Studies in American Political Development* 3 (1989): 74–87.

2. See H. Jefferson Powell, "The Original Understanding of Original Intent," *Harvard Law Review* 98 (1985): 885.

3. See Ian Shapiro, "Richard Posner's Praxis," *Ohio State Law Journal* 48 (1987): 999–1046; Rogers M. Smith, " 'Don't Look Back, Something Might Be Gaining On You,' " *American Bar Foundation Research Journal* 1987: 297–309.

4. See Laurence H. Tribe, *American Constitutional Law*, 2d ed. (New York: Foundation Press, 1988), pp. iii, 1–2.

5. See Michael Sandel, "The Procedural Republic and the Unencumbered Self," *Political Theory* 12 (1984): 81–96; William M. Sullivan, *Reconstructing Public Philosophy* (Berkeley: University of California Press, 1986).

6. See Rogers M. Smith, "The 'American Creed' and American Identity: The Limits of Liberal Citizenship in the United States," *Western Political Quarterly* 41 (June 1988): 225–251.

7. See Rogers M. Smith, "After Criticism," in *Judging the Constitution*, ed. M. McCann and G. L. Houseman (Boston: Scott Foresman, 1989), pp. 92–124.

8. See Mark V. Tushnet, "A Conservative Defense of Liberal Constitutional Law," *Harvard Law Review* 100 (1986): 423–434; Sotirios A. Barber, "Review," *Political Theory* (1987): 657–671.

9. Smith, "New Institutionalism," pp. 75, 80–81.

10. Other liberal writers in recent years have argued powerfully for a more purposeful liberalism. See Joseph Raz, *The Morality of Freedom* (Oxford: Clarendon Press, 1986); Thomas Spragens, "Reconstructing Liberal Theory," in *Liberals on Liberalism*, ed. Alfonso Damico (Totowa, N.J.: Rowman, 1986); William Galston, "Liberal Virtues," *American Political Science Review* 92 (1988): 1277–90.

· Contents

· Introduction

In his acclaimed 1955 study of the American liberal tradition, Louis Hartz wrote that "law has flourished on the corpse of philosophy in America, for the settlement of the ultimate moral question is the end of speculation about it." Hartz believed that an unreflective consensus on Lockean principles in American society, made possible by the absence of a class-ridden feudal past, explained why a vast range of American political issues could be dealt with as matters of settled law. That consensus also made profound philosophic reflection on politics unnecessary and un-likely in America. The point, according to Hartz, was not that Lockean principles were so clear and decisive that American lawyers could me-chanically deduce legal doctrines and decisions from them. He knew, as constitutional scholars would protest for some time to come, that Lock-ean liberalism was in many ways inconsistent and outdated, compelling lawyers of his era to eschew formal reliance on it in favor of "prudential" or "pragmatic" approaches to constitutional issues. Hartz maintained, however, that it was only because Americans still subconsciously clung to liberal values that this "pragmatism" could seem a suitable substitute for the philosophy of the past. "It is only when you take your ethics for granted that all problems emerge as problems of technique."[1]

Today, the relationship between law and philosophy in America looks quite different. Although legal arguments still pay little careful attention to political or moral philosophy—perhaps because of a continued belief that the ultimate moral issues are agreed upon, a conviction that at any rate philosophy provides no useful guidance, or a sense that the issues are just too complex for routine exploration—many academic lawyers, at least, are now much more inclined to explore philosophy than in the past. The immediate cause for this development seems to be the break-down of agreement on the New Deal's governmental objectives and, more broadly, a dissatisfaction with the pragmatism by which those objectives were defended. Those reasons should lead us to question Hartz's general historic portrait of American law as blissfully unconcerned with its static, unchanging philosophic premises. That portrait was, after all, written in the "end of ideology" period of considerable apparent consensus, when it was quite natural to see prevailing opinions as representing ideological unanimity. Hartz's view therefore might well have understated past lawyerly dissatisfactions with America's inherited liberal principles, just as it failed to anticipate our own.[2]

The first task of this study is to confirm that suspicion. It examines four topics in American constitutional law in order to demonstrate that, at least in regard to legal doctrines, America's original liberalism has proven a restless corpse. From the nation's inception, its body of basic constitutional principles has been agitated by painful difficulties, both philosophic and political, that have never been finally laid to rest. Efforts have repeatedly been made to heal these wounds in the nation's public philosophy by grafting on to constitutional law features taken from rival intellectual and political positions. Yet despite these many operations, the national corps of political principles remains more unsettled than ever. This is the lesson of the new spirit of philosophy displayed in much current legal discourse, for it arises out of what many are proclaiming to be the grave of traditional legal thought.[3] No doubt many traditional lawyers, confronted by this proliferation of unfamiliar, speculative analyses, would prefer the grave. But if Hartz was right about the conditions under which legalism flourishes, they are not likely to get their wish soon. Only if the new philosophizing gains some success will it once again be able largely to disappear from sight, while secretly animating a renewed rule of "settled" law. The second major task of this work is to consider what philosophical route is most likely to lead to such a renewed constitutional consensus.

Hartz's own text acknowledged that his contrasting stress on the unchanging, "absolute and irrational" moral unanimity of Americans was largely prompted by his fear, in the midst of the 1950s Cold War, that a militant "Americanism" would generate harsh, foolish, and ultimately self-destructive policies of intolerance at home and abroad. Viewed without the obscuring darkness of McCarthy's shadow, the landscape of American political thought now exhibits a less unbroken horizon. Writers in the 60s and 70s showed persuasively that Hartz's thesis neglected, for example, the non-Lockean republican and religious strains in early American thought. It also failed to recognize the full political radicalism of Populism or the major philosophic changes wrought by pragmatism.[4] Even so, Hartz's essential contention, that American politics and law have always been characterized by unusually extensive agreement on liberal values, has not been effectively dislodged. But it is clear that the story of American political ideas and their relation to law must now be revised to take into account various competing strains and the ways in which they have succeeded in modifying the prevailing liberal consensus.

The present study contributes to such a revision by considering in detail the question of how the liberal principles contained in American constitutional law have been altered over time, to meet both new circumstances and criticisms and their own continuing dilemmas. In Part One it describes the political principles of the more moderate Lockean Enlightenment liberals, and it analyzes the philosophic and substantive weaknesses of their views. In contrast to the common stress on the novel premises of Enlightenment political thought, the account here emphasizes how these views constituted a new understanding of political purposes. Although their priorities varied, proponents of the political vision of the moderate Enlightenment, including most of America's founding generation, accepted that government should be redirected away from prescribing religious, moral, or martial virtue to secular ends of peace, economic growth and prosperity, intellectual progress, and personal liberty.[5] The American Constitution represents perhaps the greatest success of the Enlightenment in turning political life toward these goals.

But this liberal vision was flawed from its inception. Their concern to oppose the moral hegemony of the medieval Christian world led many liberals to avoid any definite statement or defense of their own alternative ends, for they did not wish to appear to be offering simply an exchange of orthodoxies. The arguments they did provide were multiple and contradictory, designed to appeal to supporters of the old faith as well as adherents of the era's new rationalism and empiricism. Consequently, their basic justification for their new positions, whether consent or some form of higher law, was uncertain, and their proposed political directions were far from unambiguous. Even more significantly, the pursuits they favored, as well as the institutions they established to achieve those ends, proved over time deeply dissatisfying to many people, who to greater or lesser degrees turned to different values. Chapter 2 canvasses some of the major alternatives—communitarian, romantic, and egalitarian—that were embraced by those who came to oppose early liberalism.

In Part Two, the study analyzes four constitutional issues: the debate over positive and natural law interpretations of the criminal procedures required for due process of law, freedom of speech, voting apportionment, and the national government's constitutional responsibilities for economic welfare. In each area the law begins as a fairly clear articulation of early liberal aims, in keeping with Hartz's thesis. But the study goes on to trace how the difficulties of those aims have been played out in the course of America's constitutional development. This analysis reveals that, instead of preserving an essentially unaltered Lockeanism, the legal doctrines display several patterned and more or less extensive transformations in those original principles. The changes, wrought by legislatures, amending processes, and courts, are recognizable as efforts to meet criticisms engendered by the frequently disappointing experience of life in America's liberal society, efforts that mirror theoretical alternatives posed to early liberalism. The historic fluctuation between higher law constitutional theories and more positivistic, utilitarian views; the expanding legal emphasis on consent as the sole source of political legitimacy and hence on fuller democracy; and the recent judicial expression of a broader, more romantic conception of personal liberty and of a greater commitment to social equality—all are shown to be explicable as aspects of these transformations. These doctrinal innovations, however, amount to only a superficial patchwork of often contradictory solutions that have temporarily cloaked but never resolved the continuing dilemmas of the liberalism expressed in American law. As a result, constitutional doctrines in each area today represent accommodations among different versions of liberalism and different senses of basic political ends—accommodations that are often ambiguous, even incoherent, as well as substantively debatable.

After completing this revisionist portrait of the fate of the liberalism embodied in America's law, the study turns in Part Three to its other major task, the consideration of what all this suggests for the future directions American constitutional and political thought might pursue. The very real persistence of the American liberal consensus indicates that, even today, only a relatively narrow range of alternative understandings of American political principles is likely to prove potent in legal doctrines and public policies. The basic alternatives that seem currently available include the democratic relativism predominant since the 1930s, revived higher law traditions, and finally the neo-Kantian liberal egalitarianism prevalent in academia today. Each of these alternatives possesses attractions; yet when measured against the continuing difficulties of America's liberal principles and laws, all possess serious flaws. Fundamentally, all respond to liberalism's long-standing failure to define its conception of political purpose clearly by either proposing alternative ends or eschewing any sense of purpose entirely. As a result, they fail to capture the substantive commitments that, however implicit, seem the most enduring and compelling aspect of liberalism's impact on American constitutionalism.

In its final two chapters, the study therefore returns to the early liberalism of Locke in order to develop the underlying sense of purpose that was crucial to liberalism in its first phase. In doing so, the analysis underscores the great problems of philosophic and political persuasiveness that may have led Locke and later liberals to shun more unqualified advocacy of their substantive values. But those problems indicate instead how the essential goal of early liberalism should be reformulated in order to serve as the basis for a more credible contemporary liberal constitutionalism. The conception of political purpose thus defended is liberalism's dedication to promoting the capacities of all for reflective self-direction, or "rational liberty." Properly conceived, this standard can respond to the basic philosophic dilemmas of American liberalism more adequately than can an alternative commitment to democracy, to religious or moral virtue, or even to egalitarian justice per se. This neo-Lockean, rational liberty conception of political purpose also provides more practical guidance for contemporary American law on the four constitutional issues. It suggests that many of the most significant judicial decisions of the last two decades were appropriate, but it offers a fuller and more consistent theoretical foundation for them than have either the justices or commentators employing alternative constitutional perspectives. Furthermore, where a concern for rational liberty calls for different results, its conclusions appear not only to promise philosophic and legal consistency but to be intrinsically desirable as well.

The prime motivation for this study is a belief that American political values need to be more carefully identified and then rethought and restated if they are to be defensible today. It also arises from more particular concerns about how that task should be pursued. In brief, it seems to me that many of the analyses of liberalism made by political theorists are at best loosely grounded in empirical assessments of contemporary American political or legal thought and practice. Thus, while theorists often develop critiques of liberalism and propose solutions that have great theoretical power and elegance, it is usually far from clear whether their views articulate significant strains in actual governmental discourse or can hope to do so. Hence it seems preferable to begin an analysis of contemporary American liberalism with a fairly detailed assessment of the ideas expressed in an actual arena of political debate, such as constitutional law. When, on the other hand, one looks at constitutional discourse, on the bench and in the scholarship, it is obvious that the recent increased interest in philosophy has yet to produce any profound changes. For "practical" reasons, most conventional legal scholarship still pays little attention either to the fundamental dilemmas of America's inherited liberalism or to the alternative versions of it presupposed by the very steps an author may be proposing. The result is that the full complexities of the theoretical problems and different views of liberalism influencing the law are not adequately brought out.

This study therefore explores actual constitutional decisions by means of a framework constructed from historical presentations of early liberalism and its later opponents, in order to determine how far judicial decisions display liberalism's characteristic difficulties or any opposing values. The approach allows competing constitutional views to be described in terms of the political theories they presuppose, and it shows which versions of liberal or illiberal political thought are important strains in American constitutional discourse today. Thus, it sheds light on the deeper roots of existing governmental practices spawned by prevailing constitutional doctrines, while providing some indication of what changes are likely to be practically feasible. And although here our current circumstances are held to point to the rational liberty theory of American constitutionalism described in Part Three, the descriptions this approach provides should also be useful to those who would choose differently among our basic contemporary alternatives.

The study's dual effort—to clarify liberalism's theoretical precepts and difficulties and to identify the notions that are actually forces in current affairs—reflects certain assumptions about the relationship of political theories to political experience. It does not assume that constitutional arguments are representative of all American political thought. Such discourse forms only a small portion of the nation's debate over public issues, and a portion with its own special traditions, constituencies, and concerns. But while legal discourse is produced by distinctively socialized elites, it expresses significant strains in American political thought as a whole, if for no other reason than that judicial decision-making both reflects and structures broader political and economic activities. Similarly, judicial decisions, to say nothing of political decisions more broadly, plainly involve far more than conscious efforts to apply fully elaborated theories to immediate problems. A wealth of more or less conscious notions, of internal psychological factors and personal interests, and of external social, economic, and political forces influences all political conduct, including the judiciary's. However, the behavior of political actors, and of the institutions they construct and participate in, is influenced in part by the nature and adequacy of the ideas they possess, and the basic ideas of a given period and group often have a discernible structure, which may be articulated in revealing fashion by political writers of the day. The descriptive aspect of this book focuses on how such structures of ideas have been manifested in the decisions of the Supreme Court. In principle, the method could equally be used to analyze the evolving structure of the court system, or the institutional structures and policies of other parts of the regime, such as the Congress, the Presidency, or the federal system. But the very thing that makes constitutional discourse distinctive, its unusually self-conscious effort to connect decisions on immediate conflicts with the first principles of the political order, means that if the approach can be usefully applied anywhere, it should clearly be of value here.[6]

Yet with all the recent writing that can be placed under the heading of "law and philosophy," connecting constitutional issues with liberalism may still strike some readers as a familiar enterprise; so it is necessary to stress why the approach adopted here, though certainly not unprecedented, is distinctive. It obviously has considerable affinity with what has been termed "traditional" or "interpretivist" constitutional scholarship, which prior to the ascendancy of legal realism in law and behavioralism in political science, often discussed constitutional issues in terms of political philosophy and intellectual history. The works of Edward S. Corwin, Alpheus T. Mason, and Robert McCloskey are examples. But their emphasis tended to be more historical than philosophical: they did not fully develop the structural principles and problems of the varieties of liberalism, nor did they use such a framework systematically to describe and analyze distinct constitutional positions. More recently, the many legal scholars who have heeded Ronald Dworkin's call to turn to contemporary political and moral philosophy have generally sought to use philosophy only to provide solutions to current legal problems, not to diagnose their origins.[7] Here, in contrast, the different historical versions of liberal theory are laid out, and their appearance in constitutional arguments is charted.

A smaller, but significant, group of legal scholars, including Roberto M. Unger, Duncan Kennedy, Morton Horwitz, and Mark Tushnet, has undertaken such historical analysis, though they have been most concerned with the "private" law of the economy. Like this study, their work rejects any sharp division between legal and political or ideological discourse. They place much less stress, however, on the ways the current law represents an (often inconsistent) mix of competing political visions. Instead, the Critical Legal Scholars at times treat American law as a startlingly thorough elaboration of an internally contradictory but essentially monolithic liberalism.[8] The account here instead describes the unity that exists in law as areas of agreement among related but significantly different views.

More fundamentally, however, these scholars take as their starting points the more radical, postliberal conception of freedom discussed in Chapter 2. They evaluate liberal theory, law, and practice as responses to what at least some of them see as the "fundamental contradiction" of modern (if not human) existence—the impossibility of realizing our conflicting aspirations for both personal and communal freedom. Since I am skeptical about the understandings of freedom these postliberal views advance, and particularly about the relative merits of the ill-defined alternative institutions they imply, I have tried to begin instead with the early liberals' own sense of their objectives and the problems liberals have since experienced in defending and applying them. This analysis therefore describes liberalism's root problem as its failure to prove the appropriateness of its particular conceptions of liberty, without assuming that the failure arises because those conceptions distort some other ideal of "true freedom" or autonomy.[9] To the contrary, this review of America's constitutional evolution suggests that liberalism's basic goal may be formulated more persuasively today.

As a liberal, I hasten to add that all these other endeavors, as well as institutional and behavioral research into judicial processes, attitudes, and impacts, are unquestionably useful enterprises. But the approach here produces several valuable results that cannot otherwise easily be achieved. First, it shows specifically how the internal difficulties of liberal premises and purposes contribute to particular constitutional problems. It does not relegate the Constitution's liberalism to the background, nor does it simply catalogue liberalism's failings according to the index of another, hostile system. For example, conventional legal scholars often deal with the obvious connections between constitutional issues of political equality and liberal theory by merely reciting the adage that liberalism displays an unresolved tension between its conceptions of liberty and equality, making perfect majoritarianism controversial. Radical legal scholars argue instead that liberal conceptions do not generate "true" political freedom or equality. But the joint historical, philosophical, and legal analysis here shows why liberals lost their belief that their purposes could be rationally shown to be obligatory even in the face of contrary majoritarian sentiments. It also identifies more precisely the difficulties presented by pure majoritarianism, as well as the recently proposed limits on it, as alternative, postliberal theoretical guides for legal doctrines governing electoral institutions. This knowledge makes it possible to identify what needs to be done at several levels to achieve constitutional rules on these issues that will better satisfy prevailing substantive and philosophic concerns. And however hard meeting those concerns may prove to be, I think it ultimately wiser to address them than to evade them pragmatically or to start anew from some nonliberal notion of modern man's fundamental dilemma.

Admittedly, a focus on the predominant currents of existing thought means that, when considering future alternatives, the analysis gives much less attention to radical positions than to more mainstream views. But while some radical perspective, on the right or the left, may yet prove to be the wave of the future, such a view seems unlikely to wash away much of the status quo while flowing through the channels of constitutional argument. By their institutional nature, courts tend to follow broader political changes, not to initiate them.[10] And the approach here at least shows how the deeper problems of liberalism, which prompt turns to radicalism, are involved in constitutional conflicts.

Furthermore, categorizing constitutional doctrines in terms of their theoretical responses to early liberalism identifies patterns of ideological development that cut across traditional doctrinal lines. The major contemporary free speech positions, for instance, presuppose theories of the Constitution as concerned chiefly with promoting autonomous self-realization, or majoritarian democracy, or a more absolutist liberal egalitarianism. This makes it possible to decide more confidently whether doctrines in different areas, such as the new rights of privacy under due process and the Fourth Amendment, express similar constitutional philosophies, and to build up comprehensive evidence of the types of general constitutional theories that individual justices, courts, or eras have tended to apply.

These identifications have value in themselves. They show that the Burger Court, which has been difficult to categorize, typically interprets the Constitution in light of a political philosophy of conservative democratic relativism, in tune with much mid-century American thought and contrary to a more stringent egalitarianism.[11] But most important, empirical identification of the competing theories in current law through analysis of particular areas makes it possible to evaluate those theories in terms not only of their philosophic potency but also of their concrete results. The approach thus seems well designed to assist judgments on the broader directions that should be pursued in legal discourse today.

Many constitutional scholars may find the characterizations of the nature, strengths and failings of various constitutional positions most useful, while other readers may be more interested in the evaluation of current general theories and the defense offered for a particular version. But I hope that in either case, all parts of the analysis will be seen as interdependent—for our current political institutions and policy problems cannot be adequately described without understanding the difficulties of the principles embedded in them, while clarification or advocacy of political ideas remains arid unless it is linked to their articulation in current forms of political life. Only by striving for such a united view can we obtain a full picture of the nature and prospects of the nation's continuing constitutional enterprise.

I · *The Aims of Liberalism*

THE WRITINGS of John Locke, taken as a whole, remain the best examples of the Enlightenment liberalism that most heavily shaped the framing of the American Constitution. And the weaknesses of that liberalism are best described in the writings of its major historical philosophical critics, such as Hume, Rousseau, Burke, Emerson, and Marx. Together, these sources richly illuminate the liberalism, with all its failings, that has pervasively influenced America's constitutional evolution.

There was, of course, never any single, authoritative version of liberalism, and recent scholarship has shown that many sources besides the liberalism of Locke contributed to early American political ideas. Bernard Bailyn and Gordon S. Wood stress the colonists' devotion to the works of the opposition Whig radicals; more broadly, J. G. A. Pocock has emphasized the contributions of the whole Atlantic republican tradition; Henry May, Morton White, and Garry Wills have underlined the impact of the Scottish Enlightenment on American moral philosophy. Scholars generally have noted that colonial political writers referred less to Locke's *Second Treatise of Government* than to other English sources, such as Algernon Sidney, John Milton, Thomas Gordon, and John Trenchard, and to continental authorities, such as Montesquieu and the public law theorists Hugo Grotius, Samuel Pufendorf, Jean-Jacques Burlamaqui, and Emmerich de Vattel. American political thought was also shaped by deep-rooted and distinctive Protestant traditions.[1] It cannot therefore be reduced to any set of influences or sources. In many respects Americans—the Constitution's framers most of all—provided important new syntheses of all these views. And if Americans initially were not perfect Lockean liberals, they have become even less so since, at least in their constitutional law.

Although such diversity belies Louis Hartz's portrait of the American political imagination as completely dominated by Locke, these various currents share a framework of political values and concepts, distinguishable from those of most other times and places, that expresses the fundamental elements of "liberalism." Most of the patriot leaders and framers held what Henry May terms "the moderate Whig ideology" of "liberty" and drew on radical Whig writings, the Scottish philosophers, the continentals, and various strains of Protestantism for support. They were able to do so because, as Bailyn and Wood acknowledge, the "intense liberalism" of the radical Whigs rested on "common political and social assumptions" and was distinctive only in its "emphasis" on the omnipresent danger of "corruption"; the Scottish theorists were primarily concerned to short-circuit the dangerous moral and epistemological implications of Locke's work while generally endorsing his liberal political objectives; the public law treatises increasingly emphasized rationalist, liberal doctrines over medieval legacies; and much of the clergy came to believe that the "law of God" could best be advanced by accepting its identity with the liberals' "law of nature." As Herbert Storing concludes, not only the founding Federalists but even the Anti-Federalists, who were influenced by the civically oriented republican tradition, still were liberals in the "decisive sense" of seeing "the end of government as the security of individual liberty, not the promotion of virtue or the fostering of some organic common good."[2]

Liberalism's most distinctive feature is thus its insistence that government should be limited so as to free individuals to undertake private as well as public pursuits of happiness, even if this option erodes public spiritedness in practice. While this characteristic is often traced to an inherent methodological, psychological, or philosophical individualism in liberalism, for the early liberals it was at bottom a normative political commitment, an espousal of a society that would promote some public and personal goods and not others. As a political ideology at least, Enlightenment liberalism rested not so much on the vulnerable philosophic premises that liberals reshuffled freely in different contexts as on the basic ends that they shared, despite their important differences over relative priorities, immediate means, and ultimate justifications. Those ends were not always prominent on the surface of the liberals' writings, for it was often more persuasive to focus on particular features of their views that were attractive, rather than on their controversial ultimate aims. This was probably true even for liberal thinkers themselves. Yet only by keeping those aims in view can we explain their advocacy of particular measures.

To a surprising extent, early liberals conceived of popular governance, religious tolerance, the rule of law, and other forms of liberty only as means to their basic goals. They also did not equate liberalism with fair legal and constitutional procedures, or with pursuit of the maximum freedom imaginable, as many modern liberals do. Instead, liberals originally held that only a specific and limited conception of liberty deserved to be an end in itself. And they were attached to other specific ends, for which liberty was a means—essentially peace, prosperity through economic growth, and intellectual progress.

But though early American political thought displays a consensus on these liberal aspirations, other widely read theoreticians besides Locke clarify liberalism's typical aims and difficulties, including Francis Hutcheson, David Hume, Thomas Paine, Montesquieu, and Sir William Blackstone. Locke is crucial, however, because the political philosophy of liberalism is historically linked with a whole range of distinctive developments that are best encompassed in his writings, such as parliamentary movements, new constitutional limits on government, economic mercantilism and nascent capitalism, the social rise of the bourgeoisie, and the Enlightenment's rationalist and empiricist attacks on medieval scholasticism. Both Locke's *Second Treatise on Government* and his first *Letter Concerning Toleration* are classics of political liberalism. The *Essay Concerning Human Understanding* marks Locke as a founder of modern philosophy, the "Father of the Enlightenment." *Some Thoughts Concerning Education* holds a similar place in modern pedagogy. He also wrote and worked actively on behalf of religious liberty, parliamentary rule, and commercial expansion.

It is true that Locke has little to say about specific constitutional mechanisms and institutions, the area of political discourse that might seem most pertinent. Although Locke's contribution to the evolution of the notion of separation of powers was not insignificant, the authorities on whom the colonists relied most often for such devices were the liberal heirs of the classical and Florentine tradition of republican discourse, such as James Harrington, Montesquieu, and Hume, and also the continental publicists, especially Vattel and Burlamaqui. Pocock suggests, moreover, that the republican tradition understood political liberty in terms of active citizenship, and feared private economic pursuits as corrupting—in stark contrast to seventeenth century Lockean liberalism, which equally valued liberty but associated it less with political participation than with just such unimpeded private activities. Pocock has not, however, explored in detail the relationship of the republican tradition to the liberalism of American political thought. While their common concerns for political freedom may have made it easy for these traditions to combine into "liberal republicanism," most accounts agree with Storing's view that, by the time of the Constitution at least, the liberal strain predominated. Pocock's own discussion suggests that latter-day republicans, from Cato to Montesquieu and Hume, increasingly accepted that in the modern civilized world commerce must be embraced and made to serve as a basis for disciplining desires and achieving a kind of private virtue compatible with a peaceful, free public life. Bailyn similarly indicates that even the radical Whig concept of political liberty did not stress participation but rather the concern of the governed to be allowed to exercise their natural rights as they wished, free from the oppressions of a corrupt tyrannical government. Hence the liberal tradition still seems most expressive of the ends of the framers.[3]

Locke, in turn, remains the most exemplary liberal theorist precisely because—as the founding generation recognized—he reveals most powerfully the fundamental ends that early liberalism proposed for political life and that America's constitutionalists promoted. It is common to disparage Locke's importance by citing Benjamin Rush's remark that "Mr. Locke is an oracle as to the principles, Harrington and Montesquieu are the oracles as to the forms of government," and Jefferson's admonition that "Locke's little book on Government is perfect as far as it goes. Descending from theory to practice, there is no better book than the Federalist." Yet these statements precisely capture Locke's intent. He defines the principles liberals pursue; and Americans have always evaluated constitutional doctrines and devices largely in terms of their serviceability for liberal ends. As a result, disputes over the relative ordering and the desirability of those values, rather than debates about the mechanisms for achieving them, have most influenced particular constitutional doctrines and probably constitutional law as a whole. Furthermore, while the *Second Treatise* may not always have seemed such a crucial "oracle," the aims of early liberalism pervade all Locke's works, which had a massive collective impact. Hence, early American liberalism is best understood if we correct the conventional concentration on Lock's *Two Treatises* at the expense of the *Essay Concerning Human Understanding, Letters on Toleration, Some Thoughts Concerning Education,* and other works; but nothing can be gained by abandoning Locke entirely.[4]

The fact that early liberalism must be understood in terms of its substantive Lockean purposes does not mean that attention to its philosophic foundations is unnecessary. On the contrary, Locke's own strong attachments to his political ends led him to ignore incompatibilities and difficulties in the arguments with which he advocated them. He left unresolved the question of whether his doctrines were based on divine will, reasoning on nature, or human desires alone and, correspondingly, whether consent or some higher law was the ultimate foundation for political legitimacy. He thereby failed to justify definitively his preferred conceptions of human fulfillment, which others have found excessively individualistic, narrowly rationalistic, and crassly materialistic. Locke was also unduly optimistic about how far economic liberties would contribute to prosperity for all, and so he gave little attention to the inequalities they involved. Philosophic critics of Locke have offered alternative visions of political life that dramatize what such liberalism does not attain. Rousseau and Burke showed how liberal thought neglected the claims of community and civic virtue; Emerson and Thoreau explained how it stifled full emotional and spiritual self-realization; Marx assaulted the social and economic inequalities it entailed. Not only the weaknesses of early liberalism but also these alternative senses of political purpose have shaped the transformations wrought in the liberalism of American constitutional law.

1 · Principles of Early Liberalism

Four goals were central to Locke's original vision of liberalism: civil peace, material prosperity through economic growth, scientific progress, and rational liberty. Intentional governmental obstruction of any or all of these goals was regarded as tyranny. Liberals differed significantly on how these goals were to be achieved, particularly on how much positive governmental activity was needed to secure them. And their quarrels over means usually reflected differences over which goals should be given priority. At the time of the Constitution's adoption, for example, American liberals were most divided on whether democratic political liberties should be risked for the sake of material prosperity. But in the initial phase of opposition to surviving medieval values and institutions, these conflicts among liberals were not pressing.[1] All agreed that their shared purposes required that government be explicitly limited in its ends and that disputes be settled in a regular and widely accepted manner. Hence they carried with them an emphasis on liberty in many forms, on constitutionalism, and on the even-handed rule of law. This stress on both liberty and legalism separated early liberals from the views of their chief philosophic predecessor, Thomas Hobbes, who shared most of their values but did not see liberty or the rule of law as means to their attainment.

Above all, early liberals like Locke were concerned to provide for lasting civil peace and physical security. Every aspect of liberalism finds part of its motivation in this goal. This concern is not surprising in view of the constant political turmoil that raged during most of the seventeenth century. As Locke says of himself, "I no sooner perceived myself in the world, but I found myself in a storm which has lasted almost hitherto." Like Hobbes before him, Locke's response is to make peace the first object of his natural law. Specifically, Locke contends that the law of nature "willeth the Peace and *Preservation of all Mankind*"—the last phrase expressing his quarrel with Hobbes's more purely egoistic natural law. Also like Hobbes, Locke is particularly concerned to achieve peace by ending the intense disputes over religious issues that had long characterized European political life, from quarrels between church and state to struggles between religious sects. His first *Letter Concerning Toleration* was motivated largely by "all the bustles and wars that have been in the Christian world upon account of religion," and in the *Essay Concerning Human Understanding* he blames religious "Enthusiasm" for many of the "untractable zealots in different and opposite parties."[2] Both works express a deep belief that a new and more stable solution to the problem of religious disputes was vital to the attainment of civil peace. This concern, widespread in the seventeenth century, was a constant feature of liberal thought. It was shared by most of America's founders, particularly James Madison and Thomas Jefferson, who exhibited an ongoing preoccupation with the problem of religious strife.

Because Locke regards the task as central, he tries several ways to keep religious and moral beliefs from becoming politically divisive. He attempts to make religious beliefs a strictly private affair, removed from the legitimate concern of others, by asserting a right to freedom of conscience that allows all to hold what moral principles they will. Contending that "the care of souls does not belong to the magistrate," Locke argues that "liberty of conscience is every man's natural right," so that "nobody ought to be compelled in matters of religion either by law or force." The state, Locke insists, can legitimately be concerned only with those "outward things . . . belonging to this life." Not even "the consent of the people" can entitle the magistrate "to compel anyone to his religion." In support of this position, Locke reasons that force is ineffective in controlling men's minds and that no man should or even can give to another the power to judge the means to his ultimate good, salvation.[3]

But Locke also explicitly grounds his case for toleration on the cause of civil peace, and here he directly attacks Hobbes's belief that religious tumult can best be avoided by empowering the sovereign to impose opinions. Locke claims that "the common disposition of all mankind . . . when they groan under any heavy burden" is to "endeavour naturally to shake off the yoke that galls their necks." When religious toleration is denied, "oppression raises ferments and makes men struggle to cast off an uneasy and tyrannical yoke." Hence, only the establishment of toleration "would take away all ground of complaints and tumults upon account of conscience; and these causes of discontents and animosities being once removed, there would remain nothing in [religious] assemblies that were not more peaceable and less apt to produce disturbance of state than in any other meetings whatsoever."[4]

Locke's call for general tolerance and freedom of conscience reflects in part a strategic dispute with Hobbesian absolutism over the means to defuse religious issues. This is shown by the fact that Locke's toleration is not complete. Although the realms of church and state are as "absolutely separate and distinct" as "heaven and earth," this does not mean civil magistrates have nothing to do with moral and religious issues. On the contrary, magistrates are entitled to regulate "moral actions" when those actions affect the "outward things" that are their concern, and they can even curb "opinions" if those opinions are "contrary to human society, or to those moral rules which are necessary to the preservation of civil society." When religious and moral opinions and acts conflict with the attainment of civil concerns, particularly when they lay claim to "any peculiar privilege or power" and thereby threaten civil peace, it is legitimate for the civil authorities to restrain them.[5]

Locke's confident defense of this civil power reveals a less obvious means by which he tries to prevent divisive religious quarrels. Although through his lifetime Locke's writings increasingly stress tolerance over enforcement of any orthodoxy, he tries repeatedly to combat such divisions by establishing a moral system that can claim to be genuinely authoritative, settling definitively the moral questions that impinge on political life. The mature Locke, to be sure, presents himself above all as a student of the limits to human knowledge. The *Essay* elaborates how human understanding "comes exceeding short of the vast Extent of Things." This skepticism is itself related to Locke's concern for civil peace, as shown by his views on overconfident religious enthusiasm and the advisability of toleration. Reason must be the judge of revelation and religious opinions, or else men will "let loose their fancies and natural superstition." Such superstition "most powerfully produces the greatest mischief" in human affairs.[6]

But Locke is not immune to the promise of the Enlightenment's new modes of reasoning to provide surer guides for human conduct, and he is willing to claim morally authoritative status for what he thinks can be rationally ascertained. It requires, after all, considerable faith in one's system of reason to make it the measure of revelation. Locke insists in the *Essay* "that *Morality is capable of Demonstration,* as well as Mathematicks," if only a similar method is used. As the comparison with mathematics suggests, Locke actually shows only how to clarify the consequences of moral ideas, not how to show them to be true. Nonetheless, he insists that great "improvements" would be possible if moral beliefs were open to rational examination, perhaps again chiefly to combat those who "cram their Tenets down all Men's Throats." His position suggests a degree of moral certainty not unlike that of his opponents.[7]

These instances of Locke's moral authoritativeness in the generally skeptical *Essay* help explain the puzzle of his seemingly inconsistent claims elsewhere for certainty in his moral principles. Even in the *Letter Concerning Toleration,* he gives liberty of conscience the high status of a "natural right" which cannot be contravened by popular consent, while assuming the primacy of other civil concerns when they are threatened by exercises of conscience. Locke's more noted claim of certainty for his moral principles comes in the natural law doctrine of the *Second Treatise on Government.* Like Hobbes in *Leviathan* but more emphatically, Locke bases the obligatory character of natural law on its divine sanction: we must preserve ourselves and others because we are all the "Workmanship" of our divine "Maker." Yet Locke acknowledges that his doctrine of the rights and duties of men in the state of nature is not readily apparent in Christian teachings and may seem "very strange." He emphasizes, therefore, that "Reason" teaches his law of nature even more plainly than positive laws, although, as with the rational demonstration of morals, it is beside Locke's "present purpose" to give "the particulars."[8] His substantive emphasis on tolerance and free inquiry thus should not obscure the diverse ways in which he tries to give these principles an authoritative status that can resolve disruptive religious and moral issues definitively.

Acceptance of these freedoms to believe and to question is characteristic not only of Locke but of liberalism in general. That is why it is important to see how greatly these freedoms are inspired and limited in Locke by his concern for civil peace. The limits confirm that Locke argues for these freedoms as much from certainty about the aims of civil life as from doubt: whenever the freedoms conflict with, instead of contributing to, attainment of the concerns that Locke assigns to civil society, they are curtailed. His effort to make religious values purely private matters while establishing goals for public life that can override the claims of private conscience characterizes early liberalism more than its later forms.

Peace and personal safety are high among such authoritative Lockean public values, but other values are central as well. Locke's judgments are justified by the new modes of reasoning he and his "enlightened" contemporaries regarded with such confidence. Most notably, Locke advances an empiricist, sensationalist account of the operations of the human mind that identifies good and evil with what gives pleasure or pain. To be sure, he again emphasizes that because God designed "our constitution and frame," we can be certain that our natural inclinations direct us to ends truly good for us. He emphasizes as well that he does not mean "only bodily Pain and Pleasure," and that the greatest delights are intellectual pleasures. But however immaterial and divinely fostered our leading pleasures, "Pleasure operates not so strongly on us, as Pain."

Hence our wills are determined not by our greatest good but by our "most pressing *uneasiness*." We are usually first inclined to care for our physical discomforts, which announce themselves most forcibly, a circumstance that Locke sees as providential.[9] Given this psychology, Locke naturally regards the acquisition of material goods as another basic public concern, for material well-being is thus a central human value. This end advanced by Locke has long been identified as vital to most liberals.

Hobbes similarly contends that civil society ought to aim not just at "bare Preservation, but also all other Contentments of life" which men acquire "by lawful Industry." But he stresses the necessity of this goal for "the common Peace and Security." Mony, Hobbes says, is "the Bloud" that nourishes the commonwealth by its circulation, and if the commonwealth is to be healthy enough "to sustain . . . the common Peace," it "can endure no Diet" in the things that sustain it. While Locke focuses even more sharply on material prosperity as a chief concern of civil society, he believes that this end is not well served by allowing the civil authority absolute power to direct its pursuit, and he does not subordinate it to the goal of civil peace. He insists that civil societies are established for, and can "only" properly aim at, not just "peace," the life and health of the body, and "strength against foreign invasions," but also "outward prosperity," "riches," "the possession of outward things, such as money, lands, houses, furniture."[10]

Locke argues accordingly that "the Preservation of . . . Property," broadly conceived, is the *"chief end"* of the commonwealth. At the same time, he limits the power of civil magistrates to regulate property as they wish, even though this limitation may endanger civil peace. Whereas for Hobbes "the Introduction of *Propriety* is an effect of Common-wealth," so that sovereigns always retain "Dominion" over the property of their citizens, for Locke property is authorized by "the Law of Nature" in the state of nature, "out of the bounds of Societie." The acquisition of property out of the world God gave men "in common" is dictated, Locke says, by both "God and Reason," which again provide a dual source of authoritativeness for Locke's principles. God intends man to "subdue the Earth" in order to "improve it for the benefit of Life," and "the penury of his Condition" also makes it reasonable for man to do this. Property serves this end because, when the "industrious and Rational" appropriate and cultivate parts of nature, they make their possessions up to a thousand times more valuable and productive, thereby creating abundance out of what was previously virtual "wast." Locke assumes both that such productive appropriation enables each to live on a smaller share of nature's resources, leaving more for others, and that eventually, through exchange, this greater prosperity serves to improve the lot of all.[11]

If the right to property is authorized by God and reason essentially as a means to economic growth and general prosperity, it might seem legitimate in civil society to direct property centrally in order to assure this end. Locke in fact contends that, while property rights originated in nature, once men contract to create a civil society, they agree to define such rights by social arrangement. Yet while civil authorities may regulate property, they do not have *"absolute power"* over it. Men had a natural right to their property before they entered civil society, and since they entered society to make their property more secure, they can never be understood to have given the magistrate carte blanche to "dispose of it as he thinks good." Property can be regulated only on behalf of the subsistence and developmental interests that led to its establishment, and consent is always required for its taking by public authorities.[12]

Locke, who merely alludes to the tendency of violations of the natural right of conscience to inspire insurrection, goes further in relation to property rights, arguing that "whenever the *Legislators endeavour*" to *"destroy the Property of the People,"* the People have "a Right" to rebel and establish a new government.[13] In fact, since God commanded us to acquire property, we have a sacred duty to protect our property rights against an oppressive government. Locke makes the protection of the property that leads to prosperity even more essential for his government than does Hobbes, and so he limits civil authority over property, with full recognition that this limit can serve to justify civil war. Peace at the cost of liberty of property is not acceptable.

But again, this difference is partly strategic. Locke's statement that "the increase of lands and the right imploying of them is the great art of government" not only gives the expansion of material prosperity a more pivotal place than does Hobbes but also suggests that his defense of liberty of property is not due solely to its origins beyond civil society. Locke believes that this "great art of government" calls not for extensive regulation but for liberty, because liberty is usually a more effective way to promote economic growth and reach the goal of material prosperity, just as in the case of religious beliefs and the goal of civil peace. This prosperity, in turn, serves to guarantee adequate power, in part to preserve peace, as in Hobbes, but also to acquire further wealth. As Locke suggests, "that Prince who shall be so wise and godlike as by established laws of liberty to secure protection and encouragement to the honest industry of Mankind against the oppression of power and narrownesse of Party will quickly be too hard for his neighbours."[14]

In short, the "Industrious and Rational" "improve" the earth most when they are given liberty to acquire property and security in their acquisition, and so a government that limits its regulation of property is likely to grow both rich and strong. Once more, while Locke emphasizes the goal of material prosperity more than Hobbes, his insistence on liberty as part of this goal represents to some extent only a different estimation of how their common goals of peace and prosperity can best be secured. This effort to turn the focus of political life away from religious concerns to matters of material well-being again characterizes early liberalism. And as indicated by the long and close historical connection between "economic" and "political" liberalism, Locke's view on the means to this goal were widely successful.

For all their concern with peace, personal security, and material well-being, neither Locke nor Hobbes were economic entrepreneurs. They were, above all, innovative philosophers, and so each was vitally interested in propagating the new understandings of science and reason that are evident in their arguments for their political and moral principles. Liberalism, as the chief political theory fostered by the philosophic movements of the Enlightenment, was not only justified by but also dedicated to the advancement of such intellectual doctrines and enterprises.

This commitment is most evident in Hobbes's *Leviathan,* where he denounces the "Vain Philosophy" of the medieval scholastics and insists that the method of the modern "Geometrician" and "the Astronomer" should be applied to politics and morals. Hobbes understands "the end" of his science to be not metaphysical knowledge of "Abstract Essences" but rather the ability "to produce, as far as matter, and humane force permit, such Effects, as humane life requireth." The new scientific method is concerned to acquire a knowledge of the properties of things that can allow us to manipulate them for our purposes. In fact, the "Encrease of *Science*" is above all "the *way*" by which we reach the ultimate "*end*" for men, "the Benefit of man-kind."[15]

But for Hobbes the attainment of this end again depends upon the commonwealth and the civil peace it supplies: "*Leasure* is the mother of *Philosophy;* and *Commonwealth,* the mother of *Peace,* and *Leasure.*" Consequently, civil peace remains the fundamental end, and despite the benefits that true philosophy can engender, the civil sovereign must be empowered to control philosophy, too, if civil peace is to be assured. The sovereign can legitimately punish those "that against the Laws teach even true Philosophy."[16]

Despite Locke's emphasis on the limits of human reason and his political differences with Hobbes, he gladly inherited Hobbes's enthusiasm for the new Enlightenment philosophic modes—while again denying that absolutism is the condition for their increase and differing in his sense of what they entail. Locke indicates that man's understanding "is the most elevated Faculty of the Soul," which "is employed with a greater, and more constant Delight than any of the other," although he recognizes that many men favor different pleasures. For Locke, rational inquiry is "a sort of Hawking and Hunting, wherein the very pursuit makes a great part of the Pleasure . . . he who . . . sets his own Thoughts on work, to find and follow Truth, will (whatever he lights on) not miss the Hunter's Satisfaction . . . and he will have reason to think his time not ill spent, even when he cannot much boast of any great Acquisition."[17]

Since Locke places intellectual pursuits at the top of human pleasures, true science is not for him, as it is for Hobbes, merely that which enables us to master beneficial "Effects." Rational inquiry can be an end in itself, and Locke even puts as the end of "natural philosophy" "bare speculative truth." Again, however, the difference is less than it seems, for Locke, too, is skeptical about whether we can ever gain much "general Knowledge" about the "real *Essences*" of natural substances. He even suspects that "natural Philosophy is not capable of being made a Science." For Locke, unlike Hobbes, science's greatest promise comes not as a system of general, demonstrated truths but rather as a compilation of "Experiments" and empirical "Observations" which can give us only probable, not certain knowledge. Like Hobbes, however, Locke holds this knowledge to be valuable because it serves to "increase our stock of Conveniences for this Life."[18]

While accepting the fact that pure natural science aims at abstract "speculative" truths, then, Locke emphasizes that experimental inquiry is "a surer way to profitable Knowledge" and is preferable to abstract systems. Correspondingly, he defines the end of "practical philosophy" or "Ethicks" as "the Attainment of Things good and useful," and he is confident that men's faculties are "fitted . . . to lead us into a full and clear discovery of our Duty, and great Concernment."[19] We are best suited to practical matters, even in speculative subjects and in our speculative abilities.

In the cases of both practical and natural philosophy, Locke insists on the importance of "questioning" and "examination" of any "general Maxims" advanced, this being the only way to avoid "Mistake and Error." There must be freedom of intellectual inquiry if there is to be intellectual progress: "truth certainly would do well enough if she were once left to shift for herself . . . she will be but the weaker for any borrowed force." Again, liberty is a more effective means than absolutism to attain the various goods science can offer. Locke's concern to promote peace and freedom through toleration instead of the quarrels and repression bred by zealotry is also evident in his arguments for new approaches to science. He warns against overestimating our abilities in natural science because we may be led to take "unintelligible Notions for scientific Dem-

onstrations," and like Hobbes, he openly criticizes the Aristotelian reasoning of "the Schools" for allowing this to occur. Principles taken up
without examination, particularly moral principles, are *"dangerous,"* and
recurrent abuses of clerical authority prove that the dangers go beyond
the realm of the intellect to politics. Because of the fitness of our faculties
for moral reasoning, contrary to the scholastic claims of exclusive intellectual and moral authority, morality is *"the proper Science, and Business
of Mankind in general."* Thus, all principles can properly be widely
questioned, again assuring that the moral doctrines of the advocates of
tolerance and free inquiry will have practical ascendancy.[20]

Even in the *Second Treatise,* where Locke says little directly about
scientific and intellectual progress, the promotion of man's rational capacities is at the heart of his views on political goals. He makes clear
that "liberty," which is part of the "property" that governments are to
secure, is not liberty *"for every Man to do what he Lists"* but rather
liberty under "the Law of Reason." It is only man's "capacity of knowing
that Law" which makes him "capable of being a Free Man." Our liberty
is "grounded on" our "having Reason." Locke's faith in the clarity of
this "Law of Reason" parallels his faith in the rational demonstrability
of morality, by and for all. Hence, his promotion of liberty, understood
as a capacity to direct ourselves in accordance with the law of reason,
includes freedom for the sort of rational moral inquiry he calls the *"Business of Mankind in general."* Indeed, this rational inquiry seems integral
to the instruction in the law of reason which men require to have true
liberty.[21]

Locke is therefore an even greater advocate of the benefits of modern
philosophy than Hobbes, though in regard to natural philosophy Locke
has more confidence in the attainment of those benefits by means of
empirical inquiry than by rationalist deductive demonstrations. Locke
gives reasoning itself a high status as a pleasure and argues that both
science and civil society will flourish if men are left to pursue this pleasure
in liberty. In holding intellectual inquiry to be both intrinsically satisfying
and practically useful, Locke was undoubtedly inspired by the "Master-
Builders" of the growing "Commonwealth of Learning," especially by
his friend, "the incomparable Mr. Newton."[22] Most early liberals shared
the enthusiasm of Locke and Hobbes for some combination of the modern
rationalist and empiricist philosophic approaches, most agreed that they
formed the most promising road to mankind's well-being, and most felt
that they would prosper best under conditions of intellectual freedom.

Locke's understanding of liberty leads to the final goal of early liberalism, often considered the essence of liberalism, its intent to prevent
tyranny and provide for personal and political freedom. Although Locke's

emphasis on liberty separates him from Hobbes, many liberties are justified for Locke only as means to the other goals he shares with Hobbes,
not as ends in themselves. Liberty is a better means to avoid violent
religious conflict and preserve peace, to provide for material prosperity,
and to advance science. Locke is even willing to curtail liberty of conscience, which overlaps the freedom to engage in rational moral inquiry,
when it is exercised in ways that threaten his other goals, particularly
civil peace. Nor does Locke make liberty of property absolute. Property
can be regulated, if not taken without consent, to ensure that it serves
to bring about prosperity. Does Locke, then, mean by "tyranny" only
the failure of governments to preserve the types and degrees of liberty
needed for the pursuit of these other ends? Does he attach any importance
to either personal liberty or to political self-governance as ends in themselves?

For Locke, any government that is not confined to pursuing the ends
he designates as proper is indeed a tyranny. But personal liberty has an
independent place among these ends, and some measure of popular self-
government is deemed necessary to preserve it. Official actions must
always possess, at the least, tacit consent, and the people always reserve
the ultimate right of revolution.

Locke discusses liberty chiefly in terms of the private freedoms upon
which governments might intrude, holding that such liberty is as essential
to man as is life itself. In fact, men have no right to let governments
eradicate it: "This Freedom from Absolute, Arbitrary Power is so necessary to, and closely joyned with a Man's Preservation, that he cannot
part with it, but by what forfeits his Preservation and Life together. For
a Man, not having the Power of his own Life, *cannot,* by Compact, or
his own Consent, enslave himself to any one." Men cannot give up their
liberty because it is essential to the life God gave them and commanded
them to preserve, and they cannot be sure of that life's preservation if it
is in the absolute, arbitrary power of another. Those who think men's
lives can be protected only at the cost of liberty, by setting up an absolute
ruler, must ask themselves, "What Security, what *Fence* is . . . in such a
State, *against the Violence and Oppression of this Absolute Ruler?* The
very Question can scarce be born . . . This is to think that Men are so
foolish that they take care to avoid what Mischiefs may be done them
by *Pole-Cats,* or *Foxes,* but are content, nay think it Safety, to be devoured
by *Lions.*"[23]

Locke's concern for personal liberty produces a ban only on absolute
governments, not an insistence on any particular form of limited government, democratic or otherwise. But he indicates that systems con-
taining a measure of popular self-governance are preferable for avoiding

tyranny. Since he also legitimates ultimate popular overthrow of oppressive governments, some minimal degree of political liberty, understood as participation in ruling, seems advisable.[24]

Locke's contention that it is illegitimate for men to enslave themselves, personally or politically, might still be taken as an essentially prudential argument that personal security is better guaranteed under a limited government than an absolute one. His visible effort to make liberty more than that, to insist that it is so "closely joyned" with human life that it can never be surrendered, might only be taken as a way of placing beyond challenge what he regards as the correct means to personal safety. Similarly, his argument that liberty of conscience is a "natural right" might be regarded as a prudential contention of liberty's value for civil peace. The "common disposition of all mankind" is to be "uneasy" in the vulnerable and insecure situation that loss of liberty represents, to the point where men are "willing to ease themselves" even at the cost of personal danger and civil strife. This view is consistent with the claim of Locke's psychology that "uneasiness" determines the will and that "life itself, and all its Enjoyments, is a burden cannot be borne under the lasting and unremoved pressure of such an *uneasiness*."[25] It is characteristic of human nature to feel so anxious and miserable when one's life is absolutely subject to another that risking that life seems preferable to perpetuating it in servitude. Clearly, if most men have such a nature, absolutism will not bring peace but constant unrest.

Yet a feeling of liberty, even apart from its connections with personal preservation and civil peace, is in itself a basic component of human happiness. To be content, men must believe they have at least some power over themselves and their fates. Locke in fact defines liberty as a "power," holding that "so far as a Man has power to think, or not to think, to move, or not to move, according to the preference or direction of his own mind, so far is a Man *Free*."[26]

Locke argues that this power is twofold: it involves a power to withstand all forms of external coercion but also an internal power over ourselves to ensure that our minds really do direct our actions. Since true liberty does not involve doing as one "lists" but rather means obeying the law of reason, people can and should direct their preferences by rational deliberation. The *Essay* describes how the mind can suspend its desires and, through consideration of the various goods it might pursue in its situation, raise its level of desire for the greatest good available to the point where that desire determines the will. Only when we obey this rational judgment, only when it has power over us, do we truly have liberty. For Locke, such rational determination is "the source of all liberty . . . This is so far from being a restraint or diminution of *Freedom*, that it is the very improvement and benefit of it: 'tis not an abridgement, 'tis the end and use of our *Liberty;* and the further we are removed from such a determination, the nearer we are to Misery and Slavery."[27]

Locke suggests that this capacity for rational self-determination is the distinctive feature of human nature and also the essential element of moral responsibility. Understanding "sets Man above the rest of sensible Beings, and gives him all the Advantage and Dominion which he has over them." It also gives us dominion over ourselves, which Locke terms "the great privilege of finite intellectual Beings." Rational self-determination is our "privilege," because it enables us to overcome our bodily instincts and do what is best for us. Just as he insists that the law of reason is morally obligatory, so Locke contends that when we have determined our will according to our rational judgment, "we have done our duty." Accordingly, anyone who says that "he cannot govern his Passions" short of extreme duress is sinfully mistaken. Locke's later work, *The Conduct of the Understanding,* is devoted to teaching men how they can increase the power over themselves that is the source of true liberty.[28]

In sum, for Locke liberty is essential to human happiness as both an end and a means. It is essential in itself, because without it we feel so uneasy that life becomes miserable, and it is a means, since with it we progress toward all our goods. It is also a defining characteristic of our humanity, an exercise of the capacity that sets us above animals, and the part of our human nature that enables us to act in accordance with the determinations of our reason. This compatibility between what gives us pleasure and what is necessary for us to do God's will is predictable. Our pleasures are given us by God to direct us in the right way, though not all pleasures are divinely authorized at all times, and preservation of our liberty is not simply felicitous but also morally obligatory. When we abandon our political liberty by placing ourselves in the hands of an absolute ruler, or when we abandon our personal liberty by accepting physical slavery, by habitually yielding to untempered impulses, or by putting our opinions in the keeping of a dogmatic zealot, we not only leave ourselves vulnerable, and hence miserable. We also give up our ability to act as our own reason tells us we should for the greatest good, and we have no right to do any of these things. Although it is possible to limit liberties so that men's other proper temporal ends can be attained, to leave men absolutely enslaved and powerless is not merely politically imprudent and dangerous but morally evil. Locke's praise for Lord Shaftesbury applies equally to himself: he had "a mind that abhorred slavery, not because he could not be the master, but because he could not suffer such an indignity to human nature."[29]

Just as Locke expresses the goals of early liberalism in giving primacy to peace and security, prosperity, and scientific progress, his esteem for mankind's special capacity for rational liberty captures its developing moral vision. Although he makes this point largely to argue only that men should not be enslaved, it implies a limited measure of political self-governance, and other liberals stressed this consequence more strongly. But Locke's position falls far short of any Rousseauean call for a fully participatory, democratic polity.[30] It is also distinct from the more demanding readings of Kant's contention that rational nature makes each man equally a moral end in himself. And it is positively opposed to those later defenses of liberty that do not identify freedom with reason.

Indeed, in the first edition of the *Essay,* Locke himself presented a more straightforwardly mechanistic utilitarian psychology in which the will was determined directly by the greatest good in view, without deliberation. Only when it was argued to him that this denied free will did he arrive at the account of rational self-direction just described. However much he wanted to demystify human values and ground them firmly in rational modern philosophy, he could not accept that the understanding which gave such insights and provided people with their worldly dominion nonetheless left them powerless over themselves.[31] Locke's refusal to accept any position belittling the significance of human strivings for reflective self-direction suggests that of all his ends, this aim is for him morally fundamental. But he places an arguably equal stress on liberty's value as a means to his other ends, and he allows it to be curtailed, if not sacrificed, for their attainment. While he provides the seed for the notion of freedom as the sole human value that was to characterize much subsequent liberal thought, Locke himself cultivates a greater variety of ends.

Locke's emphasis on man's capacities for rational self-control suggests that liberalism would abolish government if men could only be brought to conduct themselves properly. This implication becomes a visible dream for Thomas Paine and an open call to rational anarchy for William Godwin.[32] But Locke himself, though not entirely free of this dream, insists that appropriate governmental measures are prerequisites for his other, inevitably social goods of peace, prosperity, and intellectual progress. And though he thinks these measures usually involve granting citizens considerable liberty, he dismisses conduct that runs contrary to his objectives as being not free but licentious and properly subject to constraint. Furthermore, Locke and other early liberals call for limited government under the rule of law, and hence for constitutionalism, out of concern not just for extensive personal liberty but for the multiplicity of goals they regard as rational and proper for both political societies and individuals to pursue. Thus, the important place of constitutionalism and legalism in early liberal thought is qualified by its overriding concern to secure fundamental liberal ends effectively.

Although medieval thought, too, can be termed "constitutionalist," liberal constitutionalism originates in its normative rejection of the basis of medieval political principles. Liberals deny the medieval political tradition's claim that men are subject to a higher law that sanctions life in political societies under divinely and naturally authorized rulers. That is the point of the "state of nature" doctrines in both Hobbes and Locke who, despite their differences, see all men as "naturally" in "a *State of perfect Freedom,*" "without Subordination or Subjection" to anyone. This view fosters a new sense of human equality and liberty, but it does not mean that all social purposes must forever be subordinated to individual freedom, with governments confined to an umpire role aimed solely at maximizing freedom for all. Liberals maintained only that, as men naturally have no governors, governments must be constructed by men for certain specific ends, with the scope of government defined by what is necessary for those ends. Locke, like other early liberals, dramatizes this conception by arguing that governments are formed as a result of an *"original Compact"* or social contract among individuals. Later liberals usually dispense with this unhistorical notion but retain the characteristic liberal view of government, though not of society, as a human artifice, limited by and to its proper purposes.[33] They also insist with Locke that no reasonable governmental end supports an absolute civil sovereign. Rather, reason prescribes substantial restraints upon what governments both prudentially should and legitimately can do. These distinctive substantive restraints, whether explicitly embodied in law or not, form the heart of the liberal understanding of constitutionalism.

Although Locke's limits on government include other goals besides preserving liberty, he argues that the parties to the original social contracts could not have legitimately authorized governments to go beyond his aims because this would have given up their God-given liberties arbitrarily, without reason, as no man has a right to do.[34] This assertion continues an appeal to divine authority that seems jarring today, but in the context of its time its most striking feature is its normative content, its disavowal of the state's traditional concern with human moral fulfillment. For some of the more rationalist or materialistic of the early liberals, this stance may have represented a conviction that only mundane intellectual and physical pleasures were real human goods, as their opponents claimed. But it certainly represented a belief that liberal constitutional governments must pursue more restricted aims than medieval ones, so as to attain civil peace and well-being.

For Locke, these restrictions are so essential that whenever "the Power" of any government "is applied to other ends," it "becomes Tyranny" and can be legitimately opposed. *"Tyranny"* is the *"the exercise of Power beyond Right,"* and there can be no right to act against or beyond government's proper goals. This position again accepts some risk to one of government's purposes, civil peace, out of the belief that Locke's other ends are also necessary for life to be worthwhile. Whenever governments "impoverish, harass, or subdue" citizens by "Arbitrary and Irregular Commands," they can "be resisted." The fundamental place of these limits in Locke's constitutionalism is confirmed by the fact that they apply to all "Forms of Government," not just to "Monarchies." A government that pursues unauthorized ends is tyrannical whether it is a government of "one or many," kingship or democracy.[35] Government is limited, however, only in its ends, not its powers. Locke insists as firmly as Hobbes and the *Federalist* that governments must have power adequate to their ends.

Besides rejecting medieval political notions and supporting a new understanding of limited, constitutional government, the liberal concept of a formative social contract supports the last major argument used to legitimate liberal ends, their origin in the consent of the citizenry. Even though men cannot rationally consent to governments of unlimited or improper aims, they have no obligation to any particular government unless they consent to give up the appropriate extent of their natural liberty and obey it. Since for Locke there is a real possibility that men may be even worse off under a specific government than in the state of nature, each man must personally consent to submit to the government of a civil society, although a man's consent can be assumed to have been given tacitly under certain circumstances. Once a man has done so, his government can muster powerful arguments to demonstrate his obligation to it, as does Hobbes in support of his own social contract.[36] The government can claim to be acting by the individual's authority, hence according to his will, and thus to be doing no injury when it constrains him, so long as the constraint is in pursuit of an established end. The liberal view of the state as originating in consent thereby provides a strong support for the legitimacy of liberal governments and their goals, which can compensate for liberalism's abdication of any direct divine authorization. This aura of legitimacy can significantly aid in stilling discontent and advancing the civil peace that forms a profound liberal hope.

The notion of an original contract, along with the other justifications for liberal ends, contributes to another means by which liberalism attempts to achieve all its ends, especially the peaceable settlement of disputes. Liberal regimes promise to decide a wide range of controversies fairly through decisions based on established, known, impartially applied rules and procedures—to provide, in short, the rule of law. The very notion of government as originating in a "contract" already gives liberal political theory a legalistic cast. When the original contract is understood to set standards for what government may do, and when it requires officials to apply those standards in nonarbitrary, regular, and equitable ways, then even the governors can be said to be governed by the laws. When the purposes and provisions of the original contract are held to embody principles of natural justice sanctioned by both untrained and methodical human reasoning as well as by God, then the laws men consent to in forming that contract can claim to be binding in every sense. All the points of liberal theory combine to make credible the notion that liberal regimes genuinely provide the "rule of law."

Locke frequently points up the promise of his position to provide such rule. He remarks that governments established by contract solely to secure the rights, liberties, and civil interests of all are in large part "Umpires" who decide disputes "by settled standing Rules, indifferent, and the same to all Parties." Furthermore, because each person has consented to be governed by the laws of civil society, "every single person became subject, equally with other the meanest Man, to those Laws." Hence, *"No Man in Civil Society can be exempted from the Laws of it,"* and "the Ends of Political Society and Government" only authorize fair and impartial legal rule. The Commonwealth "is bound to govern by establish'd *standing Laws,* promulgated and known to the People, and not by Extemporary Decrees; by *indifferent* and upright Judges, who are to decide Controversies by those Laws; And to imploy the force of the Community at home, *only in the Execution of such Laws* ... And all this to be directed to no other *end,* but the *Peace, Safety, and publick good* of the People."[37]

Locke lays particular stress on the importance of applying laws equally, of having "one Rule for Rich and Poor, for the Favourite at Court, and the Country Man at Plough." However, this emphasis arises not from any ambition to abolish social and economic inequalities. It stems again from Locke's primary goals. He favors legal equality both to ensure that his basic rights are secured for all and to promote civil peace.[38] Men are only likely to be satisfied by the rule of law—indeed they are only likely to regard it as the rule of law—when they believe that the legal system serves to protect everyone's liberties without granting anyone unfair advantages.

Locke's concern for legalistic rule leads him to say that *"where-ever Law ends Tyranny begins,"* though he adds the qualifier, "if the Law be transgressed to another's harm." He thus goes far toward making legal rule the definition of nontyrannical government, but he does not quite go all the way. As in the case of the prerogative power, Locke does not equate the requirement that government be legitimate with the requirement that it be regular, nonarbitrary, impartial—in short, truly "lawful." While he relies on the appeal of such proceduralistic legalism to buttress the legitimacy of the liberal state and indeed makes the rule of law a central liberal tenet, government is still ultimately legitimated only by its ends, however lawful it may be. Since these ends include avoiding governmental intrusion on personal pursuits as much as possible, Locke suggests that some laws may be transgressed if no harm is done. Similarly, if the proper ends of government truly require it, the executive has a legitimate prerogative to act "without" the authorization of the law "and sometimes even against it."[39]

Early liberals often had to fight to restrain the arbitrary actions of monarchs, the privileges of aristocrats, and the biases of the courts, and to promote the supremacy of the Parliament that was their most constant means to governmental power. Hence, they often stressed equal justice under the rule of law. But Locke's example demonstrates that at least some early liberals were unwilling to subordinate their other goals to this emphasis on legalistic rule, even though they saw it as essential to the attainment of those goals under most circumstances. Thus, liberal constitutionalists were liberals first, choosing governmental forms and procedures and stressing adherence to them on the basis of characteristically liberal ends. Locke's arguments for constitutional government, the social contract, and the rule of law itself all aim at avoiding governmental oppression and achieving peace, and his definitions of what constitutes oppression reflect his further goals of material prosperity and scientific progress, as well as his sense of the dignity of liberty.

While Locke has limited use as a guide to specific constitutional institutions, his legalistic aspects, reflected in the liberal emphasis on constitutionalism and combined with the colonial tradition of written charters, helped lead Americans to the project of a written constitution. Lockean goals are, moreover, pervasive in American constitutional thought. They dominate early judicial doctrines on constitutional issues and persist as major influences to the present day. Madison's dedication to peace and stability, Jefferson's to scientific progress, Hamilton's to material prosperity, and even Adams's concern to avoid corruption and governmental oppression all display elements of Locke's vision.[40] Each of these founders, like all individual liberals, pursued a unique and complex combination of these and other goals. They also quarreled over the aims to be emphasized, and eventually a constitutional order stressing stability and commercial growth came to prevail over Jefferson's focus on less restrained democracy and his elitist intellectual concerns. But underneath their differences all these statesmen shared an abiding commitment to certain typically liberal goals.

American constitutionalism, too, is thus an effort not only to subject governmental activities to fixed legal limits but also to provide authoritative liberal standards and directions for many basic issues of political purpose. The American Constitution strives to limit government and to provide the rule of law, but that rule of law has a specific content. This close connection between liberal ends and American constitutionalism means that efforts to change the goals of the regime inevitably cause the whole structure of America's liberal constitutionalism to shake—a fact of continuing concern to those who share the deep liberal fear of civil strife.

2 · Problems and Criticisms

American values and institutions still display the imprint of early liberal purposes. But changes have occurred, not least in constitutional law, which reveal in part the weaknesses of early liberal thought. Four basic difficulties have especially influenced constitutional issues: 1. early liberalism's ambiguous philosophic justification; 2. the consequent puzzle of the source of political obligation in liberal theory; 3. liberalism's much-decried individualism; and 4. the equally controversial ends that liberalism sets for political life.

The problem of liberalism's true philosophic foundation arises because of the multiple arguments that early liberals used to render their ends authoritative. Locke, like Hobbes before him, advances principles that he claims are at once laws of nature, divinely sanctioned, and based on methodical reason. But the rational premises and methods employed by Locke do not seem to establish his natural law and natural rights, or even to be compatible with them. Locke gives a naturalistic psychological explanation for the origins of human values that leads him to equate good with pleasure and evil with pain. In taking a similar stance, Hobbes concluded that, since men have different pleasures, human values are relative, "For these words of Good, Evil, and Contemptible are ever used with relation to the person that useth them: There being nothing simply and absolutely so; nor any common Rule of Good and Evill, to be taken from the nature of the objects themselves." Yet Hobbes argues for the legitimacy and primacy, not of all human desires equally, but of the desire of men for peaceful self-preservation. Locke, on the contrary, suggests that some pains and pleasures are universal, "to be found in all Men," implanted in us by God to point the way to our well-being. Perhaps, then, they provide more constant standards of good and evil. However, Locke also acknowledges the diversity of the objects men may desire—

"the relish of the mind is as various as that of the body, and like that too may be altered"—and Locke's empiricist reasoning poses even greater problems for his natural law than does Hobbes's. Locke, after all, gives natural right status not only to the preservation of life but also, within limits, to personal liberty and property. For him, a man can never be understood to have consented to the destruction of any of these rights. Locke's natural law also requires men to defend these rights not only for themselves but for all men: it "teaches Mankind . . . that . . . no one ought to harm another in his Life, Health, Liberty, or Possessions," and "everyone has a right to punish the transgressors" of this law.[1] This view gives to an even wider range of values a special obligatory status above mere personal choice, and these values are not so obviously prerequisites for pleasure as is Hobbes's simple right to life.

Locke recognizes that "degenerate men" in their "corruption, and viciousness" do not always wish to act according to his natural law. Reason nevertheless makes it "plain and intelligible" to men, if they reflect honestly, that their most profound desires are best achieved by such obedience. Yet Locke's insistence that his are the only proper ends of government makes them the standard for our "true" pleasures, and not the reverse. Intelligent men simply do not always conclude on the basis of their desires that liberty of mind, body, and original property are inviolable natural rights. Locke asserts that morality can be a matter of rational demonstration, and that reason can reveal the law of nature, but he never enters into "the particulars" of these tasks. In fact, he never attempts to vindicate the claim that his natural law, while not innate, follows so plainly from human preferences and moral ideas as to be "writ in the hearts of all mankind"—undoubtedly because he has little hope of doing so.[2] But if our desires define our goods, and neither our preferences themselves nor our reasoning upon them dictates an absolute status for Locke's ends, then they are not obligatory even on his own grounds. The agreement between his natural law and sensationalist arguments is shattered. And the threat posed to all natural law positions by equating human values with human pleasures is compounded in Locke's case by his claims that a relatively wide scope of duties to others ought to be recognized.

Locke would doubtless reply that his natural law and rights are divinely sanctioned and so are obligatory. But this cannot solve his problem, for he also holds that our pleasures and pains are divinely established for our own good, even as he recognizes that we must deliberate on which of our desires should be gratified. It is left unclear how, on the basis of our preferences, we are to decide which of our God-given pleasures are divinely preferred. We are again confronted with Locke's failure to derive his ends from our desires. If our un-Lockean impulses are also divinely inspired, they refute our obligation to Locke's ends.

The traditional guides to divine intentions are not human sensations but revelatory texts. At times Locke claims to rely on these authorities to prove the divinity of his principles, but in fact he never derives his position directly from scriptures. Instead, he makes reason the measure of revelation, holding that it alone can determine if a revelation is genuine, and that nothing contrary to reason can be revelation.[3] Since reliance on reason makes it possible to judge what in scripture is divine law, revelation cannot truly be the basis for Locke's rational standards.

In the *Second Treatise*, promisingly enough, Locke grounds his divine natural law on neither preferences nor revelation but on reasoning about man's natural condition. This approach is not an aberration, for Locke consistently maintains that divine law can be manifested to reason "by the light of Nature" as well as by revelation. But again his portrait of man's state of nature varies sharply from the traditional Christian understanding of the concept, and it also does not derive simply from our natural preferences, for its law overrides many of those preferences.[4] Since this doctrine is "very strange" and is not immediately drawn from either revelation or experience, there is no certainty that its law is actually divine law as revealed by the "light of nature." Locke knew his reasoning opposed traditional religious scholarship, and his doctrines were attacked by orthodox religious leaders. It is thus far from clear whether his natural law is any more compatible with the tenets of the religion whose God he claims as his sanction than it is with his psychological empiricism. While Locke's justifications for his principles are consistently aimed at the same ends, they do so inconsistently with each other.

The vulnerabilities of early liberal theory caused by these varied justifications hardly went unnoticed. The seminal thinker of the Scottish Enlightenment, Francis Hutcheson, responds to the hedonistic implications of Locke's empiricism by arguing that moral values are derived not from reason but rather from feelings experienced by a special faculty, the "moral sense," which delights in virtuous and benevolent acts.[5] David Hume accepts a version of this position, albeit without Hutcheson's faith that the virtues naturally pleasurable to our moral sense are divinely authorized. Hume, however, uses the positivist and empiricist elements in Locke and Hobbes to discredit their rationalist doctrines of divinely sanctioned natural laws and natural rights.

Agreeing with his predecessors that a "science of man" devoted to the operations of the human mind and human behavior is "the only solid foundation for the other sciences," Hume calls for "the application of experimental philosophy to moral subjects." He accepts that "moral good and evil" are known by "pains or pleasures," while insisting, with Hutcheson, that moral sensations are "of a particular kind," experienced in a complex way he described. But since morality originates not in reason but in "feeling," there can be no "eternal rational measures of right and wrong" or "external laws, *obligatory* on every mind." Correspondingly, the *"state of nature"* which supposedly reveals such laws is "a mere philosophical fiction," and the reasoning that led to the notion of an original contract is "fallacious and sophistical." Certain moral preferences are intrinsic to human nature, but justice and property are instead the products of human "artifice." Hume understands why earlier philosophers tried to supply "a stronger foundation for our political duties" by identifying a *"natural* obligation" to them, but he terms this search "fruitless" and confusing. It is better to recognize that men *"invented"* the laws of nature out of a sense of their "advantages" for society, since those advantages in themselves justify government. Hume dispenses with arguments of divine sanction for any particular political order by contending that whatever actually happens must have been intended by Providence, so that everyone can always claim to act "by a divine commission."[6]

Going further than Hume, Jeremy Bentham dismisses "natural rights" as "nonsense on stilts" and insists that those who speak of "the Law of Nature" simply express their personal "sentiments" on what is right and what is wrong. Bentham's philosophy of utilitarianism formalizes the trend developing from the empiricist elements in early liberalism by designating pain and pleasure to be "the standard of right and wrong," the "two sovereign masters" of mankind. Both Hume and Bentham, rejecting natural law, accept the Hobbesian position that all true laws are positive commands created by human authorities who have acquired the power to make laws. Bentham's associate and fellow utilitarian John Austin developed this position most influentially, providing the seminal work for the jurisprudential school of legal positivism. Ironically, the self-same "new modes of reasoning" that gave Hobbes and Locke such confidence in their natural laws also gave rise to the philosophy that most vociferously opposed any such notions, at least any detached from the principle of utility.[7]

The tensions in liberal thought that led to this opposition did not, however, destroy political liberalism. Both Hutcheson and the later Scottish moralist Thomas Reid continued to defend doctrines of natural rights and liberties that are not substantially different from Locke's.[8] Reid achieved enormous influence in nineteenth century America by appealing from the subtle speculations of the philosophers not to a special moral sense but to our common sense belief in the reliability of both our physical senses and our moral judgments. And while most of the later British empiricists and utilitarians criticized early liberalism for its reliance on notions of natural law, natural rights, and an original contract, they too still advocated essentially liberal goals.

Hume, who did more than anyone to discredit those elements of Lockean political theory, claimed he was undertaking to reach essentially the same conclusions regarding political ends and political obligation "on more reasonable principles." He argues that political societies are established for "protection and security," "peace and order," and the "advantages" they make possible, particularly the "advantages" of "commerce" and "the sciences," which flourish best in political liberty. "Zealots," especially "priests," are "enemies to liberty." In fact, all the aims of early liberalism find expression in Hume's thought, even though he is reluctant to disturb the existing social order too greatly in their pursuit. He contends that his critique of fallacious and dogmatic natural law doctrines places the pursuit of liberal purposes on firmer ground, freed from dubious and controversial reliance on eternal laws of reason and divine sanctions.[9]

Bentham's utilitarianism pursues similar goals, since material well-being is the basic condition for the greatest happiness of the greatest number, "the only legitimate and universal end of government." This end is to be achieved by pursuing the "particular ends" of "security, subsistence, abundance, and equality"—the latter understood as "practicable" not "absolute" economic equality, pursued because "through the medium" of the other ends it contributes to happiness. The liberal concerns with peace, personal security, and material prosperity are evident here. By and large, Bentham believes that their attainment requires liberty; laws should be primarily concerned to secure legal and political rights, leaving the attainment of happiness to individual prudence. Bentham, like Locke and Hume, contends that liberty is particularly required in the case of religion, or else the result will be contention and persecution. But he believes natural law doctrines similarly serve "as a cloke, and pretence, and aliment to despotism," another form of irrational dogma which can be exploited to justify oppression. Natural rights also impose limits on governments which might rule out measures to maximize utility, "prohibiting the making of the most necessary laws."[10] Although the attempt to limit governments and prevent bad laws is laudable, inviolable natural rights are too rigid and unadaptable to do the job properly. While there are real differences in the politics of Locke, Hutcheson, Reid, Hume, and Bentham, especially over how far to disturb the status quo in order to achieve a greater measure of liberty or happiness, the similarities indicate that utilitarianism's critique of early liberalism comes from "within" liberalism. That critique argues above all that natural law and natural rights hamper more than they aid the attainment of peace, prosperity, liberty, and intellectual progress. Men are more likely to feel obliged to government when they recognize rationally that it serves to maximize their happiness than when they are indoctrinated with the "nonsense" of higher law.

The problems posed by the multiple justifications for early liberalism lead in turn to its second dilemma, its ambiguity as to the ultimate source of political obligation. That ambiguity is already evident in Hobbes, who says of the obligation to civil obedience: "there being no Obligation on any man, which ariseth not from some Act of his own . . . And because such arguments, must either be drawn from the expresse words . . . or from the Intention of him that submitteth himselfe to his Power (which Intention is to be understood by the End for which he is so submitteth;) The Obligation . . . of the Subject, is to be derived, either from those Words . . . or else from the End of the Institution of Sovereignty; namely, the Peace of the Subjects within themselves, and their Defence against a common Enemy." The problem is whether the fundamental source of obligation is our act of consent or the end for which we give that consent. The end for which we consent might require things that we do not think we are consenting to, and conversely, we might want to authorize acts that are unnecessary or opposed to that end. In the passage just cited, Hobbes appears to treat obligation stemming from consent as fundamental. There can be "no Obligation" except that arising from our own acts, and the end for which we submit obliges us because it is our "intention," even if not expressly stated. This suggests the end obliges because we implicitly consent to it. Yet the ambiguity remains, because we interpret a person's "Intention" according to the end for which we hold he consented, and our notion of that end need not be defined or even limited by the "expresse words" of his consenting statement. Hobbes writes that a person "cannot be understood" to give up his right to self-defense, no matter what "words, or other signes" he may use indicating his consent to precisely that.[11]

It is obvious why Hobbes wants to display consent as the fundamental source of obligation. Although the nature of the ends and means appropriate to political life are controversial, acceptance of Hobbes's psychological claim that each man is the best judge of what is good for him makes it plausible that "nothing done to a man, by his own consent can be Injury." This view allows Hobbes to assert of the commonwealth constituted by consent that, "because every Subject is by this Institution Author of all the Actions, and Judgments of the Soveraigne Instituted;

it followes, that whatsoever he doth, it can be no injury to any of his Subjects; nor ought he to be by any of them accused of Injustice."[12] Thus, obligation based on consent is the most effective way to legitimate the actions of the sovereign and obligate the citizenry to obey.

Nonetheless, consent cannot really be so fundamental for Hobbes. He is unwilling to accept that people might not pursue his end of self-preservation, no matter what they say. Thus, no one can be understood to give up his life voluntarily for his country, and this is a problem for Hobbes, as some people have to be willing to do so if his broader end of civil peace is to be attained. Here Hobbes is willing to use the end to construe the intention and obligation of subjects, even though their express words cannot so oblige them: "No man is bound by the words themselves, either to kill himselfe, or any other man; And consequently, that the Obligation a man may sometimes have, upon the Command of the Sovereign to execute any dangerous . . . Office, dependeth not on the Words of our Submission: but on the Intention: which is to be understood by the End thereof. When therefore our refusall to obey, frustrates the End for which the Soveraignty was ordained; then there is no Liberty to refuse; otherwise there is."[13]

Hobbes again tries to suggest that obligation is a form of implied consent, saying we are obliged by the intention of the original contract. Yet when we are obliged regardless of the words we originally expressed or our explicit refusal now, the end is clearly what Hobbes regards as obligatory. It both limits what we can be understood to consent to and obliges us to perform acts to which we do not expressly consent. Even so, Hobbes never explicitly says we are obliged by the legitimacy of his ends whether we consent to them or not. He presents the obligatory nature of the end as arising from a different sort of consent, preserving the ambiguity as to the ultimate source of political obligation.

This ambiguity runs equally deep in Locke. He seems to make consent even more essential to political obligation than does Hobbes. Hobbes maintains that all members of an assembly which decides to declare a sovereign are obligated to that sovereign, even the minority who vote against the action, but Locke requires "the consent of every individual" to make them all one community. Hobbes feels that all who enter such an assembly have "tacitely covenanted " to obey its majority decision, but Locke demands an actual "yes" vote on membership in a new political society before a man is bound by its majority, as he is in the actual establishment of the society's form of government. Correspondingly, Locke stresses that nothing is able to put a man "into subjection to any Earthly Power, but only his own Consent."[14] Consent appears unequivocally to be the sole source of obligation.

Yet according to Locke, anyone who continues to live under an existing government, enjoying its benefits, has tacitly consented to be "as far forth obliged to Obedience to . . . that Government . . . as any under it," even though he can only become a member of its political society by "express Promise and Compact." While express consent is required for permanent citizenship, tacit consent is enough to bring on the full force of political obligation—a position not far from Hobbes's. And again, Locke goes further than Hobbes in setting limits on what people can be understood as having consented to. Men cannot authorize government to do more than protect their lives, liberties, and estates because "no Body can transfer to another more power than he has in himself; and no Body has an absolute Arbitrary Power over himself, or over any other, to destroy his own life, or take away the Life or Property of another."[15] The range of consent is limited by natural law and by those natural rights that Locke makes the standards for political life. These limits mean that rebellion is legitimate when a government goes beyond the aims to which the people can consent, and such a government is illegitimate even if people purport to consent to it. Locke sees all forms of government as liable to "Tyranny," even those that act by popular will. His consent requirements, moreover, do not include demands to obtain popular consent continuously or even regularly, since any form of government may be established so long as it is limited to the authorized ends.

If, in turn, authorized ends are the objects of a government, Locke regards that government as legitimate, even when the people have not consented to the means by which the ends are sought. Locke's executive can act against popularly established laws if it is necessary to attain the aims of the commonwealth; and the people should not rebel even if the government commits "Great mistakes" in pursuit of its ends, so long as the ends are proper.[16] Again there remains substantial ambiguity concerning the true source of political obligation. While Locke lays greater stress than Hobbes on consent as the sole basis of obligation, he is not much more concerned than Hobbes to secure it practically. Both are willing to assume "tacit" consent if their ends are met and to consider apparent consent invalid if it opposes them. Perhaps this amounts to employing an illusion of consent to provide legitimacy to their regimes and to support a rigid adherence to their ends, even when this rigidity produces severe and unresponsive government. Both Locke and Hobbes appear genuinely to believe, however, that their ends are all that people can rationally authorize. This might explain their willingness to construe a wide range of behavior as just such consent.

This same position on obligation is visible in the Declaration of Independence. It asserts that governments derive "their just powers from the consent of the governed," but it also says that governments "are instituted among men" to secure certain "inalienable rights," and that "whenever any form of government becomes destructive of these ends," it can and should be altered or abolished. For most of the Declaration's signers, democracies were included among the forms that can become destructive of proper ends, however much they might elicit consent.

This ambiguous understanding of the sources of obligation is mirrored in early liberal theories of representation. Contrary to many recent treatments, representation is not solely a device for transmitting popular opinion, so that decisions can claim to be grounded in consent. That view makes democratic representation presumptively valid.[17] But because early liberals treat political obligation as arising at least as much from a government's ends as from its consensual basis, their design of all types of governmental institutions reflects their concern to ensure that liberal ends are pursued—and these may call for less egalitarian systems of representation. Although Locke, in keeping with his focus on principles instead of institutions, does not dwell on representation, he is affected by both these sorts of considerations.

Locke describes the formation of government as a two-stage process: everyone must consent to membership in a political society, though conveniently, the consent of latecomers can be tacit. Then a majority can adopt whatever form of government it believes most likely to achieve the proper ends, given its circumstances. Democracy, oligarchy, hereditary monarchy, elective monarchy, or almost any government may be chosen, so long as it is not absolute. Locke does not explain which forms are desirable under various circumstances, but the test for the forms seems to be not what will maximize consent but rather what will maintain the proper ends.[18]

Locke's arguments that legislative and executive functions must be separate, that property must not be taken without some form of consent, and that a popular assembly is preferable for this purpose are explicable in terms of his ends. A separation of powers and a popular assembly can help to avoid absolutism and keep government confined to its proper concerns, especially where, as in Locke's situation, a popular parliament means added influence for the commercial bourgeoisie, who were opponents of feudal restraints and advocates of economic expansion. Locke does not, at any rate, insist on a purely consensual system of majoritarian democracy. If there is to be an assembly, the executive should revise its electoral districts periodically to ensure "fair and *equal*" representation, since "People, Riches, Trade, Power, change their Stations," a statement that reflects a concern to keep the channels of consent accessible on a just basis. But Locke's notion of a fair and equal representation does not focus on population alone: he points to the absurdity of a deserted district receiving as many representatives as a whole county not only "numerous in People" but also "powerful in riches." To Locke, both elements call for representation. Hence, when he says that "no part of the People however incorporated" can have "a right to be distinctly represented" except "in proportion to the assistance which it affords to the publick," he probably does not mean this "assistance" to be measured only in terms of numbers of inhabitants. Most early liberals treat material property as a natural measure of the public "assistance" that a citizen or district can provide, particularly since property qualifications help ensure respect for the property rights thought to benefit all. While Locke believes that governments should be grounded on consent, he also believes that the "forms" of government, including representation, should be designed so as to direct the governors toward their proper ends.[19]

Today representation is often treated only as a vehicle for consent, perhaps because liberals, influenced by the various difficulties now under discussion, have come to stress even more emphatically than Locke that consent is the sole basis of legitimacy and obligation. The criticisms made by the utilitarians against early liberal natural law doctrines lent weight to the view that values are derived only from human preferences; other criticisms of early liberal substantive values similarly made consent the only respectable defense for liberal governments. The trend toward greater democracy in America and other Western nations over the past two centuries has certainly been fueled in part by this discrediting of the other legitimating doctrines that limited the significance of consent in Locke and early liberalism.[20]

While contemporary liberal theory thus conceives of representation largely in terms of its function of expressing popular preferences and not of achieving set ends, this does not mean that the ambiguity of liberal thought in regard to the true source of obligation is a problem of the past. Most liberals still regard some choices as beyond the legitimate authority of even a fully democratic decision-making process, and so they continue to require rationales for limits on permissible popular choices, as well as institutions that can uphold the limits credibly and effectively. These circumstances shape much of the continuing debate over judicial review in constitutional law. They also indicate more broadly that the problems of liberalism's true philosophic foundation and its ultimate source of political obligation remain ongoing burdens for contemporary liberal thought.

Liberalism continues to be criticized for a third problem evident in early liberal theory, its excessive individualism. The accusation that liberal theory is too individualistic has meant a variety of things, but I will focus on two of its basic forms. Liberalism is often held to regard people as naturally and essentially independent individuals, without an intrinsic group identity. It is also held to regard human satisfaction or fulfillment as fundamentally individual—perhaps not as inaccessibly subjective but as essentially unshared and personal, not collective. Often, these two elements are linked, and liberalism is said to be wrong not only in seeing people as fundamentally isolated individuals but also in failing to recognize that true human happiness comes only in man's common life.

Several aspects of early liberal thought are often identified as contributing to this "individualism." Some argue that it stems from Hobbes's adoption of Galileo's rationalistic "resolutive-compositive" method. This method involves imagining the components that might make up complex phenomena and then constructing a model of the interaction of these components that can account for observed behavior. Hobbes's construction of human behavior, beginning with the senses and passions in the individual and moving to individuals in nature and then to men in society, seems to embody this procedure.[21] The method is held to produce an inevitable tendency to view people originally as isolated units which can only be artificially bound together, when in fact their existence "originates" not just as a complex of smaller components but as an integral part of a human group or groups. Regardless of how strictly Hobbes actually follows this procedure throughout his philosophy, both Hobbes and Locke clearly develop their ethics from analysis of the operations of individual human minds and contend that ideas of good and evil originate in individual pleasures and pains.

Each also accepts that everyone has his own notions of what his good is. While Locke, who is not so overtly relativistic as Hobbes, maintains that certain things are universally regarded as good, he still acknowledges that, though "all good be the proper object of *Desire* in general; yet all good even seen and confessed to be so, does not necessarily move every particular Man's desire; but only that part, or so much of it, as is consider'd and taken to make a necessary part of his happiness." One man might desire "sensual Pleasures" and another "delight of Knowledge," and while each recognizes the other's pleasure as a good, it forms no part of his own good. Furthermore, a man, at least in relation to his "present Good," "never chuses amiss; he knows what best pleases him."[22] Men may misjudge their long-range good by not deliberating on whether their choice serves it, but they are nonetheless the best judges of what gratifies them and hence of what is best for them at any moment in isolation. So Locke to some extent presents human satisfaction as an individual experience individually defined, and this view may stem from the methodology he uses to explicate the origin of human values. At any rate, he produces an ethics with a substantial strain of individualistic hedonism, although it also contains values that are not held to be simply products of human preferences or subordinate to them.

In his political writings, moreover, Locke, like Hobbes, portrays men as "by Nature, all free, equal and independent." While men may associate with each other in the state of nature, they are still in a fundamental sense "on their own"—according to Hobbes, because each has a right to everything and the result is a constant struggle; according to Locke, because each is an "Executioner" of the law of nature.[23] Further, since men are in some sense naturally independent, political societies can arise only as artificial human constructions, designed to achieve what are still individual goods, be they individual preservation or a more expanded set of individual rights. The governments that men construct serve chiefly as "Umpires" for Locke, and their laws serve as "hedges" for Hobbes, to regulate the clashes of citizens in the course of what remains an essentially personal pursuit of happiness. Governments are also designed to advance men's "civil interests," but the extent to which they should do so actively is unclear, and these interests are presented far more as individual purposes collectively pursued than as truly common concerns. The portrait of political life characteristic of early liberalism, then, does explicitly depict men as naturally independent individuals and their fulfillment as equally individualistic.

Although early liberalism has been criticized from all along the political spectrum, critics generally take exception to the individualistic cast of its methodology, ethics, and politics. Even Locke's liberal successors dissociate themselves from extreme claims of man's natural individualism. Hutcheson, Burlamaqui, and Blackstone all argue that men are naturally inclined to pursue a social existence. Montesquieu similarly describes man as "formed to live in society," and the manner in which he analyzes political life from the standpoint of different social and political structures marks him as a forerunner of modern sociology. Indeed, the distinguishing feature of sociology is sometimes said to be its departure from the individualistic analyses attributed to early liberalism, in favor of a focus on the interrelations of social groups and institutions.

Theorists of widely different views have similarly emphasized man's social nature. Edmund Burke, on the one hand, sets his sights firmly on "civil social man," insisting that men are naturally members of a "partnership" between the living, the dead, and the unborn—"the great primeval contract of eternal society." He scorns those who instead see society as resolvable into "an unsocial, uncivil, unconnected chaos of elementary principles," a view which reduces men to "loose counters," "little better than the flies of a summer." Karl Marx, on the other hand, attacks the liberals' division of human life into "public" and "private" realms and their treatment of the private realm as more fundamental, more truly "real." To Marx, this "bourgeois individuality," by portraying man "as an isolated monad, withdrawn into himself," leads men to see their "authentic" selves as "*egoistic* man," not as social beings. By relegating their "true" communal identities only to their "abstract, artificial" roles as citizens, liberal individualism serves as an ideological barrier to human fulfillment.[24]

There is, in sum, virtual unanimity that liberalism's atomistic view of man fails to recognize human nature's social aspects and consequently does not do justice to deep human needs for social life and a sense of community. Nonetheless, while early liberalism's commitment to individualism is problematic, its portrait of human nature is not quite so one-sided as charged. Although early liberals may have been taken with mathematical and empiricist methodologies—which in any case have to be misapplied to produce a neglect of man's sociality—there are other motives for stressing that men are naturally independent individuals.

Both Locke and Hobbes criticize not only the reasoning but the political morality of the tradition of medieval Aristotelianism. According to Aristotle, "man is by nature an animal intended to live in a *polis,*" and consequently "every *polis* exists by nature." Aristotle also holds the polis to be the "most sovereign and inclusive association" to which men naturally belong, one that attains "full self-sufficiency" and therefore exists to provide not simply "mere life" but a "good life." If men are naturally meant to live in a political society so they can attain a fully self-sufficient "good life," it is only natural for the political community to concern itself with the moral and spiritual fulfillment of its members. A political society would be inadequate if it did not do so, and any individual who found moral fulfillment outside the life of the political society would be "either a beast or a god."[25]

In this view, it is inevitable for a state to involve itself intimately with moral and religious issues. Such Aristotelianism served well the authorities of the medieval Christian world, but for early liberals, who were concerned to keep divisive religious and moral issues out of political life and to redirect the state toward concerns of "mere life," it posed a formidable obstacle. Hence, early liberal theory stresses men's natural independence and the artificiality of political societies, while tying these arguments to efforts to limit governmental ends and to keep religious and moral issues from becoming politically controversial.

Perhaps, then, these aspects of liberal theory are not so much products of simple analytical error as deliberate efforts to combat positions antithetical to liberal goals. Again, the *Second Treatise* is meant not as an analysis of actual governance but as a statement of proper political purposes. Even so, Locke's discussion of the "Beginnings of Political Societies" demonstrates that he did not really think political societies began through a formal contract among independent adult individuals. Rather, he describes actual societies as growing up out of family units and tribes which were gradually compelled to adopt more formal political structures. He merely insists that however political societies grew up, the principles implicit in their structure are always those he describes as established in a formal social contract: "which ever" of any of several ways a commonwealth may have grown up, "certain it is that no body was ever intrusted" with governing power "but for the publick Good and Safety" as Locke understands it. This point is echoed by later liberals who profess to improve on Locke's natural individualism.[26] Thus, to criticize early liberal theory for falsely regarding men as naturally purely independent beings is an exaggeration at best.

This does not entirely answer the charge that early liberalism is excessively individualistic. Liberalism indeed denies that moral or spiritual fulfillment can be attained only in our common life, and it limits the state to protecting individual rights which allow each person privately to pursue his own sense of his happiness, so long as that pursuit does not seriously violate basic liberal values. Human fulfillment thus seems to be regarded as ultimately an individual experience. Although the state must devote itself to attaining certain ends for all, including peace, security, liberty, enlightenment, and prosperity or "living well" in not an Aristotelian but a modern sense, this can amount to no more than the collective pursuit of essentially individual pleasures. If these are the only proper common ends, this liberal view defines the purposes of political life far too narrowly for many. It still places little emphasis on the human need for satisfactions provided by common memberships and endeavors, which are held vital to well-being. Thus, in its ends more than in its analysis of political life, early liberalism may be too individualistic. This problem is intimately related to the final and most important difficulty of early liberal theory, the goals it sets for political society.

The vision of early liberals was an optimistic one. They believed that after centuries of superstition, stagnation, and misery, they had found the methods of reasoning and the political and moral principles that would lead to a new era of peace, wealth, scientific advancement and personal freedom—in short, the well-being of all mankind. Theirs was a persuasive and powerful vision that helped shape a new stage in the history of Western culture which has not yet ended. Nonetheless, almost from its inception this vision was criticized as inadequate, and alternative values were set forth. Three such critiques will be described here. The "civic" critique was made on behalf of the claims of political community; the "romantic" critique was made on behalf of the human need for self-realization; and the "social egalitarian" critique was made on behalf of the materially and socially disadvantaged. While each of these three critiques endorses values that have corollaries in liberal theory, all reject the primacy that liberalism gives to its specific individual rights and offer radically different versions of those values, which are nonliberal if not in fact antiliberal.[27]

The civic critique is closely related to the criticism of liberalism's excessive individualism. It is a chief theme not only of Edmund Burke, the great conservative, but also of Jean-Jacques Rousseau, the philosopher most identified with the very revolution in France that Burke was assaulting. The civic critique also attacks liberalism's emphasis on the individual pursuit of happiness in private life and its identification of happiness largely with personal material well-being or, at most, personal intellectual attainments. These views are claimed to render the state and public life mere mechanisms devoted to mundane necessities. Liberalism therefore undermines the sense of the moral worth of one's political community and the feeling of affection for it that inspire patriotism and an ethic of civil service, elements that are vital not only to the flourishing but to the very survival of political society. In its strongest form, this critique stresses the primacy of the community over the individual, but it is compatible with a view of political society as either natural, as in Burke and nationalist writers, or artificial, as in Rousseau and later participation theorists.[28] Its characteristic element is a belief that liberalism gives no support to the public-spirited civic consciousness and civic virtue that are necessary for political life.

Rousseau attacks the whole of Enlightenment thought that spawned early liberalism for undermining such civic virtue. He maintains that the Enlightenment sciences have actually been borne of "vices," of "ambition ... avarice ... vain curiosity ... human pride," so a man who devotes himself to such "sterile speculations" is a "useless citizen." And not merely "useless"; because such men try to win fame via intellectual novelties, they are "enemies of public opinion," who "smile disdainfully at the old-fashioned words of fatherland and virtue" and thereby undermine patriotism and good morals. Rousseau has little more regard for the liberal attachment to material well-being. Insisting that "good morals" are "essential" for political "stability" and that "luxury is diametrically opposed to good morals," he scorns the dedication of liberal regimes to prosperity: "Ancient politicians incessantly talked about morals and virtue, those of our time talk only of business and money."[29]

According to Rousseau, the particular virtue endangered by such an ethics involves the capacity to defend one's country. He points to examples of poor nations conquering decadent rich ones, for "with money one has everything, except morals and citizens." In addition, "cultivating the sciences is harmful" to the "warlike qualities" needed for "military virtue." Enlightenment society showers prizes on "noble discourse" and admires the rich, but the "noble actions" of virtuous "defenders of the country" are left "without honors." The result is that society has many learned men, but "we no longer have citizens." So duties go unfulfilled, nations are weakened, and "the people" are left "vile, corrupt, and unhappy."[30] The very attainments that bring happiness to individual liberals are responsible for destroying the qualities that bring a people health. This critique presupposes the greater satisfaction of being a dutiful, contributing member of a thriving political society. At least some of the time, then, Rousseau praises the virtues of the good citizen, which place the good of the community over individual pleasures, as the truest virtues.

Burke's alternative defense of the primacy of civic virtues harkens back to the Aristotelian view that civil societies should be concerned with all aspects of the "good life." Like Rousseau, Burke disdains the view that a state is a contrivance for merely material goals: "the state ought not to be considered as nothing better than a partnership agreement in a trade of pepper and coffee, callico or tobacco, or some other such low concern, to be taken up for a little temporary interest, and to be dissolved by the fancy of the parties." Rather, the state should be regarded "with other reverence," because its province includes all aspects of human attainment and fulfillment: "it is not a partnership in things subservient only to the gross animal existence of a temporary and perishable nature. It is a partnership . . . in every virtue, and in all perfection."[31]

Again like medieval Aristotelians, Burke makes evident that the "virtue" promoted by the state includes not just military but religious virtue. More emphatically than Rousseau, Burke gives priority to the civic virtues not merely because they enable the community to be strong and healthy but because they provide for men's spiritual rectitude. While both Rousseau and Burke call for a publicly established religion, Rousseau argues for a "civil religion" defined essentially according to the needs of political society, holding that without a religion which makes a citizen "love his duty," "neither the state nor the government will ever be well constituted." Burke, too, recognizes the political values of a public religion in combating "the lust of selfish will" and giving the state "an wholesome awe" upon its citizens that persuades them of their duty toward it. Yet when he says that "religion is the basis of civil society, and the source of all good and of all comfort," he does not mean the good of the commonwealth alone. A religious public life is needed if men are to attain their full perfection in all its aspects. Of "religious establishments," Burke says: "Every sort of moral, every sort of civil, every sort of political institution, aiding the rational and natural ties that connect the human understanding and affections to the divine, are not more than necessary in order to build up that wonderful structure, Man."[32]

For Burke, man can become all he ought to be in his spiritual as well as his physical nature only through life in a society that is devoted to all facets of human fulfillment. This view elevates the civil virtues above individual pursuits not simply because they are higher than purely personal satisfactions but because they entail all virtue. The private liberties that liberalism seeks are worthless if they eliminate higher spiritual concerns from public life: "But what is liberty . . . without virtue? It is the greatest of all possible evils; for it is folly, vice, and madness, without tuition or restraint."[33]

Burke and Rousseau are nevertheless united in insisting that dedication to the well-being of one's political community and willingness to sacrifice for it—the elements of public virtue—constitute an ethic superior to early liberalism's dangerous individualism. This critique is manifest in many varieties of modern nationalism and conservatism, and it probably reached its most radical statement in that exaltation of the "fatherland" which formed an essential theme of modern fascism. Yet as Rousseau and Burke indicate, it can readily be given more civilized and humane formulation. It currently finds expression in both the participatory, communitarian politics of the American Left and the religious patriotism of the New Right.[34]

In contrast, the romantic critique on behalf of the needs of the inner person regards the values of early liberalism as narrow and ignoble, not because they do not recognize man's social nature, but rather because they do not allow for the full development of his individuality. Men's liberty to choose their actions gives them a certain moral dignity in Locke's eyes, and for him men can be obligated only by their own choices. The romantic critique more tightly unites and then radicalizes these views. It holds that men's moral worth consists solely in acting in accordance with their own internal dictates, so the only values that are truly binding are self-generated and self-imposed. A value is valid only when it is personally and sincerely embraced. And whereas for Locke, man's inner liberty consists in his ability to be determined by reason and not simply by passion, the romantic critique holds that reason is only part of human nature, and not the highest part. With Hume, the romantic critique holds that morality is essentially a matter of feelings and sentiments. As a result, it objects to rational constraints on feelings that can render value choices insincere. Furthermore, in accordance with aesthetic theory going back to Plato, the critique sees human creativity as something not essentially rational but imaginative, even inspired; and because values, too, are human creations, moral freedom is a matter much more of the spirit and the emotions than of reason. From this viewpoint, liberalism's attachment to security, material prosperity, and science, in preference to the individual's pursuit of self-defined ends, seems at best mundane and pedestrian, at worst stifling and oppressive. For the romantic critique, the only true values are those of authentic self-expression and self-realization.

This second critique drew inspiration from Rousseau's *Reveries*, but his position is far too complex to be simply identified with it. There are few political writers in whom the romantic critique appears in unmixed form, for such a view leads away from political life. It is, however, articulated in mid-nineteenth century America by Ralph Waldo Emerson and Henry David Thoreau. Whereas the rationalists of the Enlightenment and the Benthamite utilitarians tend to analyze men as kinds of flesh-and-blood machines, romantics such as Emerson argue that men are in fact organisms which must be allowed to grow according to their own natures. Using the archetypal romantic image, Emerson terms man "that noble endogenous plant which grows, like the palm, from within outwards." Consequently nothing should interfere with human self-development, with man's "unfolding." As Thoreau puts it, "if a plant cannot live according to its nature, it dies; and so a man." And since a man's good depends on his own unique nature, he must follow its lead if he is to do as he ought. "Right ethics . . . go from the soul outwards," says Emerson, so "a man should learn to detect and watch that gleam of light which flashes across his mind from within, more than the lustre of the firmament of bards and sages." It is not just the light of reason that men should heed, as that is not what is deepest and most "generative" in human nature. "Thinking is a partial act," Emerson observes, and "character is higher than intellect," so "leave your theory" and "trust your emotion." The "essence of genius, the essence of virtue, and the essence of life" is "Spontaneity or Instinct." To conform to dusty conventional morals denies one's nature and hence is immoral. Therefore, in a phrase that had a future, "do your thing, and I shall know you."[35]

Given these sentiments, Emerson and Thoreau find early liberalism's preoccupation with the practical concerns of this world cramped and shallow. Emerson takes "materialists" to task for seeing only how nature can be exploited for human purposes: "Economical geology; economical astronomy, with a view (to annexation, if it could be) to navigation; and chemistry and natural history, for utility . . . is there no right wishing to know what is, without reaping a rent or commission . . . their natural history is profane . . . This charge that I make against English science, that it bereaves Nature of its charm, lies equally against all European science." Locke's advocacy of forms of science that can "increase our stock of conveniences" places him squarely with the "English science" that Emerson here indicts. Thoreau, too, insists that "this curious world which we inhabit is more wonderful than it is convenient; more beautiful than it is useful; it is more to be admired and enjoyed than used." Thoreau, however, directs his criticism less toward liberalism's practically oriented sciences than toward the "commerical spirit" it has encouraged. He writes that "there is nothing . . . more opposed to poetry, to philosophy, ay, to life itself, than this incessant business," and the "luxuries" and "comforts of life" are "positive hinderances to the elevation of mankind."[36]

All this is much removed from the concerns of the defender of the right to property, a right that is looked to, in Emerson's view, from a "want of self-reliance." Romantics even go so far as to attack the central liberal goals of peace and security. For Emerson, "every individual strives . . . to impose the law of its being on every other creature," and so he is "ashamed" when men shirk this task and timidly "capitulate" to the demand for order. Any change, "no matter how violent and surprising, is good when it is the dictate of a man's genius and constitution." Thoreau describes his own "genius and constitution" as quite capable of violence: "I found in myself, and still find, an instinct toward a higher, or spiritual life . . . and another toward a primitive rank and savage one, and I reverence them both. I love the wild not less than the good."[37]

Men who see change and struggle, even violent struggle, as natural and fulfilling are not likely to be concerned about the liberal attachment to the rule of law, either, and Emerson and Thoreau each contend that the law is of less moral worth than the dictates of one's own nature. Emerson asserts that "the only right is what is after my constitution; the only wrong what is against it." But in a more moderate and characteristic mood, he finds that the "moral identity of men" "expresses itself" in law as well, and so he recommends respect for law as a "middle measure which satisfies all parties," insisting only that "good men must not obey the laws too well." Thoreau, however, is more uncompromising: "The only obligation which I have a right to assume is to do at any time what I think right . . . There will never be a really free and enlightened State until the State comes to recognise the individual as a higher and independent power." Unlike Emerson, Thoreau never retreats from this insistence that an individual's self-chosen values override any and all claims of civil obligation. To him the state, even in its best imaginable form, is something wholly inferior to sincere adherence to one's own principles.[38]

Although elevation of the individual seems the logical consequence of romantic precepts, Emerson finds it impossible to apply those views consistently to politics. He admires most those "noble" individual natures, the "geniuses" or "heros," who are able to create their own laws and conform the world to themselves. Consequently, he sometimes asserts an intensely hierarchical view of humanity, arguing that the majority of men are "bugs" who contribute most to man's glorification when they are used, shaped, and sometimes destroyed by "great men." Even if the average man should adhere to the law's "middle measure," a "hero" is above laws: "his greatness will shine and accomplish itself . . . whether they second him or not."[39]

On the whole, Emerson is too much of an American democrat to persist in such a stance. He decides in the end that "there are no common men," that "each is incomparably superior . . . in some faculty" to all others, and he is thereby able to remain essentially a political egalitarian. Yet this is a vulnerable position, so like Thoreau, Emerson commonly resorts to decrying politics altogether. For example, Emerson holds that "all public ends look vague and quixotic beside private ones. For any laws but those which men make for themselves, are laughable." So he advises to "leave governments to clerks and desks." Thoreau is even blunter: "What is called politics is comparatively something so superficial and inhuman, that practically I have never fairly recognised that it concerns me at all."[40]

Once one accepts that individually defined self-realization is the highest value, a life amid the constant compromises and public pressures of politics may well seem wasted. Thus, Emerson and Thoreau each call for the individual to seek his perfection privately, a call that restores a certain amount of practical compatibility between their views and liberal regimes. Thoreau took this position to the extreme of his (relatively short-lived) retreat to Walden Pond, while Emerson remained a private lecturer, not a political leader.

The romantic critique of liberal ends thus can have multiple political implications. It may turn men toward private pursuits and thereby generally harmonize with liberalism, but its assertion of a superior moral status for self-imposed values can serve to justify anarchism, a tack it has sometimes taken historically. This critique can also lead to adulation of a political leader who seems to be a great man or hero, and it may then be combined with a belief that personal self-realization is naturally bound up with the destiny of one's people or nation. This is the role that romantic views quickly came to play in European thought, transforming romanticism from an anarchical to a conservative vision, though there were also many European romantic liberals in the Emersonian mold. Romantic conservatism then laid the groundwork for the ideal of a great man leading his people in the imposition of the law of their nature upon the world, as is visible in Nazi ideology.[41] In recent decades romantic thought has instead been increasingly egalitarian, proclaiming the equal right of all to "do their thing," as did elements of the American New Left in the 1960s. Common to all these stances are the key elements of the romantic critique: its rejection of the early liberal effort to give priority to security, material enrichment, and a practical sense of rationality, and its assignment of the highest good to the actualization of one's inner potentialities.

In its egalitarian manifestation, the romantic critique is often joined with the third, social egalitarian critique of liberalism on behalf of the socially disadvantaged. The social egalitarian critique does not, however, necessarily assert that the highest values are self-established. Nor does it scorn the values of material well-being, science, liberty, and security. Instead it complains that they are not being fulfilled for all, though this contention often involves challenging the liberal understanding of these values. The critique maintains that the sciences which support liberalism's political and economic systems are ideological distortions, that societies based on liberal principles therefore cannot attain true prosperity or true liberty for all, and that the security of liberal societies shields oppression. Liberal individual freedoms, in particular the right to private property, inevitably result in extreme economic, social, and political inequalities which are both inhumane and unjust. Marx is the most influential exponent of this critique, but Marxism is far from its only form.

To be sure, early liberalism makes no pretense of providing full equality. All men are held equal in their right to consent initially to a particular civil society, but there is no requirement for the subsequently established form of government to provide for equal political influence. If a structure that includes inequalities in political power seems most likely to achieve liberal ends and wins majority approval, it is perfectly legitimate. Moreover, Locke knows that the right to property, combined with the existence of money, means there will be "an inequality of private possessions." He simply contends this situation arises with the "tacit and voluntary consent" of men, since they chose to create and value as money durable materials which can be stockpiled and then translated into a much larger supply of perishable goods than could otherwise be rightfully possessed.[42]

The original choice to accept gold and silver in exchange for useful goods causes Locke some difficulty. It seems traceable either to a "Fancy" for useless baubles or to a far-sighted but avaricious desire to circumvent natural limits on personal wealth by acquiring durable commodities that others can be persuaded to accept. Neither desire is acceptable in Locke's eyes. "Ambition and Luxury" breed an "evil Concupiscence" that corrupts society's prepolitical *"Golden Age,"* making government necessary. Yet Locke seems ambivalent about the moral value of money, for he indicates that, since money makes commerce possible, it encourages additional industry and leads to improvements in both production and culture by drawing in rare and useful goods from other parts of the world. Because this outcome serves the ends that property is meant to promote, Locke finds money on the whole to be morally acceptable.[43]

Although Locke continues to accept that certain charitable duties are owed to all, he does not admit that the increased inequalities which money entails will extend to the impoverishment of many. Instead, he believes that, whatever inequalities might exist, a "day labourer in England" with its commercial economy will be fed, lodged, and clad better than "a King of a large fruitful Territory" in still uncultivated America, despite his recognition of the fact that wages for labor respond to the market and that many in his own time, with labor in oversupply, live a "hand to mouth" existence. Locke believes that the lot of laborers will eventually progress if the rights of all are defended, though he never provides any economic rationale for this assumption. Later classical economists claimed that over time economic growth would combine with equilibrating forces to bring about improvements for all, but Locke failed to elaborate any such argument.[44]

If Marxists are correct, Locke could not, for the economic inequalities he embraced inevitably involve class antagonisms between those who control the process of production and those whose "surplus labor" is utilized in that process by the controlling group for its own benefit. In themselves these economic inequalities foster human *"estrangement,"* and according to Marx, the advantages of reducing labor costs in a profit-motivated capitalist system drive employers to assign laborers repetitive tasks under rigidly controlled conditions at wages that approach subsistence level, while the employers expropriate all further value the laborers create. These inequalities mean that rights to equal political participation, even if granted, do not significantly alter matters. Actual political influence mirrors actual economic power, however much this may be concealed by forms. Marx thus holds that "the modern representative State" is "but a committee for managing the common affairs of the whole Bourgeoisie." Its vaunted "right of property" is "already done away with for nine-tenths of the population," so that only "bourgeois property" is preserved. Its freedom is really only freedom for capitalist economic pursuits in which a shrinking few dominate, whether or not liberals themselves intend this situation. Its legalism is only the will of the bourgeoisie "made into a law for all"; its "eternal laws of nature and reason" are only the products of "selfish misconception." While contemporary Marxism paints a more complex portrait, the wealthy owners of capital are still thought ultimately to be much more able to manipulate liberal political systems on key issues. As modern liberals like Robert Dahl admit, "extreme inequalities in income such as now exist in the United States mean extreme inequalities in capacities to make personal choice effective," thereby impairing "political equality."[45] And those who control the means of production have available a whole range of mechanisms for the protection of their interests that are not available to the majority.

Marx believes that the liberal capitalist state, caught in the inherent contradictions of its economic and political exploitation of the proletariat that is also its market and its citizenry, will eventually collapse, to be replaced by "a vast association of the whole nation" that will provide perfect equality and permit "the free development of all."[46] One need not, however, accept either Marx's contention that all economic and political inequalities involve exploitation or his prophecies in order to hold liberal inequalities unjust. If Locke's optimistic distribution assumptions do not hold—if those inequalities, instead of improving conditions for all, entail some measure of poverty and deprivation—they can be deplored on grounds of human compassion alone. While Locke's social conscience in regard to the poor may be harsh by modern standards, it at least goes this far.

Some social egalitarians insist that economic and other forms of inequality are unjustified whether they involve exploitation and suffering or not. John Schaar, for example, argues that "the ideal of democratic equality" is "based on a philosophy of equal human worth transcending both nature and economics," and he therefore rejects even inequalities that rest on demonstrable economic efficiencies or different capacities. While similar conclusions have been based on religious faith, Schaar's position rests on the claim that the material and psychological conditions of an inegalitarian society make it impossible for many to achieve the "self-realization" or "personal validation" that is the romantic critique's highest value. Those deprived of material resources and leisure are obviously restricted in their opportunities for such self-development. Schaar, along with other "participatory democrats," argues specifically that the lack of opportunity for genuine self-government is most stifling: "insofar as any man does not participate in forming the common definition of the good life, to that degree he falls short of the fullest possibilities of the human vocation." Consequently, he rejects "all claims for political authority based on technical competence" and calls for "the widest possible sharing of responsibility and participation in the common life."[47] While this insistence that values be self-defined is romantic, the additional contention that such self-definition requires intense political activity is not accepted by all romantics. It thus marks Schaar's position as fundamentally social egalitarian.

Social egalitarianism, then, usually combines both an extreme form of the consent rationale, holding that nothing less than a fully egalitarian social and political democracy can be legitimate, with a view of self-realization that entails ardent political participation. Such participation promises for some people the communitarian "warmth and intimacy," and the excitement of zealous involvement, that liberal societies lack; for others, it represents simply an attractive ideal of the human personality.[48] The problems of achieving a fully equal political and social system are immense, and the solutions range from intensely centralized collectivist planning to highly localized political and economic self-governance. The social egalitarian critique, like the other critiques, can thus be elaborated in many ways, of varying compatibility with America's liberal constitutional institutions.

II · Constitutional Issues

*F*OUR KEY ISSUES in American constitutional law are discussed here: whether to interpret the Constitution, particularly the requirements of due process for criminal procedure, by positive or natural conceptions of law; what the purposes and extent of freedom of speech are; what the requirements of political equality are for legislative apportionment; and what the extent of national responsibility is for individual and social economic welfare. The judiciary's efforts to devise appropriate doctrines on these four topics have been complicated by the continuing problems of America's inherited liberalism. The courts' responses to these problems display three significant patterns, discernible to varying degrees in each constitutional area. These patterns demonstrate that in its attempts to meet early liberalism's dilemmas the judiciary has moved in directions explored by influential political theorists. Thus, the judicial decisions are incidents of broader philosophical developments in American thought, developments that stem in part from the failure of early liberalism to justify definitively the aims it proposed for modern political life.

The first pattern of response stems from the recurrent breakdowns of legal doctrines premised on the early liberals' effort to combine multiple philosophical justifications. Judges have repeatedly abandoned higher law doctrines for more empiricist positions, but higher law views have then been revived, usually to challenge policies that are supported by powerful legislative majorities. This is especially apparent in the recurring debate between natural and positive law theories of the meaning of due process. The second pattern of response, which reflects the lessened credibility of higher law, is the increasing judicial agreement that consent is the basic justification for the legitimacy of the American constitutional system. This has fostered greater democracy on balance, but expert guidance has sometimes been thought necessary to satisfy popular wishes. The increased striving for consent in government particularly affects decisions on legislative apportionment, although it influences virtually every area of the law. Finally, the third pattern expresses the qualms about liberal individualism and liberal ends that both arise from and assist the discrediting of higher law doctrines. These qualms have led to litigative and judicial attempts to incorporate new sorts of values into the law, especially more romantic and egalitarian ideals. The impact of these substantive ideals is visible in all legal areas, especially in relation to existing and proposed reformulations of free speech and welfare rights.

These developments probably have many causes, but they plainly express deep dissatisfaction with the early liberals' claim to be able to demonstrate rationally that the desires and purposes they favored are most appropriate for political life. This claim was the linchpin in liberalism's union of absolutist, rationalistic natural law and a more relativistic, utilitarian empiricism. It lay at the heart of the American framers' liberal constitutional enterprise, their effort to design a popular system that would obtain the "blessings of liberty," the fruits of the "self-evident" rights that defined the bounds of governments based on consent.

This early liberal claim about rational political choice was open to epistemological and substantive objections, and all the worse for liberalism, these objections were often related historically.[1] The epistemological objection does not invalidate liberal purposes, but it can assist substantive challenges if it prevails. Once liberal theorists admitted with Hume and Kant that empiricism alone gave no proof of the rational necessity of liberal ends, all purposes could seem equally legitimate. To the Benthamite utilitarians, this conclusion justified a calculus of popular desires that was generally held to confirm liberal objectives, and for many modern liberals it has pointed to a concern for fair and democratic procedures that can give any outcome consensual legitimacy, while perhaps including safeguards for individual rights. But to others these relativistic reformulations have only underlined the substantive poverty of liberalism, while the abandonment of the claim that liberal values can be rationally demonstrated has cleared the way for the primacy of different goals, which have been justified by postliberal rationales. Although these alternative values are sometimes held to be consistent with liberalism, they also have often heralded calls for radical transformations in liberal societies.

These three responses—the long-term ascendancy of empiricism accompanied by periodic revivals of liberal higher law, the increased stress on consent as the sole basis of legitimacy, and the advocacy of new substantive ideals—have together produced a potentially misleading general configuration in American constitutional law and political thought.

Natural law doctrines have frequently undergone joint empiricist and democratic assaults, as they did in the Jacksonian, Progressive, and New Deal eras, only to be recast and renewed by opponents of majoritarian policies, such as the abolitionists, advocates of laissez-faire, and modern defenders of social equality and autonomy. These disputes have produced a cyclical historic oscillation between liberal empiricist and higher law views, perhaps suggesting that the original consensus on early liberal principles, with their attendant tensions, has never been fundamentally altered or overcome. But the cycle is only an appearance. In reality, the renewed antimajoritarian principles have always been changed in significant respects, moving from the rationalistic liberty of early liberals and many abolitionists to the property rights of the late nineteenth century, then to modern egalitarianism and libertarianism. The justifications for these antimajoritarian ideals have also increasingly been accommodated to the dominant stress on empiricism and consent. The process reached a turning point with the triumph in the late New Deal of the relativistic, democratic, pragmatic political beliefs that originated in large measure with the Progressives. This strain of American political theory has since generally been treated as authoritative. The Court of the *Lochner* decision, upholding laissez-faire as a constitutional requirement, could still defend its economic "absolutes" by invoking both divine law and natural laws of economic development.[2] But when activism arose again in the 1950s and 1960s, replacing the largely deferential judicial stance of the late New Deal, its rationales had changed. The Court not only promoted substantively different ideals, but did so through a more pragmatic and democratic appeal to evolving social values. This effort to base activism on empiricist and consensual premises has had noteworthy consequences: the Burger Court has shown that appeals to fundamental social values can easily be made to serve a somewhat more deferential and decidedly more conservative democratic relativism instead of the near absolute libertarian and egalitarian principles of the Warren Court.

Despite a significant evolution in the Court's treatment of constitutional issues, the early liberal framework of rationales and ends, and its attendant difficulties, remain at work. The principles of early liberalism illuminate the Court's initial treatment of most constitutional issues, while their problems and their theoretical successors are expressed in later doctrinal developments. The three patterns are visible throughout the law, but they are manifested somewhat differently in each area. Enduring majorities on the Court tend to revise constitutional doctrines in accordance with their general outlook, but they do not modify all areas at once. Their own substantive concerns and the issues that events bring to their bar mean that they are more likely to alter some inherited positions than others. Therefore, each doctrinal area displays a distinctive evolution.

In due process litigation, the rebirth of higher law theories in the Civil War period and the Gilded Age persisted uneasily through the post-New Deal era of relativism and judicial self-restraint to the present. A shift also occurred in the content of due process, which came to be informed by new concerns for autonomy and equality, especially in the 1960s. The Burger Court has partly retreated to a stance that defines substantive due process guarantees in terms of conventional social mores.

In free speech, a recognizably early liberal set of categories for the scope of permissible speech expanded after World War I as a result of relativistic arguments about the functional needs of a democratic process. When these positions proved too responsive to majoritarian intolerance in the 1950s, however, a more demanding political egalitarianism, and also a new focus on personal self-expression, became prominent in the activist free speech decisions of the Warren years. These views, too, have given way to doctrines that draw standards from conventional morality, while reemphasizing the importance of maintaining an open democratic system.

Apportionment adjudication moved from theories that permitted considerable inequalities on behalf of early liberal concerns for political and economic stability—to the extent that no constitutional challenges to malapportionment were heard—to a deference to the political processes justified by the democratic relativism of the mid-century, and then to an insistence on fuller political equality in the 1960s. Again the Burger Court has partially retreated from this last burst of egalitarianism and moved toward the more relativistic stance of the Court in the 1940s and 1950s.

Views of the nation's responsibilities for economic welfare have evolved from an early liberal national mercantilism accompanied by the protection of vested rights, to a Jacksonian deference to state economic regulatory and promotional measures, to the judiciary's protection of property rights during the *Lochner* era, and finally a post-1937 period of acceptance of extensive national power to promote economic welfare. The Burger Court has only slightly shifted this stance, but it has refused to encourage efforts to expand welfare entitlements that began in the Warren years.

In no era, however, did the prevailing doctrines coherently articulate any single view. Today, the law in each area mixes vestiges of all the preceding stages. These persistent difficulties and current responses suggest the possible future developments for each legal issue.

3 · Due Process and Concepts of Law

The problem of how or even whether to interpret the Constitution is crucial to all constitutional analyses, and one central aspect of the question historically is whether to read the document merely as positive law or in light of some higher law principles. Clashes between these two approaches have occurred in most areas of law, and especially in connection with the due process clause of the Fourteenth Amendment. Through the doctrine of substantive due process, the clause has served as the textual foothold for some of the most controversial judicial appeals to higher law. But the clash between positive and higher law conceptions surfaces even in such apparently nonsubstantive matters as the adjudication of criminal procedures.

This ubiquitous clash is traceable in large part to the basic tension between the empiricist and rationalistic natural law theories that were combined in early liberalism and American constitutional thought. That nexus made early liberals feel able to draw on both positive and natural conceptions of law without any sense of contradiction, and American liberals did so in regard to the procedural as well as the substantive content of due process. Precisely because due process was often thought to serve higher law principles of justice, it was not so customary in the nineteenth century to distinguish procedural from substantive due process cases. Justifications of higher law approaches to all the clause's requirements drew on both sorts of precedents. In fact, judicial activism on behalf of procedural requirements was more an effect than a cause of substantive due process decisions, despite the venerability of reliance on unwritten law to determine due process procedural rights. The common distinction today between procedural and substantive due process, as well as the heightened anxieties about substantive review, reflect the reduced credibility of higher law views in law as in contemporary theory, traceable to both the epistemological and the substantive objections to early liberalism. But just as the early liberals' confidence in the self-evident worthlessness of some desires has not been wholly abandoned, neither has the corresponding notion that due process embodies determinable but inexplicit principles of justice.

The historic oscillation between higher and positive law views in due process as well as in other constitutional areas demands explanation because of both its significance and its endurance. The most common explanation is to cite Aristotle on the impossibility of always adhering to established general rules, and to view the appeals to natural law as efforts to justify inevitable exercises of judicial discretion. Many scholars, following Edward Corwin, add that it is because Americans inherit both positive and natural law legacies that they tend to respond to the dilemma with higher law appeals. But this explanation does not go far enough, for it does not indicate why Americans originally thought that they could combine these two legal conceptions, which now seem so antithetical, nor why this belief has been progressively undermined yet not eradicated.[1] The answer lies in the conviction of Americans that liberal theory had successfully united empiricism and a rationalistic natural law.

Locke exemplifies how both legal conceptions found seemingly secure grounds in liberal political thought. In Locke's state of nature each man is sovereign over himself, and so legitimate civil societies and laws can result only from a compact among these individuals, who form themselves into a sovereign people. All valid laws must accordingly be traceable to popular consent. The people may assign the lawmaking function to a legislature or other governmental agency, but that body can legislate only on behalf of its authorized ends, or else the people can rightfully alter or abolish it. Hence law may seem ultimately to be positively established, as in Hobbes, though created now by the sovereign people instead of their government.

But Locke's natural man is not simply sovereign over himself, free to do as he likes. He is a divinely created rational being, and in his natural condition his reason can and should restrain his discretion with a moral law that is also the law of God. The rights and duties visible in the state of nature set limits on what men can authorize in forming civil societies. Governments can properly be dedicated only to securing those rights and duties, thereby fulfilling the objects of the law of nature. If legislatures should act beyond or against such ends, even with popular consent, their acts would not be valid. Thus, the laws that must be established by positive human authorities are in turn limited by natural law. Indeed, it is natural law which holds in the first place that laws must be posited, or at least consented to, by the people.

Although Locke's politics consequently involve a synthesis of positive and natural law conceptions, they are not aimed at achieving such a synthesis. Both sorts of conceptions simply happen to follow from Locke's philosophic premises and to be useful for his broader aims. Locke describes valid laws as both originating in the actual choices of free men and expressing transcendent standards for the same reason that he holds each man to be sovereign over himself, the final judge of his own good, and yet limited by natural law. The key in each case is that Locke does not believe men are truly free or sovereign unless their reason rules their passions and desires, and he treats reason as a substantive as well as an instrumental guide. For Locke, "the source of all liberty" is the power of rational deliberation to give weight and hence effect to desires that can generate genuine long-range happiness.[2] He is confident that if we will but reflect conscientiously, we will discern not only how to relieve our various "uneasinesses" but also which longings lead to the most intrinsically worthwhile satisfactions. The apparent tension between human desires and the demands of natural morality, and so between will and reason, is thus dissolved. It is only those who do not deliberate as their reason says they should who experience such conflict, and if they go on to violate the law of nature, they have immorally enslaved themselves to their immediate inclinations. If possible, it is then proper to impose obedience to natural law upon them regardless of their own preferences. In short, valid civil laws must be derived from the consent of truly free men, but on some points consent is not required and dissent is not permitted.

The *Federalist Papers* show that similar premises were involved in the view of many framers that the Constitution embodies both positive and natural law. The *Federalist* authors state emphatically that the proposed constitutional system will rest on "THE CONSENT OF THE PEOPLE," the "pure, original fountain of all legitimate authority." At the same time, they stress that not "every sudden breeze of passion, or . . . every transient impulse," but rather the "reason," the "deliberate sense" of the people, must be deemed the ultimate authority. The Constitution is valid precisely because it is the embodiment of rational popular desires, and it includes numerous devices to ensure that the rights it guarantees do not succumb to the "occasional ill humors" of the popular will. Most pertinent, the power of "judgment" is entrusted to the judiciary to "safeguard" the rational limits imposed by the Constitution on popular measures wherein "the *passions*," not "the *reason*, of the public" have held sway. While expressing faith that any "dangerous innovations" against the "rights of individuals" will be abandoned by the people upon "more deliberate reflection," the *Federalist* agrees with the Declaration of Independence that even popular action inimical to such rights is illegitimate.[3]

To be sure, for most early Americans this did not mean that the judiciary could regularly overturn legislation in the name of the reason of natural law. Most agreed that the ultimate authority for determining the objects of natural law and the means to secure them was the "deliberate sense" of the people, and since the Constitution expressed their considered judgments, judges had merely to apply it. But many early American judges accepted that, when the positive law was unclear, it was proper to resort in interpretation to the natural law that the legal framers had meant to embody. Blackstone argues as much in the *Commentaries* when he holds that "the most universal and effectual way of discovering the true meaning of a law . . . is by considering the reason and spirit of it," for he shows that the English constitution is animated by the "spirit of liberty" and so is "principally" aimed at the security of absolute natural rights. This position was elaborated in American jurisprudence by the first two great constitutional judges, John Marshall and Joseph Story.[4] Although the framers' insistence on a written constitution might instead seem to represent greater stress on the notion that law must be positively established, the judiciary they created in fact proved a new and more practical means for maintaining the rational limits on positive law that were demanded by natural law.

Locke's synthesis of diverse philosophic justifications ably served his political ends, and the American Constitution's combination of positive and natural law conceptions had similar utility. Locke's effort to derive human values from our sensations furthered his attempts to discredit supernatural doctrines that sparked conflict, stifled intellectual progress, and justified violations of human liberty. It also gave weight to the goods of this world, which Locke felt had to be made central to political life if happiness were to be achieved. In contrast, Locke's claim of natural law status for his principles enabled him to hold them to be unchanging and to link them with traditional religious teachings. Together, these varied justifications allowed Locke to sanction his views as expressive of our truest desires, our reason, and divine commands. They also supported his doctrine of government as originating in a positive compact expressing natural law and therefore aided his presentation of liberalism as the fullest realization of the rule of law. All this had obvious value in promoting peaceful, productive, law-abiding behavior by citizens and officials alike.

Similarly, the positive law strain in American liberalism justified substituting the "sovereign people" for any spiritual authorities with claims to temporal power, and this substitution in turn directed American government toward concern with the public's earthly "general Welfare." American constitutional theory was at the same time able to state these directions as fixed purposive limits on government sanctioned not only by popular will but also by divine natural law, thereby lending credibility to Paine's promise that in America the law, not human governors, would be king. The unity of philosophic justifications that made possible the American reliance on positive and natural law notions thus produced many of the same advantages in the United States that it did for Locke and liberalism generally, and it did so in the service of the same basic ends. The Constitution was more immediately concerned with security and "the prosperity of Commerce" than with either equal political liberties or intellectual progress, but this was a matter of emphasis within the political goals of Enlightenment thought.

Yet Locke left unredeemed his apparent claim that reason could show that the desires favorable to his principles were more worthwhile than all others. Perhaps the advantages provided by his synthesis of positions kept him from explicitly exploring the tensions among them, but since he did not, it remains a hard question whether and how Locke resolved them in his own mind. The prevailing view is that Locke could not have genuinely achieved such a resolution. Roberto Unger, for example, holds that because Locke, like all liberal empiricists, regarded desires and values as rationally arbitrary and subjective, his efforts to claim objective status for certain ends were "incoherent." He also maintains that modern American lawyers similarly continue to speak "as if rational choice among competing values were possible" while claiming that "values are subjective."[5]

While more might be said on Locke's behalf, it is true that liberals found it increasingly difficult to uphold their claim to be able to prove rationally which desires should be preferred, and this problem pervades American law, including adjudication of the due process clause. This guarantee has usually been a battleground when quarrels have arisen over the Constitution's higher or positive law nature. Both types of responses to early liberalism's views—epistemological challenges to liberal higher law and to the limits its sets on means, and challenges to liberal ideas of governmental ends—are seen in the long-standing debates over what due process demands.

The phrase "due process of law" was given prominence in English renditions of the Magna Carta as a substitute for the Latin phrase *"per legem terrae,"* literally "by the law of the land." This suggests that "due process" meant only "in accordance with the (positively) established procedures" of municipal law, but because English common law was sometimes held to embody higher principles of "right and reason," it often meant much more. In particular, Sir Edward Coke, who revived both higher law notions and Magna Carta as their embodiment in the seventeenth century, argued that the "law of the land" included certain fundamental principles of liberty that should guide the construction of all statutes. Coke meant by these principles largely procedural maxims, such as no double jeopardy, no denial of *habeas corpus,* and indictment by grand jury, but he included among them security against monopoly and the demand for taxation only by consent.[6]

Because it appealed to natural law principles of reason, including some substantive liberal principles, the legalistic, largely procedural higher law tradition of Coke was easily combined in America with the more substantive and rationalistic natural law theories of the Enlightenment, the defenses of "life, liberty and property" exemplified by Locke. The federal Bill of Rights, for example, like many preceding state Bills of Rights, united the political freedoms of the First Amendment, heirs of the "natural right" of conscience expounded by Locke, with a set of fundamental procedural guarantees in most of the remaining provisions, including the Fifth Amendment's due process clause. Since to early liberals the notion of nonarbitrary, reasonable government invoked both purposive and procedural rational principles, it was natural to list substantive political liberties with largely criminal procedural rights. A similar blend was already evident in Blackstone.[7]

This is why, although the due process clause in the Fifth Amendment refers chiefly to procedural concerns, it has always been possible to claim that due process stands for a broader, more purposive ideal of minimally rational governance. And through the history of the clause's adjudication, most justices have accepted this contention.[8] The quarrels have been over what those substantive purposes are, whether they are protected directly or by guaranteeing appropriate procedures, and how the substance and procedures are to be ascertained. Until the mid-twentieth century, due process actually figured more prominently in conflicts over substantive liberties than in debates over means to liberal ends, despite its apparent concern with "process."

To be sure, while in the first half of the nineteenth century the Fifth Amendment due process clause was generally regarded as aimed at protecting all basic liberties, it was usually held to do so only by guaranteeing certain procedures. The fullest antebellum discussion by the Supreme Court, *Murray's Lessee* v. *Hoboken Land and Improvement Co.,* argued that these procedures were found either in the Constitution itself or in "those settled usages and modes of proceeding existing in the common and statute law" of both England and America. Anglo-American legal history was sufficiently diversified, however, to allow permissive readings of acceptable "modes of proceeding," and the Court adopted such a reading in the case.[9] Hence, the clause seemed to add little to the Constitution's procedural requirements, and it was not even much litigated in this regard. The importance of the clause was also limited because it did not apply against the states, which had the major responsibility for criminal law. As the Court held in 1833 with almost undisputed historical accuracy, the entire Bill of Rights was intended to apply only against the federal government.

In contrast, from early on, state courts sometimes used law of the land clauses in state constitutions to protect property rights against legislative revocation. By the midnineteenth century, temperance and abolitionist movements had provoked further judicial protection of property rights in liquor and slaves via state due process clauses. At the same time, abolitionists had claimed unsuccessfully that slavery violated due process rights of liberty and property. But the only constitutional consequence of these developments was the brief suggestion in the infamous *Dred Scott* decision that the Fifth Amendment clause provided substantive property rights protection for slaveholders. That decision obviously could not serve as a cornerstone for due process activism in the postwar era.[10]

In 1868 the nation adopted the Fourteenth Amendment, which states in Section One that "No state shall make or enforce any law which shall abridge the privileges and immunities of citizens of the United States; nor shall any State deprive any person of life, liberty, or property, without due process of law; nor deny to any person within its jurisdiction the equal protection of the laws." These words were first given judicial construction in the landmark *Slaughter-House Cases* of 1873, where former Justice John Campbell urged that they made enforceable against the states not only the entire Bill of Rights but also all the natural rights of mankind. Unwilling to embrace the radical change in federal-state relations this entailed, the Court's majority instead rendered the privileges and immunities clause, which Campbell had stressed, a virtual dead letter. The Court held that the clause referred only to those unique protections arising from the special national character of United States citizenship. Since most significant liberties could be held to be privileges and immunities of state citizenship as well, they were still subject to state regulation. Although this ruling is disputable, the Court has never abandoned it. Its opinion said little about the due process clause, however, holding only that it was not applicable to the substance of the statute in question. In dissent, Justice Stephen Field argued that the amendment as a whole was meant to secure all "inalienable rights" against needless state infringement, defining these rights in part by appeal to Adam Smith. Justice Joseph Bradley added that violations of these rights, which he identified with Anglo-American legal traditions, would constitute violations of due process of law.[11]

These dissents presented the arguments that the Court would later use to turn the Fourteenth Amendment into a shield for laissez-faire economic rights. By 1878 the Court was willing to concede that "a statute which declared in terms, and without more, that the full and exclusive title of a described piece of land, which is now in A, shall be and is hereby vested in B, would . . . deprive A of his property without due process of law," although it stressed that the clause's limits on legislative power were far less sweeping than many litigants thought. The Court also admitted that those limits needed definition, which should be provided by the courts through a "gradual process of judicial inclusion and exclusion."[12]

The justices took the same approach when defining the criminal procedural requirements of the clause, although they were much slower to stress its potential limits on state actions. In the first major procedural case, *Hurtado* v. *California* (1884), the Court upheld a state law that permitted criminal proceedings without grand jury indictment and denied the argument that this violated the Fifth Amendment, made applicable to the states by the Fourteenth Amendment. Justice Stanley Matthews rejected this contention with arguments that have ever since posed obstacles to those who would hold with Campbell that the Fourteenth Amendment "incorporates" all the Bill of Rights. Matthews's opinion for the Court refused to follow the *Murray's Lessee* reading of the Fifth Amendment clause and contended that due process did not impose any "fixed, definite" procedures to be ascertained simply through examining "settled usages and modes." It guaranteed "not particular forms of procedure, but the very substance of individual rights to life, liberty, and property." States had great leeway to experiment with new sorts of procedures so long as their new system "regards and preserves those principles of liberty and justice." The Fourteenth Amendment clause also did not require all the procedural guarantees detailed in the Fifth Amendment and elsewhere in the Bill of Rights, because the identically worded Fifth Amendment due process clause did not do so, despite the contrary implication in *Murray's Lessee*. If it had, the framers would not have needed to specify those additional procedural guarantees. Justice John Marshall Harlan in dissent insisted that attention to past practices demanded the conclusion that this was indeed a procedure vital to securing liberty and that the Fifth Amendment due process clause imposed "broad" and "general requirements" encompassing other Bill of Rights guarantees. These were spelled out only to ensure their protection doubly.[13]

The Court instead refused to impose the procedure in question on the states, and the decision appeared to allow even more state discretion in procedural matters so long as proper ends were pursued. But the majority agreed with Harlan that the clause's purpose was to require those criminal procedures necessary for the substantive "principles of liberty and justice . . . at the foundation of our civil and political institutions." Its reasoning therefore permitted the argument both that some procedures were essential to safeguarding basic rights and that material violations of such rights, by whatever procedures, offended due process. Yet ironically, *Hurtado's* argument that due process could not have been intended to include any of the rights elsewhere enumerated in the first eight amendments meant that it was difficult to give protection under the clause to any of the essential substantive and procedural guarantees of the Bill of Rights. Due process would have to protect other, unspecified basic liberties. And given the Court's view that procedures were merely instruments to achieve the clause's "substance," it is not surprising that nonexplicit substantive rights were the first to be granted Fourteenth Amendment due process coverage.

Beginning roughly in 1890, the Court began to consider under due process the substantive rationality of laws that infringed on liberties which it deemed fundamental, especially the rights to pursue a trade, make contracts, and establish conditions of employment. In the case symbolizing these developments, *Lochner* v. *New York* (1905), the Court struck down a state law restricting bakers' hours as an "illegal interference" with "the right of free contract." In line with Bradley's *Slaughter-House* dissent, this nonexplicit right was held to be part of the "liberty" and "property" protected by due process, which could not be infringed "unnecessarily" or "unreasonably." The Court also indicated that, to be "reasonable," a statute must have a "direct relation" to a "legitimate end." The law in question failed the test, because bakers needed no special contractual protection, nor did the health of the community require any such restrictions. In later substantive due process cases, the Court made clear that "legitimate" state ends did not include "the removal of those inequalities" that result from the fundamental "right of private property," and it tightened the test for a "direct" relationship, contending that even economic regulations enacted for valid health objectives required means that were not merely "related" but "necessary" to that end.[14]

The Court's willingness in these cases to find laissez-faire economic rights to be the very "substance" of due process reflected much more than the logic of textual interpretation. It stemmed from a variety of political, legal, and intellectual influences arising in late nineteenth century America. Common law traditions, the legacy of Adam Smith's economic liberalism, and the social Darwinism of Herbert Spencer and William Graham Sumner were combined into a legal ideology that justified opposition to the extensive reform legislation of the Populist and Progressive eras on higher law grounds. Those higher law doctrines were thought to be self-evident enough to dismiss as completely irrational laws violating the substantive rights at which due process allegedly aimed. These doctrines involved significant revisions in the natural law theories of the early liberals, but they appealed to those theories to justify their reading of the Constitution as intended to protect economic liberties.[15] Thus, they used the higher law tradition as the early liberals had, to defend limiting democratic governments to certain ends and means.

With such stringent protection provided to natural law economic liberties through the due process clause, many felt that the provision must also give some defense to the explicit substantive and procedural guarantees of the Bill of Rights. And the Court's acceptance of due process protection for economic rights enabled Justice Harlan to gain his only victory for incorporation of a Bill of Rights provision into the Fourteenth Amendment. In *Chicago, Burlington & Quincy Railroad* v. *Chicago* (1897), Harlan wrote for a unanimous bench that Fourteenth Amendment due process in itself required "just compensation," even though both these phrases appeared in the Fifth Amendment. He maintained that in "determining what is due process of law regard must be had to substance, not to form." Standards of "natural equity" indicated that while lawmakers might set "a form of procedure" for the taking of private property, they could not establish "due process of law if provision be not made for compensation." Harlan simply ignored the resulting redundancy problem of *Hurtado,* but his success in persuading the Court to do so was short-lived. It soon became apparent that in regard to all the other, noneconomic Bill of Rights guarantees, the *Hurtado* reasoning still applied, leaving this case an unexplained exception to the general rule of nonincorporation.[16]

The Court tried to answer this difficulty in *Twining* v. *New Jersey* (1908) by building on *Hurtado's* indication that the clause protected any procedures vital to the "immutable principles of justice" that inhered in due process. As a result, the Court stated, "it is possible that some of the personal rights safeguarded by the first eight Amendments against National Action may also be safeguarded against state action, because a denial of them would be a denial of due process of law." The Court explained this by distinguishing between due process rights and rights otherwise established as part of state or national citizenship, and then contending that at least some of the rights spelled out when the framers listed citizenship rights in the Bill of Rights might also express due process principles of justice. If the Fourteenth Amendment clause were held to protect those same rights, this would not be "because those rights are enumerated in the first eight Amendments" but because "they are included in the conception of due process of law."[17]

This argument did not really answer the *Hurtado* claim that if due process embodied those same rights, their specification elsewhere was unnecessary and illogical. But it provided grounds for the Court to impose some of the specified Bill of Rights guarantees on the states, without being obliged to enforce all of them. This point was important in *Twining,* which involved the question of whether a state law that allowed juries to draw an incriminating inference from a defendant's refusal to testify violated a right against self-incrimination. The Court did not regard this criminal proceeding as violative of anything essential to due process, and it sustained the state law.

While the Court continued to give protection to economic liberties under due process and, in 1925, found without much discussion that the clause also protected the First Amendment citizenship rights of speech and press, no rights of criminal procedure were found essential until *Powell* v. *Alabama* (1932). There, the rape convictions of several young blacks were appealed on the ground (among others) that they had been denied adequate counsel. Although ambiguous, Justice George Sutherland's opinion suggested an alternative to the *Twining* response to the redundancy problem presented by incorporation. The *Powell* opinion held merely that the Sixth Amendment right to counsel was "fundamental" in the circumstances of the case at hand, where uneducated blacks had been tried by enraged Southern whites. This suggested that due process rights were determinable only on a case-by-case basis, varying with what was needed for a "fundamentally fair" trial in the situation in question. In this view, the framers' enumerations represented a decision to strengthen certain due process rights by specifying that they be protected in every case.[18]

Not all the language in *Powell* conformed to this interpretation, but it was so understood in, for example, the second Justice Harlan's later arguments for such a case-by-case approach. In *Palko* v. *Connecticut* (1937), however, Justice Benjamin Cardozo made a further effort to respond to the incorporation issue with an approach that tried to comprehend both *Twining* and *Powell* as well as due process protection of substantive guarantees in the Bill of Rights. Arguing that there was no "general rule" that the Fourteenth Amendment had incorporated the Bill of Rights, Cardozo found in effect three levels of due process rights by looking to the principles of liberty and justice presumably embodied in the clause. Some of the Bill of Rights guarantees, such as the right to grand jury indictment, were not necessary for "a fair and enlightened system of justice" and so were not required by due process. Others, such as *Powell's* right to counsel, might be "essential" in the "particular situation" of a specific case. Still others, especially the substantive guarantees in the First Amendment, were so "implicit in the concept of ordered liberty" that "neither liberty nor justice would exist" without them. These did not depend on case-by-case determination but had been fully "absorbed" into the Fourteenth Amendment with the same force that they had against the federal government.[19]

Because Cardozo's opinion accepted some full incorporation, it did not meet the *Hurtado* redundancy problem any more than the *Twining* Court had. This failure may explain the Court's occasional suggestions in later cases that due process rights were always determinable case by case. But Cardozo's position gave the Court greater flexibility in providing the degree of protection that seemed warranted without including unwanted Bill of Rights provisions. By the same token, this whole fundamental rights doctrine gave ample play to subjective judicial discretion, and at precisely the time when the Court was retreating from its parallel higher law activism in regard to due process economic rights.

That activism had been under attack since its inception, beginning around the time of *Lochner* with Oliver Wendell Holmes, Louis Brandeis, and the sociological jurisprudence of Roscoe Pound, and taking on renewed force in the 1920s and 1930s in the work of such legal realists as Karl Llewellyn, Jerome Frank, and Felix Cohen. On the surface, these responses to the legal descendants of early liberal higher law were overwhelmingly of the utilitarian type. All these writers agreed on the fundamental step of dismissing notions of natural law limits on governmental policies and methods as "transcendental nonsense." In fact, these legal thinkers were often close readers of the classical utilitarians; but following Pound, many embraced the instrumentalist pragmatism of William James and John Dewey as the paradigm for a new philosophy of law that strove to be more empirical and relativistic than even Bentham and Austin had been. Virtually all advocates of the new jurisprudence were much less confident than Bentham that laissez-faire was usually the proper means to promote the happiness of all and were more inclined to accept regulation of its excesses. And the 1930s realists were much more skeptical than Austin about the empirical possibility of deciding cases through deductive application of previously established rules.[20]

Consequently, rather than insisting on consistent applications of rules justified by formal calculations of social utility, the new legal theorists were more inclined, with Dewey, to advise judges to examine the particular empirical contexts, the "actual situations of fact" in which problems arose, and to draw from those contexts governing standards of "social advantages." Thus, widespread actual desires were still taken as the proper guides for rule-making, but there was less stress on performing a strict utilitarian calculus, especially if prevailing sentiments were adverse to such an approach. In truth, through the 1930s the focus was on criticizing the reigning *Lochner* orthodoxy, and few legal writers explored the issue of the correct standards for judicial decision-making in any depth. Confident that the ends would be apparent once all the facts were in, they stressed both the need to compile massive "Brandeis briefs" of social data and the judicial responsibility to give weight to such materials rather than to purely legal concerns.[21]

In so arguing, these legal thinkers were self-consciously part of the widespread relativist and empiricist revolt against formalism and higher law that reshaped American thought in the first part of the twentieth century. But this common cause did not mean there were no important differences in the views of the *Lochner* era critics. The question of how judges were to weigh social advantages produced the most significant cleavages. Apart from Holmes, the *Lochner* critics were unhappy not only with the Court's formalist method of reasoning but also with the content of its decisions, which seemed inimical to any sensible pursuit of the general welfare. They did not agree, however, on what that general welfare really was or on how it was to be furthered institutionally. Most tended, like Pound, to discuss the appropriate aims of law in pragmatic, utilitarian terms, as the promotion of dominant popular desires, but Brandeis also increasingly insisted that certain rights should be upheld against contrary majoritarian legislation because they were essential to the state's "final end" of human development. Many agreed with James Bradley Thayer that since the democratic political processes were best equipped to determine prevailing desires and to explore means to their fulfillment, the appropriate stance for the judiciary was generally deference to democratic authority. Some, however, invoked Holmes in urging judges to give weight explicitly to their own judgments of the social advantages that their decisions could provide, and again these advantages could be seen in utilitarian or nonutilitarian terms. The division between those who thought utilitarian premises required democratic governmental authority and those who thought they permitted governance by experts in promoting public utility reflected an ambivalence in the classical utilitarians.[22] But the occasional expression of nonutilitarian values suggested that some of the reaction to *Lochner* always expressed the substantive type of response to liberalism's dilemmas.

That response had to await the triumph of the mainstream *Lochner* opposition before it could come to the fore. While the efforts of Brandeis, Pound, and others to show empirically that various economic regulations were reasonable had some success in the Progressive years, they did not succeed in eradicating the widespread belief that certain economic ends were inherently illegitimate. The Taft Court of the 1920s voiced this view energetically, and it was only in the wake of the Depression that the new jurisprudence prevailed at the federal level. By 1934 the Court was willing to admit that "property rights and contract rights" were not absolute, but not until 1937, the year of *Palko,* did the Court perform the famous "switch in time" and abandon its close scrutiny of economic and social welfare legislation. In the pivotal case, *West Coast Hotel* v. *Parrish,* the Court reversed its view of legitimate state ends by arguing that a minimum wage law to avoid the "exploitation of a class of workers who are in an unequal position with respect to bargaining power" represented not an illicit interference with the "natural" consequences of property rights but rather a permissible community concern for the general welfare. In later cases the Court accepted and even imagined rationales for almost all economic legislation, viewing such matters as issues not of "immutable right" but of legislative policy.[23]

At that point a profound difficulty arose. If property rights were no longer deemed basic liberties specially protected under due process, what was the basis for the Court's similar activism on behalf of other substantive and procedural rights? The problem was particularly acute in regard to First Amendment freedoms, which since the 1920s had been accorded a Fourteenth Amendment status equal to *Lochner* economic rights. Most justices wished to continue this form of activism, and some wished to increase criminal procedural guarantees as well, in the manner of *Powell.* But the Bill of Rights framers had not seen these liberties as so clearly protected by due process as to require no further elaboration, and any appeal to higher law seemed unacceptably inconsistent with the momentous rejection of *Lochner* jurisprudence. That rejection could not easily be distinguished away, since it was only an instance of the more general political turn from natural rights notions to the "relativist theory of democracy" that, in various forms, dominated American political and legal thought from the end of *Lochner* until the 1950s.[24] This theory usually followed James Bradley Thayer in denying the legitimacy of any extensive discretionary authority by so unaccountable an institution as the Supreme Court.

Numerous responses emerged in the Court and the legal literature. They represented two broad approaches: the fundamental values approach, which tried to find ways for judges to continue to distinguish some rights and liberties as most basic and protected; and the democratic process approach, which explicitly strove to define the judicial role in terms of relativistic democratic theory. The fundamental values adherents attempted to retain the advantages of liberalism's higher law tradition, while the democratic process advocates looked to its empiricist, utilitarian branch. All post-1937 adjudicatory positions fit under these two heads, although there was substantial variety within each category, and most writers attempted more or less consciously to synthesize the two sorts of views, as liberal thought has always done.

The adherents of a fundamental values approach to justifying selective Court activism tended after 1937 to look to Cardozo's *Palko* opinion, finding some rights to be more basic to "the concept of ordered liberty." This view was not only open to anti-incorporation criticism, but, more fundamentally, perpetuated the *Lochner* higher law approach, relying on rationally discernible but nontextual principles of liberty. Consequently, some realists abandoned activism in favor of deference to legislatures on virtually all matters. Their leading spokesman was Felix Frankfurter, who generally opposed any special solicitude for particular freedoms and therefore deferred heavily to the legislative "weighing of competing interests" even in religion and speech cases.[25]

Frankfurter's advocacy of a restrained democratic judiciary held considerable sway on the Court and in American legal thought through the later New Deal and Fair Deal eras, when democratic relativism was at its height. Even so, in 1938 Justice Harlan F. Stone provided three justifications for certain kinds of judicial activism that might not violate the new pragmatic, democratic legal theories. He argued in the famous *Carolene Products* footnote that "more exacting judicial scrutiny" was required first, when legislation infringed on textually specified constitutional rights. Since these rights were enacted by an overwhelming majority of the people, the Court could democratically enforce them even against contrary legislative judgments of constitutionality. Activism was justified, secondly, if "political processes" were made too unrepresentative to be democratically responsive and thirdly, when adjudicating laws that discriminated against "discrete and insular" religious and ethnic minorities, whose interests might be unduly overridden by a democratic majority.[26]

Of these three rationales, only the second was really successful in defending judicial activism in terms of relativistic democratic theory. If actual consent was the sole standard for legitimacy, it was not clear why long-dead majorities, however large, should be entitled to bind current ones, nor why there were substantive restraints on how greatly majorities could harm those outvoted in a truly open political process. All of the rationales also failed to address the incorporation problem, and in application they all required additional arguments as to what textual provisions meant and when the political process was improperly limited or minority interests were invidiously ignored. But First Amendment freedoms could be given heightened protection on all three grounds, and often criminal rights could be as well, since they were frequently claimed by blacks and other minority litigants.[27]

This affirmation of the results of Cardozo's "concept of ordered liberty" analysis led some justices simply to speak of First Amendment rights as having a "preferred position" without much discussion. Consequently, much First Amendment and some criminal protection continued despite the judiciary's new and generally deferential posture. But Justice Hugo Black was not satisfied to let it go at that. He defended broad free speech protection by relying on a literalist, "absolutist" reading of the First Amendment's text and argued for extensive procedural guarantees, contending that the American people *had* meant the Fourteenth Amendment to apply all the Bill of Rights against the states. Believing only such positivist arguments to be democratic and legitimate, Black attacked the vestiges of what he saw as *Lochner* analysis in the Cardozo approach to procedural issues. His ire was most aroused because this approach usually led to criminal procedures that were less protective than those of the Bill of Rights.

Consequently, in *Adamson v. California* (1947), Black turned the jurisprudential arguments that had opposed the Court's protection of non-explicit economic rights against the similar approach to due process procedural guarantees elaborated in *Twining* and *Palko. Adamson's* facts parallelled *Twining's,* and the Court again held that the self-incrimination permitted by state procedures had not rendered the overall trial "unfair" and so had not violated due process. Black in dissent offered controversial historical evidence to justify his belief in Fourteenth Amendment incorporation and hence in the applicability of the Fifth Amendment to the case at hand. He attacked the Court for relying on "a constitutional theory spelled out in *Twining* . . . that this Court is endowed by the Constitution with boundless power under 'natural law' periodically to expand and contract constitutional standards to conform to the Court's conception of what at a particular time constitutes . . . 'fundamental liberty and justice' . . . that decision and the 'natural law' theory . . . degrade the . . . Bill of Rights and . . . appropriate for this Court a broad power which we are not authorized by the Constitution to exercise."[28]

Black was correct in arguing that the *Twining* approach tended to deny fundamental status to explicit Bill of Rights provisions while allowing the Court to give much weight to unspecified higher law rights. The fact that *Palko* allowed for "absorption" of some of the Bill of Rights' guarantees made it more palatable to Black, but he objected to any Court selectivity. This, he maintained, allowed justices to "roam at will in the limitless area of their own beliefs." Instead, they must adhere to the popularly ratified provisions of the framers, enforcing all, and only, the Bill of Rights against the states under the Fourteenth Amendment.[29]

The fullest defense of the Court's approach came, ironically, in the concurring opinion of the Court's leading advocate of judicial restraint, Frankfurter. While he, too, took his bearings for the judicial role from democratic theory, he could not accept Black's claims for incorporation nor the fixed due process procedures it entailed. Frankfurter maintained that it would have been "extraordinarily strange" for the framers to incorporate the Bill of Rights "in such a roundabout way" and reiterated that this made the framers of the Fifth Amendment clause guilty of "meaningless redundancy." Frankfurter agreed that *Palko's* efforts to select Bill of Rights provisions for full incorporation were "subjective," and so he insisted with the *Twining* Court that due process had an "independent potency," which neither "comprehends . . . nor is . . . confined" to the Bill of Rights. Appealing to the Cokean legal tradition of enforcing certain procedural maxims as requirements of "common right and reason," Frankfurter claimed that in regard to procedure, "natural law" had a historically determinate legal meaning that did not leave judges "wholly at large." He was, however, unwilling to engage in substantive due process analyses by using the Lockean natural law tradition to define the clause's requirements.[30]

In Frankfurter's approach, the clause was not confined to historically established criminal procedures but only took guidance from them, while maintaining flexibility in coping with unforeseen problems. He gibed that Black's approach could be made adaptable only through "warped construction" of existing clauses. No doubt in response, dissenting justices Frank Murphy and Wiley Rutledge largely embraced Black's incorporation doctrine while refusing to concede that due process was "entirely . . . limited by the Bill of Rights."[31]

Nevertheless, Black's criticisms of the alternative, reliance on judicial determinations of fundamental fairness, also had force. This became clear in three subsequent cases that raised the question of whether illegally obtained evidence could be used in state courts. The Court followed Frankfurter's lead in the first two cases but disagreed with him about what they implied in the third. In *Wolf* v. *Colorado* (1949), Frankfurter's opinion for the Court held that peacefully but illegally seized evidence could be used in a trial if the state so provided. But in *Rochin* v. *California* (1952), Frankfurter found "conduct that shocks the conscience" in forcible police administration of an emetic to obtain swallowed capsules, and he threw out the conviction based on evidence thus obtained. Then in *Irvine* v. *California* (1954), an illegal bugging case, the Court's majority felt bound by these precedents to uphold the conviction because there had been no physical coercion. Frankfurter dissented, arguing that the key element was simply "conduct which the Court finds repulsive."[32]

For police, lower courts, and Frankfurter's fellow justices, fundamental fairness had become too unpredictable and subjective a test. Hence, in another exclusionary rule decision, *Mapp* v. *Ohio* (1961), the Warren Court adopted a new approach to procedural due process, modifying the fundamental fairness test without abandoning it. It held that the right to "security of one's privacy against arbitrary intrusion by the police" accepted in *Wolf* was "in reality" withheld if illegally seized evidence could ever be used in state criminal trials. Justices Harlan and Frankfurter argued in dissent that in many cases fundamental fairness would not demand such exclusion. Justice Black decided for the first time that the Fourth and Fifth Amendments collectively required the exclusionary rule, an argument Frankfurter undoubtedly saw as the sort of "warped construction" he had warned against.[33]

Although *Mapp* did not announce its ruling as such, it was immediately treated by the Court as implying that any Bill of Rights privilege that had some sort of corollary in due process was so fundamental that it must, in *Palko* fashion, be "absorbed" into that clause in its entirety. By *Duncan* v. *Louisiana* (1969), the Court noted that under its "new approach" various First, Fourth, Fifth, and Sixth Amendment rights had without qualification "been held to be protected against state action by the Due Process Clause." No longer would due process be held to contain only rights of "independent potency" which happened in some cases to be similar to Bill of Rights guarantees. Either a provision of the Bill of Rights was present in full force, or it was not present at all. A few of the Bill of Rights guarantees, such as the right to grand jury indictment, seem destined always to remain in the latter category, though most have been found fundamental, at least to any "Anglo-American regime of ordered liberty." But as *In Re Winship* (1970) showed, criminal due process was still not limited to the contents of the Bill of Rights. In that case a right to "proof beyond a reasonable doubt" was proclaimed which had no corollary in the first eight Amendments. Even so, the Court found this right to be required by "fundamental fairness."[34]

The Court has since subjected the exclusionary rule to what Justice William Brennan describes as "slow strangulation," and the issue of its force remains unsettled. Justice Lewis Powell has continued to raise the Frankfurter-Harlan objections to full incorporation, with apparently increasing support. Nonetheless, the *Duncan* approach remains predominant today. Hence the Court continues to employ a test explicitly aimed at ascertaining criminal procedural standards of fundamental fairness that are treated as basic principles of liberty and justice even when they are not called natural law. While the justices generally identify these standards with the Bill of Rights, they remain unconfined by this restraint.[35]

The Court's increased protection for procedural rights from *Mapp* onward was only partly a response to the practical difficulties of Frankfurter's case-by-case fundamental fairness approach. The rejection of his limited activism in procedural due process was one aspect of a broader rejection of the stress on Frankfurterian self-restraint throughout constitutional law. Especially after the desegregation decisions of 1954, the same year as *Irvine*, American courts undertook a heightened activism in a wide range of areas. This activism championed more egalitarian and romantic values, embodying the substantive type of response to liberalism's dilemmas.[36]

These judicial innovations came when they did for complex reasons. The recurrent utilitarian pattern in which critiques of higher law forms of liberalism clear the way for more substantive responses held here, with the activism in all areas challenging social and economic inequalities and restraints that would previously have been seen as natural and legitimate. But modern judicial activism has many other roots. At first it represented a reaction to the spectacle of totalitarian abuses overseas, and it was fueled by the heightened sense of injustice in returning black veterans. For many people, however, these elements only reinforced a more general dissatisfaction with views of the American system as aimed at nothing more than fulfilling prevailing majority preferences.[37]

Whatever their substantive motivations, these developments posed many problems for the reigning theories of constitutional interpretation, particularly in regard to due process. One problem was that the dominant strain in the triumphant *Lochner* opposition was a relativistic pragmatism which lent itself most readily to support for majoritarian democracy. The Cold War of the 1950s added to this view intense fears for national security which reinforced beliefs that national self-preservation had to override all other concerns. This attitude temporarily undermined judicial activism even in free speech cases. And because the prevailing relativism denied that there were absolute standards for political outcomes, it focused attention on legitimate procedures for decision-making and hence on rule of law ideals as well as democracy. Judicial innovations are, however, difficult to present as simply government according to established law. This era thus saw renewed controversy not only over the judiciary's renascent activism but also over the very institution of judicial review, and it produced significant elaborations of the two main approaches for defending the function, even when activist, against its democratic critics.[38] Both fundamental values and democratic process theories were developed more powerfully by legal scholars, with visible consequences for judicial arguments.

The most significant development for due process adjudication, and perhaps for constitutional jurisprudence as a whole, was the reformulation of the fundamental values approach to make it more compatible with the reigning democratic premises. In its *Palko* form this approach seemed vulnerable to charges that it amounted to reliance on nonsensical higher law doctrines, and this indictment gained force from Frankfurter's willingness in *Adamson* to defend fundamental fairness as a kind of resort to natural law. Yet the methodology Frankfurter proposed for determining due process rights did not in fact appeal to transcendental standards but rather to an historical exploration of the criminal guarantees long deemed fundamental in America's relevant social traditions. This approach was arguably more consistent with the requirement that decisions rest on democratic choice, for it seems wholly democratic to demand conformity with the community's basic values. The next step was to maintain that because democratic political processes tended to focus only on immediate material needs and to negotiate compromise policies, legislators might neglect the bearing of their decisions on these more deeply rooted and long-term social ideals.[39] Hence, judicial intervention could be justified.

This approach was most fully elaborated by Alexander Bickel in *The Least Dangerous Branch*, probably the most influential work to emerge from the 1950s adjudicatory debates. Bickel drew considerable inspiration from the opinion of his mentor Frankfurter in *Sweezy* v. *New Hampshire* (1957), one of the few cases where Frankfurter turned the approach he had developed for procedural due process cases to the defense of substantive rights. The case involved a challenge to academic freedom, and Frankfurter thought the rational relativism he espoused did require judicial activism for the freedom of intellectual inquiry that had produced it. He maintained that by looking to America's "political and legal history," judges could discern "fundamental presuppositions" of the society, still possessed of "widespread acceptance," which could stand as a more legitimate basis for judicial activism than reliance on any justice's own "preference." Bickel relied on this reasoning to justify both substantive and procedural fundamental values activism, heavily restrained by considerations of prudence. Similarly, those justices inclined toward a fundamental values position increasingly stressed this historical methodology while omitting all overt claims to be looking to higher law. The employment of history and tradition, at least rhetorically, to justify judicial discovery of fundamental rights came to characterize most of the 1960s justices, and it has been perpetuated by the Burger Court.[40]

This methodology, which remained prominent in the Court's fundamental fairness approach to criminal procedure, was explicitly turned from procedural to substantive due process rights by a frequent Frankfurter ally, the second Justice Harlan, in the 1960s contraceptive cases that established the "right of privacy." Because the Court had never clearly endorsed Black's view that the Fourteenth Amendment incorporated the Bill of Rights, its ongoing application of First Amendment freedoms against the states had always been a form of substantive due process; but this was rarely stressed by the justices. Then in *Griswold* v. *Connecticut* (1965), the Court once again openly conferred special due process protection on substantive rights not explicit in the first eight amendments. Justice William O. Douglas's lead opinion in *Griswold*, striking down a Connecticut law that banned contraceptive use, did explicitly disavow substantive due process and relied instead on the view that the Fourteenth Amendment incorporated the Bill of Rights and that the "penumbras" and "emanations of explicit Bill of Rights guarantees" generated "zones of privacy" sufficiently broad to cover the conduct in question. This argument, however, was widely found unpersuasive, and five justices joined three concurring opinions, each of which in various ways conceded that the decision rested on substantive due process protection of a nonexplicit fundamental right. Justice Arthur Goldberg, joined by Chief Justice Earl Warren and Justice Brennan, appealed to the Ninth Amendment to buttress his belief that the Fourteenth Amendment's "concept of liberty protects those personal rights that are fundamental, and is not confined to the specific terms of the Bill of Rights." Imitating Frankfurter's approach to criminal due process requirements, Goldberg argued that substantive rights also could be discerned in the "traditions and . . . conscience of our people," and he found therein a right of marital privacy infringed by the law. Justice Harlan used the same approach while relying exclusively on the Fourteenth Amendment's due process clause, without any reference to the Bill of Rights. Justice Byron White concurred because he felt the statute could not stand even minimal due process scrutiny. But Justice Black could find no pertinent right stated or "implied" in the Bill of Rights, and he therefore attacked the judgment as more "natural law due process" in the *Lochner-Twining* mold.[41]

Although still controversial, the right of privacy established in *Griswold* has since become one of the most prolific areas of judicial concern. Its most dramatic application came in *Roe* v. *Wade* (1973), overturning a Texas abortion statute. Justice Harry Blackmun's majority opinion in the case did not pin the right of privacy on any particular constitutional provision, but it indicated a preference for finding the right "in the Fourteenth Amendment's concept of personal liberty," and Justice Potter Stewart's concurrence indicated that he, too, was now explicitly employing substantive due process to uphold the right in question. Since then, the right of privacy has been sustained in a variety of childbearing, marital, and familial contexts, serving as the cornerstone for a whole new constitutional area of family law. In one of these cases, Justice Powell argued that the Court was maintaining "appropriate limits" to its discretion in the area by using "the teachings of history" and "the basic values that underlie our society" as its guides in the "treacherous field" of "substantive due process," just as Bickel, Harlan and Goldberg had urged.[42]

But whereas in the 1960s the principles found to be basic to American society usually supported liberal activism, more recently justices have reached relatively conservative judgments regarding America's fundamental values. Their focus on protecting only rights that are clearly ranked fundamental in America's traditions means that they have avoided the broad reading of privacy put forth in Justice Douglas's concurrence in *Roe* and have protected only more conventional forms of behavior. Similarly, the Court has not followed Douglas's expansive view of the privacy protected by the Fourth Amendment as including an absolute "zone that no police can enter," so as to protect "the choice of the individual to disclose or to reveal what he believes, what he thinks, what he possesses." The Court has instead taken the concurrence of Justice Harlan in *Katz* v. *United States* as its Fourth Amendment lodestar, protecting only actual subjective expectations of privacy that "society is prepared to recognize as 'reasonable.' " Consequently, the Burger Court's Fourth Amendment decisions have usually been less protective than Justice Douglas advocated.[43]

Partly in response to this increasingly conservative conformity to social traditions, Ronald Dworkin carried the fundamental values approach a step further in the 1970s, establishing a position that appears to be the most influential current scholarly statement of the fundamental values stance. He argued that, to ensure responsibility and consistency, judges not only should ascertain enduring American principles by examining American institutional and social traditions but also should construct from these materials a comprehensive theory of American constitutionalism that would indicate which historic strands are to be given most weight today, generating consistent constitutional decisions in every doctrinal area. In constructing and applying such a theory, judges would inevitably have to make value choices, and to do so credibly, they ought to inform their theories with the efforts of contemporary liberal philosophers such as John Rawls. Dworkin has not applied his approach extensively to due process issues, but he has called for such applications, and he has suggested that most criminal guarantees can be analyzed in terms of his fundamental right to equal concern and respect.[44] Thus the fundamental values approach, which in its due process origins drew first on higher law doctrines, then on history and tradition, now calls for reliance on modern theories of liberalism, though most justices still prefer the Frankfurter-Harlan historical mode. While the approach still tries to set near-absolute limits on majoritarian choice, the legitimacy of both of its current versions is ultimately defended through the democratic and relativistic contention that the principles upheld simply represent the deeply held values of the American people.

Judicial activism has also been justified by relying more directly on democratic theory itself. In the 1950s and early 1960s both Charles Black and Eugene Rostow tried to show that judicial review was compatible with democracy on three main grounds: the institution had been tacitly accepted by the people; it worked, as the first of the *Carolene* footnote rationales held, to further their constitutionally posited aims; and perhaps most important, it often worked to achieve more democratic processes and results, as the *Carolene Products* footnote had also held.[45] The appeal to tacit consent was open to all the long-standing objections against such conjectural justifications for individual obligations, and the point about the democratic legitimacy of judicial enforcement of positive constitutional provisions led to probably the weakest line of defense for the activist decisions of the 1960s. To claim that the innovations proposed were plainly demanded by long-familiar constitutional passages was often difficult, as in Justice Douglas's effort in the *Griswold* opinion to derive a right of privacy encompassing contraceptive use from the First, Third, Fourth, Fifth, and Ninth Amendments. Such expansive textual readings could be used to reach almost any result, and Douglas's argument failed even to convince his usual ally and the Court's leading positivist, Justice Black. There was also still no clear democratic argument as to why past majorities should be permitted to bind present ones.

But the third claim of these scholars, that judicial review may be needed to promote democracy, has continued to show vitality. Its restatement of the *Carolene Products* rationale for court intervention to assure a democratic political process has often been cited to justify much of the Warren Court's activism, though more often by commentators than by the Court itself. John Hart Ely has elaborated it into a full-scale theory of constitutional interpretation, arguing that as long as the judiciary confines itself to enforcing explicit constitutional rights, guaranteeing democratic political processes, and weeding out any products of such a process which reflect prejudices against minorities, its activism is perfectly democratic. Accordingly, Ely eschews substantive due process entirely, restricting the clause to procedural guarantees, while agreeing with Frankfurter that the Constitution largely entrusts the judiciary to define what criminal procedures are "fair" and "reasonable." He also suggests that these requirements can be defined largely in terms of his standard of democratic equal protection.[46]

Yet in attempting to give content to the result-oriented *Carolene Products* concern for minorities, Ely's "democratic process" view is able to defend activism against procedurally correct democratic majorities only by asserting that democracy rests on a fundamental "ideal" of "equal concern and respect" which invalidates majoritarian biases. Ely offers no justification for this ideal, conceding that it is a means to avoid the consequences of his otherwise utilitarian position, and while it may be essential to many democratic theories, it does not seem required by democratic process theory alone. Such theory demands only that the majority be entitled to decide what degree of concern and respect must be given to others.[47]

Thus, while in Ely's hands the democratic process approach supports most, though not all, of the Warren Court's activism, efforts to define the Court's role through appeal simply to consent still tend more naturally to support judicial deference. In his later years, for example, Bickel increasingly agreed that judicial decision-making should be concerned most of all to ensure a truly consensual governmental process. But because he did not incorporate so strong a notion of a right to equal concern and respect and because he emphasized the generation of long-term consent, he left the Court much less leeway to oppose inegalitarian majority actions and to promote participation than Ely.[48]

These two leading types of response to contemporary adjudicatory difficulties, the fundamental values approach of the early Bickel and Dworkin, and the democratic process approach of the later Bickel and Ely, illustrate both the persistence of early liberal premises in American constitutional thought and the historic movement toward acceptance of liberalism's empiricist, consensual components over its higher law elements. The insistence of the early Bickel and Dworkin that fundamental values should be upheld even against contrary democratic choices attempts to play the role that doctrines of natural rights did for the early liberals. This approach is a lineal descendant of the higher law methodology used in the procedural due process cases. Even so, since these theories ultimately defend the protection of fundamental rights not on any transcendental religious or natural law grounds but simply on the basis of society's commitment to such rights, they accept the prevailing view that all values must be traced back to the consent of those they oblige. The same is true of the Court's historical fundamental values approach. In taking the promotion of democratic political processes as the only goal that can justify judicial activism, Ely and the later Bickel accept this position as well. But Ely cannot resist injecting a more demanding egalitarian restraint on majoritarian actions drawn from Dworkin's opposing "fundamental values" theory, and Bickel, too, called for limiting majoritarian "whim" through upholding principles he could only defend as "indispensable . . . illusions."[49]

While all these positions take it for granted that empiricism, consent, and democracy have superseded natural law as standards, they would all continue to resist some majoritarian decisions even if the democratic process were shown to be open to all. This resistance is a legacy of the early liberal belief that some desires can be rationally shown to be worthless and illegitimate, but like most of their contemporaries, these writers have abandoned that belief, leaving them without any clear basis for their lingering counter-majoritarianism. The problem is particularly acute for these scholars, who would like to be able to uphold an egalitarianism more stringent than that of early liberalism and current law. While Dworkin relies more on the higher law legacy of faith in inviolable rights, and Ely on the positivist legacy of popular consent, both positions display the same persistent difficulty in legitimating judgments about the worth of competing desires, and neither really addresses, much less resolves it. Consequently, the tension between higher and positive law constitutional theories that has existed throughout American history continues to plague even the most sophisticated theories.

Whether contemporary thought has the resources for finally overcoming this recurring difficulty is questionable. Any solution will require a response to the fundamental weaknesses in liberalism's philosophic foundations. It is necessary either to find a way to do what the early liberals thought they could do, indicate credibly why some desires do not deserve to prevail and why other interests occupy a preferred place, or to accept on consent theory grounds a majoritarianism bridled only by the requirement to keep the democratic process open. Unless this underlying normative and philosophic quandary is addressed directly, constitutional theories, with their particular doctrines of due process, seem destined to provide only further types of temporary, patchwork solutions.

4 · Freedom of Speech

Freedom of speech deals with one aspect of the liberties of mind and spirit that were central to the early liberals. Justices have set forth different rationales for preserving this freedom, including not only the original liberal goals of peace, intellectual progress, and personal freedom but also more utilitarian democratic goals and more egalitarian and romantic ideals. The purposes and problems of early liberalism nevertheless remain the starting point for constitutional principles of freedom of expression.

Locke never argued for free speech per se, either as a natural or as an instrumental right. This lacuna only demonstrates that for Locke the issue grew out of a more fundamental concern for freedom of spiritual and intellectual conscience. His understanding was shared by early liberals, such as John Milton and Benedict de Spinoza, who did write on freedom of expression. Locke's ascription of natural right status not to free speech but to freedom of conscience reflected his concern to weaken the influence of superstitious medieval ideas. In the *Letter Concerning Toleration* and *Essay,* he stressed that liberty of conscience, by opposing dogmatism and dogmatists, helped both to curb social "tumults" over speculative and moral issues and to promote "truth." These two goals reflected the liberal ends of furthering peace and intellectual progress, ends that were held in turn to advance personal liberty. Advocacy of governmental tolerance was in fact a crucial element in Locke's effort to redirect political life from questions of moral fulfillment to more practical, temporal concerns. Leonard Levy has noted that these justifications of liberty of conscience depended on Locke's great skepticism about the merits of holding, much less imposing, the traditional religious and moral principles that had for long ordered European thought and life.[1] Only if such precepts were doubted could it be deemed both useful to think beyond them and improper to require them.

But like many others, Levy overstates the case when he contends that

Locke's skepticism amounted to a belief that truth is inaccessible to men, who should therefore pursue more mundane concerns. This fact explains differences between contemporary rationales for free speech and those of early liberals. Locke's skepticism fell short of making him a modern moral relativist, and his defense of freedom of conscience in no way relied on such a stance. He maintained that "How short soever" human knowledge "may come of an universal, or perfect Comprehension of whatsoever is," it nonetheless suffices to secure men's "great concernments," to show them "Whatsoever is necessary for the Conveniences of Life, and Information of Vertue." His view that moral principles could be determined rationally accorded with this claim, and again, he advocated widespread moral inquiry not so much because it would lead to needed new discoveries in true morality but because it would implement and advance the principles he had already ascertained. The acceptance of such inquiry in itself involved acceptance of the principle of tolerance and promoted its attendant benefits.[2]

Locke's rejection of relativism was most apparent in his denial of tolerance to beliefs and arguments that would threaten those benefits, claiming for his principles the decidedly nonskeptical status of natural rights and allowing the magistrate to punish all who advocated positions inimical to those principles. Locke's position on intellectual freedom is therefore distinguishable from later defenses of freedom of speech that do rely on more complete skepticism and relativism. It is distinguishable as well from subsequent claims, shaped by the romantic critics of liberalism, that free speech is a necessary vehicle for emotional expression. Locke accepted the central place of emotion in human psychology and conduct, since he defined good and evil in terms of human desires and held that reason's task is to fulfill those desires that can provide the truest happiness. He did not, however, treat all human emotions as equally legitimate or deserving of expression. His great, if questionably supported, claim was that people can rationally determine which of their desires ought to prevail. He therefore condemned those "wicked Men" who by "shameful neglect of what is in their power" allow "heat and passion" or "sloth" to control their behavior instead of rational judgment. For Locke, "the moderation and restraint of our Passions" should be our "chief care"; to succumb to a "too hasty compliance with our desires" is to behave not only irrationally but immorally.[3] It is not likely, then, that Locke would have placed much value on communication that gave vent to unchecked passions and desires. Any such expression that conflicted with Lockean ends, including civil peace, would have been punishable.

Most early liberal theorists similarly justified free speech in terms of

its contributions to peace and intellectual progress, and similarly restricted its scope. In 1670 Spinoza defended "freedom of judgment" on
philosophic as well as religious matters, claiming that it not only aided
truth but also enabled men to "live together in harmony." He permitted
speech against the state, however, only when it rested on "rational conviction," not "fraud, anger, or hatred," or any effort to impose one's
"private authority." Milton's tolerance, like Locke's, did not extend to
"Popery and open superstition" or "impious or evil" communication. It
amounted, as Levy notes, to protection only for "the serious works of
intellectuals, chiefly scholars and Protestant divines."[4]

Like these early liberal theorists, the American founders gave freedom
of religious conscience pride of place among rights and argued that it
aided the triumph of truth and social stability. Jefferson, in fact, placed
more stress than Locke on the claim that truth would prevail if intellectual
liberty were allowed, "errors ceasing to be dangerous when it is possible
freely to contradict them." This emphasis may have reflected Jefferson's
unique abundance of Enlightenment optimism, but both he and Madison
also maintained that such liberties would help promote "moderation and
harmony" and hence "the preservation of free government."[5]

The tasks faced by the founders, first to justify revolution and then to
construct a free government, moved them beyond religion to concern for
freedom of speech and of the press. Here America's oracles were the
early eighteenth century Whig writers John Trenchard and Thomas Gordon, who collaborated as "Cato." Their opposition to High Church and
Court led them from the standard defenses of religious toleration to more
politically focused liberal positions. In their 1720 essay "Of Freedom of
Speech," which was enormously popular in the colonies, they stated the
central arguments of early American discussion of the issue. They agreed
that free expression encouraged "Genius" but emphasized that liberty
for political speech exposed the "Mischief" of "Governors" and informed
the people on "publick Measures." These political functions of freedom
of expression dominated libertarian discourse of the revolutionary era,
with the Jeffersonian focus on scientific progress being the leading secondary theme. Trenchard and Gordon did not, however, depart significantly from early liberal thought on intellectual liberty, for they also
stressed reason as that which placed "a *Man* above the *Beasts*" and
checked "tumultuous Passion, the greatest Enemy to the Peace of the
Mind and to the Peace of Society." They thus defined liberty as adherence
to the "reasonable" dictates of one's mind and argued that its security
was more important than life itself, serving to promote not only peace
but "industry," "property," and "Arts and Sciences"—all that made life

worthwhile. But their elaboration of the political value of free expression was a major and fairly original contribution to liberalism.[6]

As Levy has shown, most Americans believed that these arguments supported freedom only for political speech that conveyed "liberal sentiments," not speech inimical to the security of natural rights.[7] Few challenged the legitimacy of the common law of seditious libel, at least when used to defend free governments; not even Trenchard and Gordon went quite that far. Madison himself argued that while free governments had to be ultimately subject to the sovereign people, they did not need to be and indeed should not be fully democratic, since "pure" democracies could "admit of no cure" to majoritarian tyranny. Consequently, he viewed as acceptable any limits on political participation that were essential to preserving liberal government. For most Americans, these included constraints on some illiberal political expression. Not until after passage of the First Amendment, during the controversy over the Alien and Sedition Acts, did Madison argue that it was unconstitutional to make seditious libel a federal crime in the United States, and most Jeffersonians believed that such prosecutions were permissible at the state level.[7] The Supreme Court never ruled on the constitutionality of the 1790 Sedition Act, but justices sitting on circuit enforced it. Hence American law continued into the nineteenth century to accept some restraints even on political speech, though they were most acceptable at the state level and few federal restraints on political expression were imposed.

This legacy of suppression derived in part from the confidence of early liberals that certain ends were self-evidently valid and certain beliefs and emotions were immoral and licentious, forming no part of free and rational expression. The framework of early liberal thought on freedom of expression survived through most of the nineteenth century, guiding the thinking of American courts. State governments became, if anything, less tolerant of speech that seemed to endanger the ends or existence of free government. But the liberties of speech and the press were still defended primarily as a means to keep popular governments free by keeping the electorate informed, especially about abuses of their representatives, and tribute was generally paid to the contribution of free discourse to the arts and sciences, as well as to the right of free conscience. The same exceptions, based on liberal premises, were also made to the scope of protected expression. Not only was seditious libel, or speech that threatened America's free governments, still punishable, but private libel, which harmed the reputation that was an essential part of one's liberty, could also be criminal, and various types of material contrary to public morality, including obscenity, blasphemy, and expletives, were considered to express irrational and improper desires and hence to be punishably licentious.[8]

Nineteenth century courts contributed more specific tests to determine when speech fell within these punishable categories, which often expanded the exceptions and narrowed the range of protected expression. The general standard, applied especially to political communication, was the "bad tendency" or "natural tendency" test: any speech which could be held to tend naturally and reasonably to bring about a forbidden effect could be prosecuted. There was no need to show that actual harm had occurred or was likely to occur, and while it was sometimes suggested that the harmful effects had to be intended by the speaker, the presumption was that one intended whatever was the reasonable and natural tendency of one's speech. Consequently, this test made speech convictions easily attainable. In regard to obscenity, most courts in the later nineteenth century adopted some form of the rule established in the English case *Regina* v. *Hicklin* (1868). *Hicklin* was generally treated as holding obscene all matter that tended to "deprave and corrupt" those most susceptible to its influences, with the validity of the work as a whole to be judged on the basis of its most disturbing passages. This test, too, could be used to ban almost any challenged expression. At that time some began to argue for a broader scope of free speech protection, but they did not offer any theoretical innovation. Instead, they relied on a broader reading of what was required to preserve free expression's traditional political and intellectual functions of disseminating necessary governmental information and encouraging the growth of the arts and sciences. Apart from seditious libel, the exceptions themselves were rarely challenged.[9]

But outside of American law, in response to the problems of early liberalism, currents of thought were developing that would lead to revisions in this framework for free speech. Once Hume's notion that reason could not by itself demonstrate morality was accepted, it became increasingly difficult to present speech borne of certain passions as self-evidently licentious. Perhaps if everyone had had only the moderate, practical, and peaceful passions of Hume himself, the new view that all pleasures could be deemed good would not have much altered the prevailing modes of expression. But there were many who agreed with Emerson and Thoreau that the traditional concerns of liberalism were shallow, cramped, low, and unfulfilling. The boundaries that liberal values set for expression prevented what for romantics was the highest end—the unconstrained unfolding of one's innate faculties.

In the mid-nineteenth century, even many committed liberals shared the romantics' feeling that the early liberal vision did not provide a satisfactory account of human purposes. And since in certain forms the romantic value of personal authenticity seemed compatible with the liberal value of individual freedom, efforts were made to join the two views into a revised romantic liberalism. Ironically, the Benthamite utilitarians' most carefully groomed disciple, John Stuart Mill, made the leading attempt at this synthesis. His conclusions on free speech had a significant influence on Justices Holmes and Brandeis and hence on American constitutional law.

In *On Liberty* Mill claims to defend "liberty of thought and discussion" on the basis of "utility" but adds that this must be utility "in the largest sense, grounded on the permanent interests of man as a progressive being." The concept of "permanent," "progressive" interests suggests that Mill's judgments of utility are not intended to accord equal validity to all human desires and pleasures. The values that justify the liberties of thought and expression reveal his sense of man's permanent interests. Although these liberties are vital for "political freedom," especially for developing a competent citizenry and preventing excessive centralization of power, they are especially required to avert the dangers of nonpolitical "social tyranny." Social tyranny is dangerous not so much because it can jeopardize political freedom, although it can, but because it is even more likely to stifle other aspects of men's permanent interests. Of these, Mill singles out the danger to the "development" of "individuality."[10]

Mills's concern is nevertheless an ambiguous one. His first defense of the liberties of thought and expression is that they contribute to the attainment of truth, which is held inseparable from utility in opinions. But Mill does not share Jefferson's faith that truth will succeed in open competition, although he is as yet unwilling to regard truth relativistically, as whatever opinion prevails. He merely hopes that these liberties will preserve the chance for truth to be rediscovered if it is defeated. But this hope raises the further question of when one can be sure that truth has at last prevailed, and on this point Mill seems fairly relativistic. He holds with Hume that "there is no such thing as absolute certainty." At best, there is only "assurance sufficient for the purposes of human life," and the opinions to be regarded with this assurance are those that currently prevail. It is precisely because present majority opinions are not finally certain that intellectual liberties must be maintained. Mill believes that, in modern societies at least, these liberties will in the long run lead to progress, even if truth may lose individual contests. This belief presents an even deeper difficulty, characteristic of all such intellectual relativism: if we can never be sure that truth has finally prevailed, how can we claim to know that liberty fundamentally abets its discovery and contributes to progress? It is impossible to place utter confidence in any standard for truth, for utility, or for permanent, progressive interests.[11]

This problem may explain why Mill emphasizes the importance, not of truth itself, but of the development of "open, fearless characters, and logical, consistent intellects." If we cannot be certain of truth, perhaps we can at least distinguish between those who have developed their mental faculties and those who have not. For Mill, the worth of individuals is their development in this way, their attainment of "mental expansion and elevation." Those who are most mentally developed "are best entitled to trust their own judgment," and this development comes only from the questioning that freedom of thought and discussion promote.[12]

This contention does not resolve all the problems of Mill's relativism. For example, while we may be able to assert confidently that an adult is more mentally developed than a child, how can we tell which of two mature adults is wiser or more correct? But this contention does show how Mill tried to incorporate into his free speech defense a romantic view that the development of our faculties is an end in itself, which becomes even more apparent when Mill defends the liberty of individuality, of living according to one's own "tastes" and "plan of life." Mill cites the German romantic liberal Wilhelm von Humboldt in support of the view that the end of man "is the highest and most harmonious development of his powers to a complete and consistent whole." Mill then describes human nature in characteristically romantic terms, not as "a machine to be built after a model," but as "a tree, which requires to grow and develop itself on all sides, according to the tendency of the inward forces which make it a living thing."[13]

This position produces further difficulties for Mill. Although in the bulk of his essay he treats the development of men's intellectual faculties as the key to their worth, here he quite explicitly holds that "all human faculties" should be "cultivated and unfolded" to make human beings "noble and beautiful." Moreover, all humans, not just mental superiors, are entitled to live "in their own way," and some "require" a "different" "moral . . . atmosphere and climate." If this is so, and if the "cultivation" of every human's individuality "brings human beings . . . nearer to the best thing they can be," then mental faculties have no special claim to development except in those so inclined, and the traditional liberal elevation of reason over the other aspects of human nature is completely lost.[14]

Mill does not equate the moral worth of "Socrates" with that of a "fool" who has thoroughly cultivated his passions for gluttony and debauchery. Nonetheless, Mill does not succeed in reconciling the contrary implications of his liberal attachment to rationality and his romantic attachment to emotive self-expression. Indeed, his position has further problems. He insists that individuality is to be cultivated only "within the limits imposed by the rights and interests of others," and that "the strong man of genius" who "forcibly" seizes the world and makes it "do his bidding" cannot be countenanced. Yet "improvement" may require "despotism" under certain conditions, and the need of some people for their own moral climate, combined with the doubtful accessibility of certain truth, provide elements that could be used to justify virtually any behavior. It is therefore questionable whether Mill manages to fuse liberal and romantic thought successfully, or whether he succeeds in avoiding the aspects of the romantic critique that are most disturbing from the liberal viewpoint.[15]

Despite its difficulties, Mill's position responded powerfully to the felt needs of many liberals for a long time afterward. It began to influence American law in the course of the Supreme Court's first major confrontations with free speech issues. During World War I, Congress passed the Espionage Act of 1917, which regulated "reports or statements" that could subvert the war effort. Subsequent litigation prompted the Court to deal more fully with freedom of speech and led to Justice Holmes's development of the "clear and present danger" test, beginning with *Schenck v. United States* (1919).[16]

The defendants in *Schenck* had printed and distributed pamphlets attacking the draft. The government did not contend that the draft had actually been hampered by these measures but rather relied on the traditional "natural tendency" test of the state courts to show that these measures were of a sort that could reasonably be thought dangerous. Holmes's opinion for the Court upheld Schenck's conviction on the basis of something very like natural tendency reasoning and appeared only to rephrase that rule by using the words "clear and present danger." Thus, it seemed no great innovation when Holmes first argued: "The most stringent protection of free speech would not protect a man in falsely shouting fire in a theatre . . . The question in every case is whether the words used are used in such circumstances and are of such a nature as to create a clear and present danger that they will bring about the substantive evils that Congress has a right to prevent. It is a question of proximity and degree." Nor did Holmes's opinions for the Court upholding convictions in two subsequent Espionage Act cases, *Frohwerk* and *Debs,* where he continued to use clear and present danger language to reach natural tendency test results.[17]

Holmes's wording began to take on an independent, more Millian meaning when he dissented in *Abrams* v. *United States* (1919). That case involved five Bolshevik sympathizers convicted in part of violating a 1918 amendment to the Espionage Act which outlawed urging any curtailment of production of war materials. The defendants had published pamphlets claiming American-made munitions would be used against the Soviets. Although these circulars were not aimed directly at the war with Germany, the Court ruled that, if effective at all, they were "likely to produce" damage to that effort, and so this must have been intended. The opinion was straightforward natural tendency reasoning, but Holmes in dissent argued first that "intent" must be taken more strictly to mean only the "proximate motive" of an act, which in this case had not been to hamper the German war. More significantly, he gave teeth to the clear and present danger test by stressing its "immediacy" and "gravity" requirements for threatened dangers.[18]

Holmes justified such broad protection of speech by his famous contention that "the best test of truth is the power of the thought to get itself accepted in the competition of the market" of ideas which free speech creates. This recalls Mill's claim that competition among ideas is necessary to preserve truth, but it takes the argument a step further, reflecting the more relativistic, evolutionary philosophy that led to Holmes's innovations in legal theory. Holmes at least appears to be saying not merely that an open marketplace keeps alive the possibility of truth prevailing but also that marketplace success is the only standard for truth that we can have. This position might suggest that if a majority has decided certain restraints on speech are political "truth," they must be taken as correct, and for a long time this was Holmes's conclusion. Eventually, however, probably due to the influence of Louis Brandeis and Learned Hand, Holmes accepted that opportunities to engage in the competition must be kept as open as possible.[19]

Holmes therefore contended that statements cannot be suppressed unless they "so imminently threaten immediate interference with the lawful and pressing purposes of the law that an immediate check is required to save the country." This demand for a danger so serious and immediate that the country can be saved in no other way than to halt the speech is far more stringent than the relatively vague requirements of the older test. It is still debatable whether Holmes was biding his time in the earlier cases, as Professor Zechariah Chafee suggested, or whether his thinking had since evolved.[20] Regardless, the *Abrams* dissent was the first of a series of dissents by Holmes and Brandeis that refined the clear and present danger test, and these opinions were eventually largely adopted by the Court.

The two justices' next dissent came in *Gitlow* v. *New York*, the case where the Court first held the free speech guarantee of the First Amendment applicable against the states by means of the Fourteenth Amendment. Here, as in subsequent cases, Holmes dropped the emphasis on intent that had arisen in the peculiar circumstances of *Abrams* and focused the test solely on the issue of whether the "Left Wing Manifesto" involved produced a "present danger of an attempt to overthrow the government by force." Holmes believed that the manifesto posed no such danger, that any success it might have could come only "at some indefinite time in the future," and that this threat was "too remote" to warrant restraint. Indicating how much more relativistic his defense of free speech was than that of early liberalism, he also maintained that if "in the long run the beliefs expressed in proletarian dictatorship are destined to prevail, the only meaning of free speech is that they should be given their chance and have their way." This claim is greatly removed from the early liberals' belief that the rectitude of free government as they understood it was so plain that "illiberal" sentiments could be deemed criminally licentious. Moreover, because Holmes's position accepts that a free political process may rightfully be transformed into a dictatorship if a majority so chooses through constitutional processes, it continues to display his doubts about whether free speech is truly permanently required, even as it upholds the open marketplace in the circumstances at hand. Against Holmes's call for a showing of immediate danger, the Court's majority argued that the legislature had determined that certain sorts of speech inherently produce "the danger of substantive evil," that this was not unreasonable, and that therefore deference was appropriate. The Court denied there was any need to review the actual danger of the utterances in particular cases once the legislature had declared the class of speech involved to be dangerous enough to be curbed.[21]

Brandeis eventually responded to this argument and added the most significant elaboration of the danger test in his opinion in *Whitney* v. *California* (1927). Contending that "where a statute is valid only in case certain conditions exist, the enactment of the statute cannot alone establish the facts which are essential to its validity," Brandeis tried to derive what those conditions had to be from the purposes he saw underlying the free speech clause. In an important departure from the previous emphasis on the freedom's instrumental value, Brandeis claimed that the framers had "valued liberty as an end and as a means." Free speech was an end in itself because it was an integral part of the state's "final end," which was "to make men free to develop their faculties." This echo of the ideal of individualistic romanticism was not coincidental. Brandeis came from a family of German romantic liberals and was an admirer of Emerson as well as Mill. And in elsewhere advocating the "right of privacy" and "the most comprehensive of rights and the right most valued by civilized men," Brandeis expressed his belief that the ultimate liberty was freedom to seek fulfillment of not only one's intellect but also one's feelings and emotions.[22]

But here, as for the Court for a long time to come, most of Brandeis's attention was still devoted to the instrumental political value of speech. Avoiding the ambiguities raised by Holmes's suggestion that truth was simply what prevailed in the market, Brandeis referred only to the way speech's informing role promoted "the discovery and spread of political truth." These functions helped to preserve not only "freedom" but also "stable government," since "political repression breeds hate." The goals of free and stable government still implied some boundaries to freedom of expression, but they were wide indeed. They required the presence of an evil "so imminent that it may befall before there is opportunity for full discussion," and this evil had to be not only imminent but "relatively serious." Brandeis defined relative seriousness by expanding on Holmes's *Abrams* dissent: "Prohibition of free speech . . . is a measure so stringent that it would be inappropriate as the means for averting a relatively trivial harm to society . . . The fact that speech is likely to result in some violence or in destruction of property is not enough to justify its suppression. There must be the probability of serious injury to the State." This test exempted almost all speech, and Brandeis's insistence that this "probability" could not be determined by the state in advance made it even stronger.[23]

Although after *Gitlow* the justices were willing to extend First Amendment guarantees against the states via the Fourteenth Amendment, the call by Holmes and Brandeis to interpret clear and present danger as putting speech, in effect, in a preferred position only gradually gained acceptance on the Court. The delay occurred partly because the freedom seemed less central to the judicial activists who saw economic liberties as most essential, and partly because free speech advocates had to search for independent grounds for their activism. Holmes's defense of speech in terms of its role in generating the market of ideas that decided truth, as well as Brandeis's romantic view of speech as an end in itself, provided background presumptions in favor of unrestrained expression. But when the Court gave more protection to speech, it, like the libertarians of the early twentieth century, chiefly stressed the liberty's political value for popular government, as Holmes and Brandeis had done. The *Carolene Products* footnote also fell into this mold, since denials of free speech rendered the political process less open and might therefore be deemed presumptively suspect.

But while these defenses of free speech focused on the political functions of speech as liberals had done since Trenchard and Gordon, changes were taking place beneath the surface. Most twentieth century writers on free speech did not share substantially in the early liberal belief that the ends of government were self-evident and that desires contrary to them were irrational. They were generally legal realists, proponents of modern relativistic thought, who defended the American government more as a democratic system responsive to the actual desires of the majority than as a liberal system protective of natural rights. Brandeis's romantic stress on individual self-development differed from both early liberalism and the realists' focus on democracy alone, but it was rarely alluded to by the Court from the 1930s through the 1950s. The move toward democratic relativism explained in part why the long-standing emphasis on political function now seemed to demand more speech protection: it was harder to claim that illiberal political sentiments were valueless, as Holmes's comments in *Gitlow* show. Even so, modern democratic premises could be used to justify majoritarian speech restraints. This, again, is why the democratic arguments against such majoritarian action in the *Carolene Products* footnote seemed both new and especially useful.

In 1937, just as the Court was retreating in earnest from its economic activism, a majority at last overturned a state conviction for "inciting insurrection" on explicit clear and present danger grounds. The Court soon made clear, however, that its political focus did not mean quite as much protection as Holmes and Brandeis had proposed. Whereas for them "some violence" or "destruction of property," without direct danger to national security, could not justify speech constraints, the Court held that any danger to "a substantial interest of the state," such as "public peace and order," did suffice. The scope of the Court's expanded protection for speech thus had to be defined in a wide variety of speech cases in the 1930s and 1940s, including some involving allegedly subversive "symbolic speech," picketing, expression held to endanger the government's ability to provide a fair trial, and "commercial speech," as well as a few cases falling outside these categories.[24]

None of these cases presented any innovations in the Court's basic rationale for protecting speech. The challenged expression was still usually political, or else religious, and the defense was that this sort of "discussion of public questions" was vital to the American political system. The Court was willing to construe such public questions expansively enough to include, for example, labor disputes, but as two 1942 cases indicate, the early liberal conceptual framework for free speech, with its attendant restrictions, had not yet been repudiated, despite its erosion. In *Chaplinsky* v. *New Hampshire,* the libertarian Justice Murphy, writing for the Court, indicated that the traditional exceptions to free speech coverage still applied: "lewd and obscene, the profane, the libelous, and the insulting or 'fighting' words" were all held to be classes of expression that formed "no essential part of any exposition of ideas," had minimal if any value, and consequently could be restrained without special judicial scrutiny. Both the particular categories of worthless speech and the exclusion of noncognitive expression recall the rationalistic views on the scope of free speech in Milton, Spinoza, Locke, and Trenchard and Gordon. In *Valentine* v. *Chrestensen,* the Court added an additional category of communication outside full First Amendment protection. Commercial speech was held to be essentially private economic activity, not discussion of public questions, and so the Court indicated it would treat restrictions upon it with the same deference it had adopted toward other economic regulations.[25] This decision, while raising more complex issues than the Court addressed, was consistent with the early liberal understanding of free speech largely as cognitive political, intellectual, and religious discourse.

The increased pragmatic emphasis on national self-preservation during the Cold War in the early 1950s made unrestricted speech seem more dangerous than at any time since World War I. The result was the prosecution of Communist Party members under the Smith Act, as well as dismissal of public employees for refusing to answer questions about their political affiliations and legislative contempt citations of those who refused to give similar information to congressional investigating committees.[26] In *Dennis* v. *United States* (1951), six justices were persuaded that the clear and present danger test's demand for an *immediate* threat would not justify constraint of subversive communications until it was too late to be of any benefit. The government successfully argued that American Communist organizations would not undertake overt resistance until the country was under attack from foreign Communist powers and all too vulnerable to internal resistance. Since speech had always been held illegitimate if it presented the probability of serious injury to the state, the justices thought that to restrain Communist activities under such circumstances was not a radical departure.

In fairness, these decisions partly stemmed from real fears of imminent global conflict, which made the costs of excessive tolerance seem far too high. When the Court examined whether the record showed that specific defendants actually presented concrete threats of the sort the government described, a question it took as proven in the lower courts in *Dennis,* it soon found the documentation lacking, and the government won very few cases.[27] Yet the repression of domestic Communism was pervasive, and the Court's part in it reflected not only a sense of the inappropriateness of an immediacy test but also the frailty of the Holmesian view of free speech in resisting majoritarian persecutions.

As the opinions in *Dennis* illustrate, the increased relativism of American constitutional thought, which mitigated against fixed substantive limits on procedurally valid popular decisions, made it easy for the justices to uphold the new restraints. The Court agreed that free speech was not some sort of higher law absolute but rather an aspect of democratic procedure that could be restricted through such procedures to preserve democratic government. As Frankfurter put it, "absolute rules" and "dogmas" could not be used to define "the demands of free speech in a democratic society." Typically, he defended the Smith Act on grounds of judicial deference to the legislature, concluding that by such legislation "the democratic process at all events is not impaired." This argument allowed democratic relativism to undercut free speech protection, although most subsequent commentators have argued from the democratic grounds of the note in *Carolene Products* that special judicial action was required to keep the political processes truly unimpaired.[28]

In rejecting that view in *Dennis*, Chief Justice Fred Vinson argued for the plurality that "nothing is more certain in modern society than the principle that there are no absolutes . . . all concepts are relative." Preservation of "the Government" was left as "the ultimate value of any society," for without it "no subordinate value can be protected." While this claim recalls the traditional liberal argument that rights can be infringed to preserve the government that aims at securing rights generally, it again expresses modern pragmatic relativism. No early liberal would have applied this argument to "any society." The United States began, after all, with a revolution proclaimed legitimate because the existing government had become destructive of its proper ends. Locke's account of the circumstances that justify revolution, which the Declaration of Independence strove to meet, does admit that all states can defend themselves against revolt; the issue is to be decided via combat, by an "appeal to heaven." Even so, Locke, like Jefferson, thought that there could be a duty to rebel against an unjust government.[29]

Vinson argued in response to these concerns that the claim of "a 'right' to rebel" was "without force where . . . the government provides for peaceful and orderly change." His position still differed significantly from that of the early liberals: Locke and Jefferson both insisted that any "Form of Government" may pursue "other ends" than those authorized and so can be legitimately opposed.[30] The fact that a government is democratic and provides channels for electoral change does not override its obligation to secure the rights for which it is established. But the pragmatic relativism of Vinson found no difficulty in holding that national security outweighed the need to preserve certain rights. Although nineteenth century American liberals would probably have reached similar conclusions on grounds of the threat to free government as they saw it, Vinson's reasoning thus reflected major underlying philosophic changes.

The mood expressed in *Dennis* was by no means universal. In reaction to the Court's increased willingness to accept suppresssion of political discourse, more tolerant democrats sought stronger grounds for broad speech protection. The commonest alternative was Alexander Meiklejohn's 1948 defense of the First Amendment as an "absolute." This view was by no means a return to higher law doctrines. In keeping with the orthodoxy of the day, Meiklejohn "derived" the principle of free speech not from "some supposed 'natural Right' but from the necessities of self-government by universal suffrage." He insisted, however, that all "public speech," broadly defined, must be permitted if democratic decision-making was to be an effective reality. His argument was not new, although contrary to his rather sketchy historical claim, it did not date back to the *Federalist,* which did not advocate the "universal suffrage" on which Meiklejohn's argument relied. The position essentially elaborated the familiar second paragraph of the *Carolene Products* footnote, defending the necessity of free speech for a truly democratic political process. But Meiklejohn's insistence that this logic demanded absolute protection for public speech and his stress on actual participation showed some movement from the first, utilitarian response to natural rights to the second, substantive type of reaction, in this case the more absolutist attachment to democracy of the social egalitarian critique. Meiklejohn's position was in fact too absolutist on political matters, and too exclusive of claims for speech as an end in itself, to win widespread support during the 1950s on the Court or in the legal literature.[31]

Eventually the heightened fears of the McCarthy period began to recede, permitting a striking historical irony. The relativism that had so recently justified the suppression of speech was again employed to argue for the broadest protection of speech in the nation's history. Not only did the Court begin to look much less favorably on various sorts of Communist prosecutions, but the dominant relativism greatly broadened notions of what constituted public questions and pertinent expression. It therefore undercut traditional arguments for exempting from First Amendment protection libel, obscenity, other offensive speech, and commercial speech. Since it seemed increasingly obvious that free speech had to be conceived expansively, Harlan could remark offhandedly in *NAACP v. Alabama* (1958) that "Of course, it is immaterial whether the beliefs sought to be advanced . . . pertain to political, economic, religious or cultural matters." The extension of protection to much literary and economic expression had not been so clear even a decade before.[32] Consequently, from the late 1950s to the present, the Court has engaged in a slow but definite process of narrowing or eliminating all the traditional exceptions to First Amendment coverage summarized in *Chaplinsky* and *Chrestensen.*

The process could not have stemmed from the logic of relativism alone, however, for that logic derives substantive commitments from prevailing preferences. The development also reflects new substantive values, able to gain influence here, as elsewhere, because of the triumph of instrumentalist views. Especially during the 1960s, both the egalitarian values of Meiklejohn and the romantic individualism of Brandeis worked for stronger protection of all expression, even that formerly excluded from the First Amendment entirely. The use of laws banning obscenity and offensive speech to suppress literary works was a subject of particular moral indignation for those who felt, with the romantics, that creative self-expression was the highest human value. Sensitive to such concerns, the Court entered the area of obscenity adjudication for the first time in *Roth* v. *United States* (1957), promising "ceaseless vigilance" against needless restraints on communication. And although Justice Brennan, writing for the Court, continued to hold that "obscenity is not protected by the freedom of speech and press" because it is "utterly without redeeming social importance," he accepted that sex was a matter of "public concern," and he rejected the old *Hicklin* obscenity standard as too restrictive. Instead, the Court adopted a more recently proposed test: "Whether to the average person, applying contemporary community standards, the dominant theme of the material taken as a whole appeals to prurient interest."[33] The reliance on the average person, instead of on those particularly susceptible, and the consideration of the whole work instead of especially objectionable passages, meant more materials could be protected. But the appeal to community standards left unclear whether this test was ultimately to be applied by the local trier of fact or by the justices. This problem, along with the ambiguities of the test as a whole, meant that the Court soon found itself entangled into obscenity adjudication so convoluted that it can only be highlighted here.

Before the review of that adjudication, note should be made that the Court's tasks were further complicated because at this time it also began interpreting the old political function arguments to give heightened protection to speech on all matters of public concern. In *New York Times* v. *Sullivan* (1964), Brennan's opinion for the Court endorsed the verdict of "history" that prosecutions for seditious libel were unconstitutional and significantly restricted the scope of private libel. Asserting that shielding "criticism of official conduct" was the "central meaning of the First

Amendment," Brennan held that public officials could recover damages for libel only by proving the statement was made with "actual malice," either with knowledge of its falsity or in "reckless disregard of whether it was false or not." The decision was widely seen as a significant move toward Meiklejohn's democratic theory of free speech, although the *New York Times* test distinguished between public and private figures, not between public and private expression, and it did not grant absolute protection. The concurring opinions were closer to Meiklejohn's approach. Taking as his standard "the political ends of a self-governing society," Justice Goldberg advocated "absolute, unconditional" protection for criticism of "official conduct," but not for defamation of the "private conduct" of officials or citizens. Black simply called for absolute protection of criticisms of public officials.[34]

Even as the Court was responding to Meiklejohn's egalitarian, democratic defense of more absolutist protection for speech, his position as the leading academic theorist of free expression was being superseded by law professor Thomas Emerson, who made perhaps the most comprehensive effort since Mill to incorporate romantic ideals into a liberal doctrine of freedom of expression. Emerson still agreed that First Amendment liberties serve to further universal "participation in decision making" and "in the building of the whole culture," as well as to advance knowledge and promote social stability. He emphasized anew, however, that free speech is an end in itself, an essential part of individual self-fulfillment, the proper end of man. Emerson thus strove to combine all the main rationales for free speech in the "final, composite form" of the liberal theory of free expression. But it is doubtful whether all these views can be consistently united, and the distance between Emerson's view and that of the founders is evident in his dismissal of the *Chaplinsky* exceptions, which were consistent with early liberal premises, as "totally incompatible with modern first amendment theory." In fact, Emerson eventually acknowledged that his emphasis on self-expression had not been "as fully articulated in colonial times" and was only stressed in Brandeis' *Whitney* opinion.[35]

Whatever its historical pedigree, this new academic focus on self-expression, as well as the heightened judicial solicitude for all expression on matters of public concern, soon found echoes in the Court's efforts to define appropriate obscenity standards. One key development came in *Memoirs* v. *Massachusetts* (1966), where a three-justice plurality made the *Roth* ruling that obscenity was utterly without redeeming social importance part of the test for deciding whether materials were obscene, along with the requirements that "the dominant theme of the material taken as a whole appeals to prurient interest in sex" and "the material is patently offensive because it affronts contemporary community standards relating to the description or representation of sexual matters." It was difficult to hold that any expression was "utterly" without social value, especially since some might feel that affronting community standards and even appealing to prurient interests were worthwhile. This ruling left the Court so divided that from the time of *Redrup* v. *New York* in 1967 to 1973, it was forced to employ the practice of "Redrupping," whereby materials were suppressed by per curiam decisions only when five members of the Court, applying their own tests, judged them obscene.[36]

The difficulties engendered by this confused situation, combined with other developments during this period, led to the prediction that the Court would abandon obscenity restraints altogether. This seemed particularly likely after *Stanley* v. *Georgia* (1969), where Justice Thurgood Marshall, writing for the Court, held that while states might regulate the distribution of obscenity, they could not outlaw its private possession. Marshall argued that there was a First Amendment right "to receive information and ideas, regardless of their social worth," a position never before applied to obscene expression. He also maintained that the right of privacy, recently established in *Griswold,* provided an "added dimension" to the First Amendment when an individual attempted to "satisfy his intellectual and emotional needs in the privacy of his own home."[37] It seemed but a short step to a holding that traffic in sexual materials could not be regulated regardless of their social worth, at least among consenting adults.

In *U.S.* v. *Reidel* (1971), the Court ruled to the contrary that the restraints on obscenity distribution upheld since *Roth* were still valid. It treated *Stanley* as resting essentially on privacy considerations. Nonetheless, the impression that the traditional free speech restrictions were gradually being abandoned was reinforced by the Court's treatment of the numerous protest and symbolic speech cases produced by the civil rights and antiwar movements of the 1960s. Many of the protestors, imbued with radical romantic ideals, claimed the right to convey their messages through forms consistent with their personal "authenticity," regardless of how offensive this might seem to others. And their views had some impact on free speech doctrine, notably in *Cohen* v. *California* (1971). The case involved a protestor who had worn a jacket bearing the words "Fuck the Draft" in a courthouse and had been arrested for offensive conduct. Harlan in his opinion for the Court defended this expression on the grounds that it both possessed political content and gave an offense that could easily be avoided. But he went on to add contentions that seemed to repudiate *Chaplinsky's* rationales for punishing offensive speech. Harlan first made the relativist argument that "principled distinctions" were hard to achieve in this area, since "one man's vulgarity is another's lyric." And he rejected the long-standing rationalist insistence that protected expression had to involve some "exposition of ideas," for "much linguistic expression serves a dual communicative function: it conveys not only ideas capable of relatively precise, detached explication, but otherwise inexpressible emotions as well. In fact, words are often chosen as much for their emotive as their cognitive force. We cannot sanction the view that the Constitution, while solicitous of the cognitive content of individual speech, has little or no regard for that emotive function which, practically speaking, may often be the more important element of the overall message sought to be communicated."[38]

How protection of the "emotive force" of speech could be consistent with repression of language that gained its force precisely from its offensiveness to others was hard to see. Hence, while the Court never explicitly overruled *Chaplinsky*, it showed in later cases that the fighting words exception, at least, has little vitality. When in 1972 the Court either reversed or vacated and remanded convictions in a set of cases involving activists who had used highly provocative language, it indicated that the governing statutes must be closely scrutinized for "overbreadth."[39] No law banning such expression has proved narrow enough to withstand the Court's scrutiny, for it has not subsequently sustained any fighting words convictions.

While these cases centered on the emotional aspect of political communications, the suggestion in *Cohen* that the emotive function of expression might be more important, combined with the Court's reluctance to judge social worth, implied that obscenity, with its undoubted emotive force, might be protected as well. Brennan, the author of the *Roth* and *Memoirs* opinions, finally reached that conclusion in a set of landmark obscenity decisions in 1973. He advocated that the *Stanley* approach of permitting obscenity to consenting adults be applied to obscenity distribution. Under Chief Justice Burger's leadership, however, the Court rejected the implications of the recent cases. Burger's opinions in 1973 established a new standard for obscenity, putting an end to Redrupping, and elaborated on the traditional assumption that obscenity, once defined, could be suppressed. In determining obscenity, Burger held in *Miller v. California* that the "basic guidelines . . . must be: (a) whether 'the average person, applying contemporary community standards' would find that the work, taken as a whole, appeals to the prurient interest . . . (b) whether the work depicts or describes in a patently offensive way, sexual conduct specifically defined by the applicable state law, and

(c) whether the work, taken as a whole, lacks serious literary, artistic, political, or scientific value."[40]

By relying on the average person and the work as a whole and by assigning full First Amendment status to literary and artistic expression, Burger retained the added protection established in *Roth*. Indeed, in calling for forbidden depictions to be specifically defined by state law, he provided a further obstacle to successful prosecutions. Nonetheless, insistence on serious value for sexual expression was a retreat from the holdings in *Memoirs* and *Stanley*, and so Burger had to address directly why obscenity could be deemed sufficiently unworthy to be restrained.

Burger took on this task in a companion case, *Paris Adult Theatre*, which involved pornographic movie houses that refused admission to those under 21 and did not employ any offensive external advertising. Burger held that displays of obscenity could be banned even for these establishments' adult, consenting customers. The expression in question did not occupy a preferred position, in part because places of public accommodation could not claim privacy interests and in part because such communication lacked serious value and was therefore "distinct from a control of reason," "the intellect," or "ideas." Since the expression did not merit heightened protection, the state could regulate on a showing of merely legitimate, not compelling, state interests. Burger found such state interests to reside both in the possible connection between obscenity and criminal or antisocial acts and, particularly, in the community's concern for a "decent" environment. Citing Alexander Bickel, Burger maintained that "what is commonly read and seen and heard and done intrudes upon us all, want it or not."[41]

Burger's insistence that suppression of obscenity was distinct from restraint of reason and ideas resembled the early liberal and *Chaplinsky* distinctions between rationally directed and illicit actions, but the affinity with those nonrelativistic positions was blurred by his confusing claim that the state's power to "maintain a decent society" involved a "morally neutral judgment." Burger's clarification of the permissibility of obscenity restraints seemed to Brennan insufficient to prevent use of the *Miller* guidelines against legitimate expression, especially because the guidelines would be applied by local authorities. In subsequent cases the Court found it necessary to review local interpretation of its new obscenity rule, despite Burger's continued calls for deference to the varied standards of different communities.[42] But the *Miller* standards for judging materials to be obscene and punishable remain in force.

The Court has also continued to uphold some regulation of nonobscene offensive speech, though not fighting words, despite considerable ambiguity about its grounds for doing so. Justice John Paul Stevens has advocated a two-tiered approach to offensive (and obscene) speech that would distinguish between "dissemination of ideas of social and political significance" and "material that is on the borderline between pornography and artistic expression." He would not make even obscene expression criminal, but he also would not give preferred position protection to profanity and erotica, since "society's interest in protecting this type of expression is of a wholly different, and lesser, magnitude" than the interest in political speech. Hence he has upheld extensive civil regulation of the time, place, and manner of obscene and offensive expression. Although Stevens has often obtained a majority for his result in offensive speech cases, a majority of the Court has usually insisted that, outside the obscenity area, all offensive speech has preferred status and so regulations must be content-neutral.[43] It is only because Powell, in particular, has repeatedly found time, place, and manner regulations to be content-neutral, despite the fact that they are triggered only by certain forms of expression, that Stevens's results have been adopted by the Court. So it appears that, officially at least, the Court no longer accepts that it can distinguish some nonobscene offensive expression as unworthy of full First Amendment protection.[44]

The Court's reluctance, even as it upholds restraints, to admit to anything but a morally neutral stance toward different types of speech reflects the relativism that has undermined all exceptions to First Amendment coverage. It may not be surprising, therefore, that the Burger Court has undercut the last intact exception, commercial speech. The pivotal decision was *Virginia Pharmacy Board* v. *Virginia Consumer Council* (1976), where the Court struck down a ban on pharmaceutical advertising of drug prices. Blackmun's opinion for the Court found significant social interests in enabling consumers to be informed in their "private economic decisions" and in their judgments about how the free enterprise system "ought to be regulated or altered." Hence commercial speech could not be denied "all protection" under the First Amendment.[45]

Blackmun acknowledged, however, that commercial speech was not "wholly undifferentiable" from the traditionally protected forms, and in subsequent adjudication the Court has significantly limited the reach of the *Virginia Pharmacy Board* ruling. It has indicated that commercial speech generally receives only "limited" protection in keeping with its "subordinate" status, and that some forms of commercial expression receives less protection than others. The prevailing test, laid down in *Central Hudson Gas* v. *Public Service Commission* (1980), protects commercial speech only if it concerns lawful activity and is not misleading. Any restrictions upon such speech must promote a substantial governmental interest, directly advance that interest, and infringe upon expression only to the extent necessary to achieve its aim. The area remains, however, in the early stages of evolution.[46]

And just as the Court continues to show some responsiveness to pressures to expand the types of speech given First Amendment protection, it also continues to give expression to the more recent rationales for free speech. For example, in *National Bank of Boston* v. *Bellotti* (1978), both Powell writing for the Court and White in dissent cited Thomas Emerson's contention that one of the First Amendment's concerns is to protect individual "self-expression, self-realization and self-fulfillment." The case raised the question of whether corporations have the same right to speak on political issues, in this case a state tax referendum, as individuals. While acknowledging the importance of personal self-expression, the Court, looking to the First Amendment's concern to promote "free discussion of governmental affairs," granted the bank the protection sought. But White noted that some considered promoting self-expression to be the "principal function" of free speech, and he maintained this function is "not at all furthered by corporate speech." He also argued that corporate expression is more likely to imbalance than to serve the democratic political process.[47]

The Court's contrary conclusion shows that, while it remains willing to strike down legislated restraints on speech in the name of an open political process (in keeping with the second paragraph of the *Carolene Products* footnote), its democratic egalitarianism does not extend to guaranteeing full and equal opportunities for political expression and participation to all. This has been affirmed in a variety of contexts. In *Buckley* v. *Valeo* (1976), the Court struck down limits on campaign expenditures, although not on campaign contributions, as violations of rights of political expression. In *Citizens Against Rent Control* v. *Berkeley* (1981), it banned limits on personal contributions to committees supporting or opposing ballot measures. The Court also narrowed the scope of those who are counted as a "public figure," and thus of expression that can be made without fear of libel suits, under the *New York Times* v. *Sullivan* rule. And the Court has repeatedly denied that the press is entitled to any more immunity from grand juries subpoenas and search warrants, or any more access to governmental proceedings, than the general public.[48]

Seen in the light of the different conceptions of free speech in the American constitutional tradition, the Burger Court's treatment of First Amendment issues appears confusing, if not confused. It endorses the relativistic modern emphasis on content neutrality, and its decisions have in some ways expanded the types of expression protected by the speech and press clauses. The Court is willing to strike down majoritarian legislation to preserve political democracy, as in the fighting words cases, and it pays continued tribute to the new focus on self-expression. But it refuses to further the trend toward elimination of all suppression of obscenity, offensive speech, and libel. Instead, the Court has to some extent revived traditional restraints on these types of communication. This pattern has caused the current Court to be described as "particularistic," "pragmatic," or simply incoherent.[49]

However, the Court's treatment of First Amendment cases is consistent with the view of the Burger Court's jurisprudence as predominantly a democratic relativism that emphasizes judicial protection of long-standing basic social values. In disagreement with Frankfurter and in line with the *Carolene Products* footnote, the Court believes that this very relativism justifies giving political speech a preferred position, for heightened protection is needed to ensure that the political processes are truly open and democratic, that all preferences are heard. The Burger Court has rhetorically affirmed this proposition in every case involving indisputably political speech. But as indicated in the decisions denying the press special access, the Court also accepts, against more absolutist egalitarian and participatory views, that a democratic majority can set limits on full, universal participation in decision-making. And the justices have actively opposed legislative efforts to equalize political influence completely, seeing these as undue restraints on individual political and personal expression, as in *Buckley* v. *Valeo* and *Citizens Against Rent Control.*

The Court's willingness in these cases to defend individual expression against conflicting majority views on the nature of a properly democratic system, along with its solicitude for commercial and corporate speech, may also be explicable in terms of its general relativism, which arguably requires that it give full First Amendment protection equally to all communication. But again, the Court is willing to uphold some limits on political participation, so long as these do not deny all access to the process, and it has not gone so far as to rule commercial speech identical to political speech. As some have suggested, therefore, the Court's activism in this respect may reflect a belief that the conduct of private economic activities and its fair consequences are insufficiently protected in the modern state. Consequently, a departure from traditional deference may be necessary to preserve traditional laissez-faire conditions and values.[50]

This sort of activism on behalf of what the Court views as long-standing political and economic values would be of a piece with its approach to claims of self-expression. The Court has accepted this ideal as a valid purpose of free speech, but as in the right of privacy area, it has defended actively only those forms of self-expression that appear to it to be valued by social traditions and customs. Hence, while literary and artistic expression is generally given full First Amendment coverage, obscenity and child pornography can be banned and offensive speech can be regulated. The picture that emerges is again one of general deference combined with heightened scrutiny only of laws that infringe what the Court views to be the fundamental historic values of American society. This stance follows from accepting democratic relativism, but with a Bickelian emphasis on preserving those principles that have won long-term consent.

The rather conservative democratic relativism that characterizes the Court's free speech decisions displays several tensions, some due to the Court's failure to follow through the logic of its position completely, others inherent in any such relativistic approach to judicial activism. Somewhat trivially, the Court's willingness to protect equally and extensively all forms of expression except those traditionally deemed excessive seems inconsistent with its apparent abandonment of the fighting words exception. The abandonment is not wholly clear, however, and it may be traceable to the Court's ongoing concern to protect political speech. Since that concern is justified in terms of maintaining an open, democratic political process, the Court's antimajoritarian activism on behalf of corporate speech and against equalization of campaign expenditures is more problematic. Corporate political speech and unregulated expenditures have long been customary, but inclusion of them under the First Amendment has no clear judicial precedents. The cases that come closest to suggesting such protection are those of the *Lochner* era, and it has since been established irrefutably that contemporary society does not wish the courts to deem *Lochner's* values fundamental. While the Court argues that it is protecting traditional political rights, not economic ones, its willingness to overturn efforts to minimize the political influence of economic power is close to the sort of strict scrutiny of economic regulations that it officially eschews. Hence this activism in the contemporary context may be a departure from any genuine reliance on widely shared social values, toward protection of principles that are more outdated than traditional. Furthermore, the Court has not dealt adequately with arguments that these regulations are necessary to preserve the sort of fundamentally open democratic process it is committed to preserving.

The Court's claim to maintain a relativistic moral neutrality in speech cases also appears inconsistent with its protection of only more conventional forms of self-expression. But the positions are not in fact incompatible, as long as the Court adheres to activism only on behalf of values that genuinely are deeply and widely held. It is then merely enforcing those principles that have the most substantial social consent, without any prior bias as to what their content should be. While adherence to such consensual relativism is a moral position, the Court can claim neutrality on the merits of the values it finds to be prevalent. Yet such a relativistic approach involves a deeper paradox: if the Court defends, for example, the long-standing restrictions on expression of certain erotic passions, solely on the ground that such speech has always been socially disapproved, it is implicitly rejecting the traditional nonrelativistic rationalist and religious grounds for such constraints, or at least treating those grounds as in themselves arbitrary. It is doubtful that this amounts to adherence to traditional values. As with Burger's claim in *Miller* to a neutral rejection of nonrational, indecent speech, efforts to combine relativism and America's traditions are likely to be incoherent.

Reliance on a relativism that legitimates the values judicially upheld only in terms of consent involves a further inherent difficulty. Why should one who does not consent to the majority's values, tacitly or otherwise, obey them? On relativist premises, the situation appears to be one in which a large group that chooses one set of values coerces one or a few who choose another. Although there may be no credible alternative account, that description of the Court's enforcement of social values undermines the Court's authority.

But while the Court's current approach to free speech is plagued with difficulties, it remains to be seen whether any other available approach could be more workable. None of the inherited positions is wholly satisfactory without major qualifications. The early liberals used their distinction between rational and irrational expression to suppress much political and emotive communication that would be legally protected today. Even if the scope of speech necessary to preserve free government, insure stability, and promote intellectual progress is read more broadly by contemporaries than it was by the early liberals, the fundamental problem remains: drawing lines that distinguish between rational and irrational expression seems too difficult a task to avoid repressive chilling effects, if it is not indeed impossible in principle. Democratic relativism can extend protection to all types of speech, but it can just as easily justify majoritarian restraints. And if restraints are judicially analyzed in terms of concerns to maintain an open political process, then the position must be used only to defend protection of political speech, narrowly defined, or else the scope of its coverage is unlimited. The current Court's solution, adherence to limits that have long-term social consent, not only is too indeterminate to be put into effect practically and predictably. It also runs the risk of sustaining majoritarian prejudices against forms of expression, particularly those less directly political, which would be held crucial from other theoretical perspectives, including early liberalism and later romantic liberalism. A variety of scientific and artistic works, after all, have at times challenged long-standing moral beliefs of society in ways now seen as beneficial.[51]

The possibility remains of moving further in one of the two other main alternative directions by defining protected speech in terms of either the romantic ideal of self-realization or a more absolutist democratic egalitarianism. These two positions cannot be combined in their pure forms. The absolutist egalitarian view strives to equalize political influence as fully as possible. The romantic perspective calls for unbridled expression of each person's individuality, and for some that perspective will preclude political involvement, while for others it will demand political domination.

Indeed, in pure and individualistic form, the romantic ideal is wholly inconsistent with any form of external constraint. If, as Emerson said, "the only right is what is after my constitution, the only wrong what is against it," then all moral strictures that seem foreign to one's nature can be rejected. Liberals who have attempted to embrace romantic values from Mill and Emerson to the present have shrunk from this conclusion, but modern advocates of the position have had to acknowledge that, taken alone, self-fulfillment values can justify "every imaginable type of conduct," including "violence or coercion." Consequently, they have adopted a variety of standards to indicate what forms of self-expression should not receive society's deference. Mill himself distinguished between "self" and "other-regarding" actions and, implicitly, between "progressive" and "barbaric" forms of self-development. But the first distinction has proven notoriously hard to apply, and the second is inconsistent with the claim that all are entitled to follow their unique natures. Recent free speech theorists have instead distinguished between "expression" and "conduct," the "communicative" and "noncommunicative" impact of speech, and "coercive" versus "noncoercive" expression, among other contrasts. Yet all such efforts presuppose that some values are entitled to override claims of personal self-realization, and these priorities cannot be defended in a way consistent with adherence to the romantic position. The usual device is to adopt some sort of egalitarianism that requires respect for the like rights of others, as in Emerson's assertion that all are special in some respect and so worthy of consideration, or the modern assertion of a simple right to equal concern and respect. But this egalitarian restraint on claims of self-realization is usually merely assumed, not derived from the romantic ideal itself.[52] The premise of self-realization leads each person to regard his own nature as an ultimate end but does not by itself require him to treat others similarly or to be so treated by them. To adopt other values that do require this outcome would reject the romantic claim that personal actualization is the highest value.

If the unit to be actualized is not the individual but his social group, it is possible to insist that he has obligations, at least to the other group members. Such romanticism, however, usually identifies those obligations by appeal to the character of the group as expressed in its customs and traditions. In this respect the romantic view resembles the democratic relativism propounded by the later Bickel, as he recognized, and hence to the approach of the current Court.[53] And the view is open to the same objections, that it produces internal inconsistency when employed in a liberal society and that it can be excessively repressive. The latter point is only emphasized by the fact that, just as individual romanticism has difficulty generating obligations to other persons, so this group romanticism issues more often in claims to supremacy than in respect for other nations.

Among the pure alternatives, there remains the option of explicitly giving primacy to absolutist egalitarian values and deriving from them the standards for free speech. Some movement toward this philosophy is evident in the legislative effort to equalize campaign contributions and expenditures, and thus political influence. This effort to restrict political expression in the name of equality is objectionable on various grounds, such as a belief in the legitimacy of inequalities flowing from just economic acquisitions or a belief in the right to unbridled self-expression.[54] Even if the particular equalizing measures taken in *Buckley* v. *Valeo* should seem legitimate, it is widely seen as impractical and undesirable to attempt to ensure genuinely equal political influence on the part of all citizens. Resources of knowledgeability, persuasiveness, and personal allegiance are bound to remain significantly unequal, and efforts to mitigate their political significance could easily be unduly coercive. Furthermore, many citizens currently choose to exercise very little political influence, and a neo-Rousseauean requirement that they participate would also be widely seen as unjust. More appropriate standards for equalizing speech opportunities might be designed, which would perhaps be consistent with genuine opportunities for all in the marketplace of political expression. Such standards will inevitably, however, result from combining equalitarian concerns with other values, and so will be less absolutist.

A satisfactory theory of free speech must therefore be more complex than any pure form of these inherited conceptions of the liberty. The present task appears to be to combine these different values within a more comprehensive framework. Such a combination involves hard choices: because of their inherent tensions, certain values have to be given primacy over others. Much traditional legal analysis would argue that those choices are best made not by attempting a seamless, thorough synthesis of all pertinent free speech considerations. Instead, judges should prudently work out appropriate combinations to meet particular problems as they arise. To some degree, this is what the current Supreme Court has done and what sitting justices must do. But because the resulting case law displays so many normative perspectives, free speech doctrine is now widely perceived as internally confused and substantively inadequate. Since the law only reflects the broader uncertainties in contemporary American thought about the purposes of free speech and of the constitutional system as a whole, it is unlikely that the inconsistencies in current First Amendment doctrines can be reduced unless the difficulties of early liberal aims and later goals are addressed in a stronger guiding theory.

5 · Voting Apportionment

The Constitution is generally held not to confer any right to vote per se, but it does protect against infringement of the voting rights of those qualified according to state laws.[1] In the twentieth century the Supreme Court has upheld numerous constitutional safeguards against a variety of voting restrictions. Only since the 1960s, however, has the Court's activism extended to challenging state malapportionment of electoral districts. This new attention to voting apportionment again reflects the evolution of American liberalism, for it expresses both a relativistic democratic concern to ensure that all interests are counted and a partial acceptance of a more absolutist political egalitarianism. Recently the Court has inclined more toward the relativistic view, although its doctrines do not display a fully coherent position.

The Court's difficulties have been somewhat obscured because many analysts of the apportionment cases have not accurately related constitutional notions of political equality to the different historical versions of liberal theory. Even very able scholars tend to treat Locke as a clear harbinger of the modern Court's one person, one vote rule. Although he demanded majority rule in the initial selection of a form of government, Locke presented numerous forms as permissible and left the matter to be decided in the concrete circumstances of particular political societies. In discussing legislatures, Locke criticized rotten boroughs and called for representation to be based on "just and undeniable *equal measures*," but he did not hold that population alone could justly be measured in apportioning representatives. Instead, Locke, like many early liberals, seemed to contemplate that an area's "Riches" would be taken into account in assigning it representation. He only insisted, consistent with his call for uniform application of the laws, that such factors be given the same weight in determining the representatives granted to different geographical districts. If the number of an area's representatives is determined by measuring both its wealth and its population, the results will not necessarily conform to one person, one vote.[2] Locke's views on apportionment itself were too brief to justify definitive conclusions, but his general tolerance of any form of government that pursued his ends shows beyond question that he did not require a fully egalitarian political democracy.

Neither the writers of the *Federalist Papers,* which deal more fully with the subject of representation, nor the rest of the Constitution's framers actively contemplated a one person, one vote requirement. The original Constitution plainly did not impose such a standard on state legislative apportionments, and despite the Court's contrary holding, few scholars have agreed that it was mandated for congressional districts. Egalitarian sentiments were nevertheless present. Madison defended the departures from exact population requirements in Article I only as concessions to the state's rights and slavery supporters needed to ensure the Constitution's ratification. The acceptance of state representation in the Senate, the guarantee of at least one representative for every state, the counting of slaves as 3/5 persons for purposes of taxation and representation, and the proviso that the House's electors would be those qualified by each state to vote for its most populous legislative body, all fall in this category. The Constitution also apportioned representatives among the states primarily by population, and while it said nothing about the existence or character of congressional districts, the framers appeared to expect districts to exist and to be equal in population size. Madison argued that representation by population had a "natural and universal connection" with the "personal rights of the people," and he assumed that Philadelphia, with a population close to 60,000, would be assigned two equally populated congressional districts.[3]

Even so, the new constitutional system directly countenanced numerous deviations from equal population representation and left many electoral procedures up to the state legislatures, who were not subject to equal apportionment requirements. Most of the calls for equal representation in the House referred only to the numbers of representatives assigned to the states as units, not to intrastate district equality. Indeed, Madison's reference to Philadelphia indicates that he expected some conformity to existing political subdivisions, since he did not anticipate that Philadelphia might be divided up among a number of largely suburban or rural congressional districts. Madison also cited, albeit equivocally, the argument that the property as well as "the persons of individuals" might be "considered as represented" and so taken into account in granting representatives.[4]

If we try to appeal from these specifics to the general representative philosophy of the framers, we get no further toward one person, one vote. The framers, attached to higher law and property rights, feared the excesses of democracy and the tyranny of majority factions. They saw representation as a means to guard against these dangers. Since they believed that "it is the reason, alone, of the public that ought to control and regulate the government," while the passions of the public "ought to be controlled and regulated by the government," the founders sought to distance the people's representatives from the "transient impulses" and "temporary errors and delusions" of their constituents.[5]

The representative structure they created might be analyzed by discussing the representation they gave to diverse interests, providing numerous opportunities for each to oppose threatening measures. Or it could be explained by stressing their hopes that representatives would not be too dependent on particular interests and so would be able to act dispassionately and on behalf of the whole. Both lines of analysis are revealing. But the crucial common denominator to the framers' representative structures was their willingness to adopt any system that promised to preserve ultimate accountability while checking all popular desires contrary to government's proper end, the securing of inalienable rights. This willingness enabled the framers to embrace departures from individual political equality whenever these seemed conducive to social stability and the protection of legitimate economic rights and interests. Even egalitarian framers were apt to dismiss less qualified notions of democratic representation, as shown by Madison's remark that "nothing can be more fallacious than to found our political calculations on arithmetical principles." When in *Gray* v. *Saunders* (1963) Justice Douglas tried to justify historically the one person, one vote rule, he therefore had to argue that the original Constitution's view of permissible political inequalities "belongs to a bygone day," having been superseded by the more democratic principles expressed in the Fourteenth, Fifteenth, Seventeenth, and Nineteenth Amendments.[6]

The egalitarian notions expressed in the recent Court apportionment decisions thus largely reflect more modern political conceptions, born in part due to the difficulties of early liberalism. Epistemological and substantive objections to its higher law principles led liberals to deepen their commitment to consent as the ultimate basis for government, and that pattern characterizes the history of American representation. Its historical highlights included the Jacksonian elimination of property qualifications, establishment of universal white manhood suffrage, increased accountability of electoral college delegates, and creation of elective judiciaries in some states; the post-Civil War adoption of the equal protection clause of the Fourteenth Amendment and the enfranchisement of blacks in the Fifteenth Amendment; and the adoption of such Populist and Progressive democratic reforms as direct election of senators, primaries, the initiative and referendum, and women's suffrage. These egalitarian movements also prompted federal statutes in 1842, 1872, 1882, 1891, 1901, and 1911 requiring the states to construct single-member congressional districts that would be compact, contiguous, and equal in population.[7]

At the state level the Jacksonians in particular achieved considerable success in securing more equal representation for newly opened rural areas. But while many states in the nineteenth century made population the starting point in apportioning representatives, they often combined the population principle with the principle of giving some voice to each political subdivision in at least one house of the legislature. At a minimum, established towns or counties might be guaranteed one representative even if their populations were significantly less than those of most districts. This pattern prevailed even in the states created from the territories governed by the Northwest Ordinance, where Congress, in legislating for new areas free of local political traditions and customary subdivisions, had explicitly required representation to be "proportionate" to population.[8]

After 1900 a countercurrent within the ranks of democratic reformers worked against equal apportionment. The remnants of rural Populism and the middle-class Progressives often joined together to limit the legislative power of fast-growing cities run by urban machines built on the votes of industrial laborers and immigrants. Some states adopted constitutions that appealed to the "federal analogy" to justify geographically apportioned state senates or other means to assure continued strong rural representation. Some simply refused to reapportion their legislatures as their constitutions required. And in the Republican 1920s, when *Lochnerizing* thrived and the Progressive focus on scientific management snuffed democratic impulses, Congress failed after the decade's census to reapportion the number of representatives assigned to each state. Hence the states were not prompted to redesign their congressional districts. When in 1929 Congress finally adopted standards to be used after the 1930 census, the requirement for equally populated districts was dropped. Discrepancies in congressional district sizes thus reached as high as 40 percent; but for a Court deeply suspicious of urban social reformers and rising egalitarianism, these political inequalities posed no constitutional problem.[9]

The subsequent ascendancy of the deferential Frankfurterian version of democratic relativism made it difficult for this situation to change. The leading case was *Colegrove* v. *Green* (1946), where Frankfurter wrote for a plurality in the Court's first major consideration of a constitutional challenge to unequal apportionment. Kenneth Colegrove, a political scientist, had sued Illinois officials because the state's congressional districts were not approximately equal in population. Frankfurter found the issue not "justiciable," in part because authority over it was constitutionally assigned elsewhere. Congress had "exclusive authority to secure fair representation by the States in the popular House," and the Constitution "left to that House determination whether States have fulfilled their responsibilities." Even so, the judiciary might ordinarily be expected to ensure that the states' actions met constitutional requirements, but Frankfurter held that it would be "hostile to a democratic system" for the courts to act on questions of this nature. Apportionment constituted a "political thicket" of conflicting party interests and theories of representation, and no legal criteria existed that would enable the justices to pick their way among these disputes. This argument reflected Frankfurter's belief that democracy would be unimpaired if in ambiguous cases the Court upheld the political branches even when they were acting to limit political equality. He was confident that as long as no blatant constitutional violations had occurred, American representation could still adequately express the desires of the people, or at least could do so better than the Court.[10]

But by this time the rival democratic logic of the *Carolene Products* footnote existed, insisting that the Court had a special responsibility to make sure both that the political processes were genuinely open to all and that minorites were not victimized even by an open democratic process. In a series of cases involving primary elections the Court had already shown itself willing to intervene on behalf of qualified voters faced with efforts to deny them effective political voice. The author of the *Carolene* footnote, Justice Stone and his onetime clerk Herbert Wechsler, as well as lawyers Thurgood Marshall and William Hastie of the National Association for the Advancement of Colored People, were instrumental in persuading the Court to decide that constitutional protection against suffrage infringements extended to primaries and that all-white primaries violated the Fifteenth Amendment. Precedents thus existed for holding that voting rights were justiciable, and three justices argued in *Colegrove* that the Court should act against the district inequalities, either through the federal power over congressional apportionment conferred by Article I, Section 4, or under the equal protection clause. The swing vote in the 4–3 decision came from Justice Rutledge. He agreed that the Court had jurisdiction over the question but felt that the judiciary lacked clear standards for deciding apportionment issues and that the only remedy available in the case, the ordering of at-large elections, might be "worse than the disease" from the standpoint of effective representation. He therefore voted to dismiss the case for "want of equity."[11]

The closeness of the result suggests the frailty of Frankfurter's argument for deferring to an unrepresentative legislative body, an argument that did not even follow from his own insistence on the primacy of democratic processes. Yet because the problem of appropriate relief seemed insuperable, *Colegrove* v. *Green* was followed over the next sixteen years by a series of opinionless, *per curiam* decisions by the Court. In the meantime, forces were at work that would make the case against unequal apportionment more persuasive. Studies documented the extent of disproportionate representation in various states and explored possible remedies based on state court experiences. The new, less relativistic stress on egalitarian democratic values during this period also affected voting rights law. The drive against unrepresentative electoral systems was fueled in part by litigation to secure equality for blacks, as demanded by the third, result-oriented paragraph of the *Carolene Products* footnote. The same Court that was beginning to move against segregation also moved against racial discrimination in voting, with Frankfurter himself writing to overturn a racist district gerrymander in *Gomillion* v. *Lightfoot* (1960).[12] Analysis of contemporary voting litigation must distinguish between judicial arguments for democratic decision-making procedures based on relativism and contentions resting on more absolutist demands for full political equality as of right. But when the issue was gross malapportionment, both positions opposed the status quo. Hence, once the Court began deciding voting issues, it soon held that unequally populated districts violated equal protection as much as racially gerrymandered ones.

The Court took this major step in *Baker* v. *Carr* (1962), although Frankfurter, joined by Harlan, refused to follow, finding the Fourteenth Amendment's concern for equal political rights less clear than its commitment to racial justice. In *Baker* the Court confined itself to deciding whether an equal protection challenge to Tennessee's legislative apportionment was justiciable, leaving any further disposition of the case to the district court. Consequently, Brennan's opinion for the Court was essentially devoted to considering whether apportionment was the sort of "political question" that courts should not decide. Brennan listed a number of factors defining a political question, the crucial one being that such an issue involves "a lack of judicially discoverable and manageable standards for resolving it." For the case at hand, Brennan argued, "judicial standards under the Equal Protection Clause are well developed and familiar, and it has been open to courts since the enactment of the Fourteenth Amendment to determine . . . that a discrimination reflects no policy, but simply arbitrary and capricious action." This argument seemed to invoke the traditional equal protection demand that legislative distinctions be "reasonable," but Brennan's comments were too cryptic to be certain. He simply concluded that "we have no cause at this stage to doubt the District Court will be able to fashion relief if violations of constitutional rights are found."[13]

Justice Tom Clark's concurring opinion intimated what the standards might be more fully. He did discern in the Court's opinion the traditional reasonableness standard, and he defended it, finding that the Tennessee apportionment "offended" equal protection because it was "a crazy quilt without rational basis." Even so, Clark acknowledged that it would be hard to select among the wide range of possible rational apportionments, and he would not wish the Court to act in "so delicate a field if there were any other relief available." But, Clark argued, a legislature produced by malapportionment would never reform itself, and since Tennessee lacked initiative and referendum, there were "no practical opportunities for reform other than through the federal courts." This reasoning accorded with the second paragraph of the *Carolene Products* footnote: the Court had a special responsibility to intervene only when the political processes were too unrepresentative to be even colorably responsive. Reasonable inequalities might be permissible, but gross and arbitrary differences in district size were not. Justice Douglas's concurrence suggested a similar view, since it held that "universal equality is not the test; there is room for weighting."[14]

Because the Court's opinion said so little about what the appropriate constitutional standards were, the dissenters had little to attack, but they still maintained that no "accepted legal standards or criteria or even reliable analogies" existed to guide judicial judgment. Assuming that reasonable weighting was to be permitted, Frankfurter argued that this approach meant "geography, economics, urban-rural conflict, and all the other non-legal factors which have throughout our history entered into political districting are to some extent not to be ruled out." But, he insisted, judges had no way of determining to what degree such factors and others were to be given play in districting. The courts were being asked to choose "among competing theories of political philosophy," and they had no manageable standards to do so.[15]

Frankfurter's argument indicated that the justices would have to come up with credible standards for apportionment under equal protection. They did not officially do so until the six *Reapportionment Cases* led by *Reynolds* v. *Sims* (1964), but they foreshadowed their answer in two intervening cases, *Gray* v. *Sanders* (1963) and *Wesberry* v. *Sanders* (1964).

Gray involved Georgia's county unit method of counting votes in Democratic party primaries for statewide offices. Each county was allotted a set number of unit votes, all of which went to the candidate who led the county's popular vote, regardless of his margin of victory. This system was held to violate equal protection because only the votes of those who voted for the leading candidate in a county ended up having any ultimate weight. Douglas's opinion striking down the system claimed not to decide what the Fourteenth Amendment required for the construction of legislative districts. In fact, it acknowledged that the Constitution "sanctioned" the weighting of votes involved in "matters of representation, such as the allocation of Senators irrespective of population and the use of the electoral college" in presidential elections. But once the class of voters and their qualifications were specified, and once the geographical unit to be represented by an officer was designated, all qualified to participate in the election were to have "equality of voting power."[16]

This holding accepted that to some extent the Senate and even the President represent not the United States as a geographical unit but the separate states, so states can be given representation not strictly in accordance with their populations. The relevant geographical unit for the Georgia state offices, however, was the entire state, and so the primary system could not give voters in some counties more effective votes than those in others. In a closing footnote, Douglas even stated that if unit votes were assigned to the counties in accordance with their populations—if, for example, County A of 10,000 persons received ten votes, and County B of 6,000 only six—the assignment would still not satisfy the equal protection clause. The winner-take-all rule would mean that a 6,000 majority in County A would win ten unit votes while a unanimous vote in County B would still be worth just six votes.[17] Thus, within the relevant geographic unit, subdivisions not only had to be assigned votes in proportion to their population but also had to be equal in population, if the Court's standards for equal voting power were to be met.

In *Wesberry* v. *Sanders*, which concerned congressional districts drawn by the Georgia legislature, Black, writing for the Court, was unwilling to admit that he was employing a more demanding notion of political equality than that of the original framers, unlike Douglas in *Gray*. Black held that Article I, Section 2, which states that representatives have to be chosen "by the People," meant that "one man's vote . . . is to be worth as much as another's," and so congressional districts also must be equal in population. Black referred to new and more exhaustive historical documentation provided by the government showing that many framers had anticipated equally populated congressional districts. Through the arguments noted earlier, however, the evidence for this rule as a constitutional requirement was decisively criticized by Harlan's dissent and, subsequently, by scholars.[18]

Because *Gray* involved voting rights within a single electoral unit and *Wesberry* involved congressional apportionment under Article I, neither case spoke directly to the demands of the equal protection clause for state legislative apportionment. Nonetheless, the Court's willingness to read the Constitution's underlying philosophy of representation as one person, one vote suggested what the Fourteenth Amendment would be held to require. The Court's announcement of its position in *Reynolds* and the companion cases came only after extensive argument, and as a result the decisions were unusually thorough in laying out the issues.

Warren's opinion for the Court in *Reynolds* read both *Gray* and *Wesberry* expansively. *Gray* was held to establish "the basic principle of equality among voters within a state," even though it did so explicitly only when the state was the relevant unit; and *Wesberry* indicated that "the fundamental principle of representative government in this country is one of equal representation for equal numbers of people, without regard to race, sex, economic status, or place of residence." Elaborating this fundamental principle, Warren contended that each citizen must "have an equally effective voice in the election of members of his state legislature" in order to achieve "full and effective participation by all citizens in state government."[19]

This assertion seemed vulnerable in light of the long-standing American tradition of eschewing direct participatory democracy partially to safeguard minority rights. Warren argued, however, that any inegalitarian effort to "sanction minority control of state legislative bodies would appear to deny majority rights in a way that far surpasses any possible denial of minority rights that might otherwise be thought to result." He dismissed the federal analogy of the Senate's state-based representation, noting that this system was only a product of "compromises and concession" and was "inapposite" for state districting, since "political subdivisions of States" were not "sovereign entities" but "governmental instrumentalities."[20]

Even so, Warren did not demand perfect equality. He stated that it was a "practical impossibility" to achieve "mathematical exactness" in apportionment, although equally populated districts can be achieved within the accuracy of the latest census data. The Chief Justice seemed willing to tolerate other, more significant grounds of discrepancy. At first, he appeared to be advancing the traditional, highly deferential equal protection requirement of reasonableness employed by Clark in *Baker* v. *Carr*. Warren held that "so long as the divergences from a strict population standard are based on legitimate considerations incident to the effectuation of a rational state policy, some deviations . . . are constitutionally permissible." But he delimited sharply the considerations that would suffice. Rejecting most of the complicating elements Frankfurter and Harlan had held to be involved in a mere reasonableness approach, Warren said that "neither history alone, nor economic or other sorts of group interests, are permissible factors." Ironically, the criterion explicitly held to be permissible was the one that seemed precluded by *Gray* and by Warren's rejection of the federal analogy: departures from population equality to give more equal representation to differently sized political subdivisions. Warren held that "insuring some voice to political subdivisions, as political subdivisions," was "of more substance" both because much legislative activity centered on "so-called local legislation," where subdivision interests seemed most pertinent, and because adherence to traditional subdivision lines might "deter the possibilities of gerrymandering." Warren qualified these concessions, too, in a manner more reminiscent of *Gray:* "But if, even as a result of a clearly rational state policy . . . population is submerged as the controlling consideration, [the] right of all . . . to cast an effective and adequately weighted vote would be unconstitutionally impaired."[21]

Warren's opinion is puzzling. It rejects a mere reasonableness test for districting discrepancies, but it appears to accept some deviations from perfect equality in district populations. At the same time, the considerations it rules out are so sweeping as to reject any ground for departures from perfect equality except conformity to political subdivisions, and that consideration, too, cannot "submerge" the population standard. Justice Stewart, who now along with Clark argued for a reasonableness approach and therefore dissented in two companion cases, pointed out that if, as the Court's opinion ultimately suggested, only "equally 'weighted' votes" mattered, there was no wholly satisfactory solution short of abolishing districts altogether and establishing proportional representation.[22]

Reforms approaching proportional representation have long been favored by adherents of the social egalitarian critique. They have defended fully equal, participatory democracy as a moral requirement of the human vocation, however that may be grounded. Advocacy of this sort of position shaped the context of the apportionment adjudication. For instance, in 1964 political scientist Andrew Hacker dismissed the outcomes of popular referendums that rejected egalitarian reapportionments by arguing that citizens "should be given the blessings of equality whether they want them or not." The Court's furthest move toward such a nonrelativistic attachment to political equality came in a companion case, *Lucas* v. *Forty-Fourth General Assembly of Colorado* (1964). In a statewide referendum, Colorado voters had rejected a plan to apportion both legislative houses by population in favor of a scheme based on the federal analogy. This was the case that separated Stewart and Clark from the Court. Accepting only the reasoning of the *Carolene* footnote's second paragraph, they argued that apportionments merely must be rational in the light of a state's needs and must not systematically frustrate the will of a majority of the state's electorate. Because the referendum option kept the political processes open to majoritarian action, the people's choice of a rational, if imperfectly democratic system, had to be upheld.[23]

Warren saw his principle of political equality as resting on a more inflexible basis than the need for ultimate majoritarian consent. Although he noted that the Colorado referendum had given the voters only the alternative of a perhaps more unpalatable at-large system, his holding did not depend on this fact. Regardless of how well referendums might be framed, the individual's "constitutionally protected right to cast an equally weighted vote" could not "be denied even by a vote of a majority of a State's electorate." This position suggests an activism reconciled with democratic theory in terms of the first paragraph of the *Carolene Products* footnote: while the people are ultimately sovereign, temporary majorities, particularly at the state level, cannot be allowed to alter express constitutional embodiments of popular will. But consent theory provides no clear reason why past majorities should be entitled to restrict present ones if prevailing opinion rejects such restraints, and in any case the existence of a national majority in favor of this interpretation of the Constitution, in 1964 or at any other time, was unclear. Constitutional acquiescence in the decisions of state majorities on voting rights was at least as well-founded. Warren's stance was thus more akin to the third paragraph of the *Carolene Products* argument, which calls for the Court to enforce egalitarian principles regardless of a genuine majority's will.[24]

Given the Court's rejection of a test for mere reasonableness, its dismissal of most, if not all, considerations justifying unequal districts, its rhetorical endorsement of the goal of full and equally effective participation, and its finding in *Lucas,* many felt the Court was moving far toward the radical goal of constitutionally requiring full and equal democracy. Alexander Bickel exaggerated the case when he said that after *Baker* "it became irresistible dogma that no qualification for voting made any sense," but it is true that the Court went on to assault many other voting restrictions, suggesting that the *Reynolds* rule rested on a broader sense of equality than mere identity of district population size. The impression that *Reynolds* stood for, in Harlan's words, a new "constitutional absolute" was reinforced in 1969 by the Court's decisions in a set of congressional districting cases headed by *Kirkpatrick* v. *Preisler*

(1969). There, the Court held that the one person, one vote rule that *Wesberry* had found in Article I, Section 2, could not tolerate anything short of a "good faith" effort to achieve "precise mathematical equality" in congressional apportionments. Even solicitude for political and geographical subdivisions was ruled out. Thus, *Reynolds* might be read as standing for a principle of equally powerful representation, with the goal of achieving not simply formal voting equality but genuine equality in actual influence.[25]

The Court, however, never ventured so far. Despite its sweeping rhetoric, it upheld egalitarian requirements only for certain voting rights, and the prevailing justices probably never conceived of their goal as anything beyond the achievement of more genuinely equal access to electoral systems.[26] During the Burger years, moreover, the Court's partial acceptance of absolutist egalitarian values has been abandoned. Here, too, the Burger Court largely adheres to a moderate version of relativist democracy that rejects the extreme deference of Frankfurter on political process issues, but does not go beyond the minimum demand of the *Carolene Products* footnote for an open political system. This position is evident in the Court's treatment of reapportionment in the 1970s. While *Reynolds* has not been overturned, most justices have rejected any reading of its requirements as including equality of actual influence and have instead adopted the rational basis standard advocated by Clark and Stewart in regard to state and local legislative apportionment.

The Court first made clear that the fundamental principle of representation in *Reynolds* did not apply strictly in nonlegislative contexts. In *Gordon* v. *Lance* (1971), the Court upheld West Virginia's requirement of approval by 60 percent of the voters for certain sorts of referendums. Disagreeing that this demand gave approving voters a "proportionately smaller impact on the outcome," Burger held for the Court that the equal protection clause did not mean "majority control," much less proportional representation. It demanded only that "provisions do not discriminate against or authorize discrimination against any identifiable class." While this view retreated from the earlier insistence that each citizen have an "equally effective voice," Burger pointed out that the *Reapportionment Cases* had dealt with state legislatures and that the Court was not deciding whether "extraordinary majorities" were permissible for the election of "public officers."[27]

Nonetheless, for subnational legislative bodies, the Court has accepted concern for political subdivisions, in particular, as justification for considerable deviations from districting equality. The process began with *Abate* v. *Mundt* (1971), where the Court accepted an 11.9 percent total deviation from equality in a county legislature's apportionment, persuaded that this was necessary for adequate cooperation between the county and its constituent towns. The leading case was *Mahan* v. *Howell* (1973), where the Court approved a Virginia legislative redistricting plan that had a maximum variance of 16.4 percent. Justice William Rehnquist held for the Court, in line with Warren's first argument for the subdivision consideration, that the greater importance of local governments to the states justified "more flexibility" in state than in congressional districting in order to maintain the "integrity" of existing subdivision lines. The Warren Court had refused to allow as much as a 3 percent deviation in congressional apportionment. At least at the state level, according to Rehnquist, the proper test was not whether conformity to subdivisions was deemed a "necessity" by apportioners but simply whether it represented a "rational state policy." Rehnquist still maintained, however, that states could not "emasculate the goal of substantial equality" through districting that stymied genuine majorities. In *Gaffney* v. *Cummings* (1973), the Court held that, in order to promote "political fairness," the legislative shares of the two major parties could be designed to reflect their percentages of the total statewide vote. In related cases the Court indicated in effect that it would not consider deviations in state districts below 10 percent to present even a prima facie violation of equal protection. It suggested, however, that it would subject court-ordered state apportionment plans to closer scrutiny than those of legislatures, though not to the exacting standards of *Kirkpatrick* v. *Preisler*.[28]

The vitality of the political subdivisions exception gained added force in *Connor* v. *Finch* (1977). Blackmun's opinion for the Court noted that "to the extent that the attainment of precisely equal districts requires abandonment of longstanding political boundaries, gerrymandering is that much easier," recalling Warren's second argument in *Reynolds* for respecting subdivision lines. As Blackmun observed, "it is at this point that the goals of equal apportionment and minority representation may well conflict." Advocates of absolute political equality would reconcile this conflict by abandoning districts and adopting proportional representation, but the Court preferred to lessen its demand for one person, one vote. The justices remain closely divided on this solution, but recent reapportionment cases indicate that at least at the state level the trend continues toward deference to deviations justified in terms of representing political subdivisions. In *Brown* v. *Thomson* (1983), Powell, writing for a 5–4 Court, sustained the Wyoming Constitution's guarantee to each county of at least one seat in the state House of Representatives, even though this meant granting a seat in a county with less than half the population of the state's ideal legislative district.[29]

Although concerns about gerrymandering, if not subdivision representation, apply equally to congressional representation, the Court has continued to hold that at this level political subdivisions merit less solicitude. It has nonetheless suggested its willingness to consider other factors, such as the interest in maintaining the seniority of incumbents and their established relationships with constituencies. And while *Karcher* v. *Daggett* (1983) followed *Kirkpatrick* v. *Preisler* in refusing to tolerate even a less than 1 percent deviation in New Jersey's congressional districting, that decision also rested on a 5–4 majority. Furthermore, Justice Brennan's opinion for the Court similarly maintained that a number of factors, including "respecting municipal boundaries" and avoiding contests between incumbents, could justify departures from perfect equality. But the Court found little evidence for the state's claim that the plan was drawn to avoid splitting black urban neighborhoods into different districts, viewing the plan instead as an obviously partisan gerrymander.[30] Consequently, future litigation may yet relax one man, one vote requirements even at this level, and if so, most considerations found sufficient to justify deviations in the populations of congressional districts will probably in turn be deemed rational at the state level. Thus, while the Burger Court's treatment of apportionment issues is not as relativistic as its position on free speech, the Court is moving as far in that direction as it can without sharply departing from the *Reynolds* precedent.

The justices confirmed their aversion to more absolutist notions of political equality in a case related to the apportionment area, *Mobile* v. *Bolden* (1980). The at-large system in Mobile, Alabama, for electing the city's three commissioners was alleged to have prevented Mobile's black citizens, approximately 35 percent of the population, from electing any black commission members. Housing patterns were sufficiently segregated so that a district system probably would have made the election of a black candidate much easier. Stewart's plurality opinion maintained that an at-large system violated equal protection only when it rested on demonstrably discriminatory intentions. He found that both the evidence in the record and the district court's standards of proof were inadequate for demonstrating such intent, and so the decision was reversed and remanded for further proceedings. Stewart treated *Reynolds* as standing essentially for protection against dilution of the vote by unequal apportionment, and he perceived in Marshall's dissent a belief that every minority group "has a federal constitutional right to elect candidates in proportion to its numbers." Of course, he denied that equal protection demanded "proportional representation as an imperative of political organization.[31]

Marshall cited the *Reynolds* holding that "each citizen must have an 'equally effective' voice in the election of representatives" to argue that the dilution in the effectiveness of black votes produced by the at-large structure was an "unjustified abridgement of a fundamental right" exactly like malapportionment. Consequently, he insisted, the intentions of those maintaining the system, racist or rational, were irrelevant.[32] But Marshall claimed he was not calling for full proportional representation, only for more minimal protection of a "discrete political minority" against being "effectively locked out of governmental decisionmaking processes." For the Court to find an at-large system guilty of "unconstitutional vote dilution," minorities must show not just that there had been a lack of electoral success but also that "historical and social factors" had rendered them "largely incapable of effectively utilizing alternative avenues of influencing public policy." The blacks in *Mobile*, Marshall believed, passed this test of "effective lock-out."

Marshall's language was clearly that of the protection for minorities demanded by the third paragraph of the *Carolene Products* footnote, but he tried to prove that its egalitarian implications, while demanding, could be confined short of the absolute logical extreme. He would uphold any electoral system in which minorities had some route to public influence that could partly negate their inevitable electoral failures. Nevertheless, since any reasonably cohesive group can qualify as a discrete political minority and since for many unconventional groups electoral power is a necessary precondition for winning any serious hearing, it remains questionable how far Marshall's logic can avoid supporting extensive claims for group representation in at least rough proportion to their numbers.[33]

Regardless of how closely Marshall approached a call for political equality via proportional representation, *Mobile* shows beyond question that current justices are generally unwilling to enforce any strong standard for equality of actual political influence. The holdings of the Warren Court were open to the charge not only of stating a more demanding political egalitarianism than the Constitution clearly expressed but also of failing to acknowledge the implications of that egalitarianism once adopted.[34] Warren wished to stop short of saying in *Reynolds* that absolutely equal weighting of votes was demanded, but he did so equivocally and without indicating persuasively why the one other factor he admitted, conformity to political subdivisions, was more important than other traditional considerations. Hence the Court's refusal to go all the way to proportional representation seemed inconsistent, as Stewart pointed out. But by moving back toward the mere reasonableness standard of Clark and Stewart, the current Court is open to the reverse charge. Under its approach, there is no clear reason not to admit deviations in congressional districts as extensive as those in state apportionments, so long as they have a rational basis, such as the prevention of gerrymandering, and do not render the system ultimately unresponsive to majority will. The mandate of Article I, Section 2, is surely not so unequivocal, and such remnants of the Warren Court's concessions to egalitarian absolutism seem to have no place in the prevailing relativistic Bickelian philosophy of demanding only long-term consent.

The Court may yet achieve a consistent position by loosening the *Reynolds* requirements in all contexts. But the question remains whether to do so would be the wisest path to a credible and coherent constitutional theory, or whether one of the other alternatives influencing constitutional thought should be adopted. As to the oldest alternative, the notion of representation in early liberal thought, Douglas argued correctly in *Gray* that America's constitutional development showed a declining acceptance of the types of inegalitarian devices defended by the *Federalist*. This decline related both to doubts about early liberalism's higher law principles which called for limits on democratic choices, and to the proven potential for abuse in inegalitarian structures. The state's rights federalism reflected in the Senate was a bulwark of slavery and, as such, was significantly rejected by the postwar amendments, which established equal protection for all and allowed for its enforcement by the nation against the states. The concern for an elite Senate more sympathetic to property rights was also rejected by the move to direct elections, as well as by the abolition of property qualifications and poll taxes in state and national elections. As these and other amendments extending the franchise suggest, if one looks to the structure and spirit of the modern Constitution to illuminate its representation requirements, the conclusion must be that all inegalitarian electoral structures are now constitutionally suspect.[35]

Even so, many of the original inegalitarian aspects of the American system persist, not least its federal nature and its activist, appointive, independent judiciary. The rise of the activist liberal state has generated numerous new centers of administrative and regulatory power that are subject to limited democratic controls. The survival of the older inequalities may reflect no more than a reluctance to tamper with a satisfactory status quo, and the new inequalities surely reflect the vast impracticalities of direct democracy under modern conditions. Whether fuller democracy via proportional representation would generate results more expressive of popular will is doubtful as well. It might allow excessive political fragmentation and thereby prevent any effective governmental action, even though this would be the least preferred alternative of all the participants.[36] American legal and political thought also still displays fears that pure democracy would endanger rights that majorities may not violate, however much Americans may quarrel over the nature and sources of those rights. Thus, the radical alternative of absolute political equality put forth by the social egalitarian critique lacks not only constitutional foundation but also widespread support.

Romantic notions of representation, drawn from the other major substantive critique of early liberalism, have had little influence on Supreme Court adjudication, a failure that is understandable and likely to continue. Given the romantic view's insistence on wholly autonomous, authentic self-direction, it tends either to deny, with Rousseau, that representation can ever be legitimate or else, in its collectivist, organicist variants, to embrace the notion of a great man who embodies the spirit of his people.[37] Both of these positions pose great difficulties for preserving peace and personal liberty, and they appear well outside the practical range of American constitutional discourse for the foreseeable future.

If early liberal notions of representation and modern social egalitarian and romantic precepts seem equally unacceptable, perhaps the current Court is correct in moving toward a relativistic, democratic, mere rationality stance that justifies activism only if apportionments are wholly arbitrary or destroy all democratic accountability. Yet this position gives little weight to the historical constitutional dynamic toward greater political equality. The popularity of the apportionment decisions suggests that the Warren Court's partial move toward more absolutist egalitarianism, however inconsistently realized, captured the prevailing values of the American polity. The correct approach might therefore be to subject deviations from one person, one vote, if not political inequalities more broadly, to strict scrutiny as the Warren Court did.[38]

This approach would make it necessary to articulate more fully the grounds that justify all remaining departures from full political equality and to indicate why they are sufficiently compelling to survive strict scrutiny. Here is where the Warren Court failed, in *Reynolds* and the later apportionment cases, for identification of the appropriate, compelling interests requires substantive arguments as to both what are the most important purposes of the constitutional system, which cannot be threatened in pursuit of full political equality, and why these purposes deserve such status.[39] What is required, in other words, is an integration of the theory of representation with a credible modern theory of the foundations and objectives of the Constitution's liberalism. This task requires, once again, that we confront the basic difficulties of principle that have burdened liberalism and American constitutionalism since their inception. There is no escaping this task by adopting the reasonableness approach of Clark, Stewart, and the current Court. Their position still designates a particular political theory, a moderate democratic relativism, as the proper constitutional philosophy, a choice that must be justified in this area and throughout constitutional law.

Thus, apportionment reveals the same lesson as do the other areas. The law reflects uncertainty about the proper purposes and foundations of a liberal constitutional regime. The current alternatives range from the surviving liberal notions of self-evident ends to a relativistic democracy to a more demanding political egalitarianism. A persuasive doctrine of electoral equality can again come only from a comprehensive reappraisal of America's constitutionalism.

6 · Economic Welfare

Constitutional cases involving the commerce, contract, and equal protection clauses exemplify the attitudes of Americans on a broad and complex topic: the national government's responsibility for the economic welfare of society at large and of individual citizens. Views on the state's role in the economy within both Anglo-American thought in general and American law in particular reflect the same evolution as in the areas of due process, free speech, and voting apportionment. Early liberal notions of self-evident rights—in this case property rights—gave way in stages to more democratic, utilitarian views, in a process that culminated in the New Deal. In the late 1950s and 1960s more absolutist pressures developed for economic equality. The current Court has rejected this egalitarian absolutism for a more relativistic stance that defends values ranked fundamental by long-term social consent. So far, this position has generally not included activism for laissez-faire economic values, but in the past, notably in the *Lochner* era, egalitarian democratic impulses frequently provoked assertions of both old and revamped inegalitarian economic rights. There are hints of such notions in the Court's recent jurisprudence.

The American Constitution was ratified during the historic transition from agrarian feudal economies to modern industrial capitalism, although still at a time when liberal thinkers were working out the principles of classical political economy. The nature of liberal economic policies was far from settled. Differences of opinion were inevitable, because the liberal goal of achieving prosperity through promoting productive labor, exchange, and investment had conflicting policy implications. On the one hand, liberals were concerned to guarantee the security of existing property rights, so as to provide the stability that encouraged investment. On the other hand, they wished to curb outmoded property uses and forms that stood in the way of more productive innovations.

America's constitutional law of the economy began with these diverse and unsystematic notions of early liberal thought and subsequently oscillated between protection of vested rights and acceptance of legislative and common law alterations in the existing economic order. At times, both the defenders of established economic rights and the proponents of change have found higher law and positive law arguments useful for their causes. The role played by economic concerns in America's constitutional debates has thus been exceedingly complex. Crucial to that role are the various views on the responsibility of a national government for economic welfare put forth by the historic versions of liberalism.

The English feudal view, maintained by the Tudor and Stuart monarchs, placed responsibility for the general economic welfare with the hierarchical governing order. Economic measures were often undertaken by local nobles rather than directly by the crown, but their acts usually reflected similar aims. In the era's near-subsistence economy, the ruling aristocratic class thought that it was necessary and appropriate to regulate the production and quality of basic commodities and their marketing. The overriding concern, however, was to protect the existing social order against all changes, including not only those wrought by famine and hardship but also those following upon greatly increased production. They strove to maintain a static economy, so as to ensure that the traditional or "natural" value of goods and services would not be altered.[1]

But as new trade routes expanded economic opportunities, the English rulers, nobles, and gentry recognized the gains to be made by enhancing commerce. Government economic interventions became mercantilist, aimed at a favorable balance of trade. This development was controversial: many "Country" adherents of the old agrarian order saw fixed real property as the basis for traditional English liberties. They objected to any involvement of the Court and its circle in trade and credit, for the government might then finance a standing army, corrupt Parliament into dependency, or become dependent itself on manipulative stockjobbers. And the resulting intrusions on ancient rights might not be resisted by a people absorbed in private commercial gains. Country opponents of commerce therefore constructed a rival ideology that unhistorically glorified England's "traditional Gothic Constitution" as a balanced, land-based republic protective of political liberty.[2]

Because it was impossible to oppose the rise of commerce for long, those who wished to protect the English republic against political corruption became increasingly concerned with the question of how a commercial society could maintain public virtue and freedom. They were both aided and hindered by the fact that in the mid-seventeenth century many merchants, impeded by governmental monopolies and commercial regulations, began arguing for free trade, as a natural political right as well as an economically advantageous policy. The natural rights argument blended fairly well with Country desires to set limits on the economic reach of potentially corrupt governments by establishing economic rights that could safeguard political independence. But the policy argument, promising accelerated economic growth, raised the specter of a people lost to the unhindered pursuit of private profit and hence of an economic and political anarchy that could harm the country and provoke a repressive reaction. These fears were reinforced late in the century by the merchants' lack of concern for the effects of their overseas trade on unemployment and vulnerable industries—problems that were paramount for the manufacturing and landowning employers. These two groups thus came to oppose free trade and worked for the establishment of an explicitly mercantilist state, achieving it in the early eighteenth century.[3]

While the economic thought of manufacturers and landowners was mercantilist, it was also recognizably liberal. They accepted the basic notions that both natural property rights and laws of economic behavior limited the advisability of regulation. They expected people to seek profits and hence to pursue the new opportunities in trade and commerce, and they thought that these activities were generally beneficial. But they had no faith that unlimited trade would always benefit England's producers, believing that unemployment and national decline might well result. Hence, they favored both protectionist policies, in order to promote a favorable balance of trade and encourage domestic industry, and poor laws to prevent unemployment.

Theorists of the era also came to accept the new commercial pursuits on the ground that prosperity was necessary for intellectual and cultural advances. So they tried to discover how commerce could be combined with political virtue, and they speculated that devotion to commercial activities might induce a concern for peace as well as habits of self-discipline. Both self-discipline and respect for property rights were the kinds of private virtue that might stave off corruption in commercial republics. That delay was a worthwhile achievement even in the eyes of those who, like Montesquieu and Hume, believed in the inevitability of corruption.[4] Governmental promotion of commerce in the national interest was thus justified even by many theorists concerned with public virtue, and new attention was devoted to how the economy operated so that commerce might be encouraged effectively.[5]

Locke's treatment of property rights and economic issues typified these emerging themes. Characteristically combining higher law and utilitarian views, he justified property rights in terms of both divine and rational natural law and social benefit. He supported governmental favoritism toward more productive forms of property against landlord rights of idle enjoyment or the interests of distributive middlemen. He also advocated protrade mercantilist measures in colonial and international economic policy. Although he was deeply skeptical of the propriety and efficacy of most domestic governmental economic interventions and so contributed to the relatively laissez-faire theories favored by merchants, he accepted a minimal social and governmental responsibility to provide work and subsistence for all, on both Christian and nationalist grounds.

Locke's mercantilism called for promoting a favorable balance of trade through a governmental Board of Trade, "encouraging" domestic manufactures, and giving landholders, assumed to be employers of productive agricultural laborers, as much of "the favour of the law" as the "public weal" permitted. He also suggested nationalist policies toward England's colonies, recommending that Ireland, for example, be required to grow linen so as not to compete with the English woolen trade. Locke thus has been properly described as one of the chief architects of mercantilism in the late seventeenth and early eighteenth centuries.[6] But his call for governmental economic controls stemmed chiefly from his liberal concern to promote economic growth, not from feudal Christian paternalism. Despite his traditional identification of national wealth with relative surpluses in bullion, he was not a simple metallist. He valued bullion only because mankind had agreed to exchange it for useful "conveniences," so that its possession ensured the acquisition of things needed for further production and consumption. He also denounced extensive governmental involvement in the economy. Private property was not to be regulated arbitrarily nor taken without consent, for God had effectively commanded people to acquire it "for the benefit of Life," and reason showed that, since private property originated in rational labor, it inherently served to increase abundance.[7] The divine and rational injunctions to create and protect property set limits on what people could be understood to have authorized when they contracted to give up their natural properties to political governance.

Locke thought that laws which upheld property rights but otherwise left the rational and industrious free to pursue their own interests were most likely to be nationally advantageous, enabling the kingdom to prosper and the prince to become rich, powerful, and so "too hard for his neighbours." Mercantile regulations should be employed only when productive forms of property required protection or encouragement. Indeed, since Locke's rationales for property consistently pointed to its productive benefits, he did not allow for any fixed, permanent property in unused land in the state of nature; only ongoing rational labor entitled one to possession. Civil society could establish such property if it chose, but Locke warned against the idle wealth that might result if political communities agreed to permit ownership of large, relatively undeveloped estates. He even criticized merchants and shopkeepers as unproductive middlemen who slowed the healthy circulation of money, although properly regulated foreign trade was required to sustain genuine production.[8]

Locke's arguments against regulatory measures rested on assumptions of "natural" market behavior that were coming to be commonly expressed. He claimed that attempts to set lower interest rates would be unsuccessful because market forces determined the price of money and people would find ways to get around any artificially established rate. He maintained less plausibly that, because coinage inevitably tended toward the commodity value of its gold or silver content, as determined by the worldwide quantity of these metals, efforts to revalue the currency would be futile. Generally, he opposed all regulation of private economic interests unless it was "manifestly advantageous of the public," and to prove it was constituted a considerable burden. Regulation might, however, be justified not only in the case of native manufactures but also in the case of interest rates, whenever either a monopoly had extracted exploitative credit agreements from needy purchasers or private contracts had not included rate agreements so that adjudication was required. Locke also knew that market forces did not really impose a universal common value on commodities, including currency, automatically. The value of currency varied in different parts of the world, depending both on local demand for its use in trade and on the trust possessed by the government warranting the currency's value. Because he believed that involvement in foreign trade would move the value of all currencies toward the commodity price of their metal content, he still generally argued against imposing any contrary valuation. Thus, he expressed both the liberal wariness of governmental economic intervention and the conviction that government had some role in promoting liberal economic values.[9]

Locke also recognized a duty to support the needy and to limit contracts that enriched one party at the cost of the "destruction" of the other. Although he was generally uninterested in the domestic distribution of wealth, assuming that so long as it was employed productively, the whole nation would benefit, he insisted that "common charity teaches, that those shall be most taken care of by the law, who are least capable of taking care for themselves." Thus, the duties of charity, which he never fully elaborated, justified at least some governmental redistribution and oversight of contracts. Locke's "charitable" measures, however, were keyed to making the poor, too, more productive, and they were harsh

by modern standards, including restrictions on the mobility of unemployed persons, the assignment even of children to government workhouses, and the free provision of subsistence food and housing only to
those wholly incapable of work.[10] Both considerations of right and expediency limited the state in its economic role, although governments
had the authority to promote, as well as to protect, productive forms of
property and to guarantee minimal assistance against absolute material
privation.

Essentially the same economic views characterized state governments
in the late colonial and early American periods. The governments had
previously engaged in the extensive paternalistic economic regulation
characteristic of England in the Middle Ages. Roads, ferries, mills, bridges,
and other enterprises of public concern, as well as standards for wages,
prices, and the quality of basic commodities, were likely to be established
by government and strictly regulated. By the eighteenth century, some
forms of intervention had been found unworkable, such as the regulation
of wages, which was ignored because of the shortage of labor. With the
frontier beckoning, Americans also began to transform English land law
so as to facilitate the acquisition and alienation of land. Treatment of
the poor, however, followed the English model; in fact, in some colonies
the Elizabethan poor laws were applied unchanged. All the able-bodied
poor were required to work, and indentured servitude was a common
means for them to do so. Residents unable to labor were publicly supported, often reasonably well, since these poor were seen as a natural
social responsibility. But the responsibility was a local one, and many
towns attempted to shift the burden to their neighbors by denying that
indigents were residents. Consequently, as in England, treatment of the
poor was often in practice severe.[11]

The American Revolution did not change attitudes toward the poor,
but the vestiges of feudal economic views gave way to a republican or
"Commonwealth" ideology decidedly like that of the late seventeenth
century Lockean English Whigs. The "Commonwealthmen" favored governmental economic intervention when required by the "public interest"
and thus accepted the mercantile promotion of an expanding economy
through measures to assist food production, manufacturing, and trade,
especially in light of the similar actions of other nations. At the same
time, it continued the republican fear about governmental corruption and
so was concerned to build legal "bulwarks around property" that could
guard against "overreaching coercive political authority." The Declaration of Independence, which detailed a variety of grievances against the
economic intrusions of the British, nevertheless assigned "Commerce" a
prominent place among governmental "Powers," and the new Consti-

tution was inspired largely by the experience of protectionist state economic legislation under the Articles of Confederation, which worked against commercial progress for Americans as a whole. Because the Constitution particularly augmented the commercial and taxing authority of Congress, it is aligned with both the commercially oriented strain of Commonwealth thought and the views of Montesquieu and Hume that a commercial republic would attain peace and prosperity in part through the disciplined devotion of its citizens to economic pursuits.[12]

Such views were by no means universal. Anti-Federalists stressed traditional republican fears about a powerful central government involved with corrupting financial interests. Because of these concerns, the Constitutional Convention did not adopt a number of suggested economic powers. Proposals for explicit authority to issue charters of incorporation, establish canals, and provide public institutions to promote agriculture, commerce, and manufacturing all failed. Many of these powers were nonetheless held by Hamilton and his successors to have been implied. After ratification, Jeffersonians and Jacksonians continued to speak for the preservation of an agrarian economy against the development of trade and manufacturing, holding to the ideal of freely held "fee-simple" land as the basis of political independence and hence of public virtue.[13] While both opponents and supporters of commerce favored some government involvement in the economy to advance the public interest and safeguard property rights, they did not agree on what constituted the public interest, which level of government should take action, or which forms of property most deserved legal protection.

Even the Jeffersonian and Jacksonian spokesmen for agrarian republican ideals were not united on the economic role of the national government. Despite Jefferson's depiction of urban manufacturing as a "canker" on the body politic, he came to accept the fact that both foreign policy and domestic prosperity required the growth of American industry. But agrarian virtue could be maintained only if new lands were opened up to counterbalance commercial and industrial development. Hence, he set aside his constitutional doubts and made the Louisiana Purchase. Later Jeffersonians favored the national construction of roads and other transportation improvements in order to reach the frontier lands more easily. The national government generally pursued land policies aimed at making public lands available in such a manner as to promote the development of a free, landholding citizenry.[14]

On the whole, however, rural and democratic partisans still feared national economic intervention and trusted the states, regarded as closer to the people, to undertake the measures needed for prosperity without corruption. Thus, the federal program of internal improvements never came close to completion before the Civil War. State governments granted the franchises for bridges, canals, and toll roads, chartered the corporations, and in general adopted the mercantile measures to promote economic growth. They had few of the qualms about promoting a diversified economy, including industry, expressed by agrarian republicans about economic intervention at the national level. The enhancement of productivity in all its variations was the overriding aim of all governmental involvement in the infant American economies. While Congress shared this goal, federal legislation after the adoption of Hamilton's Bank of the United States was concerned largely with conducting foreign commerce and preventing protectionist state actions.[15]

The predominance of the states in economic matters extended to care for the poor. Social welfare remained a nonfederal responsibility, except in cases of disaster relief or care for veterans and disabled seamen. After 1815, as the influx of immigrants increased the needy population, some counties in northern states began to assume responsibility for indigent care in place of smaller localities, the towns; later, states established homes for poor who were unable to care for themselves. This new trend to institutional "indoor relief" stemmed partly from the laissez-faire view that poverty was a personal responsibility and public aid was self-defeating. Home relief thus seemed unduly indulgent, while institutional aid, if granted at all to the able-bodied, was accompanied by punitive work requirements. And because few communities would fund separate facilities for the different classes of indigents, it often happened that the aged, mentally ill, handicapped, and children shared the harsh living conditions of the workhouses. Only in the 1830s did institutional specialization begin. In most areas almshouses were judged to be too expensive, and paupers were farmed out to bidders interested in cheap labor. Gradually, the alternative of centralized poor farms arose, because the treatment of the laborers could then be supervised. Home relief was generally left to sectarian or ethnic organizations. Because the traditional fears about national power were reinforced by the new laissez-faire attitudes, federal responsibility for individual economic welfare was contemplated only by the most ardent reformers.[16]

The emphasis on promoting production extended to the decisions made by American courts about property rights in the early nineteenth century. Ideology and self-interest spurred conflicts over the different forms of property that should be given priority by the courts. Some people emphasized the protection of agrarian interests; others favored the defense of the transportation, manufacturing, and financial corporations that had been established as part of the state efforts to promote growth; and still others favored opening the way for new and potentially more productive competitors to these initial enterprises. According to Morton Horwitz, common law courts of the early nineteenth century were engaged in transforming inherited feudal property conceptions, which emphasized "static agrarian" rights to "undisturbed enjoyment," into doctrines favoring the "productive use and development" of property.[17] Similarly, the commerce and contract clause decisions of the Marshall Court, which were the first major contributions to constitutional adjudication of economic issues, encouraged commerce and production while safeguarding them from excessive governmental encroachment.

Indeed, Marshall's jurisprudence was dominated by his conviction that the law ought to foster commercial development and ensure to all "the freedom to make use of one's acquisitive skills" in a competitive national market. These commitments were demonstrated by *Gibbons* v. *Ogden* (1824), which involved a New York state grant of monopoly rights to Ogden's steamboat service operating between New York and New Jersey. Gibbons, who had vessels licensed under a 1793 federal coasting trade act, started a service in competition with the monopoly, and Ogden sued successfully in the New York courts. In adjudicating the monopoly issue on appeal, Marshall broadly defined both the nature of commerce and Congress's power over it. Rejecting claims that commerce encompassed only "traffic," "buying and selling," or "the interchange of commodities," he held that it included "navigation" and all other "commercial intercourse between nations, and parts of nations, in all its branches." Moreover, Congress's commercial authority, the power "to prescribe the rule of which commerce is to be governed," was "complete in itself, may be exercised to its utmost extent, and acknowledges no limitations, other than are prescribed in the constitution." Hence it extended to all but "the completely internal commerce of a state."[18]

Marshall was evasive on the question of whether this authority over interstate commerce was so sweeping as to preclude any state regulation in the area, although he found that position attractive. Instead, he rested his decision on the primacy of the federal coasting trade law, which was well within Congress' power and in conflict with the state monopoly grant. The federal act was concerned more to protect American shippers against foreign competitors than to protect internal shipping, so Marshall's construction of it emphasized not only his acceptance of broad national commerce powers but also his willingness to act against state interventions that restrained free interstate trade.[19] The fact that the restraint took the form of a monopoly may have heightened Marshall's opposition, although like Locke, he never held that all government-sponsored monopolies were improper, doubtless recognizing that in a precarious new economy they could be necessary initially to establish enterprises.

Previous decisions had already made clear Marshall's willingness to go to great lengths to establish legal bulwarks against excessive state economic intervention, particularly to restrain the states from threatening people's rights to engage in productive endeavor and retain the fruits of their labors. His chief instrument was the clause in Article I forbidding states from impairing the obligation of contracts. Contracts were just beginning to gain prominence in Anglo-American law as it adapted to a growing market economy, and the contract clause's framers probably had in mind only a limited range of private agreements. Marshall helped expand the notion of contract to the point where contract doctrines "greedily swallowed up other parts of the law."[20]

His broad view of contracts was typified in *Fletcher* v. *Peck* (1810), involving the Georgia legislature's repeal of the Yazoo land grant because virtually all the legislators who had originally passed the grant had held shares in or been bribed by the recipient companies. The land had since passed to innocent purchasers, and Marshall held the repeal act to violate the contract clause. Previously such state grants had rarely been deemed to be "contracts." Marshall, perhaps aware of the historical vulnerability of his textual interpretation, suggested that his ruling might be supported by "general principles that are common to our free institutions," as well as by "particular provisions of the Constitution." The clear reference was to Lockean notions of natural rights against the arbitrary, unauthorized taking of property; and while Marshall subsequently tended to rely on textual provisions rather than on general principles to defend his results, he nonetheless read those provisions with liberal natural law ends in view.[21]

In 1819, for example, Marshall made two signal efforts to expand protection of acquired property rights against infringements by Jeffersonian state legislatures. In *Sturges* v. *Crowninshield* he struck down a New York insolvency law that retroactively relieved debtors of contractually obligatory debts. In *Dartmouth College* v. *Woodward* he construed a royal charter to the college as a contract which could not be constitutionally altered by the state assembly. These decisions made it more difficult for the states to undercut the power of the financiers and corporations which had benefited from legislative efforts to spark new development. But prospective bankruptcy legislation was not ruled out, and as Justice Story pointed out in *Dartmouth*, legislatures had the option of inserting clauses in subsequent charters permitting their terms to be altered. Nonetheless, the Court to a considerable degree was taking upon itself to decide how far state legislatures were allowed to disrupt expectations of secure property rights in favor of other developmental means and social interests. Perhaps reflecting the influence of the less mercantile Scottish political economists, the Court ordinarily leaned even more than Locke toward protection of the results of market transactions and private enterprises, however commenced.[22]

Marshall's decisions thus displayed the early liberal attachment to natural rights limiting government's economic role, though they also accepted the government's power and responsibility to protect and encourage productive property forms.[23] Because of both philosophical shifts and substantive dissatisfactions, these natural rights views gave way to more democratic and utilitarian positions with the ascendancy of Jacksonian democracy and the reconstitution of the Supreme Court under Chief Justice Roger B. Taney. Increasingly the franchises bestowed early in the century were seen only as bulwarks of privilege that stifled further economic progress and the general welfare, and state legislatures, though still not Congress, acted to combat such privileges and promote new competitive enterprises. The Taney Court countenanced these developments to a greater extent than did Story, the leading Marshall Court survivor.

The new Court's lead case on the contract clause was *Charles River Bridge* v. *Warren Bridge* (1837), where Taney refused to concede that the Constitution prevented the Massachusetts legislature from chartering a second bridge on the Charles River simply because it had bestowed a previous franchise. Taney argued that "the object and end of all government is to promote the happiness and prosperity of the community," and while "the rights of private property are sacredly guarded, we must not forget that the community also has rights." Consequently, where there was no explicit grant of a monopoly, no such implied grant should be inferred, contrary to the public interest. Such an inference would tie the states to "the improvements of the last century," denying them "the light of modern science" whose benefits were adding to "the wealth and prosperity . . . of every other part of the civilized world." Although Taney's doctrine of construing charters strictly to preserve public prerogatives had been expressed in Marshall's later decisions and the Taney Court continued to uphold explicit charter provisions as obligatory contracts, the *Charles River Bridge* case signified a greater willingness to defer to the regulations of democratic state legislatures.[24]

Taney's opinion, with its Jacksonian stress on the promotion of the community's interests, happiness, and prosperity, evoked Bentham's utilitarian standards for legislation. But since the Court still maintained some contract clause protections and since Taney could still write of "sacred" property rights, early liberal notions of divine natural rights were by no means generally abandoned. Rather, the Taney Court's priorities differed from those of Marshall and Story in putting less emphasis on defending vested rights against contrary community desires to provide for economic innovation. This change was due in part to Taney's explicit concern for further economic and scientific progress and in part to his Jacksonian desire to combat privilege and provide more genuine equality of opportunity.[25]

The Taney Court's deference to state legislation extended to commerce clause cases as well. In *Mayor of New York v. Miln* (1837) the Court upheld as a legitimate exercise of the state's police power a New York statute requiring ship masters to report on their passengers so that the state could identify indigent immigrants. Story thought this was an impermissible burden upon foreign and interstate commerce. While the Taney Court continued to construe the police power expansively, it found the concept of little help in defining state authority over what appeared to be interstate commerce. Consequently, in *Cooley v. Board of Wardens of the Port of Philadelphia* (1851), the Court adopted a different approach. It held that states could regulate interstate commerce in the absence of preemptive congressional action only if the subject matter was essentially "local" in nature, as in determining harbor navigability, and not "national," as in setting interstate railroad rates. In this formula, which has proven difficult to apply, the Taney Court did not move far toward limiting federal power, though it did rule out some limits on state actions. The Court continued to uphold the national commerce power whenever it was exercised, though it was still not used heavily.[26]

Federal land policy was another major area where the law was used to foster development. Following the precedent of the Northwest Ordinance (1787), federal land law included grants to promote higher education and railroads along with the devolvement of lands to individual private owners, often depicted as the virtuous yeoman farmers of the future. These grants foreshadowed increased federal intervention on behalf of the traditional liberal goals of intellectual advancement and, particularly, economic growth. Yet these endeavors remained so heavily dependent on implementation by state and local authorities that they fostered no new sense of national responsibility for economic welfare. The poor, too, remained a state, local, and private concern. Although in 1859, Congress passed Dorothea Dix's bill granting federal land to the states for mental hospitals, President Franklin Pierce vetoed it, saying the Constitution gave no authority "for making the Federal Government the great almoner of public charity throughout the United States." Even at the state level, the prevailing ideology of providing genuinely equal opportunities but no special privileges continued to limit public assistance, though it supported calls for more public education. Indeed, egalitarians were increasingly concerned that state governments, too, might be corrupted by powerful financial interests, and so the states began adopting new constitutions that limited legislative powers to grant special charters, monopolies, and other privileges or to establish banks. Legislators eventually circumvented most of these provisions, sometimes because of widely perceived economic needs, sometimes because of the influence of special interests.[27]

Passage of the post-Civil War amendments reflected a concern to enhance the national government's authority, but what this enhancement meant for its economic role was far from clear. The answer had to be worked out in subsequent political and legal practice, and initially the Supreme Court, still influenced by Jacksonian state's rights jurisprudence, was reluctant to find that much change had occurred beyond the emancipation of blacks.[28] But in the late nineteenth century the Court began to give expression to a new legal ideology that was more laissez-faire than any it had previously endorsed. The Court defended its enhanced protection of corporate and employers' rights by appeal to Locke, Smith, and the narrow common law categories of regulatable activities. In a familiar pattern, the economic elite reemphasized the natural law strain of liberalism in order to set boundaries to the range of legitimate democratic choices.

The justices went far, however, toward embracing a novel philosophy of social Darwinism that was more stringent than any previous version of liberalism. Locke had claimed, however unpersuasively, that the protection of property rights worked to the benefit of everyone in society, while social Darwinists were willing to let "day labourers" fall by the wayside as part of a natural social process that would benefit the race in the long run.[29] Adherents of this view did not find the contract clause a useful legal tool, for legislatures had learned both to insert provisions permitting future modifications in corporate charters and to legislate only prospectively. That is why the courts turned the due process clause into an even broader constitutional shield for economic privilege.

These developments occurred just as Congress, concerned by the growing power of the private corporations which the courts often defended, began to use its vast but largely dormant commerce powers for regulatory purposes. Given the weight of precedents, the Court did not act against these federal measures as vigorously as it did against state economic legislation, especially since some of the federal measures seemed designed to aid commercial and industrial growth. But in response to genuine congressional regulatory efforts, the Court began to devise and enforce limits on the reach of the commerce power. At the same time it used the *Cooley* doctrine to strike down state legislation on national commercial subjects. These interventions, along with the rise of substantive due process, collectively rendered much business activity effectively exempt from regulation.[30]

In *U.S.* v. *DeWitt* (1870) the Court for the first time found a congressional action, the regulation of local sales of lamp oil, to extend beyond the reach of its power over interstate commerce. As with substantive due process, however, not until the 1890s did the Court restrict regulatory power significantly. In *Wabash, St. Louis, & Pacific Ry. Co.* v. *Illinois* (1886), the Court had indicated that the states could not act on the national subject of long-haul railroad rates, and in 1887 Congress created the Interstate Commerce Commission for such purposes. But after the Commission had been operating for almost a decade, the Court ruled in *Cincinnati, New Orleans and Texas Pacific Railway Co.* v. *Interstate Commerce Commission* (1896) that rate regulation had not been authorized by the original Interstate Commerce Act. This began a period in which the I.C.C. lost some fifteen cases on the extent of its statutory powers. The era ended only when Congress passed additional legislation, culminating in the Heburn Act of 1906, which established the I.C.C.'s powers so incontestably that in 1910 the Court felt obliged to acknowledge the breadth of Congress's purpose.[31]

Similarly, in 1890 Congress passed the vague but potentially powerful Sherman Antitrust Act as a vehicle for more general action against the new centers of concentrated economic power. The Court narrowed the act's applicability to corporations in *U.S.* v. *E. C. Knight* (1895), the Sugar Trust Case. Chief Justice Melville Fuller's opinion for the Court dismissed a government action to set aside the acquisition of four other refineries by the American Sugar Refining Company, even though the acquisition gave the company control of 98 percent of the nation's sugar refining. Fuller reasoned that refining was "manufacture," which preceded and was not part of the "buying and selling" and "transportation" that constituted commerce. Consequently, whatever the "extent" of the refining monopoly's effect on commerce, that effect was analytically "indirect" and so could not be reached under the commerce power. Subsequently, the justices held that a labor union's boycott of a manufacturer who sold in interstate commerce was a "combination in restraint of trade" forbidden by the Sherman Act. The Court's willingness to extend the act to labor unions but not to manufacturers was reiterated through the 1920s. Its lack of sympathy for labor was underscored by the Court's treatment of the Employer's Liability Act of 1906, which made railroads responsible for injuries to employees caused by the negligence of their fellow workers. The Court found that this act reached intrastate commerce and so was unconstitutional.[32]

The Court's commerce clause adjudication was not, however, all one way. To the concerns of the rural Grangers and Populists about the economic power of railroads, banks, and commodity marketing firms were added the fears of the Progressives about financial and industrial trusts. The Progressive era was also characterized by the rise of a more pragmatic jurisprudence that opposed the older deductivist, natural law legal theories as so much antidemocratic obstructionism. This view scored some successes not only in getting anti-big business legislation passed but also in getting it upheld. The Court acquiesced in the 1906 strengthening of the I.C.C. and also accepted the Employer's Liability Act of 1908, which was explicitly limited to interstate commerce. The influence of the new jurisprudence, together with the constitutional tradition of an expansive federal commerce power, prevented the Sugar Trust decision from entirely crippling the Sherman Act's applicability to productive industries. After indicating that the act covered railroads, the Court discerned "direct" restraints on commerce even in the anticompetitive agreements of pipe manufacturers.[33]

In *Swift Co.* v. *United States* (1905), Holmes succeeded in interpreting the commerce clause's limits by a more pragmatic inquiry into whether a combination of meat packers was in the regular "stream of commerce," however local their activities might be in the abstract. This test, which gave more scope to the Sherman Act and the commerce power, continued to be used occasionally up to the New Deal. But the Court never directly addressed or reconciled its inherent conflicts with the more restrictive doctrines of the Sugar Trust case.[34]

When in the late nineteenth century Congress had begun to use the commerce power for a variety of "progressive" public health and moral objectives, the Court was also generally receptive to these actions, even though they came close to turning the clause into a national police power. As long as the objectives did not infringe too heavily on what the Court viewed as legitimate economic pursuits, they were not opposed. Laws providing for meat and livestock inspections, for example, received no judicial rebuke; and in *Champion* v. *Ames* (1903) the Court upheld a federal ban on sales of lottery tickets via interstate commerce. The Court read the I.C.C.'s authority over railroads quite broadly, notably in the Shreveport Rate Case, *Houston E. & W. Texas Railway Co.* v. *United States* (1914), where Hughes's opinion for the Court suggested a further approach to the limits of the commerce clause, one also in tension with the Sugar Trust ruling. The I.C.C. had ordered several railroads to cease charging lesser rates for purely intrastate hauls than those charged for similar interstate trips. Although the railroads argued that this order regulated intrastate commerce, Hughes found that the rates had a sufficiently "close and substantial relation to interstate traffic" to justify their enactment. The test seemed to be one of effect, not of the analytical nature of the activity or even its place in the regular interstate commercial stream.[35]

But the Court never explicitly abandoned the more restrictive doctrines of *E. C. Knight,* and as the Progressive impulses ebbed, the Court renewed its concern to define limits on the commerce authority, particularly when used in ways hostile to employers. While upholding the antitrust action in the Standard Oil case of 1910, the Court ruled that the Sherman Act did not prohibit reasonable and useful monopolistic combinations, and subsequently it sustained as "reasonable" the tobacco, shoe manufacturing, and steel trusts.[36] The Court's other major limitation on the commerce power in this era came in response to the Child Labor Act of 1916, a congressional effort to curb child labor, which the justices struck down in *Hammer* v. *Dagenhart* (1918). The law had forbidden the interstate shipment of goods manufactured by firms employing children of certain ages. Justice William Day held that while the act regulated commerce, its aim was to prevent various practices in production, which were properly matters for state regulation. He distinguished this case from precedents such as *Champion* v. *Ames* on the grounds that they were aimed at preventing traffic in items thought to be harmful in their resulting uses, while here the evil was confined to the original locality and had ended by the time the items entered interstate commerce.

The Court failed to adhere to this distinction in later cases such as *Brooks* v. *United States* (1925) when it sustained the National Motor Theft Act, prohibiting transportation of stolen cars. This ruling thus perpetuated the prevailing pattern of the 1920s, in which the restrictive doctrines of the Sugar Trust and Child Labor cases were employed alongside the more permissive stances of *Swift* and the Shreveport Rate Case, and no genuine effort was made to unify these conflicting approaches. Thus, after President Franklin Roosevelt came into office during the Depression, the Court had two sorts of commerce precedents upon which to draw in adjudicating the tidal wave of New Deal commerce clause legislation.[37]

The New Deal dramatically changed the national government's role in providing for both social and individual economic well-being. The *Lochner* era of restrictions on state and national economic powers obviously had not been conducive to a broader view of federal responsibility on these matters. Although the Civil War had given the federal government a short-lived role in providing for the welfare of the freedmen and a much longer role in providing benefits to veterans, the subsequent rise of social Darwinism militated against commitment to public assistance at all levels. The trend toward centralized indoor relief had resumed, and although the states built more specialized institutions for children and the mentally ill, poor houses became even more stigmatized and punitive. According to Josephine Shaw Lowell, a leader of the moralistic private charity organizations of the period, their focus was on character reform. "Outdoor relief," or assistance via poor farms and other employment, was provided only under circumstances that would "repel" all but the most desperate, and relief work was designed to be "continuous, hard, and underpaid." Although the Progressive era produced private movements aimed at social reform and state legislation providing for improved working conditions, workmen's compensation, and aid to widows and dependent children, it had little impact on the federal government's welfare role beyond the establishment in 1912 of a research agency, the U.S. Children's Bureau. Congress enacted the Infancy and Maternity Bill in 1921 which included grants to the states, but in 1929 the law succumbed to President Herbert Hoover's opposition.[38] Soon, however, with half the nation poor and almost all of it suffering in the Depression, attitudes shifted.

Yet while Roosevelt's programs clearly represented a break with the past, the nature and extent of its innovativeness are still disputed. Some have argued that the New Deal represented no genuinely new governmental philosophy but merely experimentation with moderate reforms in the face of crisis. Others have seen in it a more revolutionary departure from traditional liberalism. It was long conventional for constitutional scholars to disregard the question of the substantive novelty of New Deal thought and to declare that its constitutional theory was simply a reversion to Marshall's broad view of national powers, and especially the commerce clause.[39]

However, the New Deal's constitutional ideas were fundamental, if moderate, innovations within liberalism. They abandoned liberalism's natural law traditions in favor of a more pragmatic utilitarian position that set no fixed limits on collective powers and responsibilities for the general welfare, but which still conceived of such welfare as the aggregate of the society's material wants. Roosevelt embraced Bentham's goals when he defined his basic aim as trying "to increase the security and the happiness of a larger number of people in all occupations of life," especially since he thought it most important first to assure security. Given these emphases, the New Deal did not represent a major move toward nonliberal communal, social egalitarian, or romantic ideals. But in abandoning natural law, it accepted intellectual relativism more fully than had any previous version of American democratic theory. New Deal thought was also not identical to the classical liberal utilitarianism of the Benthamite circle. Pragmatism was the more modern philosophic expression of this type of response, and the New Deal is commonly characterized as "pragmatic," though not in a technical philosophic sense. The New Deal embraced the experimentalism and the lack of formal system defended by the philosophical pragmatists, but it did not move far enough in its social experimentation to satisfy such pragmatists as John Dewey.[40] On balance, New Deal thought was an only partly conceptualized synthesis of the rationales for social action provided by Bentham and American pragmatism.

Bentham had feared that a fanatical attachment to equality would blind people to calculations of utility, and thus he tended to treat even great economic inequalities as "unoppressive." But his belief that the task of the modern state was to provide the maximum possible satisfaction of human desires, which made the provision of minimal economic security vital, led him to call for "direct state action" to "seek the causes of poverty, and to effect precautions, and relief." Although Bentham, with the classical economists, did not think such relief required extensive state intervention, his rejection of any right that could not be justified by the principle of utility left no principled ground for opposing such regulation if experience showed it to be useful. Despite Bentham's own preferences, later liberals drew the conclusion that such intervention was necessary, a view to which John Maynard Keynes gave economic expression in the 1920s after the experience of repeated recessions and depressions. The New Deal was never wholeheartedly Keynesian, however, for in pragmatic fashion, it mixed monetary, regulatory, planning, relief, and public works programs at varying levels of centralization. Occasionally, too, it gave voice to the ideal inherited by Dewey and Brandeis from the romanticism of Mill and Emerson, that the state's aim should be the promotion not simply of material well-being but the self-realization of all. Its main emphasis, however, was on the material concerns that dominated the general public.[41]

In adhering to a generally pragmatic, utilitarian philosophy, New Dealers brought about basic changes in the dominant view of the national government's proper economic role. Roosevelt asserted in 1932 that the federal government had "a continuing responsibility for the broader public welfare" and owed "to every one an avenue to possess himself of a portion of that plenty sufficient to his needs, through his own work." This assertion of public duties to provide not only for general but also for individual economic welfare justified the Democrats' numerous new national initiatives, from the National Industrial Recovery Act and the

Public Works Act through the establishment of the social insurance and public assistance programs under the Social Security Act, the U.S. Housing Authority, the National Mental Health Act, and the Full Employment Act. The last measure, passed in 1946, has been viewed as signaling definitively the people's acceptance that the federal government should provide "protection against massive impersonal forces, such as poverty, unemployment, the business cycle, and the general level of economic security."[42]

Despite these landmark bills, the New Deal's break from early liberal principles was moderate. For one reason, these measures fell short of more radical proposals then circulating. For another, the government's new role was generally understood to represent nothing more than a current legislative choice of the majority. Hence, it officially rested on new judgments of expedient policy for the general welfare and not on new claims of unqualified fundamental or constitutional rights. The government made major efforts to indicate that it was maintaining the traditional liberal commitment to economic self-reliance. The Social Security program was misleadingly portrayed as a self-supporting insurance scheme rather than as a welfare program, and unemployment assistance continued to be limited only to those poor who proved themselves willing to work. Instead of endeavoring to give Social Security benefits the status of a constitutional right, Roosevelt insisted on a payroll tax as the official funding device in order to stimulate moral and political pressures to maintain the program. This strategy reflected a pragmatic effort to use democratic majoritarianism to preserve his policies rather than claiming new absolute rights against the majority.[43]

Thus, there was no clear acceptance that the new governmental welfare role was fixed as a matter of postliberal principle. If the New Deal measures proved burdensome or undesirable to the majority, no higher law social egalitarian duties stood in the way of their abandonment. Indeed, the New Dealers remained divided both about how much national action, especially planning, was appropriate and about how far such action should tilt toward the underprivileged at the expense of business. The New Deal was also influenced by the long-standing federalism and state's rights claims and by the newer Brandeisian belief that excessive centralization and institutional bigness stifled democratic self-government, diversity, and social experimentation. Thus, after 1935 its leaders opted for a more decentralized and regulatory approach that left the implementation of welfare measures largely in the hands of the states.[44]

Since the New Deal programs were extensively influenced and staffed by legal realist lawyers (and Richard Hofstadter even deemed one leading realist, Thurman Arnold, the best theoretical exponent of New Deal thought), it is not surprising that the legal doctrines the Supreme Court came to accept after 1937 also viewed the Constitution as embodying a pragmatic social utilitarianism. In now-infamous fashion, the Supreme Court opposed the early New Deal legislation largely by relying on the restrictive commerce precedents of the Sugar Trust and Child Labor Cases, but then reversed its field dramatically in the 1937–1938 terms. Although it also relied on doctrines limiting the delegation of powers and taxing powers, the Court's refusal to read the commerce power expansively, despite all the precedents permitting it to do so, underlined its opposition to the new federal role. In 1935 the Court even found that a railroad regulation, the establishment of compulsory retirement and pension plans for interstate carriers, was an invalid social welfare law, not an action concerned with "commerce as such." One of the chief blows came in *Schechter Poultry Co.* v. *United States* (1935), which invalidated the National Industrial Recovery Act of 1933. The act authorized trade associations to form codes covering wages, hours, and practices that the President could make mandatory. Schechter, a Brooklyn poultry dealer who bought from out of state but sold only locally, claimed successfully that the New York City Live Poultry Code was invalid because it reached his trade, which was outside "the flow of interstate commerce." The Court added that the "wages and hours of employees" had only an "indirect" effect upon commerce, maintaining that if the commerce power extended this far, "all the processes of production and distribution" would be within its scope.[45]

The frequently submerged direct/indirect distinction was further elaborated in *Carter* v. *Carter Coal Co.* (1936), which dealt with the Bituminous Coal Conservation Act of 1935. The act laid a tax on mining that could be reduced through compliance with a price, wage, and hour code. Sutherland's opinion for the Court held that "mining," like all production, was a "purely local activity," whatever might be done with the products, and as a result, its effect on interstate commerce, "however extensive it may be," was logically still "secondary and indirect."[46] Yet opposition to this reliance on formalistic distinctions to throttle the government's new interventionist posture soon swayed the Court, and it changed its reading of the commerce clause at almost the same time that it abandoned its obstructionism via economic due process.

The pivotal commerce case was *National Labor Relations Board* v. *Jones & Laughlin Steel Corp.* (1937), handed down shortly after the corresponding due process *West Coast Hotel* case. The National Labor Relations Board case involved an order of that two-year-old board requiring the steel company to cease discharging employees engaged in union activities. Hughes responded to the objection that the employees were engaged in manufacturing by invoking the substantial effects doctrine of his *Shreveport* opinion. He maintained that if the stoppage of manufacturing by "industrial strife" would have a "serious effect upon interstate commerce," it could be regulated. In sharp opposition to Sutherland's reasoning in *Carter,* Hughes declared that the direct/indirect distinction was not one of kind but of "degree." His reasoning moved toward a jurisprudence that, with Holmes, Pound, and Llewellyn, looked to social and economic realities, not formal categories. Subsequent cases involving the board made it clear that few, if any, labor issues would be found too remote from interstate commerce to be regulated.[47]

After sustaining the Labor Relations Act, the Court majority had no difficulty upholding the landmark Social Security programs. These decisions did not directly concern the commerce power, for the provisions considered by the Court were challenged chiefly on the ground both that they arbitrarily taxed one group, employers, to aid other groups, the unemployed, their dependents, and the aged, and that they infringed on state sovereignty by pressuring the states to adopt assistance programs in return for federal funds and by preventing the states from preserving the sort of individualistic economic climate that they might prefer. Cardozo's answers to these contentions in two cases confirmed the Court's new economic philosophy.

In *Steward Machine Co. v. Davis* (1937), Cardozo argued for the Court that it was "too late" to tolerate arguments that "in a crisis so extreme the use of the moneys of the nation to relieve the unemployed . . . is a use for any purpose narrower than the promotion of the general welfare." "Natural rights" notwithstanding, any and all could be taxed to that end. He added that since the states were not required to create cooperative programs, no state prerogatives were violated. Justice Sutherland's dissent stressed the state sovereignty argument, based on the Tenth Amendment; Justice McReynolds simply quoted at length from Franklin Pierce's veto of the 1859 mental health bill. In *Helvering v. Davis* (1937), Cardozo stated, in realist fashion, that "the concept of the general welfare" was not "static" but evolving, and if Congress decided this welfare now required "paternalistic" measures, state efforts to create a more "self-reliant" climate must be overridden.[48] The national government's power to act in the name of changing notions of public utility was thus sharply affirmed.

The Court made some effort to preserve Marshall's denial of congressional power over intrastate commerce, as it continues to do today, but some cases have undercut the importance of even that qualification. In *U.S. v. Darby* (1941) the Court upheld an act that both banned the shipment in interstate commerce of goods produced in violation of wage and hour regulations and directly required employers to conform to these regulations with respect to their employees engaged in production for interstate commerce. The ban on shipment was deemed to be a regulation of commerce, and its motive, to affect production practices, was held not to be a matter for judicial inquiry. The Child Labor Case was thus overruled. The Court sustained the wage and hour regulations by arguing that since the ban on shipment of goods produced in violation of these standards was a legitimate goal for the commerce power, that power could control even intrastate activities that interfered with this goal. Therefore, Congress could directly regulate any intrastate activity that interfered with a goal for which Congress was otherwise regulating commerce.[49]

The import of this ruling was reinforced by *Wickard* v. *Filburn* (1942), in which the Court permitted the Agricultural Adjustment Act of 1938 to reach wheat, grown in excess of a marketing quota, that was intended solely for consumption on the farm itself. Jackson's opinion recognized that the wheat was local production which seemed to touch interstate commerce only indirectly, but proclaiming a "return" to the "breadth" of the commerce power defined by Marshall in *Gibbons*, he objected to all limitations drawn from "mechanical . . . legal formulas." Even if the excess wheat was in itself trivial, this type of activity, taken in the aggregate, could reasonably be held to exert a "substantial economic effect" on commerce, and so could be regulated.[50]

By thus holding that any intrastate activity which collectively affected commerce could be reached by Congress, and for purposes essentially concerned with production, these decisions laid to rest the limitations created in the Child Labor and Sugar Trust Cases. While they claimed to return to Marshall's view of the commerce clause, they left no significant limits on what Congress could regulate, with a little skillful drafting, via the commerce power. Consequently, while no decision of Marshall's was explicitly overturned, the Court's new doctrines conflicted not only with his stated concern to limit regulation of intrastate commerce but, more fundamentally, with his belief in some natural law limits on the extent of legitimate governmental economic interventions. The New Deal decisions resounded with a pragmatic utilitarian belief that older notions of absolute natural or vested property rights were without foundation and should not be permitted to stand in the way of whatever measures a democratic government deemed expedient to promote the prosperity of all.

This New Deal view of the commerce clause remains essentially unaltered today. At first the same philosophy reinforced the Court's reluctance to scrutinize legislation closely under the equal protection clause.

There were soon hints, however, that the Court might move beyond New Deal utilitarianism toward social egalitarianism. From the late 1930s through the mid-1950s the Court willingly imagined rationales for even blatant economic discrimination and so denied equal protection relief. But the mid-1950s witnessed a new advocacy of absolutist values here, as in other areas of the law, demanding more justification for governmental actions that increased the harms of economic inequalities. Many believed the Court was taking steps in that direction in two procedural cases. One of them, *Griffin* v. *Illinois* (1956), concerned a state procedure requiring convicted criminals wishing to appeal on nonfederal grounds to furnish trial transcripts at their own expense. This requirement was held to violate both the due process and the equal protection clauses, the latter because "there can be no equal justice where the kind of trial a man gets depends on the amount of money he has." Harlan dissented, claiming that the Court's position implied, in social egalitarian fashion, that the "Equal Protection Clause imposes on the States an affirmative duty to lift the handicaps flowing from differences in economic circumstances." He viewed the case as involving only due process issues of fundamental fairness, and he did not believe basic principles of justice demanded this form of state assistance.[51]

In the other procedural case, *Douglas* v. *California* (1963), indigent convicted criminals claimed a similar right to have counsel appointed by the state for their appeals. Douglas's opinion for the Court focused even more heavily on the equal protection question, holding that "where the merits of *the one and only appeal* an indigent has as of right are decided without benefit of counsel . . . an unconstitutional line has been drawn between rich and poor." Once again Harlan dissented, attacking the suggestion that the states were obliged to limit the consequences of poverty. He denied that the equal protection clause "prevents the State from adopting a law of general applicability that may affect the poor more harshly than it does the rich." Since many state acts affected rich and poor differently, to require the state to avoid such discrimination would be to insert into the Constitution "a philosophy of leveling" that was "foreign to many of our basic concepts of the proper relations between society and government." The issue for Harlan was again an unacceptable claim of what fundamental fairness required.[52]

Douglas wrote his strongest statement yet concerning the economic implications of equal protection in *Harper* v. *Virginia Board of Elections* (1966), which found the state's poll tax unconstitutional. He held that voting was a fundamental right whose restriction required strict scrutiny. But citing *Griffin* and *Douglas*, he also emphasized that "lines drawn on the basis of wealth or property, like those of race, are traditionally disfavored." Douglas dismissed the American heritage of property qualifications by arguing, as in the reapportionment cases, that the justices were not "confined to historic notions of equality" or "the political theory of a particular era." The *Harper* ruling suggested that wealth was a suspect classification under equal protection. Harlan continued to dissent, holding that Douglas's opinion represented "an ideology of unrestrained egalitarianism" that the Court would not be able to abide by in the future.[53]

These decisions inspired many liberal constitutional scholars to explore further doctrinal innovations that would give more weight to egalitarian values. But the Warren Court never pursued the implications of its economic equal protection holdings outside cases like these, where the equal protection issues were so entangled with other claims of fundamental rights as to prevent clear-cut social egalitarian rulings. Most scholars were of course aware that the Court was unlikely to embrace any true philosophy of leveling. Nonetheless, influential articles by Charles Reich and Frank Michelman, among others, argued in the 1960s that certain forms of public assistance should be "deemed to be held as of right," so that the modern welfare state could achieve its goal of promoting a secure minimum basis for individual well-being and dignity. Such proposals sometimes suggested, in utilitarian fashion, that welfare rights should be adopted simply as a means to the New Deal goals held by the majority of Americans. More often, they claimed less relativistically that there were "certain wants . . . which justice requires shall not go involuntarily unfulfilled." Correspondingly, the Court buttressed the procedural guarantees against deprivation of some forms of public assistance; but it never treated such services as matters of fundamental right or requirements of justice.[54] Again as in the reapportionment cases, it was unwilling and unable to undertake the massive changes that commitment to an absolute egalitarianism would entail.

To be sure, the Court had no difficulty supporting the social welfare legislation of President Lyndon Johnson's Great Society, such as Medicare, the Model Cities program, and the Economic Opportunity Act. These enactments gave greater expression to the more absolutist Brandeisian themes of personal and group self-realization and social equality than had the utilitarian New Deal. Theodore Lowi has argued that the programs of the 1960s placed a new emphasis on delegating power to the affected communities and recipient groups, symbolized by the "maximum feasible participation" requirement of the Community Action Program. When the 1960s demands of groups for equality and self-determination were added to the New Deal's commitment to promote material welfare for all, the nation moved toward a new federal role of providing essentially standardless financial services to all claimants, a position that Lowi calls "interest group liberalism."[55] Given the post-1937 acceptance of all social and economic legislation, these 1960s measures could be legally justified without endorsing constitutional commitment to even minimal economic equality as a matter of right. On social welfare legislation, majoritarianism was still officially in the saddle.

Similarly, the justices permitted the commerce power to be used for purposes of racial equality, sustaining the 1964 Civil Rights Act even when it applied to places of public accommodation that seemed only remotely involved with interstate commerce. The holdings of *Darby* and *Wickard* were more than sufficient to establish that virtually all local enterprises collectively affected commerce and the goals for which it was being regulated. The Court's affirmation of the Civil Rights Act confirmed the disappearance of any real limits on the commerce power, and it also furthered social egalitarian aims, but it demanded no real departure from the deferential utilitarianism of the New Deal decisions.[56]

The Burger Court, wary of new absolutist values, especially social egalitarian principles, has been "activist" only on behalf of traditional values that can claim long-term consent. Unsurprisingly, then, in the 1970s the Court dismissed the suggestion in earlier cases that wealth was a suspect classification and that government had minimal welfare obligations. The key case was *San Antonio Independent School District* v. *Rodriguez* (1973), which considered what *Harper's* ranking of wealth classifications as suspect implied for public education, deemed fundamental in *Brown*.[57] At issue was the Texas system of financing public schools, which provided a minimum foundation of state funds but then relied heavily on local property taxes. Since school districts varied in their property tax bases, the appellees claimed that the system discriminated against those who resided in poorer school districts. And because there was a ceiling on the tax rate that districts could impose, some districts could not obtain as much funding as others even if they were willing to accept a much higher property tax rate.

Powell's opinion for the Court rejected the appellees' equal protection claims, contending that more than a varying effect on rich and poor must be shown for a wealth classification to violate the Constitution. Rather, the law must work to produce an "absolute deprivation" of a constitutionally fundamental interest for a "definable category of 'poor' people." All three things were found missing in the case: the law worked no absolute deprivation, since the poor did receive some education; it did not violate a fundamental interest, for Powell argued that education, while undeniably vital, was not an explicit or implicit constitutional right; and it did not necessarily work chiefly against the poor, since many of them resided in property-rich districts. Without these "threshold" characteristics, wealth classifications required only traditional minimal equal protection scrutiny, and application of this test showed that the law was reasonably enough related to objectives of local control to be sustained.[58]

Marshall's dissent questioned the adequacy of this argument, citing the consequences of education for the practical exercise of political and expressive freedoms, as well as the state's voluntary role in adopting such an unequal financing system. Different financing schemes were available, he contended, that would achieve the state's objectives equally well while being less adverse to the poor. The Court has not reconsidered any portion of its *Rodriguez* holding, and economic equal protection adjudication has come to a virtual halt.[59]

Because the Burger Court acknowledges that state actions which reinforce economic inequalities may be invalid if they conform to the stringent conditions laid down in *Rodriguez,* its view is removed from *Lochner's* positive embrace of inequalities as the proper consequences of exercising natural rights. But some have seen in other recent cases a move back in the *Lochner* direction. Most striking was the Court's revival of the long-moribund contract clause in *United States Trust Co.* v. *New Jersey* (1977), when it held that New Jersey and New York could not repeal a statutory covenant limiting the power of their Port Authority to subsidize rail passenger transportation. Blackmun's prevailing opinion in the 4–3 decision suggested the Court would apply stricter scrutiny when a state impaired its own contractual obligations—in this case to Port Authority bondholders—than when it interfered with private contracts. While this seemed a near-total reversal of the original aims of the clause, it at least suggested a continued deference to state regulation of private economic activity. The following year, however, the Court applied the contract clause to private obligations. *Allied Structural Steel Co.* v. *Spannaus* (1978) invalidated a Minnesota law that demanded a "pension funding charge" of employers who terminated their pension plans for Minnesota workers without providing funds sufficient for the pensions of all ten-year employees. Brennan in dissent argued that the law did not nullify any existing contractual obligations but merely imposed new ones. The majority felt, however, that the burdens imposed were too significant and the justifications for them too weak to permit deference to the state's police powers.[60]

In regard to the commerce power, too, a new restrictiveness is apparent. The Court has increased the weight given to the commerce clause's aim of promoting a free flow of interstate trade, striking down a number of inhibiting state laws. But in a manner reminiscent of its early readings of the Interstate Commerce Act, it interpreted narrowly the powers given by the National Labor Relations Act to the National Labor Relations

Board. In one education case it found that the board's authority did not extend to teachers employed in parochial schools, while in another it held that a private university's faculty was too managerial to be covered by the act.[61]

In *National League of Cities* v. *Usery* (1976), the Court once again found a congressional enactment to be beyond reach of the commerce power. The case involved a 1974 amendment extending to state employees the Fair Labor Standards Act upheld in *Darby*. Recalling Sutherland's dissents in the Social Security cases, Rehnquist argued for the Court that this amendment was an excessive intrusion on the "state sovereignty" protected by the Tenth Amendment. If the states could not structure the employer-employee relationships of those performing their basic functions, "there would be little left" of their independent existence. The Court has since retreated from *National League of Cities*, but its renewed concern for state prerogatives, visible in numerous Burger Court doctrines, is not really surprising. The Court's relativistic democratic jurisprudence, stressing the maintenance of those values that have won the lasting consent of the majority, can easily support the protection of state's rights on the traditional ground that this level of government is closest to popular opinion and control. This argument has special force in areas, such as criminal law, that historically are largely state preserves. Nonetheless, the Court's willingness to strike down state actions under the contract clause, while at the same time discerning limits on Congress's commerce authority, suggests to many observers that here, as in the speech area, it is becoming more inclined to assert limits to the reach of all governmental economic regulatory powers.[62]

How far the Court will go in setting renewed boundaries to state and national regulatory authority remains to be seen. It is already questionable whether its existing actions on behalf of corporate rights can claim to defend only long-term social values against temporary majorities. Again, American constitutional history since *Lochner* strongly rejects any notion of special solicitude for corporate and vested interests. The Court therefore cannot move much further in this direction without abandoning its general jurisprudence of democratic relativism with special solicitude for a few traditional fundamental principles. Although a move away from such relativistic deference to increased protection of economic inequalities has been a recurring pattern in American history, and one that obviously serves powerful interests, there are few currently accepted grounds for this sort of absolutist view.[63]

The Court's relativistic stance already departs from early liberalism: while Lockean economic views supported some state intervention and recognized certain charitable responsibilities, they also set fixed limits on the government's powers over property. These limits have not survived the popular and intellectual revulsion against their exaggerated reincarnation in the *Lochner* years, and they can probably not be revived today in anything like their original form. Indeed, the course of modern commerce clause adjudication suggests that, with the minor exception of *National League of Cities,* no real boundaries remain on the activities and purposes that may be encompassed by the commerce power. While this situation has thus far had no major ill effects, it contrasts with the overriding early liberal desire to maintain sharply defined limits on what governments may do.

The pragmatic utilitarianism of the New Deal has thus survived better in doctrines defining governmental welfare responsibilities than in other constitutional areas. Despite occasional flirtations during the Warren years with claims that public assistance is a constitutional right, the Court has never come close to subjecting the public sector's involvement in creating and perpetuating economic inequalities to strict scrutiny, much less to arguing that these conditions are in themselves unjust. The recently renewed inegalitarian activism has also been fairly trivial. Unsurprisingly, modern, more absolutist romantic values have had little impact here in either direction. While they could justify public assistance to promote the unfettered development of individuals or groups (and indeed this was the theme of Charles Reich's "New Property" article) romantic values could also defend economic inequality as the legitimate consequence of personal or group self-expression, and so they have no clear economic implications.[64] The real challenge to the Court's utilitarianism has come from social egalitarian concerns, as Harlan quickly detected. But his shrill opposition to even the mildest steps in this direction—steps that could as easily be understood in terms of more liberal notions of providing equal justice for all or guaranteeing personal autonomy—suggests the wariness of American constitutional thought toward principles that challenge the basic economic organization of society.

It is true that to find any philosophy of leveling in the Constitution seems not only historically groundless but contrary to dominant attitudes in contemporary American society. The task for social egalitarians must therefore be to define ways of giving leeway to such concerns while at the same time establishing limits on more radical egalitarian claims.[65] Such efforts are inevitably difficult, complex, and controversial, and they draw little direct guidance from the constitutional text. Perhaps it is understandable, then, that the Court has in this area largely retained its stance of deference, leaving to legislative action the definition of governmental obligations in regard to economic inequalities. Such judgments may indeed seem more legislative than judicial, given the lack of a clear economic philosophy in the Constitution and the diversity of views throughout American history.

At the same time, however, it runs contrary to both inherited and contemporary notions to hold either that the nation has no duties to provide for individual and social economic welfare as a matter of right or that it has unlimited power to affect these concerns as the majority wishes. Most nonrelativistic liberal theories, whether based on Enlightenment notions of liberty, romantic autonomy, property rights, or some sense of equality, see economic issues as inextricably linked to the possession and exercise of inviolable rights and freedoms that the Constitution is held to secure. The problem, again, is simply that the content of these duties and limits has been too ill-defined and controversial to serve as a basis for activism.

Thus, the evolving economic case law, like due process, free speech, and apportionment adjudication, combines successive historical versions of American liberalism, each trying to respond to the difficulties that have perplexed liberal thought since its inception. More satisfactory constitutional doctrines of economic rights and duties will again have to be drawn from a general theory of American liberal constitutionalism that deals credibly with those long-standing difficulties. The judicial and scholarly discussions on economic constitutional issues, like those on the other three constitutional areas, display the basic alternative conceptions of such a general constitutional theory that now compete in American legal discourse. Those alternatives must be the starting point for considering the possible future routes that American constitutional law may take.

III · Directions for the Future

MUCH HAS CHANGED in American constitutional thought since the nation was founded under the precepts of early liberalism. Religious and natural law traditions have lost intellectual credibility, and empiricism and consent have gained primacy as standards for both philosophical and political legitimacy. Consequently, pragmatic democratic relativism has become the chief orthodoxy, although it remains under challenge from more absolutist romantic and egalitarian values, which claim to carry out its logic to a fuller extent. Moreover, many of the values and premises of early America and early liberalism remain alongside these later positions, especially in popular opinion.[1] Americans are not prepared to abandon entirely the nation's political heritage, despite its continuing difficulties. Accordingly, inherited principles must be reformulated to meet present problems.

There are many possible versions of liberal constitutionalism. Yet modern developments in the constitutional areas of due process, free speech, voting rights, and economic welfare reveal three constitutional positions that are most influential in contemporary judicial, scholarly, and political constitutional discussions. First is the democratic relativism that gained ascendancy during the New Deal and has since been reasserted by the Burger Court. Second is the traditional higher law perspective that upholds the classical and, particularly, the religious elements in American thought, which have always coexisted with its Enlightenment strain. Third are the many expressions of romantic and egalitarian values, which are often combined in contemporary versions of liberalism, despite their potential tensions. Constitutional discourse has recently been influenced by a fourth perspective, the law and economics school, represented by scholars such as Richard Posner, Richard Epstein, and Guido Calebresi. But most of this analysis remains devoted to common law topics and to some admittedly expansive economic issues in constitutional law. Thus far, only a few have suggested that economic efficiency provides the ultimate standard for American constitutionalism or that laissez-faire economic rights, as rehabilitated by modern conservative economists, are constitutionally fundamental moral principles. Hence, this perspective is more likely to supply fruitful insights on economic constitutional concerns than to provide the sort of general constitutional theory that the other three positions represent.[2]

The central tendencies of the democratic relativist perspective are typified by the works of John Hart Ely and especially Alexander Bickel, who together show both its liberal and conservative potentialities and its underlying substantive deficiencies. The conservative perspective that reaffirms the moral absolutes of America's higher law traditions, visible in the contemporary movements for constitutional reforms on school prayer and abortion promoted by President Ronald Reagan and elements of the New Right, has been best articulated by John Courtney Murray and Walter Berns. The romantic and egalitarian perspectives range from influential mainstream scholars such as Laurence Tribe to the more radical Critical Legal Scholars. The radical positions represent these values in their purest form, but by the same token they are much less likely to win political and legal acceptance. Hence the discussion here will focus on the most philosophically developed mainstream liberal view that incorporates romantic and egalitarian themes, the neo-Kantian philosophy of John Rawls, developed into a constitutional theory by Ronald Dworkin. This view, which bases just institutions on a right to equal concern and respect, both justifies extensive autonomy in choices of the good life and retains uncompromising egalitarianism in its notion of human moral worth.

Each of these general perspectives has certain strengths in responding to liberalism's traditional dilemmas. But none is wholly satisfactory, and each involves difficulties of its own. The dedication of democratic relativism to the morality of consent and to democratic processes leaves few resources for protection against majoritarian abuses, despite the best efforts of its advocates to circumvent this weakness. The higher law tradition lacks intellectual credibility and is a proven weapon of intolerance. And neo-Kantian liberalism offers such a shallow and unsupported view of human dignity that it fails to capture many deep-rooted American moral sentiments and provides little concrete moral reassurance or guidance on worthy courses of conduct. Consequently, a further alternative position should be considered. Instead of basing contemporary liberalism on a revised Kantian commitment to human moral equality and autonomy, Americans should reformulate early liberalism's substantive purposes so as to be politically desirable and philosophically credible today. The seminal philosophic work of early liberalism, Locke's *Essay,* suggests the purpose that has always been the deepest concern of liberal thought, the promotion of personal capacities for reflective self-direction, or in a word, liberty. A liberalism dedicated to the realization of this value by all can provide practical guidance for the problems that perplex contemporary constitutional law.

7 · Alternative Constitutional Theories

The historic trend away from higher law and toward democratic consent as the cornerstone of American political thought has led to repeated efforts to derive a coherent constitutional philosophy from modern democratic theory. The most noted effort of this sort in recent years is John Hart Ely's *Democracy and Distrust*. Ely's position, self-described as an attempt to elaborate the theory underlying the *Carolene Products* footnote, has one great attraction over most other relativistic democratic judicial philosophies advanced since Holmes: it does not call for extensive deference to legislatures, as Frankfurter did. It thus promises more judicial activism against majoritarian tyranny.

At the same time, Ely claims to avoid much of the subjectivity and arbitrary judicial power that characterize attempts to define substantive fundamental values. He allows courts to overturn legislation only on behalf of two types of "process": process "writ small," or procedural fairness in the legal system, including such matters as rights of criminal suspects, entitlements to administrative hearings, and procedures of regulatory agencies; and process "writ large," or a democratic system of governmental decision-making and distribution that weighs all interests equally and provides ample opportunities for political participation. Ely admits these procedural concerns reflect a commitment to democratic "participational values." But he believes this commitment is distinguishable from any judicial imposition of substantive principles on the polity, even while it upholds judicial activism on behalf of numerous First Amendment rights, procedural due process rights, voting and other political participation rights, and equal protection rights against invidious discrimination in the distribution of social burdens and benefits.[1]

The protection of these democratic procedural values is appropriate for three reasons. First, the Constitution is itself largely concerned with such process values, not with a "governing ideology," and so it is proper for constitutional courts to act on their behalf. Ely eventually concedes instead that the original Constitution was "substantively concerned with preserving liberty," specifically religious freedom and economic liberalism. Thus it transparently did express a particular, then-novel political and social philosophy. Even so, Ely is correct in arguing that America's constitutional development as revealed in formal amendments, legal doctrines, and governmental practices has since gone in a more democratic direction. This, he indicates, is the second and "more important" point: his theory is "consistent with representative democracy" as we understand it and value it today (even if we have not realized all our aspirations.) Ely adds, third, that judges are well situated to protect democratic processes because of the courts' insulation and procedural expertise.[2]

This defense immediately runs into the problem that, while democratic theory may be the reigning orthodoxy, it has many different versions, most of which, like Frankfurter's, severely limit judicial activism against democratic majorities. A *Carolene Products* position can generate forceful activist arguments only in the case of governmental actions that effectively blockade the political processes. This type of activism does not amount to as strong a judicial role as most of those concerned about majoritarian abuses would like, Ely included. It gives little basis for overturning popularly enacted political inequalities that stop short of denying genuine access to the system, such as mild malapportionment. And it provides no check against decisions of a morally sincere and genuinely democratic legislature that violate basic rights, such as, perhaps, laws restricting unconventional intimate relations.[3]

Ely is most concerned about the latter problem. He tries to respond in process terms by insisting that democratic decision-making cannot be infected by prejudice or hostility that leads to an undervaluation of some interests in the calculus of social utility. As Ely knows well, however, determining legislative motivation is a tricky business. He elaborates a number of devices for flushing out invidious intentions, thus defining his approach to realizing the *Carolene Products* footnote's concern to combat prejudice against discrete and insular minorities. Chief among these are the stricter scrutiny invoked by suspect classifications or by legislation with disproportional impacts, which can reveal that a legal discrimination is only flimsily related to the law's stated objective or that the state goal is so trivial as to be an obvious pretext. Legislative reliance on excessively inaccurate stereotypes or actions disadvantaging those possessed of immutable characteristics may also signal discreditable motives.[4]

But as many have pointed out, these methods of protecting minorities do not ultimately save Ely from requiring value judgments about what legislative aims are "discreditable." As his discussion of gay rights indicates, one must still decide whether a law disadvantaging some is based on "a sincerely held moral objection" to their actions or on "a simple desire to injure the parties involved." If the first is true, the law supposedly must be upheld, although this position gives little protection against sharply repressive but sincere majoritarian moral beliefs.[5] Ely avoids this result only by asserting at key junctures that certain harmful intentions deny equal concern and respect. But again, it is not clear on grounds of democratic consent theory why anyone is owed any more respect than some basic access to the political process. So long as minority interests are always counted but outweighed, there are no restrictions on how minorities are treated that can be defended purely as concerns for process.

Ely's view gains much of its attractiveness because, like so many versions of liberalism, it inconsistently combines an absolute right, here Dworkin's equality principle, with claims of democratic relativism. To be coherent, it must either abandon its concern for the substantive protection of minorities, thereby moving back toward the more deferential positions of Frankfurter and the later Bickel, or it must defend itself as a variant on Dworkin's fundamental value theory. While this lack of theoretical consistency may not prevent Ely's doctrine from having great practical influence, for present purposes it will be more useful to focus on these other, more coherent stances.

The more fully relativistic position outlined by Bickel stops short of simple majoritarian democracy, on the ground that democracies can, and American constitutional democracy does, choose to protect values possessing long-term consent against the preferences of the moment. Current legislative majorities, made up of jockeying interest groups concerned about immediate material needs, may particularly fail to appreciate the impact of their actions on values that society would, on reflection, wish to prevail.[6] To avoid thoughtless infringements of time-tested norms, legal and institutional restraints on majoritarian actions are desirable. Thus for Bickel, government by long-term general consent implies above all a concern for traditional legal limits and forms with which governments must comply—and hence constitutionalism, the rule of law.

But while Bickel adhered consistently to these propositions, he shifted in his views about what they implied for judicial review. The evolution of his thinking serves to indicate the difficulties of his democratic relativism. Bickel's seminal work, *The Least Dangerous Branch*, formulated a judicial role of general deference that nevertheless left room for periodic activism. He accepted with legal realism that there are no "timeless absolutes in the art of ordering society," and, as a result, "the occasions are few" when a democracy's courts should oppose its legislatures. But Bickel still insisted, "as a moral judgment of the good society," that there were such occasions, and that judges had the capacity to recognize them and perform responsibly. Indeed, without some "process for the interjection into representative government of a system of enduring basic values," Bickel felt government would be unacceptably unprincipled.[7] So he defined a method for identifying fundamental values that judges seemed peculiarly well suited to apply. This method, as suggested by Frankfurter in *Sweezy,* was for judges to "immerse themselves in the tradition of our society and of kindred societies that have gone before, in history and in the sediment of history which is law, and, as Judge Hand once suggested, in the thought and vision of the philosophers and poets." Once immersed, judges would be "fit to extract 'fundamental presuppositions' from their deepest selves" that would be not in fact mere idiosyncrasies but rather the consensus values of the American tradition. This would be so, Bickel averred, because no one could discern any higher source of values beyond long-term human will. Hence, an intellectually honest judicial search for the "deepest controlling sources of ends" could come to rest only on values that had the requisite "widespread acceptance."[8]

The Court could nonetheless at times lead opinion. It could properly espouse values that would only eventually gain general assent—but, Bickel cautioned, it would be proper only if the Court's attempt to anticipate the evolving national consensus in fact succeeded. A court that, in face of uncertainty, chose to enforce values that finally proved idiosyncratic could fairly be accused of exceeding its authority. Only a correct articulation of what would eventually come to be widely recognized as the nation's basic principles was legitimate fundamental values jurisprudence.

This extraordinary requirement meant that the judicial search for values had to be extremely careful and rigorous, with principles "traced and evaluated from the roots up." Yet Bickel acknowledged that even so, the grounds of final judgment might remain "inexpressible." Nevertheless, in the early 1960s he maintained stoutly that his proposed method of inquiry was both identifiable and determinate in its results. Scholars could fairly decide whether or not justices were genuinely following the proper steps. And if the method was conscientiously executed, a justice not only could conclude but would *have* to conclude that *Brown* was rightly decided, in accordance with the basic premises of American society, and that *Lochner* v. *New York* was not.[9]

Subsequently, however, when Bickel observed the Court implementing a fundamental values approach, he became increasingly disenchanted with its technical performance and its substantive results. In *The Supreme Court and the Idea of Progress* Bickel stated that he had "come to doubt in many instances the Court's capacity to develop 'durable principles,' " for it seemed the techniques he had described could be used to justify too many different outcomes. The Warren Court gave some credence to more absolutist values that Bickel described as "egalitarian," "majoritarian," "assimilationist," "legalitarian," and "centralizing." Bickel himself, on the other hand, drew from American tradition a "pragmatic skepticism" that valued "diversity," "decentralization," "group autonomy," and "group participation" on a pluralist model inspired by Madison and Robert Dahl as well as Holmes, Brandeis, and Frankfurter. Yet while Bickel felt the Court had not adequately adhered to "the method of analytical reason" he had advocated, he conceded that even if it had, its results "could very well have been no different," since they did "connect with strands in the tradition of our society." But because his own conclusions were so opposite, Bickel decided that the political branches were more appropriate for these issues than he had thought: "society is best allowed to develop its own strands out of its tradition," responding "in accordance with experience, and with pressures brought to bear by the political process."[10]

Although he concluded the judicial method he had advised was after all too indeterminate to reveal society's deepest values reliably, Bickel still believed that the Court had a valid role in at least drawing attention "to issues of the largest principle," as it did in *Brown*. He knew, too, that this function was inseparable from enforcement of the principles the Court perceived. His new stance therefore could be accused of embracing mild judicial activism only when the principles he thought largest were at stake, especially since at the time his judgment that most issues should be left to the political processes also furthered the values he preferred. Precisely because those values rested on no more than "pragmatic skepticism," it was hard to see how Bickel could defend persuasively his insistence on enduring institutional roles oriented to his own ends. Similarly, it was unclear how he could so confidently dismiss as "sophistry" the common argument that democracy requires some judicial intervention on behalf of egalitarian principles. In his final, unfinished work, *The Morality of Consent*, Bickel accepted the responsibility to indicate how his relativist democratic premises justified his "enormous" but not total "reliance on the political marketplace."[11]

In this collection of essays two themes are clear: Bickel did think it terribly wrong to threaten certain values, essentially peace, stability, and the maximum freedom they permit, in the name of "abstract, absolute ideas"; and he also knew his skepticism was an uncertain defender of those values. He believed, quite plausibly, that his difficulty was universal in the relativistic modern era: "Our problem has been, and is most acutely now, the tyrannical tendency of ideas and the suicidal emptiness of a politics without ideas . . . we cannot govern, and should not, in submission to the dictates of abstract theories, and . . . we cannot live, much less govern, without . . . principles, however provisionally and skeptically held."[12]

Ultimately this dilemma was one Bickel could not solve. He could and did argue forcefully that both the Warren Court's propensity for ideological absolutes, and its unbridled democratic majoritarianism bred a politics of impassioned conflict that he saw as "an abomination." Bickel perceived that his feelings, reinforced by the turmoil of the 1960s, parallelled Burke's judgment of the French Revolution: "Such a politics cannot work as politics. It begins and ends by sacrificing peace, and it must proceed from one bloodbath to another, and from one tyranny to another." It was wiser, Bickel believed, to be flexible, pragmatic, and tolerant, like Holmes, of the seeming imperfections of American popular government. But Bickel had to admit that a "thoroughgoing agnostic" who took skepticism "to a logical extreme," might "well also be a radical democrat, believing that nothing matters and that the merest whim of the majority is as good a guide to social action as anything else." This extreme, too, Bickel fervently wished to refute. Simple majoritarianism was not only impractical. Its pursuit would render government too subject to superficial popular moods, destroying the institutional stability and familiarity needed to generate the kind of "preponderant," "long-term consent" that bonds society on an enduring basis. While Bickel found Burke's "Romantic" glorification of conventional social manners and prejudices exaggerated, he agreed that we need to rely on "custom," "our tradition," indeed "the secular religion of America" to create social unity, and so he reiterated that we must look to these sources to find "our visions of good and evil." He never relinquished his view that a simple majoritarianism endangers these vital constitutive social principles, although he might not have approved of all the enforcement of traditional values undertaken by the philosophically similar Burger Court.[13]

But Bickel was more like most of the current Court than like Burke in his refusal to claim that the values of the past are immutable truths. He recommended holding to them "provisionally only . . . as guides," because this course promotes a harmonious social order. He admitted the one value that his otherwise thoroughgoing skepticism left "irreducible" was "the idea of law." "The highest morality" was "almost always the morality of process." By this he meant a peaceful, orderly process, and he knew that valuing these qualities over other substantive ideals meant eschewing any claim to neutrality in favor of adherence "to a political position," one always near the center of moderate liberalism. And while he thought the uncertainty of claims to truth made it wiser to "hold fast to peace" than to pursue any theoretical schemes of social perfection, Bickel also knew he could not show that skepticism alone dictated this choice. Thus he ultimately disclaimed all "pretense to intellectual valor" or theoretical completeness, and admitted his beliefs led into paradoxes. His values, he said, were merely his "can't helps," or "indispensable . . . illusions," or in Conrad's telling phrase, "true lies."[14]

In retrospect, Bickel appears to have been ultimately driven to the shoals of the dilemma democratic relativism inherently involves. Its appeal to uncertainty may have force in discrediting self-righteous absolutist claims, but uncertainty cannot plausibly support alternative values. Hence, the adherents of skeptical relativism may seem hypocritical or indeed self-righteous when they inevitably uphold their own values against those who do not consent to them. Because democratic relativism seems unable to overcome this difficulty, it represents little progress in responding to liberalism's traditional dilemmas.

Relativistic democratic theory at least makes a clear choice between philosophic foundations, abandoning the early liberals' natural law in favor of their pragmatic empiricist strain. Yet in practice its advocates soon end up striving, and failing, to define principled limits on desires that they find repulsive but which have an equal empirical claim to be sources of human values. Once Bickel accepts consent, for example, as the ultimate source of obligation, it is impossible to explain why long-term social consent justifies imposing duties on those whose immediate, personal consent is to contrary principles. After all, no one can say with assurance what we will value in the long run, or even that we will be around to value anything. Even if customary values are granted pride of place over transient ones, problems remain. A court or minority may disagree with a present legislative majority over the principles that possess long-standing approval.

Although Bickel's position is not free of the problems that liberalism has always faced on issues of philosophic premises and political obligation, it may seem to have a stronger case for its ability to deal with liberalism's excessive individualism. But despite its emphasis on the importance of upholding shared values, the nation's secular religion, in order to foster a sense of common loyalty, it promotes neither moral unanimity nor the kind of all-absorbing political involvement that might satisfy the communitarian longing for *amour social*. Bickel embraces the "political marketplace" of practical, expedient, self-interested group bargaining, not a participatory democracy of fervent political action or even Burke's organic "partnership in every virtue." His is far too egoistic a vision for most community-minded critics of liberalism.

Furthermore, if social customs and traditions are used to foster a sense of national identity more energetically, the resulting attitudes may well be dangerously hostile both to different foreign traditions and to domestic dissent, as Burkean and later romantic nationalisms often have been. Both parochial, xenophobic perspectives in foreign policy and nativist domestic intolerance may then seem more credible. Even the pragmatic, utilitarian strain in Bickel's relativism does not avoid this consequence. As Vinson showed in *Dennis*, utilitarianism easily supports the view that the first principle of public policy is national self-preservation. In *The Morality of Consent*, Bickel similarly cited Justice Jackson's "principle of legitimation," his contention that "the Constitution is not a suicide pact," to support the shameful relocation camps established for West Coast Japanese-Americans in World War II.[15] Of course, Bickel did see the dangers of nationalistic tyrannies, and he therefore recognized a limited right of civil disobedience. But the potential of his premises to support less humane forms of patriotism again raises doubts about how far he succeeds in improving on early liberal constitutionalism.

Finally, Bickel's emphasis on long-term social consent over immediate personal choices, his suspicion of egalitarianism and majoritarianism, and his attachment above all to peace and stability show that in his hands, at least, democratic relativism make no concessions to the romantic and social egalitarian attacks on liberal values. While he admitted it was logically possible to draw from his principles a more absolute insistence on the complete primacy of personal self-realization or full democracy, Bickel deplored this logical "extremism." His position offers instead a moderate liberalism based on premises more initially credible than those with which the liberal doctrine began, but it does so by abandoning all claims of certainty and by accepting most of the imperfections of the status quo.[16] It therefore cannot definitively refute the romantic and egalitarian values that liberal societies have long been held to repress, while it still leaves them unfulfilled in practice.

By reasserting the legitimacy of older absolute principles, the traditional higher law approach tries to dismiss all postliberal moral perspectives and to improve on the fragile grounding that relativism gives to older American ideals. America's traditional moral absolutisms are rarely given extensive analysis by contemporary academic lawyers, for both legal theory and academic opinion more broadly have largely abandoned any overt reliance on the religious and natural law strains in American thought. But these beliefs were influential in the Constitution's creation, and they have since remained a significant, if fluctuating, force in American political culture. Sometimes in harmony with America's rationalistic Enlightenment strain, sometimes in tension, the American higher law heritage has always seen itself as providing necessary and absolute grounds for the nation's political values. Today's religiously inspired constitutional movements to restore prayer in schools and to ban abortion show that the significance of this heritage for constitutional politics exceeds its place in current constitutional theorizing.[17]

In legal circles, too, modern adherents of the higher law tradition have at times denounced the reigning relativism and reasserted theories that explicitly rely on religious and classical notions of virtue. Particularly in the 1930s and 1940s, both Catholic legal scholars and non-Catholic intellectuals, such as Robert Hutchins and Mortimer Adler, attacked legal realism, arguing that totalitarianism could be refuted only if American democracy was seen to rest on the "unchanging fundamentals" common to Thomistic theology and Aristotelian natural right.[18] Although this position remains a minority viewpoint in academia, it is sustained by Catholic law schools, by proponents of classical virtue in political science, and by powerful currents in American popular belief. Thus its alternate understanding of American constitutionalism cannot properly be ignored.

The essential arguments of the stance were endorsed early on by the greatest Catholic student of American liberal democracy, Alexis de Tocqueville. Tocqueville believed that the support given by religion to virtuous standards of behavior was indispensable for the preservation of political liberty. He also believed, perhaps even more deeply, that religion gave people a "taste for the infinite," which was essential to combat the greatest "peril" of free and materialistic modern societies. By moving men beyond their absorption in narrow, selfish, immediate interests, religion prevented them from losing the use of their "sublimest faculties" and thus from being "degraded."[19] Hence, because religion both supported the political goals of liberalism and lifted people above these goals to higher spiritual concerns, Tocqueville saw a religious foundation as essential to America. He felt that it could flourish, however, only with sufficient separation of church and state to avoid embroiling government in sectarian disputes and to prevent religion from being discredited by political entanglements.

The positions of John Courtney Murray, S.J., the leading modern Catholic commentator on American constitutional principles, and Walter Berns, the most prolific constitutional analyst from an Aristotelian perspective, both follow Tocqueville's basic points. In order to legitimate use of the writers' beliefs to interpret the Constitution, both also argue that American values have historically rested on higher law principles. Murray especially claims that the precepts of the Declaration of Independence and the Bill of Rights reflect a belief in "the sovereignty of God," held to be the "ultimate source" of American liberties. He insists more generally that American institutions and ideals are based on "the profound conviction that only a virtuous people can be free," so that unchanging standards of virtue are integral to the nation's political system. He is aware, of course, of the presence of contrary traditions in America's past, and he is explicit that it is because he sees the Constitution not as a "piece of eighteenth century rationalist theory" but as "more the product of Christian history" that he supports it. Indeed, Murray denigrates Locke, whom he accepts as the source of the Constitution's Enlightenment strain, as an incoherent philosopher who merely served as a "political weapon" of those seeking a "businessmen's commonwealth." Locke's only merits are all held to derive from the "medieval heritage" that he "did not quite succeed in destroying" in his thought.[20]

At the same time, Murray admits that Enlightenment ideas have had more influence than he would like. He accepts Tocqueville's case against formal religious establishments in the United States, but he finds America's sharp separation of church and state "exaggerated." Murray believes this separation endangers the nation's religious foundations when it precludes, for example, aid to parochial schools. But in order to make his view credible to those who do not share his specific religious beliefs, Murray stresses that the doctrine of natural law he relies upon "has no Roman Catholic presuppositions." Its precepts of moral virtue are said to be rationally ascertainable without the aid of Christian revelation, as Aristotle originally showed and as the Declaration of Independence still held.[21]

It is to Aristotle's version of this secular natural law that Walter Berns subscribes. In his initial exposition of his view in 1957, he was more doubtful than Murray about whether history showed it to be the moral foundation of the original Constitution. Berns maintained only that the Constitution's framers aspired to establish true justice, to embody "a spirit, a sense of the right, beyond the provisions themselves," and that a concern for the nation's welfare should lead Americans to interpret the document in light of this aspiration, not of the framers' specific intentions. Thus, while it might "not be true to the spirit of liberalism," it was not "un-American" to "heed the advice Charwood attributes to Lincoln and construe the Constitution . . . so as to 'render it agreeable to natural justice.'" In his recent writings, Berns has stressed, like Father Murray and contemporary religious activists, that many framers held "virtuous habits," fostered in part by religion, to be necessary to free government. Hence, while the framers were predominantly Lockean and sharply distinct from the classical and medieval tradition of higher law, Berns agrees that their thought contained elements which permit us to read the Constitution in light of those older conceptions of virtue.[22]

Both Murray and Berns also assert that religious faith is needed to maintain enduring popular allegiance to the political goals and values of

American liberalism. Liberalism itself cannot suffice, for reasons Berns has taken greatest pains to elaborate. He assaults the "liberal justices" from Holmes onward who have believed that the end of government is a certain process—democracy, or government by public opinion, which "can be anything so long as it is freely formed." Because this ideal expresses no standard beyond "what emerges from the debate in the free market," Berns argues that it makes freedom to advocate one's opinions in that market, unrestrained by any moral guides, the "ultimate good," despite the liberals' occasional talk of enlightenment and progress. Accordingly, Berns maintains, the liberal conception of law is "amoral" and "devoid of any sense of the right," a mere positivist identification of law with "the command of the sovereign."[23]

Berns has consistently viewed a relativistic attachment to a democratic process lacking "ethical signposts" as "the very center of liberalism," but he has also repeatedly argued that it prevents liberalism from maintaining itself or achieving its ends. Liberalism overlooks the fact that laws inevitably affect the character of the citizens and therefore are inextricably concerned with the virtue of citizens. Liberalism's amoral law is thus really "bad law." It promotes "license" and distrust of moral principles, which create a confused and cynical citizenry, unwilling or unable to oppose the dangers facing American democracy. If America is to preserve the peace, prosperity, freedom, intellectual progress, and justice, to which the founders aspired, "freedom cannot be the cause" of America. Instead, the nation "must promote virtue, which necessarily means that it must limit freedom." This "limiting" of freedom to avoid "license" is "justified if it is done in the name of moral principle." Murray concurs, arguing that "institutions which would pretend to be free with a human freedom must in their workings be governed from within and made to serve the ends of virtue."[24]

While both Berns and Murray believe that the American system will not survive unless faith in traditional absolute standards flourishes, each is not chiefly concerned to achieve its liberal goals, as these quotations indicate. For Murray, the promotion of Christian virtue is the higher end America ought to serve, however indirectly. While he favors some ultimate freedom of conscience as necessary to sincere faith, and also accepts the necessity of disestablishment "as an article of peace in a pluralist society," he clearly would embrace fuller official recognition of his notions of virtue if this were politically feasible. Berns, on the other hand, points to Aristotle's *Nicomachean Ethics* as a guide to the virtue America should promote, though he insists like Murray that from different perspectives most of us can "recognize" virtue's basic precepts even if "precision is difficult." Both would contend accordingly that their notions of natural virtue are fundamentally identical. They would each contend as well that their ideals spring from the human "taste for the infinite," and that they express moral aspirations higher than any of the ends liberalism consciously promotes. Hence, even if America could operate successfully without any public promotion of respective virtues, this would not be desirable or ultimately legitimate. Berns maintains that the task is rather to merge the Constitution with wisdom "on the level of wisdom," elevating it "as closely as possible to what is right."[25]

These two positions are thus at best in uneasy alliance with liberalism, which has always been wary of efforts to define and inculcate virtue publicly. The credibility of these positions, including their capacity to meet liberalism's perennial difficulties, is also obviously dubious today. Despite the contentions of both Berns and Murray and the arguments of their common authority, Thomas Aquinas, it is not certain that their notions of virtue are even compatible with each other, much less with other widespread beliefs. Whereas Christianity stresses contemplation and worship of God and peace and charity in this life, Aristotle praises philosophic, not worshipful, contemplation, and he praises a "moral virtue" crowned by "magnanimity" that has fewer qualms about pride and hence less concern about disruptive, self-aggrandizing egoism than does Christianity. As a result, the higher law foes of relativism have not generated any alternative that is intellectually convincing to those outside their camps. They thus have not improved on liberalism's traditional inability to unite persuasively its higher law with empiricism.[26]

On the issue of political obligation, the problems of the higher law approach are even more acute. Because both the religious and the Aristotelian notions of virtue claim primacy over liberal values, they appear capable of justifying extensive conscientious disobedience in liberal states. Berns in fact argues that a good man can give his loyalty only to a good regime that promotes virtue, so that "a bad regime cannot trust good men." Yet he does not wish to encourage widespread protest in America, which he views as one of the best regimes extant. Berns desires to make America conform to "moral principles," through, for example, constitutional interpretation oriented toward virtue. Moreover, he insists that while moral restraints should be "self-imposed if possible," they may be "publicly imposed if necessary." Since "the purpose of law is and must be to promote virtue," government should only permit "freedom to do good and speak the truth." People break their obligations to moral principle, and so are un-American, if they fail to oppose with all effective legal measures those who foster immoral doctrines of any sort. Berns admits that such censorship can be a danger, but he maintains that its difficulties are not great enough to justify tolerance of immoral speech and conduct. For those who do not find these standards of virtue so transparent, however, Berns' moral absolutism appears equally capable of justifying self-righteous lawlessness and unlimited governmental moral regulation, results that are hardly improvements on liberalism's traditional accounts of the scope of obligation.[27]

Higher law responses to liberalism's individualism present corresponding problems. Murray and Berns do claim to identify true and common American values beyond those of egoistic Enlightenment liberalism, and Berns particularly suggests a system of citizenship education to propagate them. But his willingness to use governmental coercion to win adherence to these standards suggests a lack of confidence that they will be easily accepted and thus raises the specter of a desperate effort to overcome disagreement by imposing "social cohesion and political enthusiasm, from above," a specter that many advocates of communitarian politics find "unattractive and even frightening." Traditional higher law views also have little patience with the more recent romantic and social egalitarian values advanced in opposition to liberalism. Murray and Berns simply try to restore the absolutist orthodoxies of the past, and while such efforts appear ever to recur in American political life, they are today less able than ever to survive scrutiny as cogent alternatives to liberal constitutionalism.[28]

With traditional religious and classical absolutes unable to provide a more powerful version of American constitutionalism, there remains the possibility of encompassing in a new liberal theory the absolute autonomy and egalitarian values of postliberal thought. This possibility is all the more promising because early liberalism treated as inviolable certain principles of liberty and equality. Many romantic and social egalitarian positions claim only to have reformulated these principles more adequately. Even so, in their pure form romantic and social egalitarian ideals are too radical to be incorporated into any view that would be recognizable as liberal constitutionalism. The romantic belief that authentic, autonomous self-realization is the highest value invalidates all external limits on conduct. Nothing could be more antithetical to the liberal rule of law.[29] Furthermore, in modern large-scale societies political and economic hierarchies are pervasive and seem inevitable. Hence a completely leveling social egalitarianism still seems impractical, and efforts to establish it are likely to be inconsistent with existing personal freedoms and general economic welfare.

But today many believe that everything worthwhile in these positions can be retained by devising a version of liberalism that gives reign to extensive personal autonomy, limited only by an ultimate equality principle which demands respect for the similar autonomy of others. This approach draws inspiration from the Declaration of Independence's original commitment to human equality and from the combination of autonomy and egalitarian precepts in Kant and Mill. Today, much constitutional discourse proceeds on the assumption that some such combination is or should be the authoritative modern version of American liberalism, even though all the historical efforts to achieve this combination contain serious philosophical inadequacies.[30] Consequently, in recent years contemporary philosophers and legal scholars have attempted to formulate and defend this position more effectively.

The most influential theory, formulated by John Rawls and applied to constitutional issues by Ronald Dworkin, rests liberalism on a "Kantian conception of equality" that provides a right to equal concern and respect.[31] There are significant differences in the versions of neo-Kantian liberalism Rawls and Dworkin provide: Dworkin is much more willing than Rawls to use their common commitment to equal human worth as a direct guide to political issues, unmediated by the elaborate philosophic reflection and refinement that Rawls provides. Their conclusions on specific matters thus can differ sharply. But both share an element basic to contemporary neo-Kantian discourse: they insist that society has a moral obligation to show equal respect to all persons and that the fulfillment of this obligation helps promote self-respect in all. In consequence, society must show equal respect, and therefore be neutral, toward all views of the good life that are consistent with justice, with equal concern and respect for all.

This neo-Kantian understanding of liberal constitutionalism has immense appeal for contemporary liberal lawyers, since it promises to redress the failings revealed by liberalism's most influential modern critics. Recent research in social psychology, however, suggests that the call for equal respect, understood as implying neutrality on the question of the good life, is unrealistic and counterproductive, because all societies develop substantive norms, and no political system can effectively insulate particular groups from the tacit values of their larger society without draconian measures. As a result, the position is counterproductive: a substantively vacuous guarantee of equal respect to all cannot prevent damage to the self-respect of the disadvantaged from the adverse social judgments that this position still allows. A liberal community must therefore define more affirmative and accessible social values if it is to promote self-respect for all.

The neo-Kantian right to equal respect position stops short of demanding absolute social, economic, and political equality for all, but it requires that everyone be treated equally in one regard: as far as possible, the situation of each person must be seen from his own point of view, thereby showing respect for him as having at least the potential for valid moral conduct. But a danger lurks in explaining why others deserve this respect. If we respond by appealing to a characteristic, attainment, or quality along which people can be shown to differ, then presumably we must admit that it can justify granting persons unequal respect, in violation of the original precept. Rawls therefore answers that everyone deserves equal consideration and respect because all have some minimal moral worth, not by virtue of birth, characteristic, merit, or even excellence, but simply "as human beings with the capacity to make plans and give justice," a capacity that constitutes "moral personality." This moral personality, which is the basis for moral worth and the right to equal respect, is defined as the potentiality for just and moral behavior, not the realization of it. Everyone who meets the minimal requirements of moral capacity deserves respect because her potential alone has worth, and to deny and thereby injure this potential by withholding the respect it warrants would be morally wrong.[32]

Many conceptions of moral worth, however, particularly theories involving ethnic or caste distinctions, deny that all have even the minimum potential for attaining such worth. Advocates of the right to equal respect are unclear on the ultimate basis of their own egalitarian claim. The dominant explanation, consistent with modern consensual relativism, is that people simply choose to accept the equality principle if they deliberate on their moral beliefs thoroughly enough. Dworkin says his principle of equal concern and respect is so "widely shared and so little questioned" in modern Western societies that it could not be abandoned without a fundamental change in prevailing "patterns of reasoning and arguing about political morality." Rawls makes the more restrained claim that it is the basic principle that people would embrace in "reflective equilibrium," through a process of testing their preconceptions and possible moral theories against each other until they reached a satisfying view. In either case, because the appeal is ultimately to moral preferences, however refined, Dworkin is correct in asserting that despite its absolutist implications, his principle rests on "no ontology more dubious or controversial" than "the various popular utilitarian theories" require.[33]

This preferential basis means that the equality principle is vulnerable to claims that people, on reflection, may choose to reject it; so both authors intimate that it may have a firmer foundation in human nature. Dworkin suggests it may arise from "innate categories of morality common to all men, imprinted in their neural structure," which cannot be denied "short of abandoning the power to reason about morality at all." Rawls originally argued that a society based on his principles of justice would allow persons to "best express their nature" as "free and equal rational beings," and he has since acknowledged that this argument relies on a particular view of what the interests of moral persons genuinely are.[34] Given the controversial nature of these assertions, however, both writers prefer to appeal to our considered moral notions more than to any doctrine of our intrinsic nature.

The advantages of so defining moral worth as a ground for equal respect are that it seems to avoid both speculative metaphysical claims, such as Kant's "noumena," and notions of merit that could serve as a basis for moral inequality. The strategy is thus to make "the concept of right . . . prior to that of the good," refusing to define any specific notion of what is involved in realizing human moral potential, while permitting only those conceptions that can subsist with the basic equality right that is at the core of justice. This aspect of the view leads Dworkin to say that governments must be "neutral on what might be called the question of the good life," though as Rawls recognizes, this overstates the point. All persons with moral potential, even the abstractions operating behind the "veil of ignorance" in Rawls's original position, still require "some notion of goodness" simply to move them to act. Yet if this notion is to be consistent with the fundamental right to equal concern and respect, it must be a minimal one that can encompass all more specific conceptions that do not violate that principle. Otherwise it would "jeopardize the prior place of the concept of right" by ruling out some moral aspirations that a just equality would permit.[35]

The answer provided by right to respect theorists is that all persons are presumed to value self-respect, a sense of their own worth. Rawls calls this "perhaps the most important primary good," since without it, "nothing may seem worth doing," and many may "lack the will to strive" that a conception of the good provides. While Rawls's "perhaps" here reflects the fact that self-respect is just one of the primary goods he lists, along with "rights and liberties, powers and opportunities, income and wealth," most scholars have concluded that it is, as Frank Michelman argues, the "preeminent" social good, "the end and objective of all the principles of justice taken together." The other goods and principles "are elaborated and justified in terms of their tendency to instill and safeguard self-respect." Because self-respect appears compatible with all more specific aims and equally available to all, it seems the suitably minimal notion of the good that can motivate persons to realize their potential without violating the primacy of the right to equal concern and respect.[36]

In fact, when belief in the good as self-respect is combined with belief in the moral worth of all, it appears that public institutions have to be designed to express equal respect for all. These theorists assume (with sound psychological supporting evidence) that self-respect "normally depends upon the respect of others." Therefore, equal self-respect is impossible as long as some people are publicly treated as inferiors. To be sure, even fair and democratic political institutions, which give equal consideration and weight to each individual's just conception of his own good, cannot guarantee that all will develop a secure sense of their own worth. But they can avoid the "demoralizing effects" of public stigma, and they will, Rawls contends, "for the most part" provide sufficient assurance to meet the human need for "social bases of self-respect." The right to equal respect advocates have given much attention to analyzing how particular institutions can be made to provide this necessary public confirmation of the personal worth of all.[37]

But Rawls acknowledges that, precisely because such institutions forego public assessments of the relative value of each citizen's way of life, they may leave an individual "unsettled as to what to do," since they "cannot provide him with instructions as to how to decide." Rawls has confidence, however, that individuals will either be able to define their own conceptions of the good or, more often, will find at least one group among a liberal society's "plurality of associations" that has an ideal they find satisfying. Once joined in the "secure internal life" of such an association, individuals will have their ideals publicly affirmed by others more concretely than by society at large, which does not distinguish among just values. Consequently, while Rawls admits that the social system largely determines the kinds of persons that citizens "want to be as well as the kind of persons they are," he denies that this means societies must publicly define virtue. Institutions embodying the principle of equal concern and respect impose constraints on unjust behavior and also help meet the need for a sense that "others value us" through the public recognition they provide to all. Any necessary additional guidance will be available in "the full and diverse internal life of the many free communities of interests that equal liberty allows," where all can pursue the virtue they find meaningful.[38]

The right to equal respect view thus seems capable of maintaining most of the advantages of early liberalism and remedying some of its persisting defects. As Rawls notes, its adoption of a view of the good that sets only wide limits on human aims is an extension of liberalism's original idea of religious toleration and an effort to "work out principles of accommodation between different moralities" and thereby render "people's secure association together possible." It may thus be even more successful than early liberalism in providing a framework for social peace, harmony, and freedom among people of widely disparate views. Insofar as the theory achieves this end only by appealing to existing moral conceptions, it is consistent with modern empirical standards of moral credibility. Yet it also claims to have clarified and refined these conceptions in a manner that indicates previously unrecognized requirements. Hence it can define limits on individuals' conduct that they are required to accept if they wish to be consistent with their own values, not just with those of society, as in Bickel. In this way the position seems able to sustain the sorts of limits on both individual and majoritarian conduct that were formerly the contribution of higher law doctrines, while employing only arguments of personal consent to prove that these limits are obligatory. Correspondingly, it suggests what sorts of principles do and do not justify civil disobedience. While it remains possible to deny that the right to respect view really does provide a coherent theoretical articulation of American values, this must now be shown to be so. For those shaped by the heritage of liberal principles, that showing may prove difficult to accomplish.[39]

Rawls has been criticized, however, for allegedly perpetuating liberalism's exaggerated individualism. He contends instead that his position remedies this long-standing deficiency as well. He argues that while his theory of the good "uses the notion of an individual's plan of life" as the chief object of respect and consideration, "this does not imply that such plans must be individualistic." Citizens are free to pursue all just social and communitarian aims, and they can make them primary so long as they do not impose them on others. Rawls has also maintained that, because people cannot hope to realize individually all their possible ideals and aspirations, to be "complete exemplars of humanity," they have to "look to others to attain the excellence" they must leave aside. In a society based on equal respect where all just excellences can be pursued, Rawls believes that the citizens will "cease to be mere fragments" and will instead feel themselves to be part of a collective activity, a "common culture" that expresses all just facets of their humanity and so is "the preeminent form of human flourishing."[40]

But because of the inevitable economic and social pressures for conformity, there is no guarantee that a Rawlsian society will display an adequate diversity in human pursuits. At any rate, his view still presents human associations as matters of artifice and individual choice, however much it may treat them as desirable. From a radical perspective, Rawls may thus still appear to assume falsely that people are fundamentally individualistic, and so he treats communitarian activities as only one type of available alternative. Instead, the claim may be made that only in social pursuits can people hope to find authentic fulfillment.[41] Yet while Rawls's response might not convince staunch communitarians, it does permit a wide range of associational pursuits and offers a vision of a culture-wide collective enterprise. It may therefore meet most lesser demands for an attenuation of liberal individualism.

Similarly, while the principle of equal respect does not fully embrace either purely romantic or social egalitarian values, it may incorporate and combine these positions sufficiently to satisfy many of liberalism's critics. Because it sets such wide limits on permissible notions of the good, the theory allows for most forms of personal self-realization; indeed, Dworkin suggests that the concept of autonomy only acquires content when it is understood to involve the equal right of others to pursue their own ideals. Consequently, the right to respect view has been invoked to support, for example, ending the restraints on obscenity that adherents of romantic values deplore. The view is even more useful in combating traditional liberal social and political inequalities that violate equal respect for each person's interests. Since a "confident sense of their own worth" must be sought for all people, even the least favored, this view imposes sharp limits on the forms of hierarchy and degrees of inequality that justice permits.[42]

Thus, the excesses of liberalism's meritocratic market society, which promises equal opportunity but rewards only the gifted, fortunate, and well-connected, are deemed unjust. Economic inequalities that do not benefit the least advantaged become indefensible, and it can be argued that certain minimum welfare rights are required, free from demeaning conditions. Similarly, educational resources should be allotted not simply to increase productive potential but to enrich "the personal and social life" of every citizen. Full "equality in the electoral process" also seems demanded, though Rawls suggests that, at least in a less than "well-ordered" society, some departures from perfect political equality may be universally beneficial. Because this view thus sustains some inequalities that seem to assist the least well off and so are consistent with the notion that everyone is entitled to respect as a person, it is not a "charter for sweeping economic leveling." In fact, given the controversies about the sorts of economic inequality that benefit the least advantaged, the ambiguities of their identification, and the difficulties of accurately depicting current circumstances, to determine the redistributive implications of Rawls's difference principle for contemporary America is almost impossible. It is commonly regarded, however, as aiming at extensive egalitarian reforms, even in its milder formulations.[43]

Overall, then, the right to equal respect theory displays considerable power in both retaining liberalism's traditional strengths and responding to its problems. It will of course not be persuasive to advocates of beliefs ranging from the most traditional to the most radical who feel that their moral intuitions would lead to very different results in reflective equilibrium, should such a critical process be found desirable. Yet in terms of predominant Anglo-American moral and intellectual standards the theory may well be more persuasive than any of its competitors. But as Ronald Dworkin has recognized, the view's success in these regards ultimately rests on "the content of the respect that is necessary" to self-respect, to a sense of personal dignity. It is questionable whether the respect that the theory accords on the basis of moral personality provides most effectively the secure sense of personal worth it promises. To further this end more capably and also to provide a stronger defense of the way of life that liberal societies seek to provide, a more substantive liberalism is required.[44]

The essential problem with the assurance of personal worth in the right to equal respect view is that it conveys no clear sense of what makes persons morally worthwhile. Mere respectful treatment may suggest only that others find it prudent to avoid conflict by humoring us, according us nuisance, not moral, value. The view holds that public institutions should express the belief that all have worth because of their moral "potentiality," but as Robert Lane points out, "like all estimations, estimation of the self requires a baseline," and moral potential is not serviceable in this regard. Without some sense of what counts as realization of that potential, the theory provides no concrete notion of what is worthy in people, even potentially, or why. Consequently, it conveys little more than an awareness that others ascribe worth to people, especially since everyone else is simply assumed equally to possess such potential. And while such an ascription of value no doubt cannot harm people's sense of self-esteem, although it may ring hollow if their conduct seems immoral in their own eyes, it is not nearly as "psychologically satisfying and effective" as a sense of attained or achieved worth. Lane notes that people generally try to present themselves as having *earned* consideration because "personhood does not feel like sufficient dress." Obversely, if a determinate standard of moral achievement or attainment is publicly adopted, it may lead some to feel inferior and serve as a rationale for invidious inequalities. Even so, it is questionable whether in the absence of such a standard most people will be able to find a secure basis of self-respect.[45]

This conclusion becomes even harder to avoid when we recognize that the refusal to provide any definite public standards for personal moral worth produces further compounding problems. It is common ground that under such circumstances citizens will look elsewhere for guides, to the values expressed in social practices and to the ideals of nongovernmental, though often political, groups and associations. The very necessity to look to these many unofficial sources of values can breed an uncertainty that mitigates against self-esteem, as right to respect advocates acknowledge. This might not seem serious if, as Rawls assumes, everyone can join a group that provides shared values and personal affirmation. However, the influence of the first source of values, the practices of society at large, cannot be passed by so quickly. Rousseau argued long ago that no society could escape establishing standards of evil and good derived ultimately from public esteem, and recent analysis supports his contention. As the social psychologist Morris Rosenberg notes, societies "tend to impose common standards on their members." In contemporary American society, race, sex, religion, ethnic and national origins, intelligence, beauty, popularity, athletic skill, and humor, as well as wealth, influence, and numerous other factors, all serve as dimensions of esteem so widely expressed as to be hard to ignore; and all promote unequal self-esteem.[46]

To Rawls the very multiplicity of such standards promises that all will be able to find some upon which they can base a sense of personal worth. Yet competing adverse social values are not easily forgotten or overcome. Rawls expects that in a well-ordered society invidious inegalitarian criteria will be publicly opposed and eventually eradicated, but this is of course optimistic in light of the tenacious "ethnocentric propensity of mankind." Rawls also acknowledges that he must confront more specifically the impact on self-respect of the economic inequalities he would continue to permit. This concession is understandable, for when modern liberalism professes to leave all free to pursue their own good, the goods most widely valued in practice are wealth and the social power it brings. When liberal governments refuse to define standards of worth concretely, the liberal market stands as the major alternative, ready to define worthy attainments in measurable economic terms. Rosenberg's research confirms that adults, at least, tend to be "highly sensitive to income differences" in their self-assessments. Whether the roots of this tendency lie in the conditioning of capitalist property relations or in human nature, it means that societies embodying liberal freedoms will predictably appear crassly materialistic, coldly egoistic and competitive, and significantly unequal in terms of the very standards of worth that the society seems to value most.[47]

Life in such a society may feel dehumanizing even for its successful members, but Rawls believes he can avoid these consequences by insisting that all economic inequalities "contribute to the well-being of the less favored" and by disentangling in the process all confusion between economic and moral value. Unequal economic rewards will be offered to, for example, "scarce natural talents" only to cover special training costs, encourage the necessary efforts, and "to direct ability to where it best furthers the common interest" as determined largely by "supply and demand." Because inequalities will thus be publicly seen to be merely social devices for organizing the common pool of abilities to the benefit of all, Rawls believes they will in fact express respect for the interests of the less well off and that no one will think "those who have a larger share are more deserving from a moral point of view."[48]

It is questionable, however, how realistic this picture is. Even limiting economic inequalities will not in itself have much impact on the problem, for "from the self-esteem viewpoint, as Rawls himself recognizes, it is not absolute but relative wealth that counts." And Robert Nozick suggests why, especially in this sort of society, people will equate quantifiable wealth with moral worth. When it is difficult to determine where a person stands along the dimension that society claims to hold central, as is true of moral potentiality, "people will come to believe that a person's score on this dimension is correlated with his score on another dimension along which they *can* determine relative positions (the halo effect). Thus, people for whom the presence of divine grace is the most important dimension will come to believe other worthy detectable facts indicate its presence; for example, worldly success." Whether for this reason or others, liberal societies are prone to this halo effect in regard to wealth, so that those who are less wealthy "feel inferior as persons." To deny any link between economic failure and moral status does not allay this tendency. After all, the relatively poor are told that their inferior economic position is justified because their talents are so comparatively limited that their condition can best be improved by giving others what they desire. While this stand may involve no logical denial of moral value, it is not a likely source of self-esteem, nor does it console people to learn that society still respects their moral potential. As Rosenberg confirms, it "is bootless for you to tell me that your wealth enhances my material well-being." The wealthy will still be resented, and worldly failure will still be a source of demoralizing self-doubt.[49]

Rawls in fact eventually acknowledges that even in his well-ordered society "to some extent men's sense of their own worth may hinge upon their institutional position and their income share." He tries to remedy this difficulty by saying that "we can if necessary include self-respect" in the index of primary goods that economic inequalities must promote for all, as he otherwise prefers not to do directly. The index would thus "allow for the effects of excusable envy." But Rawls admits that this problem is an "unwelcome complication" and that this brief suggestion does not "settle" it—as well he might, since if it is true that wealth inequalities inevitably generate feelings of inferiority and resentment, it may be that genuinely equal public support for self-respect cannot be provided without a radical socioeconomic egalitarianism. Instead of pursuing this issue, Rawls simply assumes that "as the general level of well-being rises" people become less concerned about their material statuses and more caught up in "the free internal life of the various communities of interests" through which they pursue their particular "ends and excellences." They are thus presumably diverted from dwelling too heavily on their place in the broader economic and social hierarchy.[50]

This move is certainly not arbitrary. Recent psychological research suggests that persons in all social groups do tend to judge themselves most by comparison to their immediate peers. Conventional wisdom once held that unpopular minorities were "less secure in their self-evaluations"; indeed, this was the thrust of the social psychology studies on the harms of segregation cited in *Brown* v. *Board of Education*. Yet in the 1960s blacks in particular were shown not to have less self-esteem than whites; in fact, they appeared to have slightly more.[51] Like most people, they compared themselves chiefly to others in their immediate social group and judged themselves by the attitudes of that group toward themselves. Finding themselves comparable to and esteemed by those closest to them, they had secure self-esteem.

But even though people evaluate themselves largely in terms of those around them who are similarly situated and like-minded, this finding gives an incomplete and overly optimistic picture of the social circumstances influencing self-respect. For one reason, many of the studies involved, sparked by educational issues, focused on school children. The evidence indicates that children tend to be much less aware than adults of their status in the overall socioeconomic system. For adults, moreover, socioeconomic status is regarded as something achieved, not inherited or ascribed, and it correspondingly tends to be much more important to their sense of self-esteem, although some people choose to treat it as unimportant. And while group members tend to compare themselves mostly with other members of their group, they do so in terms of society-wide criteria.[52] For example, a poor Appalachian's self-respect may be preserved only because his reference group is also poor, not because he considers wealth an unimportant indicator of worth.

Consequently, when a group's insularity is broken down, so that its members are made conscious of their relatively lower status in terms of these social criteria, self-esteem becomes less secure. Black children attending white schools and adolescents in dissonant religious environments tend to have lower self-esteem than those in homogeneous surroundings, and this discrepancy increases with age. The tendency holds true even when black children are in fact doing better educationally than their peers in all-black schools. As Ralph Alan Rovner's review of the literature on self-estimation concludes, the self-esteem of ethnocultural minority group members is at risk: (1) when living and/or working in a dissonant social (i.e. racial and/or cultural) context, and (2) when in contact with conflicting cultural values.[53]

On balance, then, we still "do not, in fact, know how important the broader society's attitude toward the minority child's group or toward himself as a group member, actually is." There are grounds, however, for thinking that throughout American history labor, feminist, and black leaders have been correct in making the enhancement of their constituents' self-esteem an early and central objective and in denouncing social inequalities as destructive of self-respect.[54] It appears likely that, if significant socioeconomic inequalities are permitted, people will take these as indicators of worth even if the system accords formal political and legal equality to all. This consequence is lessened if governments keep their poorer citizens insulated from and unaware of the remainder of society, but a solution that depends on keeping the disadvantaged segregated and ignorant hardly provides the sort of secure universal self-esteem sought by the right to equal respect view.

Of course, the theory also calls for an end to all invidious discriminations among groups and thus rules out group economic and social inequalities that do not benefit the least fortunate. However, a "difference principle" analysis is not likely to be any more effective at the group rather than the individual level. Indeed, this shift introduces additional complications. The amorphous, overlapping, and dynamic nature of social groupings makes it harder to see how the state can accord to them the same sort of political equality and guarantees of beneficial economic inequalities that it provides to individuals.

In regard to electoral institutions, a policy of equal respect toward all communities and associations logically requires a system of proportional representation for all groups that collectively seek a political voice. But there are both practical and theoretical difficulties in designing electoral systems and other representative structures that are genuinely open to all parties. Insofar as these systems are not responsive to social forces generating new groupings, established groups may become unfairly entrenched, and the concern for equal respect may remain unfulfilled. Yet if it is easy to form new associations, the existence of current groups and the stability of the overall political and social community may be undermined.[55]

Similarly, if public institutions are to ensure that economic policies benefit the least advantaged groups, there is a danger that the existing array of economic and cultural associations will be artificially sustained by their role as conduits for publicly provided economic benefits. The result might be a mild form of corporatism that discourages new groups from forming and coerces individuals into identifying themselves completely with some lucrative group membership. Policies that show equal concern and respect to all existing bodies thus might clash with efforts to show equal consideration to nascent associations and to novel individual aspirations. Moreover, the very goal of assuring equal respect to all groups may have diverse implications that are not easily reconciled in practice, whatever may be true of theory. Some groups will surely feel that their distinctive ways of life are severely constrained by the requirement that all economic inequalities serve the society's least advantaged subgroups.[56]

Moreover, if all people are to find an association that affirms their ideals and attainments, they must have a real opportunity to learn about alternative groups and to shift their allegiances. As Roberto Unger notes, this imperative implies that the state should provide an "education that instructs in the past and present beliefs and creations of mankind in their richest and fullest variety," and it may also mean that a state should intervene to limit the burdens which groups may impose on those seeking to renounce or even to gain membership. Such education and such regulation can, however, "have a permanently subversive effect on all group cohesion," discrediting beliefs and practices essential to many groups' survival. It may be argued that there is no injustice in endangering those communities that cannot withstand the light of education and the opportunities of social mobility. But since the factors that make for group cohesiveness may have more to do with contingent elements, such as ethnic origins or a prestigious antiquity, rather than the persuasiveness of the group's ideals, and since groups long thought to be legitimate, such as the Amish, might suffer under such arrangements, it is still questionable whether such a state role accords equal consideration to all communities and associations.[57]

The obstacles to a policy of showing respect for groups sufficient to reduce the demoralizing impact of social and economic inequalities are therefore large indeed. If a more radical egalitarianism continues to be rejected, people are still likely to find themselves members of socially disapproved communities, jeopardizing their sense of personal worth. The need for self-esteem is so psychologically central that most persons can be expected to find some route to it despite these difficulties. However, for many the social determinants of self-respect under the right to respect approach will still make a sense of self-worth elusive instead of secure. Some people will feel compelled to reject and despise the group to which they belong because they have internalized society's contempt. Others will choose to take pride in antisocial behavior, including criminal violence, through which they can achieve a kind of superiority over those who would otherwise denigrate them. When society objects that they must respect the moral personality of others, they may perceive this as indicating only that the government hypocritically chooses to protect the goods which others are profitably pursuing, to their own humiliation, while it prevents them from doing the things that promise satisfaction by their own lights.[58]

Thus, the right to equal respect principle either unravels into the radical egalitarianism that it wishes to resist or promotes a liberal society that will in practice appear egoistic and materialistic to nearly everyone and provide self-respect for many of the disadvantaged only by segregating them, leading them to revile those with whom they would otherwise identify, or driving them to vicious forms of domination. Although no other approach ever has or ever is likely to overcome all these problems, within the confines of liberalism a preferable alternative is available.

8 · A Liberal Theory of Political Purpose

The claim that the right to equal respect view cannot provide adequate social support for self-respect, because humiliating comparisons and cynicism cannot be effectively combated by a standardless ascription of worth to all, suggests that public institutions and policies should express a more concrete conception of why persons have worth and of how to attain a greater sense of self-worth. Governments should also pursue measures that visibly assist citizens in their efforts at such attainments, while restricting activities that seriously hinder them. Liberal institutions then might indicate more persuasively why certain routes to self-respect are unjust, why those who are economically less well off can nonetheless confidently regard themselves as morally worthy, and how all might act to achieve an enhanced sense of self-esteem regardless of their socioeconomic status. Liberal societies can provide more support and guidance for a sense of self-worth if they take as their basic goal liberalism's traditional concern to promote reflective self-direction, or rational liberty.[1] The difficulties in pursuing this course have prevented it from being adopted more explicitly, especially by modern liberal thinkers, but the ideal can be credibly formulated today.

If a more concrete standard of moral worth or the morally good is publicly adopted and promoted, and if it is one that persons may attain to varying extents, several dangers emerge. The standard may be unduly restrictive of ways of life that are in fact morally legitimate and that would further moral progress. It may lead those of lesser accomplishments to feel stigmatized and either worthless or resentful. It may be exploited by powerful interests to justify invidious discriminations against those who are alleged to have inadequate moral attainments, perhaps still judged in terms of economic status, due to the halo effect. According to Robert Nozick, some such problems are inevitable, because persons generally judge themselves and form self-esteem on the basis of "differentiating characteristics," not on their "common human capacities." If so, the establishment of a more definite moral standard along which people differ would exacerbate this tendency, leading to widespread inequalities in the sense of personal worth and in the respect that citizens show one another. Traditional societies may have been able to preserve self-respect despite extensive social inequalities out of a sense that each was doing his duty in the station preordained for him by a meaningful natural or divine order. But in liberal societies, which lack such a public faith, low attainments by society's standards of worth are often felt to be demeaning and demoralizing.[2]

As Morris Rosenberg notes, however, the evidence of contemporary social psychology suggests a more acceptable outcome. A society can chiefly value noncompetitive traits, characteristics that are attainable to differing degrees but which, unlike preeminent wealth or power, all can attain to an extent that makes everyone's sense of self-worth secure regardless of the relative achievements of others. As philosophers have recently observed, the terms *self-respect* and *self-esteem* can express two distinct notions of self-worth. One holds that people are morally responsible and worthy persons if they meet some minimum standard of personal moral attainment. The other expresses the belief that one's worth rises well beyond the established minimum and amounts to excellence in realizing the standard. All might think they possess sufficient honesty, courtesy, and cooperativeness to be morally worthwhile individuals, even though they recognize that some people exceed them in these regards. Many will feel they personally excel in these qualities. The first, more crucial sense of personal worth may be termed "self-respect," the second "self-esteem."[3] People thus may have less self-esteem because they must admit that others surpass them in these significant respects. Still, if they take the standards themselves seriously as indicators of true worth, not merely as arbitrary dimensions of social comparison, they can feel a confident sense of self-respect despite these discrepancies. It is not difficult to see oneself as an honest, considerate, valuable person while accepting that others are nearly saints. The promotion of universal, equal self-respect may therefore be a plausible goal, even if the pursuit of universal, equal self-esteem is not.

Nonetheless, once any determinate standard of moral attainment, however minimal, has been defined, some people may be viewed or may see themselves as failing to meet it. They may consequently lack a secure sense of self-respect. The right to equal respect view can more easily claim in principle to provide for the self-respect of all, since it guarantees to all who merely possess moral potential that they are worthwhile. Although a definition of moral attainment need not reject either the value of moral potential or the consideration it demands, the assurance accorded by such consideration may be undercut by the judgment of failure that can follow it.

Yet all people might display conduct sufficient to assure themselves of worth according to the standard adopted, and the right to equal respect view cannot really achieve the universal self-respect it promises. The question of what sort of approach is ultimately conducive to the most extensive self-respect, though an empirical one, is not easily examined, because it requires study of the consequences of society-wide institutions over extended periods of time. Here, I will simply try to define a liberal conception of moral worth that can plausibly claim to remedy the deficiencies in the right to equal respect view while mitigating if not eliminating the counterbalancing dangers.

Even though the early liberals pursued several goals, their advocacy of rational liberty, of the preservation and enhancement of human capacities for understanding and reflective self-direction, was the core of the liberal political and moral vision. This vision sees human freedom, dignity, and happiness as resting fundamentally on our abilities to comprehend our world and ourselves, to deliberate on the possibilities and aspirations we find therein, and to choose and execute our preferred courses to the greatest degree practicable. But contrary to many contemporary accounts of rationality, rational liberty is not only an instrumental but also a substantive standard for human conduct. It does espouse a certain process for determining our actions, namely reflective deliberation on our circumstances and on the various commitments, ideals, desires, opportunities, and constraints that those circumstances present to us. But it also includes a substantive requirement for the outcomes of such deliberation: if we value rational self-direction, we must always strive to maintain in ourselves, and to respect in others, these very capacities for deliberative self-guidance and self-control. Correspondingly, we must see the habitual exercise of these capacities as constituting morally worthy character and their enhancement as constituting morally praiseworthy action.[4]

But since the nature and degree of individual talents and inclinations along these lines vary, many different sorts of pursuits of happiness are still appropriate. In fact, the goal of promoting rational liberty not only permits but encourages considerable diversity in ways of life, even as it indicates how a secure and noncompetitive sense of self-worth can be obtained by all. The standard itself implies that all people should not make the cultivation of their rational capacities their single goal, for most persons are sufficiently multifaceted to find such a course so narrow and frustrating as to be self-defeating. Furthermore, differences in individual abilities, temperaments, and tastes mean that people will, on reflection, make different choices about the activities that are most likely to lead them to satisfactions consistent with continued self-direction. The rational liberty position therefore does not justify any public effort to transform or "educate" persons according to some single standard of proper human consciousness. For the most part, it encourages people to be themselves.[5]

But all of us, except for very young children and the severely mentally unfit, possess basic deliberative capacities and the potential for some measure of self-direction. Hence, the minimum that the rational liberty view demands for moral respectability is that we act so as not to endanger significantly the preservation of those faculties in ourselves or others. It thus values not any particular occupation, social status, or special talent but rather the sort of responsible moral character that is fostered by pursuit of this standard. It does not disavow the range of other social and personal obligations, inclinations, and values we may believe our identity involves, but it insists that we retain and exercise our critical capacities to consider our possible pursuits, their consequences, and their worth, and that we esteem this conduct in others.[6] Since this standard is attainable in appreciable measure by virtually everyone, it may provide a sense of dignity and self-respect to all of us regardless of the particular life paths, consistent with such a character, that we choose to follow.

Often liberals have focused not on rational liberty but on more immediate aims, such as peace, economic growth, or greater political and social equality, and often they have been reluctant to accept the political and philosophic burdens imposed by explicit adoption of any substantive purpose at all. But most liberal theorists and many liberal statesmen have eventually appealed to the enhancement of human potentialities as the justification for all their objectives, even though their conceptions of those potentialities have varied. The rational liberty position thus expresses deeply imbedded themes in liberal thought that are required to respond to the needs of liberal constitutionalism today.

Locke can again best serve to suggest the elements of the rational liberty view, for several reasons. The claim to discern this conception in the American liberal constitutional tradition would be crippled if it was not expressed in the early liberal thinker who most exemplifies that tradition's initial principles. There is also a misguided tendency in modern scholarship to identify liberalism's premises with Hobbes's egoistic psychology and to link any higher moral aspirations in liberalism to Kant's transcendental egalitarianism. The first assumption makes it easy to read the liberal tradition as predominantly concerned with the pursuit of hedonistic self-interest, with self-preservation and material comforts, or at most with the unleashing of human acquisitiveness and the pursuit of a hubristic, Faustian mastery of the world. The second assumption frequently provokes doubts about the credibility of liberal notions of moral personality, even among liberals themselves.[7]

Yet Locke's treatment of human nature has been the most powerful source of liberal notions of political purpose. Instead of embracing a mechanistic determinism with Hobbes or a transcendental freedom with Kant, Locke eschews extensive metaphysical claims. He takes an essentially psychological or even phenomenological approach to the ultimate character of the human self and human will, appealing to our practical experience of our selves as enduring beings with some apparent capacities for self-direction, while acknowledging that contrary accounts cannot be disproven. He believes that this basic sense of our selves, however illusory, is our inescapable starting point in moral and political reflection and the standard against which we judge rival interpretations. Therefore, he believes, it should also be our premise and standard in political morality.[8] Although he stresses goals of self-preservation, material comfort, acquisition, and mastery, at root he aspires to enhance the experience of self-awareness and self-governance that is basic to our common sense of our selves. Locke's pragmatic psychological empiricism and his basic goal are both preferable, I think, to beginning liberal theory with geometrically inspired Hobbesian reconstructions of human nature or with an assumed Kantian transcendental subject.

Numerous assertions of Locke's justify attributing to him the belief, in Geraint Parry's words, that it is not only a divine duty but also inherently right for each person to "use to the full the distinctively human capacities which he possesses—his liberty and his rationality." But Locke provides no systematic argument for the inherent propriety of this realization of our capacities. He never redeems his apparent claim that reason can indicate which of our desires are choice-worthy. He thus provides grounds for assigning to reason only the instrumental utilitarian role that it was granted by Hume. But such a reading would subvert Locke's claims that natural rights are the only proper ends of government, that the human understanding is the highest human faculty, and that in cultivating our powers of rational deliberation to guide us in the pursuit of happiness, we approach the highest perfection of intellectual nature. Locke's assertions that people may and should curb their passions and his condemnations of those who fail to do so might also express merely reason's instrumental judgment that certain desires will not in the long run maximize happiness. But they bespeak much more obviously a belief that some desires do not merit fulfillment regardless of the pleasure they bring.[9]

Yet if we read Locke as contending that the enhancement of our capacities for understanding and deliberative self-direction constitute the perfection of our natures, we must suggest why he thinks so and why he fails to show this more clearly. A number of reasons might be adduced, including Locke's lingering medieval religiosity, newer Miltonian notions of personal responsibility, or the Baconian devotion to knowledge as the source of human power, a devotion usually traced either to a concern to serve mankind or to an impious delight in human domination.[10] But I will argue for an answer implied by the psychology of the *Essay*, stressing the relief to our fundamental uneasiness provided by the enhancement of our rational liberty.

Locke rules out the most traditional argument, that we have some knowledge of the real essence of things. The limits of the human mind are such that we can know with certainty only the ideas that we ourselves form. In consequence, Locke insists that we cannot assert, as much classical and medieval thought did, that the natural essence of man is the *Animal rationale*. Nor does he accept the weaker claim that our rationality and the freedom of choice it involves are distinctively human characteristics, so that their perfection is the perfection of the unique essence of our nature. Although the understanding does set humans above all other sensible creatures and gives us our advantage and dominion over them, our apparent ability to be guided by reason is in itself morally important, regardless of whether it happens to be an exclusive attribute of ours. This ability is the great privilege not of humanity but of all finite intellectual beings, and if a monkey also had the use of reason, it would be of equal moral significance.[11]

Rationalists like Milton hold that our understanding is morally valuable precisely because it is what makes us free agents, able to judge and choose among our wishes and therefore to take responsibility for our actions as products of our own decisions. Only if we can rationally direct our own acts can we be credited with any personal moral status, good or evil. Otherwise any moral significance of our acts would derive solely from the meaning of some larger order of which we were merely helpless instruments. Since grasping the meaning of such an order requires perceiving the essence of things, this sort of significance appears impossible on Locke's premises. Perhaps it could be provided by revelation, but aside from this alternative, our capacities for understanding and self-regulation are the only available grounds for our moral meaningfulness, rendering their maintenance a moral necessity. This necessity might explain why Locke thinks that if our minds should "break loose from the conduct of Reason" and be "captivated" by our unexamined, unrestrained inclinations, the captivity would be a greater evil than even the loss of physical liberty. That is a profound evil indeed, since Locke believes we will risk life itself rather than endure the "uneasiness" loss of physical liberty entails. This weighty status is understandable if the loss of our capacity for self-direction destroys all possibility of morally valuable conduct.[12]

This Miltonian rationalist argument cannot be the whole answer, however, for it defends the cultivation of our rational faculties only as a precondition for moral significance in our subsequent pursuits. It thus renders the neglect of those abilities evil, but it does not explain why Locke regards the enhancement of our understanding and powers of self-direction as in itself something we should, after sufficient reflection, judge to be our highest delight, nor why the loss of these capacities is so definitive of misery. Locke's pivotal claim, after all, is that our sensations of pleasure and pain, properly considered, affirm his moral requirements. Yet most of us certainly do not, as Locke admits, experience rational deliberation as our chief pleasure.[13]

The only delight involved in reflection might appear to be the anticipation of future pleasures we discover that we can attain. But anticipation is not Locke's point, since he stresses the satisfaction arising from the activity of understanding itself, even if it does not lead us to acquire new means to further pleasures. Alternatively, the enhancement of the understanding might be delightful simply because it fosters an exciting awareness that we can control many aspects of ourselves and the world around us as we see fit, an awareness that may carry with it "a sense of exhilaration and power," as Charles Taylor says of the Baconian world view. This interpretation, stressing the pleasurable pride and sense of increased mastery fostered by the progress of our rational capabilities, is supported both by Locke's description of the delight of understanding as "the Hunter's satisfaction" and by his indication that a "pretty well advanced" man may "at last have a full power over his own mind, and be so fully master of his thoughts, as to be able to transfer them . . . with the same ease that he can lay by any thing he has in his hand." These passages express the sort of relish in a sense of our powers that Taylor and others see as liberalism's animating drive.[14]

Although this delight, too, is part of Locke's position, his understanding of the human condition and human psychology suggests a more fundamental aspect. Locke, who does not believe he can detect the essence of man, nonetheless thinks he can identify the core conception of our selves to which we ultimately resort in political and moral meditations. He recognizes that it is possible to theorize that man is a purely corporeal animal, or an immaterial spirit, or some union of the two, but he believes it does not matter what stance we take on the eternal mystery of the self's true nature. Since the proof of any of these doctrines is unavailable to human reason, an intellectually honest person is inevitably driven to define the self or personal identity as nothing but consciousness, the perception of what passes in that person's own mind which produces the mind's awareness of itself as itself, "the same thinking thing in different times and places." In protophenomenological fashion, Locke indicates that the notion of one's self as the same consciousness is the inescapable core idea that we form prior to any theory and which we resort to when we deliberate on whether such theories are persuasive accounts of our selves. Hence morality, which like mathematics gains certainty from employing ideas we have ourselves supposed, must posit the "immoveable unchangeable *Idea*" of *"the moral Man"* to be that of "a corporate rational Being," whatever "Shape" its incorporation may take.[15]

Locke therefore takes his moral bearings from the characteristics that consciousness gives to our condition. Consciousness involves capacities both for reflection and for pleasure and pain, and together, as an unavoidable concomitant, these capacities issue in a concern that the individual be happy. We experience consciousness, then, as including both an awareness of the possibilities of joy and misery and a sense of having the reflective capability to influence which emotion we will experience. The strongest uneasiness of which we are aware will determine our choice of action. We will feel uneasy whenever our fate seems to be outside our control, yet our control, over both ourselves and the external world, is always partial at best. Therefore, the consciousness that is both our idea of our selves and the supposition with which morality begins involves as a constitutive characteristic a profound uneasiness or anxiety—a sense that there are things, perceived and unperceived, within us and around us, which may bring us pain or, worse, come to control us so that we are helpless and vulnerable.[16]

If this portrait of an uneasy consciousness is indeed Locke's picture of the fundamental human condition, it is understandable that he believes the most genuinely satisfying experience is the relief that comes when we enhance our understanding of the circumstances that affect us and increase our ability to control not only them but our own responses to them. While heightened understanding may involve the discovery of dangers previously hidden in blissful ignorance, and while many unhappy circumstances will be impossible to overcome, we will at least have come closer to doing all we can to maintain control over our destinies and provide for our well-being.

This explanation suggests why Locke might feel that to increase our capacities for rational self-direction is the proper response to the basic, underlying, and most enduring uneasiness that moves us. It still seems a leap, however, for Locke to assert this as a moral imperative. Perhaps we *are* always forced to rely on the idea of our selves as consciousnesses, and the belief that our rational powers can assist us in fulfilling the desires that our consciousness entails. Even so, there is no logical necessity to assert that we must take the idea of ourselves as corporate rational beings as the first postulate of morality, making our desires for cognitive development morally obligatory in a way that other desires are not. There are nonetheless reasons for choosing to take this step that may at least appear persuasive. It generates a moral view that preserves a sense of our responsibility for our choices and hence of our potential moral significance. It offers an image of ourselves as capable of appreciating and accepting the limits and opportunities provided both by the world around us and by our own characteristics, an image in which we may take pride and find dignity. Furthermore, it defines a human good, the enhancement of our understanding and capacities for self-direction, that is, in principle at least, noncompetitive, available, and attainable in some measure to all of minimal cognitive capacities.

If all were to adopt this conception of moral attainment, all would accept their own responsibilities for reflective self-governance, respect the similar capacities of others, and recognize that their advancement is morally valuable. A society made up of such citizens would be one of extensive freedom, self-respect, and mutual affirmation and assistance without undue dependence. This ideal is thus one that members of a liberal society might reasonably choose as the fundamental goal of their common institutions; and if they do so, they have a right both to insist that it be upheld by all who have consented to it and to defend their shared moral purpose against those who oppose it.

The objection may be made that this ideal can never work to support social unity, for if we suspect others of threatening our plans, the desire to maintain control of ourselves may lead us into conflict, as in Locke's state of nature. Due to fears of others or to an inadequate sense of the dangers involved, we may also try to manipulate and exploit natural resources in ways that prove counterproductive, as modern experience demonstrates. But human conflict and imprudent exploitation work on balance to heighten the uneasiness of our condition. It seems possible that persons of good character could instead enhance their insights and capacities for self-direction simultaneously and, on the whole, harmoniously. Considerable tolerance and at least some social cooperation appear necessary for all to further their personal rational development, to feel they have some opportunity to influence social decisions affecting them, and to develop an ongoing, reassuring sense of social trust.

Furthermore, as Locke recognizes, people derive a sense of their moral obligations, at least initially, from the social relations and moral rules prevalent in their communities. Hence, most persons find satisfaction and feel free only by adopting a course of life that includes considerable immersion in the activities of some of these constitutive social forms. For most people, then, a moral imperative to promote the capacities for self-guidance of themselves and their peers requires the pursuit of some types of social harmony and mutual aid. No doubt some would still insist that in practice any emphasis on personal self-direction inevitably proves fragmenting, in contrast to positions that give priority to claims of social solidarity. But the stability and desirability of any social unity that depends on minimizing capacities for personal choice are equally dubious. Locke's conception of the moral man not as a mere pawn of powerful forces but as a being capable of self-understanding and of reasonable choice naturally supports conceptions of happiness and morality as things that can and must be attained in collaboration with the processes of nature and the pursuits of our fellow rational beings.[17] This portrait of the liberal character and of the moral basis of liberal community constitutes a standard that has broad and lasting appeal.

Nonetheless, despite Locke's intimations, this ideal cannot be shown to be morally obligatory by reason alone. Some may choose to pursue it only for themselves, while denying their responsibility to respect its pursuit by others. Although such egotism is inconsistent with the claim that rational development has moral rather than merely hedonistic value, not even consistency can be shown to be an objective, universal moral requirement. Moreover, some people may reject the goal of rational liberty altogether. The human condition thus pictured is, after all, inherently characterized by uncertainty and tension, which can at best be moderated, never overcome, by the activities advocated. The proper premise for morality may therefore be not the improvement of this consciousness but rather its alteration or obliteration through unquestioning allegiance to some higher authority or absorption in some all-consuming pleasure or overriding passion. As Samuel Johnson remarked, "He who makes a beast of himself gets rid of the pain of being a man." Similarly, he who becomes a devoted disciple avoids the agony of continual choices. Hence, those who conduct themselves as wild beasts by Locke's standards or who give themselves up entirely to the loyalties and leadership of their communal group may achieve a more genuine fulfillment of their deepest desires, and a more realistic sense of self, than Locke's individualistic rationalism can hope to provide. Such courses might make life not only more free and pleasurable but also more meaningful. To Locke these paths amount to a degenerate repudiation of the principles of human nature, of man's constitution as an intelligent being, but this rational constitution might appear to some to be an inverted caricature of human nature, one that generates more misery than it relieves.[18]

Such lack of foresight would be surprising in one so conscious of the limited capabilities of our rational constitution, however. Following John Dunn, many scholars have therefore concluded that Locke stresses the delights and moral worth of man's rational liberty out of his "somewhat supine religious conviction" that, since our rational capacities are God-given, their enhancement represents one of God's requirements for men. Locke repeatedly insists that we are to demonstrate morality starting not just with the idea of our selves "as understanding, rational Beings" but also with the idea of a supreme being "whose Workmanship we are." While I believe this interpretation understates how far Locke moves toward the primacy of reason as our guide, it does seem likely that Locke saw his views as at least consistent with a certain religious faith, though not with all the Calvinist orthodoxy of his upbringing.[19]

If his belief in the worth of rational liberty indeed rests simply on assumptions, religious or otherwise, it again seems understandable that Locke never attempts to show that his morality can be demonstrated on the basis of reason alone. Any such effort would lead only to an acknowledgement that his values can logically be rejected and that their enforcement amounts to the imposition of a particular faith—not something that the advocate of religious toleration and rational natural law would wish to highlight. Locke clearly does think that liberal societies have to presuppose the value of human consciousness thus understood, and that this premise requires them to punish as "Beasts" those whose choices endanger the realization of this ideal by all. He is also wary of the consequences if this premise should be thought of as a matter of choice; hence perhaps his various efforts to claim an obligatory status that he cannot prove.[20]

But the adverse consequences of Locke's inability to redeem these claims were not wholly avoided. His doubts about the persuasiveness of the ideal of rational liberty may have led Locke, along with most other early liberals, to emphasize the concern of the state with material goods and the economic benefits of property rights, though Locke defines "property" as resting on rational conduct and encompassing liberty. At any rate, the cause of economic freedom and material prosperity was a more effective political rallying cry for many early liberals in England and America than was rational self-direction for its own sake. Nonetheless, early liberals commonly spoke of a rationally discoverable obligation for people to realize their nature as "intelligent and rational" beings, "endowed with free will," and James Wilson argued at the Constitutional

Convention that the "cultivation & improvement of the human mind," not property, was "the most noble object" of free government.[21] But exponents of this goal usually still relied on a religious belief that these capacities were divinely endowed, even while empirical liberal theories undermined the intellectual credibility of religious doctrines and liberalism's secular politics held that no particular religious views should be required. In the long run the liberals' allegiance to these philosophic and political positions left them without a defense for granting any special status to the goal of rational perfection.

Some scholars have argued similarly that early liberalism presupposed a firm human reasonableness and an attendant voluntary subjection and self-control, implanted in men by Calvinist Puritanism. But, they contend, liberalism "did not create the self-control it required," since it opposed the official propagation of any religious beliefs. Students of early American political thought often similarly characterize it as still opposing "the unrestrained pursuit of self-interest as licentious," while remaining confident that the necessary ethical values of "moderation" would flourish without any potentially dangerous governmental inculcation of these virtues. Yet Jefferson, for one, was highly concerned that public education be established to form the populace "to habits of reflection and correct action," "of application, order, and the love of virtue," since "their minds must be improved to a certain degree" if the people were to be "safe" as governors. At the same time, due to his thoroughgoing rationalism, Jefferson opposed any infusion of religious content into education at any level, and this position rendered his conception of moral education not only unpersuasive but incomprehensible to many of his countrymen.[22] Liberal intellectuals, on the other hand, had already begun to concede that a self-evident morality based on reason alone was hard to discern. Consequently, Jefferson's notion of a rationalist liberal curriculum that would perpetuate morality without resorting to religion failed to gain a central place in American education.

Thus, in practice, the early liberals did not give unambiguous primacy to the ideal of rational self-direction. When liberty was defended for its spiritual values, these tended to be understood in religious terms, and often the economic aspects of liberty were instead taken as fundamental. These initial ambivalences make it clear once again why, after the claims of both religion and rationally discoverable natural law had lost credence, liberals increasingly chose not to defend any concrete notion of political purpose, such as rational liberty, and rather identified liberalism with democratic consent. This trend was reinforced by the fact that from the rebellion of the romantics onward, the emphasis in nineteenth and twentieth century thought on emotional, social, economic, biological, cultural, linguistic, and unconscious psychological determinants of human behavior made Lockean notions of rational self-direction seem naive. And because these ambiguities in early liberal thought left its practical stress on material freedoms that proved productive of large inequalities, liberals also felt increasingly compelled to respond to the social egalitarian claims that these inequalities generated. It is therefore all the more understandable that so much contemporary liberal thought denies any attachment to a substantive moral goal and instead claims to permit all notions of the good that are consistent with an ultimate equality principle reflected in fair decision-making processes.

In their religious form at least, early liberal notions of an obligation to perfect our rational natures nevertheless remained prominent in nineteenth century American political thought even while Western intellectual developments generally moved in different directions. Jacksonian working-class leaders such as Stephen Simpson and Ely Moore in fact proclaimed it labor's goal "to elevate our moral and intellectual condition" even more than "to promote our pecuniary interests," out of a belief that all must strive "to develop the full power and cultivate to the utmost perfection the human intellect." According to Robert Faulkner, Lincoln's Republicanism held that while "a common basic dignity may be conceded to all by virtue of common natural rights, the distinctive dignity of any person depends upon his or her accomplishments, the particular use each makes of his or her opportunity." Thus neither human dignity nor human rights ought to be separated from qualities of character. Moreover, Mills's praise of liberalism's role in promoting the "mental expansion and elevation" of all, Hobhouse's discussion of the "rational good," Dewey's advocacy of the "method of intelligence," and Rawls's identification of moral personality with the concern to have a rational life plan all suggest that the ideal of deliberative, self-directing persons remains deeply engrained in the thought of liberalism's modern adherents, however hard it may be to prove obligatory.[23] The next question, then, is whether this ideal can be reformulated so that it is philosophically defensible, politically workable, and practically desirable today.

The rational liberty view contains a standard for the process of moral decision-making, the requirement of rational deliberation on our alternative goals and their consequences, as well as a substantive standard, the insistence that we must strive not to endanger anyone's capacities for such deliberation. This position assumes that we have capacities for rational self-determination and that we can recognize, in ourselves and others, what is conducive to these capacities and when they have been exercised. Yet the very notion of free will based on reason has not been and perhaps cannot be coherently described, much less shown to be true:

all descriptions of psychic mechanisms of choice seemingly must be causal accounts that have no place for an uncaused agent. Modern thought has accordingly generated numerous causal theories of human behavior that have great power in accounting for human conduct. Indeed, even contemporary cognitive psychology, a discipline descended in part from Locke's psychological empiricism, has shown experimentally that the operations of our minds involve processes that are unperceived and therefore not part of Locke's irreducible consciousness.[24] Furthermore, the complexities of these accounts suggest the difficulty of identifying what constitutes rationally deliberative conduct even if it is assumed to occur.

But as Richard Rorty observes, there is also no agreement on a portrait of people's higher faculties to replace that of Locke. In the most relevant respects the common sense self-understanding of most people who make up our moral and political worlds is little changed. People still inescapably experience themselves in the way Locke describes, as partly aware and uneasy consciousnesses, with some apparent capacity for reflective self-direction. Even many who deny the reality of free will, such as the sociologist Milton Gordon, agree that "as individual human beings engaged in making decisions at virtually every moment . . . we *must* and *do* act as though we had free will."[25]

To be persuasive, any deterministic account of human behavior must make sense of such common sense understandings. As Thomas Nagel has dramatized, it must particularly deal with the appearance that subjective consciousness has for itself, and with our sense of personal agency. None has yet done so convincingly. Although this fact does not discredit determinism, the theoretical question of free will is at the least likely to remain unresolved, along with the issue of our ultimate essence. Different theoretical accounts may help us to believe that we have increased our understanding and control of our environment and our selves. But as Rorty effectively concedes, for matters of political morality the general conception of our selves that Locke provided still seems (as he argued) the appropriate court of appeal for deciding which theories we find satisfactory.[26] The tenacity of this notion in our everyday activities suggests that it may also have a pragmatic claim to primacy for more speculative purposes—although again, to show logically that no other position is tenable in either empirical or moral accounts of human personality seems impossible.

These considerations prove that the decision to take seriously our experience of ourselves as thinking consciousnesses and the goal of rational liberty that it suggests are not so philosophically naive or outmoded as may first appear. The rational liberty view can encompass and find helpful almost all existing theories of possible determinants of human behavior so long as these are not taken to deny the practical moral imperative of enhancing our conscious personal experience of rational deliberation and self-control. To be sure, in some strong versions of determinism, such as, perhaps, the oft-berated "vulgar Marxism," the subjective sensation of a capacity for self-guidance is held to be entirely illusory and morally meaningless. But the practical activity of many Marxists still presupposes that at least some can overcome the false consciousness engendered by their material circumstances with the help of knowledge, experience, and reflection and can then choose to act on behalf of a different, more universal sense of the human good. Thus, they do not deny the assertion that enhancement of our capacities for understanding and self-guidance has moral value.[27]

Some social egalitarian radicals would still insist that, while we do have meaningful powers of self-direction, any choices inimical to a radical transformation of society are substantively immoral. Few modern societies, however, display a consensus that preferences for private pursuits and for economic liberties involving some inequality seriously threaten individual and social capacities for reflective self-direction. Although the prevailing consensus may be a distortion produced by the ideological hegemony of the ruling classes, identification of those who have pierced the veil and seen the right direction is difficult, since no position can claim to be more than a partial perspective. It is therefore inconsistent with rational liberty to impose specific and controversial social egalitarian conceptions of human fulfillment on the many who do not share them, although the noncoercive advocacy of those conceptions is of course permissible. At this point, moreover, the argument between the two positions is only over what constitutes genuine "rational liberty" and how it is to be achieved, even though the differences between the positions are so great that it would be confusing to term them distinct versions of liberalism.[28] In the present state of knowledge, such differences are unavoidable, and there are no definitive grounds for discrediting the more skeptical and encompassing liberal view.

The existence of these differences raises the question of who is to decide on what counts as rational liberty, which returns to the question of how to decide what is rationally deliberative behavior and what sorts of conduct harm our capacities to attain it. After all, while certain aspects of Locke's analysis of the power of human consciousness and the means to its improvement are still practically serviceable, many conflicting psychological and philosophical accounts have since been produced. Are governments to employ psychological experts, social scientists, metaphysicians, or specialists in the wealth of other theories of human conduct for determining the boundaries of legitimate behavior?

The answer is that, because the rational liberty view takes its bearings ultimately from our personal experience of our selves as conscious, self-directing beings, it calls for us to judge what constitutes rational self-guidance not by any particular theory but by the notions engendered by that experience, as perceived and expounded by the community at large. Thus, political institutions should, through democratic processes, elicit and enforce prevailing social standards of what constitutes minimally rational, deliberative conduct and of what preserves the ability to engage in it. While the promotion of personal self-direction may be assisted by specialized expertise, it ultimately requires self-governance by the political community as a whole.

This conclusion, though reassuringly democratic, raises the specters of direct majoritarian intolerance and repression and of more subtle domination by inherited ideas that buttress what may be an unjustifiable status quo. Yet it is difficult again to know which minority views to crown as preferable, for there are many pretenders to the throne. Moreover, it is unrealistic to expect any community to avoid defining and enforcing standards of minimally rational conduct, even though these are more likely to reflect the spectrum of prevailing psychological, physical, and moral theories than any inarguable truths. The objective of the rational liberty view also sets important limits on this cultural relativism. Its vital advantage on this score is that it authorizes the community to do little more than decide on what is minimally rational. The rational liberty view cannot claim to prohibit only demonstrably insane conduct, since it cannot formally prove that that rejection of its ideal of rationally deliberative moral personality is illogical. But it authorizes the liberal political community to decide, not what behavior the community finds truly good or rationally correct, but rather what conduct expresses a process of rational deliberation and, conversely, what actions endanger persons' continuing capacities for rational deliberation. Only the latter can rightfully be prohibited. This determination is much more likely to find a broad range of individual and group behavior legitimate than is any direct inquiry into what the community thinks wise or desirable, and so this approach is consistent with both general self-government and extensive tolerance. While the rational liberty position largely calls for democratic decision-making, moreover, it can also countenance many institutions, including judicial review, that may help to prevent majorities from repressing conduct that is integral to the rational pursuits of some and consistent with the continued rational liberty of all.

A goal of enhanced understanding and rational self-direction, however, may sound like an ideal for intellectuals alone. The assertion that this goal should be viewed as fundamental in liberal societies may also evoke the image of a quasi-Aristotelian polity in which those of superior mental endowments claim primacy in a hierarchical political order devoted to imposing this view of virtue on all citizens. These possibilities revive all the fears of the right to equal respect position about a concrete notion of the moral good serving as a vehicle for narrow-minded repression, invidious discrimination against many segments of the populace, and significant demoralization of the less favored. Yet if the rational liberty view is sufficiently tolerant of nonconformity and solicitous of the least advantaged to avoid these consequences, it may seem barely to differ from the neo-Kantian liberalism that culminates in the right to equal respect and to offer few advantages over that position.

The goal of rational liberty does not in fact single out intellectual occupations as morally preferable. It is true that Locke treated the "incomparable Newton" as something of a human ideal, and that Jefferson suggested the activities of the crown were so far below the physicist that his genius would have been thrown away if turned to such pursuits. But while an increased knowledge of the workings of the natural world can benefit all, and pursuit of such knowledge is appropriate for those of suitable abilities and interests, it is ordinarily of secondary importance for the moral purposes of rational liberty. The theory's essential concern is for individuals to improve their condition by increasing their understanding of their own social and personal situations, their capabilities and inclinations, and their opportunities and limits. Insight into the natural world can assist in this endeavor, but the central task is for all to engage in the reflective deliberation that will instruct them in how best to attain happiness while maintaining, if not improving, the capacities that are inextricably linked with it for all who value a sense of conscious self-determination. Thus, a brilliant but too-ardent scientist may, like anyone else, be captivated by a single tyrannical desire that leads her to neglect other concerns and relationships that she would on reflection deem vital.[29] We might therefore hold that by improving people's grasp of their circumstances and possibilities, Locke is a greater benefactor of mankind than Newton, even if he tended to be so "captivated" himself. At any rate, the appropriate moral models in the rational liberty view are not great intellects per se but rather people of exceptional self-understanding and wise self-direction.

Only a myopic elitist would believe that intellectuals alone are capable of such attainments or find them fundamental to happiness. At the least, intellectuals are probably as likely to lack real insight into themselves as anyone else. Moreover, due to their natural diversity, people will on reflection quite properly make very different choices about the activities that are most likely to lead them to satisfactions consistent with continued self-direction. Many will prudently conclude that they are likely to be unhappy and resentful if they do not pursue economic security through the occupations most likely to provide it for them, given their particular endowments. Most will of course find it crucial to provide for the sorts of emotional outlets and support, the social and personal affiliations and recreations, that help them to function properly. But all are likely to feel more content if they are confident that these activities reflect their own considered judgments of what will best suit them, while preserving their abilities to reconsider in the future. And all are likely to find a sense of personal achievement and dignity in having realized their potential for such self-direction. It is surely not intellectuals alone who find it integral to their happiness and self-respect to feel that they have thought things through and made the right decisions.

Indeed, if the foregoing arguments are sound, few will feel that they are truly engaged in the pursuit of happiness unless they undertake periodically the sort of reflection that the rational liberty view esteems. Locke himself was so confident that this experience would eventually be felt worthwhile by all who engaged in it that he devoted his later works largely to "the cognitive responsibilities of all human beings," as John Dunn has noted, and he actually toyed with a scheme whereby all would have time set aside each day, the amount perhaps varying with ability, to engage in "systematic reflection" so that even the least favored might "be delivered from . . . horrid ignorance and brutality."[30] While that suggestion may be uncharacteristically utopian, it reflects a deep and plausible belief that virtually all who share the human condition find a sense of actual, conscious self-direction valuable.

The rational liberty view also shuns classical or medieval political hierarchies based on alleged hereditary capacities for virtue and social orders that foist one narrow view of virtue on everyone. Because the rational liberty position, unlike Thomism or Aristotelianism, makes no claim to having discovered any ultimate truths about our essence or any natural moral order, it cannot issue in any social organizational chart assigning different political stations to different human natures. It is true that, if the moral standards of rational liberty came to be widely employed in a political community, those whose characters appeared distinguished by these standards might well be regarded by the community as suitable leaders. The natural endowments and social circumstances of some would render them particularly well-situated to achieve such distinction. But the recognition would still be won by attainments during their lives, not by any inherited status. Moreover, the sorts of social origins that make these attainments more likely are far from clear. Hereditary wealth in particular seems to work against the development of responsible, self-reliant, reflective characters as often as it facilitates them.

Additionally, all are capable of the morally respectable character that renders their life plans legitimate and therefore factors to be weighed in determining social policy. Hence, again, the basic political implications of the rational liberty view are not hierarchical but democratic. It provides no basis for Mills's suggestion, for instance, that the better educated be assigned extra votes. As in the case of intellectuals generally, higher education specifically does not ensure the self-regulation and concern for others that are the crucial moral qualities to be sought in those shaping the ends of governmental action. Perhaps a different inference could be drawn if liberals thought that some were so perfect in these virtues as to be "gods" in comparison with mankind, as Aristotle intimated. But the liberal portrait of human experience is one of universal limitations, so that there can be no perfect exemplars of rational self-direction, even though some may still fall so far below this ideal as to be the "beasts" of which Aristotle also speaks.[31]

The rational liberty view does, however, advance a certain notion of morally worthy behavior that liberal societies are expected to enforce and promote in certain ways. While this notion does not approach the comprehensive moral regulation demanded by more traditional notions of virtue, it amounts to more regulation than adherents of radical autonomy or many right to equal respect advocates would accept, particularly in the case of self-regarding actions.[32] The moral good of rational self-direction cannot justify an extensive authoritative code of correct behavior because this ideal is inherently one that each person must largely pursue on his own, within his preferred forms of association. It demands that each reflect for himself on his circumstances and decide on the course that will best aid in achieving both his continued self-guidance and his distinctive happiness. Society can to a certain extent help ensure that every person has the capacity and resources for such activity, but rational self-governance must ultimately be a personal achievement if it is to be achieved at all. Furthermore, because the theory presents its values not as indisputable transcendental absolutes but as standards that people choose on reflection to accept, it again recognizes that some might reject its principles for reasons that cannot be disproven. A liberal society thus can claim no right to impose its principles on those living outside its bounds who pursue different creeds, although it can advocate its principles in the international arena and should respect them itself in dealing with others.

The rational liberty view nonetheless does permit a liberal society to insist that those who choose to dwell within it and to participate in its benefits must not act in ways that violate its basic moral standard, the insistence that it is wrong to destroy or injure the capacities for rational self-direction of themselves or others. To assert that a free society has a right to prevent its members from harming themselves is controversial, since this authority limits individual discretion in choices that may directly affect no one else. But a liberal society must express more than prudential rules of self-restraint for tactical, self-interested purposes if it is to be defensible and supportive of self-respect. Consequently, it must uphold its commitment to the belief that capacities for rational self-direction are intrinsically morally valuable. The arguments that justify restraining some from harming others thus justify keeping them from harming themselves: self-destruction also prevents society from realizing the principles that make its way of life morally worthy. A liberal society may enforce these self-regarding standards only against its own constituents, who have accepted an obligation to respect and help fulfill the liberal ideal, and in practice there are probably few whose injuries to themselves do not significantly involve others. In certain cases, moreover, legislatures may well decide that the goal of promoting rational self-direction for all is not best served by regulation, even though this abstention permits some to adopt conduct that is personally harmful.

The fact that an insistence on preserving the reflective capacities of all people rules out certain forms of behavior that the right to equal respect view permits has another important benefit. It means that the rational liberty view is more determinate than neo-Kantian liberalism, and so more useful in setting guides for moral conduct. Within the standards of rationality prevalent in a given society, the implications and realization of this goal can to a large extent be judged in particular contexts by tangible evidence. From this fact flow several advantages of the rational liberty position in comparison with contemporary neo-Kantian approaches.

One advantage is that, instead of commissioning us to act always with equal concern and respect for all, without any definite notion of the moral potentiality that warrants respect to indicate just what is required, the rational liberty view offers a different imperative. It commissions us to act so that we do not harm the capacities for rational understanding and self-control of ourselves or others, which is the minimum basis for self-respect, and to strive to realize those capacities insofar as we are able, which is the ground for greater moral self-esteem. The vague neo-Kantian notion of equality often appears able to support many conclusions beyond the liberal ones that its adherents too quickly draw from it.[33] In contrast, the rational liberty imperative poses a more specific and empirical question of whether, under the actual circumstances of a case, an action is judged likely to hamper or to promote the abilities of all involved to pursue their rational self-direction.

To answer this question, we must in practice rely on the prevailing judgments in our society about what cognitive capacities we have and what conduct indicates their exercise, as well as factual assessments of the consequences of our actions in particular circumstances. But estimations of what constitutes reflective behavior and what acts are likely to harm future abilities to engage in it are very much part of our common experience. We generally think of ourselves as capable of making such judgments uncontroversially, while even hard cases are not thought of as outside the range of credible evaluation. And one strength of the rational liberty view is to require consideration not only of the pertinent moral standard but also of the means to realize that standard by actual persons in specific social contexts. This focus avoids the sort of blind, impractical formalism that the legal realists criticized and that their successors level at contemporary neo-Kantian positions.[34]

The greater determinacy of the rational liberty standard also provides more guidance in evaluating retrospectively both our own conduct and that of others. Under the neo-Kantian approach, if we persuade ourselves that we have not denied anyone equal respect, we can assure ourselves of having acted morally by the only standard the view provides. But this assurance may ring hollow, for it captures only a narrow portion of our moral sentiments. On the one hand, we are often doubtful about the rectitude of an action even after we have reminded ourselves that "at least I didn't hurt anyone." On the other hand, despite popular injunctions against being judgmental, we often believe we must view some persons to be less morally estimable, even if they have not openly denied equal respect to others.

The rational liberty view accounts for and in some measure justifies these features of our moral beliefs. It advises us to ask ourselves not only whether we have respected others but whether we have chosen our actions through appropriate deliberation and adopted a course that, on balance, is well-suited to benefit the reflective capabilities of all affected, ourselves included. If we reflected conscientiously, within the limits of practicality, and if our decision is at all morally plausible, we have acted in a morally respectable way. If we have hit upon a particularly felicitous course of action, our conduct may be especially morally commendable. In dealing with others, we must give each person's viewpoint equal initial consideration, as the neo-Kantian view requires, for otherwise we could not fulfill our commitment to preserve and enhance the self-understanding of all. But as part of this consideration, we should estimate how seriously others take their reflective responsibilities, and we should then treat them accordingly. Those whose habitual characters display only the most minimal concern for deliberative self-direction or respect for others should receive less moral esteem, even if they have committed no sharp violations of the equal respect edict. They may, however, be those most in need of our assistance, so that they may come to act more responsibly—a fact we should weigh in determining our own actions.

Contemporary neo-Kantian positions, in contrast, offer us no clear basis to judge moral character except when people violate the principles of justice by directly harming others, and even then we must continue to respect their moral potential equally with everyone else's.[35] The course taken in the rational liberty view thus supports widespread judgments that can lead some people to feel that they have poor moral character and low moral worth, developments that the right to equal respect theory holds to threaten universal self-respect unduly. But a sense of moral attainment sufficient to justify a secure belief in one's worth still seems well within the reach of all in the rational liberty approach, and the demoralizing effects of negative social judgments are not avoided simply by eschewing any public standard of worth beyond moral potentiality.

Indeed, the rational liberty view, by providing a determinate and verifiable standard of character, is in principle better able to combat the halo effect of judging moral worth by economic status than is the right to equal respect theory, whose vagueness can give full sway to such tacit social standards. Our prevalent private moralities, along with our quest for self-esteem, already make it possible to regard the character of a wealthy person consumed by avarice as less worthy than that of a considerate and conscientious poor person, although such judgments can equally seem like sour grapes. If a liberal society's moral esteem of the conscientious character were more publicly expressed, this judgment could be made more widely and confidently. Furthermore, when we have a more specific sense of what constitutes morally responsible conduct, we can assist others with advice that goes beyond the mere injunction not to harm anyone. We can help them to judge what course is most likely to enhance the powers of reflective self-guidance of both themselves and the persons they affect. Thus, although the relative success of these views is a difficult empirical question, the noncompetitive but concrete understanding of moral value provided by the rational liberty position seems capable of providing more definite guidance and support for our sense of personal worth than the right to equal respect view, while avoiding the pitfalls that motivate the latter's indeterminacy.

If this claim holds, the rational liberty position can also be shown to respond more effectively than the right to equal respect view to liberalism's traditional dilemmas, precisely because of its determinate but universally attainable concept of the moral good. It cannot claim to have resolved early liberalism's ambivalence among religious, natural law, and empiricist philosophic foundations by showing that certain pleasures are rationally discernible as preferable or ordained. But given the central place of freedom in modern morals, it can claim, with at least as much plausibility as the right to equal respect view, to represent values we would choose in reflective equilibrium. (This can be no more than a claim because that process is too lengthy and complex ever to be executed expressly and definitively.) The plausibility of the rational liberty view is enhanced by the fact that, unlike contemporary neo-Kantianism, it explains why the liberal society it envisions is not only just but also morally good. This issue is repeatedly raised by those who deny that any version of liberalism which is neutral on the question of the good life can convincingly claim to represent their moral intuitions. Brian Barry, for example, insists that if liberalism is to be justified, liberals must defend "the proposition that some ways of life, some types of character, are more admirable than others, whatever may be the majority opinion in any society."[36]

Although the rational liberty view cannot show that its values are absolutes, it does provide an argument, based on the fundamental characteristics of the human condition as we now experience it, that neither happiness nor a sense of moral value can be attained in the long run unless we accept the personal responsibilities for systematic reflection that the early liberals identified. It maintains, too, that a society expressing this standard, which allows considerable freedom to all but enforces respect for rational liberty and seeks to promote it, is most likely to produce conscientious and self-reliant characters and a fulfilling way of life. The right to respect view hopes that all will find a moral good they can pursue to their satisfaction, but it defends only the justice, not the goodness of its institutions, and it may in practice produce an egoistic, materialistic, and still unequal society that seems hard to defend positively.

Like the right to respect view, the rational liberty position claims to identify individual and governmental obligations which bind us because they articulate values that on reflection we ourselves choose to accept. As a result, this view, too, is prey to contentions that some do not under any circumstances take its values as their own. But its assertion of a more definite moral good attenuates this difficulty also, because a society embodying this conception can make clearer to citizens the duties to which they are asked to consent. A right to equal respect community informs those who choose to join it that it will allow them to pursue their own good, whatever it might be, so long as they do not violate the equal rights, or right to equal concern and respect, of others. But its subsequent enforcement of those rights may well seem to some to represent only a hypocritical and inegalitarian preference for the goods of certain groups over those of others, especially because the view provides no clear understanding of what the moral potential is that dictates respect, or why it does so. Hence, the nature of the respect it requires may be uncertain, and its claim to represent the true values of all may be unpersuasive.

In contrast, a rational liberty society makes plainer from the outset what conduct its citizens regard as morally worthy, what conduct is impermissible, and why, so that those who consent to join it can give a more conscious and informed consent to the responsibilities it imposes. One can legitimately refuse to live in such a society, but those who do join thereby acquire obligations to help the society as a whole realize its aspirations for the rational self-direction of all its members, just as they can expect the government to perform certain services to assist them in doing so personally. It remains true that, as Rousseau showed, there must always be a tension in political theories of freedom between promoting the personal self-direction of each citizen and the rational self-government of the general society; and there are tensions as well between both these pursuits and the pursuit of a vigorous common life in smaller, more immediate social groups. For example, if too many choose to devote themselves to private pursuits or to the activities of intermediate associations, their choices, even though apparently just, may still belie the claim that the community as a body is directing its common pursuits. To others who cannot feel free unless the social determinants of their lives are under conscious collective control, these pluralistic choices can make their notion of rational self-direction unattainable.

Yet short of a consensus throughout all of a society's major political institutions that any pursuit of these notions endangers genuine freedom, all have to be deemed legitimate on the rational liberty view.[37] It does seem likely that in practice this stance will prove more conducive to privatistic conceptions of liberty, and members with more socialistic, participatory ideals may be required to assist in protecting conduct that they regard as inimical to true freedom. Furthermore, their notions of true freedom may be correct; but so long as this cannot be proven, liberals must reiterate their long-standing reply to these complaints. If public institutions are to respect individual human capacities for responsible choice, only noncoercive efforts either to keep particular social groups flourishing or to establish a social consensus in favor of more communitarian self-governance can be deemed legitimate.

Precisely because the rational liberty view compels political societies to agree publicly on the nature of activities consistent with preserving freedom, it would in practice inform citizens more precisely about the general values they are called on to support. The rights and duties of citizens could also be specified more clearly and consistently. For example, if a community decides that the range of benign rational choices includes a largely private life, it might require citizens to undergo sufficient education only to function independently, to be self-supporting so as not to burden others, to pay taxes, and to contribute to the common defense. The community in turn would be obligated to respect and protect the rational liberty of its citizens and to promote that liberty in all feasible ways, such as through education that prepares citizens for reflective self-direction and through economic and political measures that maximize their opportunities and resources for doing so.[38] It could not, however, dictate extensive political involvement. If instead participation in public decision-making is held essential to genuine rational liberty, some types of governing activity, such as voting, public service, or periodic office-holding, might be made compulsory.

The particular decisions adopted will vary with the ongoing choices of a given society as well as with its practical circumstances. But the essential point is that a community's obligation to respect all activities that it holds to be consistent with rational liberty requires and enables it to specify the values, rights, and duties that membership in it entails. Hence subsequent claims, by criminal authorities or civil disobedients, that either a citizen or the government has violated the obligations to which all consented can be more credibly asserted. A free society should permit those members who, on reflection, reject its values to expatriate themselves, but because they have led the community to expect their continued support, it may properly insist that they expatriate themselves through an explicit, established, and orderly process and that they fulfill their obligations in the interim.

Complexities remain, particularly the familiar problem of the obligations of those born into a liberal society who are held to be citizens but who have never expressly consented to its principles.[39] The Lockean solution of inferring tacit consent from continued residence in the country and participation in its benefits is questionable because of the impracticality of doing otherwise for most people, emigration being a viable option only for the rich or reckless. A rational liberty state might therefore strive to make it possible, in terms of both private resources and public law, for such citizens to leave if they so desire; but the practical obstacles are probably too great for this approach to solve the problem. A liberal state might also choose to tolerate certain violations of its principles by those who claim either not to have consented to them or to consent no longer, if no serious harm results to any person's rational liberty. But if harm does occur, the state must impose its requirements even on such dissenters. This conclusion only means that the society and the dissenters are at this point in an equivalent of Locke's state of nature, where a conflict of goals cannot be avoided and must be resolved one way or another. Again, if the society is to realize the standards it believes to be morally required, they must be defended. The dilemma of having to enforce these ideals against those who do not agree to them is regrettable, but it is one that must be faced by every viable political theory which relies ultimately on consent. The rational liberty view still has the comparative advantage of making apparent to citizens what standards they are being asked to adopt socially, and why.

In addition, the rational liberty standard appears able to provide liberal societies with a fuller sense of common purpose that can ameliorate the worst aspects of their individualism. The right to equal respect view promises only that each person can pursue associational goals if she so desires and can find like-minded fellows, although a just society may possibly result in the collective realization of all human potentialities. The rational liberty theory similarly allows for all associations and all forms of realization consistent with preserving the capacities for deliberative self-direction of all, which encompasses most sorts of collective endeavors, including the pursuit of a peaceful, consensual move to a more communal social order. Citizens who engage in serious reflective deliberation might well emerge with a renewed sense of the importance of family, neighborhood, or religious pursuits to their self-direction. At the same time, however, a rational liberty society accepts the common goal of ensuring as far as possible that each has the capacities and opportunities to attain the moral character and worth that are held to give persons dignity and to contribute to the happiness of all. It may therefore have to override commitments to groups, associations, and corporate bodies that seriously restrain their members' capacities and opportunities for reflective, independent choice, just as it restricts personal conduct that greatly endangers the cognitive abilities of the actor or others. Fundamentalist religions that oppose the acquisition of basic educational skills, cults that blockade departures from isolated communes, and employers who wield economic power coercively and unfairly, all can be subjected to regulation.

While these measures might erode the vitality of certain subgroups, citizens who not only have agreed to behave justly toward each other but also are joined in the pursuit of this common ideal are likely to have a firmer sense that it is worthwhile to belong to and participate in their broader political community. They are more likely to see their government and their fellow citizens as dedicated to advancing everyone's capacities for freedom. They may also take more pride and satisfaction in their experiences of personal self-direction. Longings for a sense of a common venture may thus be more fully satisfied in this kind of polity than in a right to equal respect society, and feelings of loyalty may be stronger toward a community that is perceived as genuinely supporting the happiness and moral attainments of its citizens. Such a system may still permit too much privatism to satisfy the more radical communitarianism that sees any retreat from realizing mankind's social identity as illusory and pernicious. But the concrete common goal of the rational liberty view enables it to fulfill communitarian aspirations as completely as any liberal position can hope to do.

As for the substantive demands for greater autonomy and equality put forth by liberalism's romantic and social egalitarian critics, they too cannot be met in their pure form. The theory of rational liberty does assert that, in promoting for all people the capacities for self-direction that it believes to be definitive of freedom and crucial to a sense of moral worth, it is providing for the most extensive genuine autonomy and is also mitigating the harms of social and economic inequalities. Furthermore, the view calls for liberal societies to alter any inequalities that the community sees as destructive of the capacities for reflective self-government in some or all of its citizenry. Even so, inequalities not demonstrated to be harmful would remain, while forms of autonomous self-realization that are judged by consensus to be inconsistent with the preservation of human deliberative abilities, such as violent conduct, dictatorial ambitions, continually unbridled emotional spontaneity, and simple raw selfishness, would frequently be constrained.

Private economic pursuits in particular are often viewed as essential means and ends of rational liberty, even though many see them as productive of inequalities that eventually make a mockery of political liberty for all. In the absence of agreement, the society must view such pursuits as within the bounds of rational choice, although they can be regulated on behalf of competing concerns. Hence significant differences in socioeconomic status would probably persist, though they should be severed more effectively from standards of moral worth. In some respects this situation is regrettable. Yet it only forces us to confront once more the sober reality of human political life, that no social system can be free of inequalities and restraints. The promise of the rational liberty view is simply that, by establishing a more determinate normative standard, liberal societies will be able to analyze their existing institutions and conditions in ways that clarify to all whatever inequalities and restrictions are permissible. This clarification should help both to defend the legitimacy of some inequalities more persuasively and to shine a brighter spotlight on those that are unjustifiable, both in political discourse generally and in constitutional law.

9 · Rational Liberty and Constitutional Problems

Rational liberty is an abstract ideal. What guidance can it provide to those who must confront the innumerable, intractable problems of constitutional government in America today? The logic of the view compels it ultimately to rely on prevailing community standards to define the boundaries of permissible conduct. Yet the ideal still contributes something vital, for it leads the community to ask, through various deliberative processes, not what behavior is truly good or wise, but what conduct is part of reflective self-direction and maintains the capacity for self-governance in the actor and others. Such determinations cannot be made without thorough consideration of the particular circumstances involved in an action or class of actions. The nature of conduct and its effects on personal capacities can rarely be judged a priori.

These features of the rational liberty position may appear unsatisfying, but on examination they emerge as its strengths. Until a seer produces genuinely incontrovertible precepts, no position can do more than suggest guides for the judgments of governors and citizens. The rational liberty view acknowledges this fact and claims only to direct the proper decision-makers to the proper questions. Furthermore, any realistic theory must recognize that it can be applied only through extensive consideration of the concrete complexities involved in actual cases. As a result, the concept of rational liberty offers no fixed and timeless solutions to the constitutional problems of interpretation and due process, free speech, voting apportionment, and national responsibility for economic welfare; and all its contemporary implications cannot be worked through here. But the general position does indicate basic principles and tests to guide these areas, which support some types of results and preclude others.

On the constitutional issue of judicial reliance on natural or positive law conceptions of due process, the rational liberty position involves two conclusions. It includes both requirements for credible approaches to constitutional interpretation generally and also basic principles to resolve the procedural and substantive due process controversies that have so often brought adjudicatory methods into dispute. It might seem natural to argue that the debate between natural and positive law theories should be settled simply by reading the Constitution as expressing the precepts of rational liberty, a course I will ultimately defend. But this claim cannot be redeemed simply by rehearsing the theoretical and substantive merits of the rational liberty view, for some may object that those qualities are irrelevant to its validity as an account of the Constitution. Consequently, a justification for addressing the four constitutional issues from the standpoint of rational liberty requires initial consideration of what the earlier survey of those issues suggests for the general problem of constitutional interpretation.

All of the previous discussion compels one basic conclusion on this issue: constitutional interpretations have always tended to reflect the interpreter's particular conception of the proper nature of the entire American political system. Marshall's Constitution was imbued with early commercial liberalism, Taney's with Jacksonian democracy, the *Lochner* Court's with economic social Darwinism, Brandeis's with romantic liberalism, Frankfurter's with relativistic democracy, and so forth. Of course, few interpreters have seen the Constitution as delineating precisely their ideal polities. Most have not articulated their political principles fully and coherently themselves, and most have also found certain parts of the text hard to explain in terms of their favorite notions. But in the cases that judges have seen either as ambiguous or as crucial to their deeper values—which is to say, most of the important cases—they have generally read the text in light of the principles they believed it must contain if it were to express a justifiable political vision.

This tendency can be presented as a psychological one, as it was by legal realists such as Jerome Frank: even the most conscientious judges cannot prevent their perceptions and judgments from being shaped by their particular values. Or the tendency can be described as logical, as it has been by Ronald Dworkin: the philosophic task of justifying a decision, or more broadly an interpretive approach, requires judges to appeal ultimately to their conceptions of the broader political enterprise in which both their activity and their results make sense. Or the two arguments can be linked, as they are by many contemporary literary theorists: an interpreter's personal values and conceptions of processes of justification are both products of the interpreter's experiences in the social milieus in which he has lived. Hence, his psychological attachments and preferred forms of reasoning both are inextricably rooted in institutional and cultural traditions that include some forms of life and exclude others. In all these views, justices who think that the political system is basically legitimate, who regard it from H. L. A. Hart's "internal point of view," are not able to separate their sense of what counts as a justification from their sense of what the system ought to be (if indeed anyone can do so).[1]

These psychological and logical claims suggest that different constitutional interpretations ultimately reveal conflicts between competing political visions, a view that American constitutional history confirms.[2] But these conflicts are sustained only because the different positions produce overlapping commitments to certain basic institutions and values, commitments that allow for compromise and agreement, however provisionally and incompletely. We might conclude, therefore, that constitutional interpretations should focus on these areas of partial agreement while discreetly obscuring, rather than highlighting, the underlying differences. The survey of the four constitutional areas shows that legal doctrines have been constructed most often by such compromises among the varied views that have won some enduring sway in America's historical development.

The quest for such syntheses must indeed be a central part of the interpretive enterprise, but legal analysts should not divert attention from the conflicting political theories embodied in the law. As Bruce Ackerman remarks, many lawyers prefer what he calls an "ordinary observer" approach to an appeal to a "comprehensive theory" of the Constitution's meaning. The ordinary observer position sees the task of judges simply as the identification, articulation and enforcement of what appear to be the system's prevailing legal norms, absolving judges of responsibility for whether or not those norms are consistent or philosophically defensible. If the norms are the standards that society has set for the judiciary, they are legitimate, and it would be an abuse of authority, as well as divisive and ultimately futile, to distort them into expressions of some preconceived abstract schemas. A more theoretically oriented approach also might blind judges to the human realities before them, once again producing an unresponsive "mechanical jurisprudence."[3]

Existing doctrines, however, display few satisfactory (if intellectually untidy) syntheses and many hopelessly ambiguous and inconsistent conglomerations of incompatible views. The indeterminacy of many current rules grants constitutional judges even more discretion than the considerable amount that they would have if the law were as definite as possible. Few judges today are willing to respond to that discretion with a Frankfurterian posture of deference. Even the Burger Court's advocates of renewed democratic relativism seem satisfied that this posture gave inadequate protection to constitutional rights and principles. The current Court's characteristic approach of protecting only values that the justices believe to have won long-term consent approximates a more activist ordinary observer model, but as a result doctrines in all four constitutional areas are amorphous and vulnerable to charges that they protect only those values and current policies that a majority of the justices happen to prefer.

In order to construct doctrines that combine prevailing norms more consistently and intelligibly, thereby confining judicial discretion, it is necessary to articulate the various "comprehensive views" or political visions presupposed in contemporary constitutional discourse. Only then is it possible to work out doctrines that largely reconcile these views, and only then can judges recognize the views that they are choosing when reconciliation is impossible and choice is nonetheless necessary. This prescription for constitutional interpretation, to develop the competing theories of American constitutionalism that illuminate adjudication, is a threefold task. First, interpreters must identify more fully than Bickel did the sources of the relevant traditions in which they are to "immerse" themselves to identify "fundamental presuppositions" of the American system. Second, they must elaborate, more fully than Dworkin has done, how they are to devise from these sources theories that have an adequate fit with past law and that are also substantively desirable. Third, they must describe how judges are to employ those theories in their decision-making.[4]

While every effort at a comprehensive theory of the American Constitution should take some stand on these questions, each position would respond to them differently. Those who stress fidelity to the long-term will of the people will demand extensive exploration of historical materials, as Frankfurter and Bickel did. Those who stress practical desirability will focus on current needs and preferences, as Pound did. And those who stress substantive moral attractiveness will emphasize philosophic persuasiveness, as Dworkin does. Still others, like the Critical Legal Scholars, will be obliged to present their views as necessary but radical departures from America's past. Each judge must therefore decide which account on balance seems most persuasive on all these issues.

Few sitting judges can be expected to explore these controversial questions in depth themselves. This understanding of constitutional interpretation thus assumes a division of labor among the bench, constitutional scholars, and the broader political community of a sort that has to some degree existed in this century. Scholarly research and debate, informed by broader community discussions, would be responsible for elaborating, at a given time, the general views that can credibly claim to be appropriate constitutional philosophies for that day. There would be innumerable variations, but history suggests that the basic types of prevalent positions would usually be few, each of which would normally have some recognized leading exponents, such as Bickel, Berns, Ely, and Dworkin today.

The judges' task would be to decide which general view of the Constitution's philosophy or spirit they subscribe to and to decide cases consistently with that view. Judges should also work collegially to construct doctrines that harmonize as many reasonably compatible views as possible, so long as this can be done without producing meaningless rules or violating their own notions of the Constitution's requirements. Compromise should be more possible, not less, once judges understand clearly what is essential to their respective positions and what is peripheral.[5] Judicial decisions should in turn be subjected to debate by scholars and the community at large. In this way judges, scholars, and citizens could all refine their understandings of the basic alternatives before them and their implications. The community could also alter any judicial doctrines that seriously violated a prevailing consensus by means of appropriately deliberative democratic processes, such as the current mechanisms of amendment and limited congressional revisions of judicial jurisdictions.

The rational liberty view offers philosophic credibility with substantive desirability through a reformulation of some of the liberal conceptions that are central to the American constitutional tradition. It is particularly attractive because it captures both the chief merit of positive theories of law, a plausible grounding in human will, and the virtue of the higher law tradition, the prescription of suitable restraints on majoritarian choices. It therefore merits consideration as a guiding philosophy of constitutional interpretation. Its appropriateness must, however, ultimately be judged by its success in addressing contemporary problems.

The rational liberty position suggests consistent basic principles for the four constitutional areas, including, first, criminal and substantive due process. The goal the theory understands the Constitution to pursue, the promotion of rational liberty for all, leads to determinate tests that direct judges to consider concretely how that goal may be most fully realized through the issue and circumstances of the case at hand. Thus, the approach does not generate a dogmatic, theory-ridden jurisprudence but instead preserves the possibility of prudential, statesmanlike adjudication. It follows, however, that a rational liberty judge may decide that, under the particular circumstances of a case or bench, this view of the Constitution's aims can best be furthered by rules framed somewhat differently from those suggested here. Nonetheless, this account indicates the general characteristics and consequences a rational liberty approach would present.

Any interpretation of the Constitution's due process clauses must resort to some explanatory conceptions, not evident on the face of the text, to decide what constitutes "life, liberty, and property" and what sorts of processes are "due" and why. The rational liberty view accordingly interprets the Constitution's procedural requirements in light of its underlying concern to respect and promote the rational self-direction of all. Herbert Packer categorized the fundamental models of proper criminal procedure as either "due process" or "crime control," a distinction that helps to identify the basic implications of the rational liberty view. The due process model, the heir of liberalism's traditional concern with individual natural rights, stresses the presumption of the innocence of accused persons until proven guilty, the burden of the state to make the case against them and hence the adversarial nature of criminal proceedings, and the need for procedural guarantees to protect individuals against unjust state coercion. These guarantees include protections against unreasonable searches and seizures and involuntary interrogations, enforced by exclusion of such evidence from trials, the provision of competent counsel as quickly as possible, limits on pretrial custody, and ample opportunities for appeal. The crime control model instead emphasizes in more utilitarian fashion the importance of enforcing the criminal law efficiently, in order to preserve the rights of all by maximizing public order and security. Whereas Packer termed the criminal justice system provided by the due process model an "obstacle course" for police and prosecutors, the ideal of the crime control model is an "assembly line," urging wider police discretion to search, detain, and interrogate suspects without warrants or counsel; high bail to keep arrested suspects in custody; informal procedures to obtain convictions without trials, such as plea bargaining; and limited opportunities for appeal. The first model is commonly identified with the Warren Court's broad interpretations of Bill of Rights criminal guarantees and their extension to the states by the fundamental fairness incorporation approach; the second model is identified with the opponents of these developments, as well as some Burger Court decisions that limit their reach.[6]

Of these two basic perspectives, the rational liberty view clearly has more affinity with the due process model. It assumes that all members of a liberal community are capable of and have accepted their responsibilities for rational self-governance, until matters are shown to be otherwise. Hence it supports the presumption that they have respected the rights of others, are innocent, and should not be subjected to state coercion, beyond the minimum reasonably required to assure enforcement of the laws, until and unless they are judged guilty of a crime. Respect for the citizens' capacity for rational self-direction also requires that they be informed of their rights, so they can make genuine choices about cooperating with the police, and that they be assisted in doing so by competent counsel, a goal that remains remote even after the Warren Court decisions.[7] Such respect similarly demands both that the courts avoid complicity in police conduct violative of civil liberties by excluding evidence thus obtained and that genuine opportunities for appeal be afforded to all to safeguard the system against error.

To be sure, acceptance of the rational liberty goal implies that all should work to rectify any violations of personal rights committed by themselves or by others, when no undue sacrifice is involved. This duty includes informing the police and courts, if that is the most effective way available. The major historical reason for instead providing rights against some forms of searches or seizures and governmental interrogations was to restrain political persecution, and this need is less pressing in contemporary America than in the days of the Star Chamber. But politically motivated prosecutions still occur, and periods of extensive political repression are not long past, so these rights have not outlived their usefulness. Furthermore, in America's complex contemporary legal system, individuals who justifiably believe they have done nothing wrong or illegal may rightly fear criminal prosecution as a result of their statements.[8] Concern for the citizens' rational freedom demands that they be allowed to judge this risk; and both the legal complexities and the emotional duress involved in police interrogations and trials mean that few citizens are able to deliberate sensibly without the aids provided by *Miranda* v. *Arizona* and the other major procedural decisions of the Warren years.[9] Barring exceptional circumstances, lesser procedural protections are inconsistent with the concern of the rational liberty view to preserve the capacities for reflective self-direction of the citizenry, who are presumed generally to have exercised those capacities and therefore to be innocent.

Accordingly, the rational liberty approach affirms the Warren Court's judgment that the goals of American constitutionalism define due process in criminal procedures in ways that require the extension of broad Bill of Rights guarantees to the states. Although unlike both the Warren and Burger Courts, the approach defines those guarantees as a means to preserve what society takes to be rational liberty, not to protect reasonable expectations of privacy, in most cases the resulting inquiry would not be significantly different. The approach similarly asks what forms of behavior citizens can reasonably expect to pursue unhindered.[10]

The rational liberty view provides these protections without advancing any controversial historical claim that the Fourteenth Amendment was explicitly intended to incorporate all or only these provisions. The language of the amendment itself, read in light of this view of the principles of the Constitution as a whole, demands similar results. This capacity to support the requirements of the due process model for state criminal procedures, without getting embroiled in the incorporationist debate, is a chief virtue of the rational liberty interpretation.

There is a-priori force, however, to the argument that, in the wake of the nation's catastrophic crime increases of the last two decades, the goal of providing rational liberty for all now requires relaxation of safeguards against suspected offenders. Otherwise, conservatives hold, enforcement will be too hamstrung to protect the preponderant rights of the vast majority, however they are construed. The goal of promoting universal rational liberty indeed justifies infringement of a few individual rights if there is no other way to defend most other rights. But there is no evidence that the procedural rights newly guaranteed in the 1960s either caused or exacerbated the heightened crime rate, despite contrary beliefs on the Burger Court. In light of the inherent tendency of the police to view their roles "professionally," in terms of efficiency in crime control, and in light of their enhanced technological resources, the due process model is instead of increasing contemporary importance.[11]

Even James Q. Wilson, often termed a "conservative" analyst of crime, agrees that strict due process protections should be provided so long as the guilt of the accused remains in question. The knottier issue is what should be done in the large majority of cases where at most the particular charge, not the defendant's guilt, is contested. This question in turn raises the issue of the purpose of criminal justice, whether retribution, rehabilitation, or general deterrence and individual incapacitation. That is a matter too large to be pursued here, although the rational liberty ideal is relevant to the debate. I will note only that the rational liberty view can justify and focus concerns for all these purposes. General deterrence and individual incapacitation and rehabilitation are important to promoting the rational self-direction of all, though as both liberal and conservative students of crime agree, no one knows how, or even if, rehabilitation can be achieved. Although the extent and nature of deterrence are controversial, virtually everyone does accept that punishment to some degree serves this purpose and so helps to secure the rights of the general citizenry. The rational liberty view also supposes that, disregarding the insane, offenders bear some responsibility for their actions, however much compassion we may (and should) have for the situation that made crime seem attractive or necessary. There are, after all, always others similarly situated who do not turn to crime, indicating that this resort, however understandable, is not inevitable. Since the theory holds that disregard for the rights of others is morally wrong, it can support, in Charles Silberman's terms, punishment "guided by the notion of desert."[12]

Because treatment of the guilty, not constitutional rights involved in investigations or trials, is the most important issue for crime control, both liberal and conservative analysts of crime were able to reach a surprising degree of consensus in the late 1970s. They agreed that the most promising immediate steps to reduce crime involved measures first to separate out, routinize, and thereby expedite handling of the bulk of cases where guilt is not disputed and preparations for a full adversarial trial are not required, and then to make sentences more uniform and predictable, especially in those cases. But they disagreed in the specific advice for sentencing reform. Wilson, for example, preferred a system that would provide some detention for all offenders, with the form varying from night and weekend confinement to assignment to treatment centers to imprisonment, depending on the severity of the offense and the rehabilitative prospects of the offender. Silberman, a liberal analyst of crime, was less critical of the variations in time served that result from plea bargaining and probation. But the consensus that these two exemplified has been sufficient to produce numerous state initiatives in sentencing reform, now being carried to the federal level.[13]

The lessons of these recent experiments remain in dispute. But regardless of the relative merits of the different approaches, the debate over crime control considerations is most appropriately focused here, not in the area of procedural guarantees. Hence, despite current problems of escalating crime, the rational liberty view today still calls for analysis of procedural issues in terms of a due process model and therefore implies support for the majority of the Warren Court's similarly oriented procedural decisions.

A Court favoring rational liberty would, however, articulate a different theoretical underpinning for those decisions. The Warren and Burger Courts have described much of their activism on criminal procedures as protection of Brandeisian privacy rights. Their decisions thus derive in part from the romantic strain in modern liberalism that emphasizes the centrality of personal autonomy, of self-defined self-realization. Romantic values call for extensive protection of both self-expression and privacy. The Burger Court has tried to draw boundaries to privacy claims by defining them in terms of conventional social standards and customs, but its decisions here, as in other areas like free speech, still give a limited voice to romantic autonomy ideals. Despite the relatively slight effect of the results in these cases on crime, and hence the probably slighter effect of their philosophic underpinnings, it is worth noting James Q. Wilson's argument that increased crime is linked to the spread of this same ethos of autonomous self-expression. He sees this ethic as surfacing in the 1920s, the period of Brandeis's most memorable opinions, and re-emerging in the 1960s, when Douglas and Marshall were reviving his themes of privacy and self-realization.[14] No doubt the parallel developments on the Supreme Court reflected broader trends in public opinion much more than they shaped them. The alternative ethos of rational liberty would, however, stress the duty and benefits of self-control more plainly than this romantic liberalism. Hence, if procedural rights, like constitutional rights more broadly, were derived from a commitment to promoting rational liberty rather than privacy, this change would represent at least a symbolic shift toward a view that appears less prone to be corrupted into a license for lawless behavior.

While the due process clauses to some extent require reliance on non-textual standards to determine the Constitution's procedural guarantees, it is far more controversial for judges to use such methods to give the phrases substantive content. Although the "due process" clauses have always been held to be aimed at securing substantive ideals, during much of the past they were thought to do so only through their procedural requirements, and so it would seem more legitimate to take this course today. If substantive guarantees are to be provided under the Fourteenth Amendment, the natural vehicle is the privileges and immunities clause which, despite the contrary holding in the *Slaughter-House Cases,* seems to have been intended to provide just the sort of warrant for judicial identification and enforcement of fundamental rights that the Court has found in the remainder of Section 1. Even John Ely, an opponent of extensive judicial discretion, terms this "the most plausible interpretation" of the privileges and immunities guarantee.[15] But the practical reality is that no modern Court is likely to overrule *Slaughter-House* and assume the task of defining those privileges and immunities more comprehensively, so it may be justifiable to continue to provide similar protection through substantive due process and equal protection adjudication.

If the due process clause is to be given substantive content at all, the most plausible reading, in terms of both its textual language and its historical antecedents, is the rational liberty one. The modern privacy approach lacks explicit textual support, stemming instead from a romantic liberalism that was foreign to mainstream American political thought at least until the twentieth century. The property and liberty of contract approach of the *Lochner* era distorts traditional liberal understandings of property rights and also fails to do justice to the place that the liberal tradition assigns to rational self-direction conceived more broadly. For most early liberals this capacity was synonymous with liberty and was both the source and the highest form of property; and Locke argued that such freedom is dearer than life itself. Since due process has thus traditionally been held to express an ideal of at least minimally rational governance, in which the rights of life, liberty, and property are not arbitrarily violated, it is legitimate to construe these clauses as meaning that rational liberty should not be infringed without reasons that are adequate in terms of the same values that support those rights.[16]

This rational liberty view of substantive due process in part tracks and justifies the predominant jurisprudence of two-tiered scrutiny in due process cases, and it supplies content for the life, liberty, and property interests that the terms of the clause protect. Whereas neither of the previous substantive interpretations offered much principled guidance as to which rights of privacy and property (and some nonproperty rights) are fundamental, and the current Court deals with this issue in an ad hoc fashion, the goal of protecting rational liberty suggests two classes of substantive due process interests. Some activities are integral to preserving and fulfilling personal capacities for rational self-direction, such as free expression, and these should be placed in a preferred position, with infringements subjected to strict scrutiny. Other pursuits are perfectly legitimate but are not essential to anyone's self-regulation, such as freedom to park on public streets. These are not to be prohibited arbitrarily, but any minimally rational purpose and means should suffice to justify their regulation.[17] Still other actions seriously endanger the capacities for rational liberty of some, and these merit no due process protection and are punishable.

When controverises arise over the categories into which specific actions fall, the rational liberty approach does not justify the sort of intermediate tier of scrutiny that the Court has now adopted under equal protection for sex classifications, or the sliding scale approach advocated by Marshall, because the multiplication of levels of scrutiny creates more room for judicial arbitrariness and is substantively ill-conceived. Again, the rational liberty view, like most other views of American constitutionalism, presumes that the legitimate form of decision-making is through democratic processes of reflective deliberation by the community of citizens. Because truly democratic processes are difficult to establish, because democratic majorities may pursue improper ends, and because the system is ultimately concerned to preserve the capacities for rational self-direction of all, there is justification for intervention by the relatively insulated judiciary when the community has unnecessarily infringed on conduct generally conceded to be essential to the rational self-governance of some persons. Barring such extreme instances, changes in disliked policies must be sought through the electoral branches.[18] The temptation to establish intermediate protections in certain areas can arise in equal protection because some classifications, such as sex, are somewhat more often relevant to compelling interests than others, notably race. This fact does not call for establishing a middle level of scrutiny; it rather calls for clarifying analytically when a classification serves compelling interests and when it does not. The same clarifications are needed when ranking liberty interests in due process adjudication, and they can be provided by the rational liberty approach. Certain types of activities are so widely thought to be integral to the rational self-guidance of most persons in American society that they should be considered to evoke strict scrutiny automatically, unless the state can show that they are actually peripheral in the case of the person claiming due process protection. The rational liberty criteria for ranking interests as fundamental involve consideration not only of whether the activities in question are directly essential to maintaining personal cognitive capacities but also of whether they are basic to the legitimate course (or in Rawls's overly demanding phrase, the "rational life plan") a person has chosen. After all, if the state prevents persons from taking actions essential to their emotional fulfillment, such as marriage, and these actions are perfectly consistent with preserving rational liberty in themselves and others, then something central to their rational self-governance, or their pursuit of happiness, has been infringed. A concern for rational self-direction does not mean that vital human emotions should be ignored, only that each should be given due weight after reflection upon competing desires, values, and circumstances. This is a requirement that should foster more emotional satisfaction in the long run.

Given the sorts of needs persons in contemporary society usually find basic, the liberties that can ordinarily be assumed to be integral to rational liberty would include, in roughly the order of personal experience, the right to live with their family, the right to an education that prepares them for rational self-direction in the larger liberal society, the right to pursue their preferred line of work subject to attaining suitable qualifications, the right to the freedoms of conscience and expression, the right to vote and to participate generally in political self-government, the right to expatriate themselves from a political community whose principles they cannot accept, the right to marry, the right to travel and reside where they wish within the liberal community, as well as the right to be presumed innocent and treated fairly by the criminal justice system.[19]

These rights are not absolute. If exercised in ways that were sufficiently harmful, they could be regulated. For such regulation to be sustained, however, it would have to be supported by a showing of compelling state interests, assertions that the capacities for rational self-direction of others would be too greatly endangered if a certain course is pursued. Thus, for example, parents who neglected their children's health and cognitive development, private schools that did not adequately prepare students to function as self-supporting and self-directing members of the general society, economic pursuits that endangered the public welfare through pollution or unsafe working conditions, or political actions that genuinely threatened the survival of liberal government could all be constrained. The state would also have the option of contending that rights of religious free exercise, for example, were not genuinely integral to the rational liberty of one whose claims to religiosity were patently fraudulent. By the same token, it would always be open to individuals to argue that a liberty not ordinarily thought fundamental actually was so in their particular cases. Thus, a litigant might ask that his right to live with a woman with whom he had a demonstrably deep and enduring relationship be accorded the same high status as another person's right to marry and live with a spouse, and if society regarded both sorts of conduct as legitimate, as modern American society increasingly does, the state would have to grant this request. In consequence, the forms of protection provided under due process by a rational liberty approach would, again, ultimately depend on what a given liberal community defines as consistent with and integral to personal rational self-direction. But precisely because the community could prohibit only conduct incompatible with the continued rational liberty of all, behavior that is desired only by a minority but is generally admitted to be consistent with rational self-direction and integral to some would be granted heightened protection by the courts.[20]

These automatically preferred rights, along with the opportunity for litigants to claim others, may seem at first glance an arbitrary, open-ended catalogue of nonexplicit Fourteenth Amendment freedoms that courts could use for extensive interference with self-government through the political branches. In fact, most of the protection defined by the approach is already being provided in some form through alternative constitutional interpretations. Even in *Slaughter-House,* the Fourteenth Amendment was said to protect a right to travel within the United States, and this right has since been held to be infringed if burdens are placed on shifting one's residence. Since the 1920s, the Court has used the Fourteenth Amendment to defend First Amendment freedoms, including nonexplicit rights of political association. The Court has also used certain *Lochner* precedents and its "right of privacy" to protect private education that meets state standards and, recently, to protect "family" rights that include rights to reside together and to marry. The Fourteenth Amendment also serves as a vehicle for extensive procedural guarantees. Although the right to vote has generally been adjudicated under the equal protection clause or the Fifteenth Amendment, and some interpretations of those provisions render voting restrictions less presumptively illegitimate than would treating the right to vote as an essential part of due process liberty, stricter scrutiny seems consistent with the democratic notions of rational self-governance that the Constitution should today be held to express. The right to pursue one's chosen vocation may in turn conjure up memories of *Lochner* jurisprudence, but numerous commentators and some judicial opinions have now concluded that adequate protection for personal freedoms must include upholding some liberties to engage in one's occupation. Recognzing this right would merely end an anomaly widely viewed as unjustifiable.[21]

Thus, the rational liberty approach would not grant to the Court any authority that it does not already exercise. Instead, it would limit potential abuses of that authority by providing a more detailed and appropriate theory of the basic liberties that can be protected under due process. The current Court's reliance on its judgments of traditionally fundamental forms of privacy to decide which claims merit strict scrutiny is inarguably unpredictable.The rational liberty approach's alternative inquiry into whether the activity in question is integral to the litigant's rational self-direction and is consistent with that of others both focuses on the proper questions and leaves less room for the operation of judicial biases. Due process aims at protecting basic liberties for all, not the majority's preferred forms of privacy; and while decisions as to whether an activity is important to an individual's life and is within the bounds of liberal values may be difficult, they do not focus so readily on what the judges themselves find fundamental in the nation's traditions.

The rational liberty theory also could still justify minimal scrutiny of infringements of interests that are not essential to the person's self-direction, such as, in all likelihood, the policeman's desire for long hair considered in *Kelley* v. *Johnson* (1976). At the same time, it could grant heightened protection to unconventional behavior that is not outside a liberal community's standards of permissible conduct, such as the cohabitation of the library employees whose dismissal was challenged in *Hollenbaugh* v. *Carnegie Free Library* (1978). The Court's tradition-oriented approach did not evoke even a review of the firings, although the employees could probably have proven their actions to be both vital to their self-direction and consistent with the prevailing bounds of rational conduct, especially since the state had repealed its antiadultery and fornication laws.[22] In sum, a rational liberty interpretation of the Fourteenth Amendment would direct attention to the sorts of concerns to secure basic freedoms that provided the amendment's chief historical impetus. It would thereby provide the weapons against majoritarian biases that most versions of liberalism have long sought. Hence, the theory of rational liberty should generate a more coherent, predictable, and principled reading of substantive due process requirements.

The rational liberty view also produces principles to guide free speech adjudication which justify placing most forms of communication in a constitutionally preferred position. Virtually all political, scientific, cultural, and artistic expression can be deemed integral to either political or personal rational self-governance, for they are essential to the cultivation of a heightened understanding of our condition both individually and socially and are also vital means of acting to shape our destinies. All the values long assigned to political speech in informing the electorate and exposing official abuse, to scientific discourse in increasing our grasp of the natural world, and to the humanities and social sciences in exploring human affairs, thus find a place in the goals of the rational liberty approach. In addition, the theory stresses the value of common discourse on all matters of public concern in furthering the community-wide deliberation that is essential to reflective self-direction in a liberal society.[23]

The rational liberty view, however, implies some limits and exceptions to preferred position speech protection. The stance does not embrace all the values put forth in modern theories of free expression, and consequently it does not regard the First Amendment as an all-encompassing absolute. Even for the great bulk of expression that would receive full strict-scrutiny solicitude, restrictions can be justified by a showing of compelling state interests, which again would usually be significant dangers to the rational self-direction of the speaker or others. That concession does not justify a great deal of suppression, for as Holmes and Brandeis proposed, such dangers must be both serious and obvious, clear and present. Political speech imperiling the very existence of liberal government, such as the revelation and criticism of secret defense plans in time of war, could still be curtailed. Speech presenting an immediate threat of violence and property damage that could be averted only by stopping the speech itself might also be restrained. The time, place, and noise level of all modes of expression could also be regulated so as to respect the liberties of others, such as their right to travel via public thoroughfares or to receive a fair trial. These regulations should be drawn to ensure that other opportunities for expression are not thereby significantly curtailed.[24]

This rational liberty view accords in the main with contemporary free speech doctrine, though not with more absolutist positions, whether couched in democratic or in self-expression terms. While the view calls for considerable democracy, it does so only as a means to realize deliberative self-guidance for the community as a whole, and insofar as certain types of even public speech jeopardize instead of furthering this goal, they can in principle be restrained. Similarly, while the theory supports forms of self-expression that are part of a person's rational self-development, it does not value modes of expression that are antithetical to respect and promotion of rational liberty for all.[25] In practice, the dangers of restricting public or personal discourse that contributes to liberal values warrant granting strict scrutiny protection in all ambiguous cases. Certain classes of speech, however, should remain on the lower tier that American law has always assigned them in the past.

Perhaps the most controversial traditional exceptions to freedom of speech are the categories of obscene and offensive speech, construing the latter to cover not words which can be shown in a given instance to have produced a clear and present danger of violence but rather expressions that are legally considered to be intrinsically harmful and denied First Amendment protection even if no such threat was apparent. It has long been customary to classify such expressions as outside the political, intellectual, and artistic discourse protected by the First Amendment, but the political category, to say nothing of the other categories, can encompass virtually all communication. Since throughout history the designation of certain concerns as "private" or "social" and hence as "nonpolitical" has served to shield racial, sexual, and economic oppression, the concern for rational liberty for all usually requires a broader definition of the political. But precisely because of its need to conceive the political broadly, the rational liberty view opposes treating expression that is inimical to the realization of liberal values as belonging to an inviolable realm of private choice. The constitutional question, then, is whether any types of expression traditionally thought to be obscene or offensive threaten those values sufficiently to justify restraint, and in principle the answer is yes.

Even though the obscene and offensive have long been held to lie outside the First Amendment, courts have rarely discussed why this is so, why such speech is worthless and harmful. Failure to address this question adequately has contributed to the difficulties in defining the scope of punishable expression in these areas. The modern Court, for example, only considered this aspect of obscenity fairly late in the day, in the 1973 case of *Paris Adult Theatre* v. *Slaton*. There, Chief Justice Burger seemed to rely, somewhat paradoxically, on a version of the position going back through *Chaplinsky* to early liberalism, that such communication is not essentially an "exposition of ideas" and hence is not part of free speech, understood to be rationally directed expression rather than a mere unleashing of emotions. Therefore, governments do not need to show a compelling state purpose to justify their restraints; they have a sufficient reason in the community's concern with ending possible sources of antisocial behavior and in maintaining a "decent" public environment.

Burger offered no guidelines, however, on what counts as a legitimate concern for a decent environment. While he would probably define such criteria in terms of the aesthetic and moral values fundamental to a given community, this definition offers few restraints on traditional majoritarian prejudices. Because he had no other doctrine of the permissible purposes of obscenity suppression from which to draw limits, he could satisfy concerns about undue censorship only by building into his standards for defining obscenity in *Miller* a number of unwieldy requirements that seem arbitrary because they are not connected with any governing First Amendment principles.

On the rational liberty view, by contrast, no conduct should ever be restrained without appropriate reasons. Even under minimal scrutiny, community wishes represent sufficient justification for infringements on freedom of action only if they are aimed at legitimate purposes. While the noncognitive nature of most obscene and offensive expression gives it a lesser value from the standpoint of promoting rational deliberation, emotive expression aimed at furthering legitimate political, intellectual, or cultural goals is still too integral to the aims of rational liberty to evoke less than strict scrutiny. Similarly, communication that is clearly an exposition of ideas but objectionable in content is nonetheless fit material to assist cognitive reflection and so merits full protection.

A lower tier of scrutiny is appropriate, then, only for expression that is noncognitive in form and which in substance conveys an emotive message that has no value or is actually immoral in terms of rational liberty standards. Such materials may influence attitudes and conduct even though they are given no conscious weight in reflective deliberation. Hence, they are sufficiently removed from the rational liberty concern with promoting thoughtful self-determination to be considered as outside the speech that the First Amendment protects.[26]

Consequently, to find any particular expression punishably obscene or offensive, the Court must decide if both its form and its content are hostile to rational liberty. This twofold inquiry rules out many traditional justifications for placing such communication beyond the First Amendment. Much of the opposition to such expression of course has religious roots: the offensive and even the obscene have been understood as the blasphemous, and sexual obscenity has been thought to glorify violations of divine commandments. Both religious and some secular moral perspectives, moreover, have at times viewed obscenity as encouraging absorption in the physical, or "animal," aspects of human sexuality at the expense of its higher communicative and spiritual significance, thereby debasing human dignity. But purely religious disapproval cannot legitimately serve as a rationale for suppressing speech or granting it lesser protection, since this amounts to a form of religious establishment; and secular moral objections have been challenged in contemporary society, so that they can no longer be deemed part of society's standards for rational and morally worthwhile conduct.[27] Many persons now believe that enjoyment of the physical pleasures offered by some human relationships need not produce any degradation of those relationships, and so noncognitive expression conveying this emotive messsage must be held to be included in prevailing conceptions of rational self-direction.

Some types of obscene and offensive speech, however, have been criticized for reasons that both are still widely shared and are inherent in any attachment to the conception of rational liberty. Some expression, such as sadistic, masochistic, and child pornography, portrays certain classes of persons as legitimate objects of coercive sexual exploitation and physical violence, which is inconsistent with any respect for their present and future capacities of rational self-guidance. Such expression insults those it so depicts in ways that may affect viewers' attitudes, but it does not expound ideas in a way that can aid cognitive deliberation. By appealing to and conflating powerful erotic and violent impulses, it may in fact glamorize inhuman conduct and thereby influence even those who consciously reject such behavior.[28] Even without the claiming that this influence produces overt acts of sexual violence, it can be held to foster denigrating stereotypes and create insensitivities that may facilitate lesser forms of immoral conduct, such as sex discrimination and neglect or abuse of wives and children.

Contrary claims can be made that this literature incidentally serves a cathartic purpose for those with such impulses and thus has social value, or that it simply has no effect on behavior whatsoever. In contemporary society both these claims have received sufficient support to be deemed reasonable, and hence legislatures might well decide that action against such expression is not appropriate. There is virtual unanimity, however, that, as the values of the rational liberty view imply, genuine acts of sexual violence or exploitation form no part of rational self-direction, deny due respect to others, and can harm others, so that they are substantively immoral.[29] Consequently, noncognitive communication that aims at glamorizing such conduct is in principle wholly without protection from rational liberty values, except perhaps for those who claim that it has cathartic value for self-direction (and in practice this claim is usually made on behalf of unspecified others). Barring cases where such value is shown, the rational liberty view assigns to this discourse lower-tier protection. If legislatures can provide merely legitimate, not compelling, reasons for its suppression, such as its possible antisocial impact, its opposition to liberal principles in form and content permits it to be restrained.

A constitutional standard for punishable obscene and offensive speech reflecting rational liberty purposes therefore might require that "the predominant theme of the materials, taken as a whole, is to render emotionally appealing conduct which overwhelmingly denies or disregards the capacities for rational self-direction of some persons or classes of persons." This definition should protect all cognitive discussion as well as those sections of literary, cinematic, or other artistic works that depict inhuman conduct in the course of conveying a larger message that has value in terms of rational liberty goals. It would, however, rule out most "snuff" pornography, visual child pornography (on the assumption that there is a social consensus on the danger of precocious sexual relationships to a child's emotional and rational development), and some glamorizations of nonsexual violence. The definition would further justify the denial of certain emotive symbolism that conveys insulting, illiberal messages, even while permitting the expression of those themes in cognitive form. Thus, Nazi speeches and tracts would have to be granted full protection, but not the wearing of swastikas in especially sensitive locales, such as the Jewish neighborhoods of Skokie, Illinois.[30]

This proposed test no doubt will raise fears of repression, but only a few would argue that the approach is dangerous because glamorizing violence and sexual exploitation is substantively valuable. Buyers or sellers prosecuted under the standard would, moreover, still have the option of arguing that exposure to their materials serves the rational self-direction of some people. The test's assumption that this is not the case legitimately reflects predominant attitudes. Most potential critics would be animated not by contrary assumptions but by an historically plausible instrumental concern—a fear that these principles could easily be misapplied in practice to communication that deserves protection. This is a realistic fear, and hence the definition insists that the dangerous emotive message must be overwhelmingly preponderant in the communication, while litigants are allowed to contend that this message relieves and does not exacerbate the tendencies it portrays. These requirements should create a buffer zone in which ambiguous materials are protected, so that only communications clearly in violation of rational liberty standards would be restrained.[31]

Even so, this problem of drawing lines might still deter legislatures from enacting even the limited restraints on expression that the definition permits. Yet the attitudes that such communication supports are substantively immoral not only from a rational liberty standpoint but from virtually all other contemporary moral perspectives. To conclude that American institutions cannot safely express these moral values because their implications cannot be reliably discerned would foster cynicism about whether those values have any practical significance at all.

Another traditional exception to full free speech protection, personal libel or slander, is also generally consonant with rational liberty principles. The dissemination of unfounded accusations performs no genuine informative function, and it interferes significantly with legitimate liberty (and often property) interests of the persons defamed, who may have to go to great lengths to combat the charges against them. Civil and criminal sanctions for such false expression thus generally are legitimate. For political discourse, however, where the "truth" of characterizations and accusations can rarely be decided by authoritative common standards, and where full information is peculiarly vital to self-governance, the government must preserve great leeway. There can be no grounds for legislation against seditious libel, at least short of a showing of a clear and present danger to the maintenance of free government; and active political participants must recognize that discussion of their lives and characters is often relevant to evaluation of their credibility and reliability in public affairs and must be extensively protected. Thus, the rational liberty view roughly parallels the current approach by suggesting that libel of political figures should not be punishable unless it concerns matters clearly unrelated to their involvement in the functions of state governance, including electoral politics, lobbying, and issue agitation, or unless the charges made, however pertinent, are not only false but either known to be false by the libeler or made with reckless disregard for their truth. Virtually all accusations against political figures could reasonably be held to be relevant to legitimate public concerns about the election and performance of governing officials; and proving reckless disregard of the truth is usually difficult. Consequently, this test should insulate political discourse extensively from the threat of libel suits.

This formulation does, however, ring two important changes on current doctrines. First, it substitutes the term "political figure" for "public figure," a change that permits more protection against libel for entertainment figures, such as actors and sports stars. Second, it provides somewhat more protection for conduct that political figures can show to be unrelated to their political activities. The alterations may seem pointless, because virtually any activity can be deemed political. The arts and even sports, for example, both reflect and shape the common culture. Influence on these enterprises is undeniably an element of social self-governance. The private lives of political actors also cannot fail to have some connection with their public functions. For most purposes it is in fact appropriate to take the political in the widest sense possible, so that no information on the competence of governors is lost, and no potentially repressive social relationships are sheltered from public debate and criticism.

But there are good reasons to define the political more narrowly in this area of law with respect not only to entertainers' activities but also to the few activities of political figures that are genuinely of only private importance. Danger to one's reputation can impair future opportunities for emotional, professional, and social fulfillment. The case for permitting almost unlimited derogation of public figures cannot rest simply on a calculation of the improvements provided thereby in society's powers of self-guidance, versus the harms imposed on the capacities of public figures to direct their lives. On many occasions the social gains are far too attenuated to outweigh the individual harms experienced from false, unfair personal assaults.

Two other elements are needed to justify a heavy presumption in favor of protecting criticism of political figures which are not applicable to public figures more broadly or to all the activities of political actors. One justification is that they have chosen their role and accepted the often excessive and unfair heat in the political kitchen. Since they have made this choice, libel rules can fairly assume that the social gains in the power of self-governance stemming from extensive discussion of these individuals overbalance any burdens on their self-direction. This fact need not be demonstrated in every case involving this category of persons. Although the element of voluntariness normally applies equally to entertainment figures, political figures engage in some activities, such as choice of family roles, personal expenditures, and recreation, that do not display this element so clearly. These types of social activity have political consequences, and the conduct of individual political figures in these areas may well be relevant to their public competence. Yet in American society persons making these decisions are not commonly thought to be engaged in political action. Hence, they are not voluntarily thrusting themselves into the political arena through these acts. They may do so in other ways, but they must have the opportunity to deny the relevance of these acts to their public functions and to require that a minimal relevance be shown. This requirement can usually be met easily, but if it were not, less demanding standards for proving libel could be applied. Thus these facets of the lives of political figures would be given greater protection than the minimal guarantees provided by the prevailing *New York Times v. Sullivan* standard of actual malice.

Furthermore, while entertainers have willingly placed themselves in the public eye and while they influence social development, their activities are nonpolitical in a different but equally crucial respect. They neither seek nor have any coercive authority to influence the lives of others. Their impact, unlike that of governing officials, derives primarily from voluntary interest in their activities. This lesser authority to shape our common destinies means that the public has a less legitimate interest in how entertainers' private lives may influence their public performances. Hence, again, greater defenses against libel are indicated. Although a measure of state discretion for experimentation with precise standards is appropriate, entertainers could, for example, be entitled to recover damages when a publication has seriously damaged their reputation with false statements, even though the publication's failure to discover the inaccuracy of its story could not be characterized as reckless.

Greater liability to libel suits would no doubt have some chilling effect on press coverage of the private activities of political figures and the lives of entertainers. But given the limited value of this information, true or false, for public deliberations on self-governance, and given the dangers posed to individual powers of self-direction by the modern media, this balance appears appropriate. Thus, for libel purposes it is proper to define the political more narrowly and conventionally to include activities of state governance and electoral mobilization. Political figures would then be those persons substantially engaged in these kinds of conduct.

The recent and still uncertain moves toward granting full First Amendment protection to some, but not all, commercial speech also can be given a foundation by rational liberty principles. Much commercial expression serves valuable informative functions by making the community aware of the nature, uses, and costs of available goods and services, knowledge that assists the reflective self-direction of most persons. These functions are served, however, only if the information provided is reasonably accurate. Much advertising also contains noninformative elements aimed solely at performing the economic activity of inducing sales by fostering favorable emotional attitudes toward the products in question. Regulations designed to assure truth in advertising thus are consistent with the principles that generally justify protection of commercial speech, and in this context standards of truth and fraudulence are more practicable than in political or artistic expression. The aim of promoting rational deliberation also suggests that the noninformative, emotionally appealing aspects of commercial speech merit no special deference and should be treated like any other economic activity. As in the case of obscenity, rational liberty goals imply that expression which is both noncognitive in form and irrelevant or antithetical to rational deliberation in content is sufficiently distant from the First Amendment's purposes to merit only minimal scrutiny protection. The means and substance of the noninformative aspects of commercial speech meet these criteria.[32] Hence their regulation, as well as rules for truth in advertising, should be sustainable simply on a showing of reasonable public purposes, although the courts would still have to scrutinize the means employed in both sorts of regulations if the informative functions of the communications were claimed to be impaired. These principles suggest, for example, that advertisement of the availability of legal cigarettes must be permitted, but that the companies advertising could be required both to inform the public fully of the harmful consequences of their wares and to eschew all noninformative emotional appeals, as defined with sufficient precision to avoid chilling effects. This requirement could reasonably be held to further the important public end of promoting health without significantly impinging on the contributions of such commercial expression to informed decision-making and hence rational liberty.

The rational liberty goal of promoting political self-government by the community as a whole suggests the need for a review of the Court's holdings concerning the First Amendment status of campaign expenditures and corporate speech. Federal and state restraints on these activities have been deemed to be impermissible restrictions of political expression, and the communications that they produce indeed serve the informing function that the rational liberty view prizes. At the same time, community deliberation on public issues may be biased, and rational self-governance may therefore be impeded, if certain points of view are made much more prominent than others due to superior economic resources. Regulations to assure the equal availability of all legitimate viewpoints are difficult to construct fairly and they raise the dangers of a chilling effect and partisan abuse. But in principle, at least, such restrictions could be designed to serve as a type of time, place, and quantity regulation which, like limits on noise levels, would be tailored to achieve on balance the maximum liberty for all.

Overall, the rational liberty view suggests standards for the scope of freedom of speech that do not depart radically from current protections. Yet it refines and clarifies that jurisprudence, defining First Amendment guarantees in terms of consistent purposes that cohere with a comprehensive constitutional philosophy and which explain why some forms of speech merit a lower tier than others, even as the view limits the permissible grounds for so classifying expression or subsequently restraining it. The approach therefore has the merit of confronting and proposing a solution to the long-standing confusion over the purposes of free speech. And it leads to workable principles that are generally consonant with the moral and intellectual standards for free expression shared widely in modern liberal societies.

The goal of universal rational self-direction implies the general desirability of democratic self-government, but different understandings of democracy are possible. Further specification is required to work out the position's implications for the political equality issues involved in apportionment. The theory calls for the promotion of both individual and societal self-governance, but that means it cannot support democracy unqualifiedly, for democratic majorities are notoriously prone to violate legitimate liberties of some or all. Indeed, if an undemocratic system served on balance to guarantee rational liberty for all most effectively, that system would in principle be justifiable; but the widespread loss of political self-governance effected by such a system makes this result highly improbable in practice. Furthermore, the experience of the last two centuries, as reflected in constitutional amendments and decisions, casts doubt on the benefits to liberty claimed for most sharply undemocratic institutions. The property qualifications favored by eighteenth century liberals to preserve rights that were thought to be preservative of all other rights came to be seen only as aids to the perpetuation of unjust economic inequalities. Mill's nineteenth century faith that educational requirements for the franchise would maximize rational governance and liberty never won wide acceptance, while traditional racial, sexual, and even age restrictions have in this century been recognized as unjust and finally abandoned.

In the modern context, therefore, the rational liberty view must hold that political inequalities are presumptively illegitimate unless they are shown to be necessary to the compelling interest of preserving the community's continued capacities for universal rational self-determination. The relevant constitutional guarantees, particularly the Fifteenth Amendment and the Fourteenth Amendment's equal protection clause, might therefore be read as subjecting all departures from full democracy to strict scrutiny. But this conclusion is too hasty, for despite these amendments, the Constitution still embodies numerous structures that make absolute equality of voting power impossible, and these structures have been and still are thought to enhance the system's capacity to promote rational liberty for all.

Both the representation by states in the Senate and the use of states as electoral units in the electoral college mean that perfect equality of voting power in these elections cannot be provided, for the same reasons that led Douglas to rule out unit voting among differently sized counties in *Gray v. Sanders*. Even the apportionment of representatives by state populations ensures some interstate inequalities, and inequalities due to intrastate districting systems persist as well. If full political equality were the only consideration, it would be better realized through undistricted national elections for federal officers, with proportional representation for the legislative branches.[33]

But no framer of any constitutional amendment contemplated such drastic changes, in part because so many have felt that popular capacities for self-governance are increased by a system that includes representation through districts and states. Among other benefits, this system permits legislators to be identified with and by more specific communities, and it ensures that the more accessible experiences of self-government at the state and local level are not rendered trivial in relation to national issues. Both features can help foster stronger and more satisfying senses of community membership. Proportional representation systems also have long been thought to foster governmental instability and ineffectiveness through the opportunities they provide for the disintegrative tendencies of electoral parties and coalitions. Americans have tried and largely abandoned such systems at the municipal level. While these negative consequences of proportional representation are in dispute, they have nevertheless raised doubts about whether such systems really advance community capacities for self-guidance. America's electoral institutions clearly give those doubts great weight.[34]

Furthermore, inegalitarian institutions, such as judicial review, can often assist a democratic system in achieving universal rational liberty by checking majoritarian abuses. Much authority is also delegated from elected policy-makers to professional administrators and regulators in the belief that their expertise and efficiency will aid the community in achieving its professed aims. Perhaps not all of these less than fully democratic political mechanisms are necessary to the attainment of rational liberty goals. Yet both the Constitution and contemporary practice express a preponderant and credible consensus that undemocratic institutional features are sometimes appropriate means to those ends.

There are few better indicators of social agreement on an institution's propriety than its constitutional enactment, and so at present the textually established inequalities must be accepted as integral to American conceptions of rational political liberty. A rational liberty reading of the equal protection clause, in particular, thus could not hold that absolute participatory democracy or even proportional representation is constitutionally mandated. However, judges should apply strict scrutiny to nonconstitutional political inequalities, which are created by sources less able to claim to represent an authoritative social consensus, even though the reasons that persuaded the constitutional framers to adopt inegalitarian devices might not survive such testing. The general movement toward democratic political principles and the centrality of political equality to free self-direction indicate that deviations must be defended by rational liberty reasons of a weight comparable to that provided by constitutional enactment. This weight would be assured by imposing strict scrutiny requirements.

The rational liberty approach, then, requires all inegalitarian political devices to be either explicitly established in the Constitution or justified as necessary to compelling liberty interests. This standard suggests, for example, that democratically elected legislatures and executives could delegate significant authority to administrative and regulatory agencies if they deemed the delegation necessary to perform governing functions effectively, as virtually all would agree to be the case in regard to some problems faced by modern states. The courts, however, could well have a role in assuring that such delegation is plausibly founded and that guarantees of due process and ultimate democratic accountability are maintained.[35] As for the power of judicial review itself, some might choose to defend it as constitutionally based, and most would accept that in some form it is now integral to the system's proper functioning. Even so, the long-standing debate over its precise nature and extent in a largely democratic society would still be appropriate and salutary, especially since it has often ensured that the function is performed responsibly.

In regard to apportionment, the one person, one vote rule is the obvious candidate for a political equality standard once it has been granted that proportional representation is constitutionally disavowed. But the goal of assuring universal political liberty, usually presumed to require political equality, may not be best served by a simple mechanical insistence on satisfying this requirement. A legislature might believe, for example, that certain minorities long prevented from participating politically would be more likely to attain representation in proportion to their actual population percentages if an apportionment plan with moderate violations of one person, one vote were adopted. Or it might think that because of regional tensions only a plan departing from the rule in order to give geographical and political subdivisions united and balanced representation could assure that those tensions would not lead to majoritarian repression or excessive intergovernmental conflicts.[36]

In each of these cases it would be difficult for the state to prove that the deviations were truly required to ensure rational self-governance, since most concerns can be accommodated consistently with the one person, one vote requirement, and since disproportionate representation, of smaller subdivisions in particular, can be plausibly construed as sanctioning excessive minority veto power. However, in principle such arguments could be made in particular contexts. If so, the rational liberty view would permit the unequal apportionment to be sustained. The theory provides no support for the current approach of subjecting state legislative apportionments to lesser scrutiny than congressional ones. This difference is admittedly not so significant, because concerns to represent political subdivisions can more easily be shown to be compelling at the state level. Arguments for deviations would also be more powerful in the context of special elections not involving the choice of governing officials.

Similarly, while a state majority is not entitled to deprive a state minority of rights held fundamental by the national consensus reflected in the Constitution, in some cases the sort of popularly adopted federal analogy legislatures struck down in *Lucas* v. *Colorado* could be upheld.[37] The courts would have to undertake a review of the legislative and political debates accompanying the adoption of such a plan to determine whether the system was justified in terms of specific needs of rational self-governance in the particular state, such as regional concerns, or in terms simply of a vague admiration for the federal Constitution. Since the Senate's system of representation was presented by Madison and most other framers as essentially a compromise, its imitation alone hardly qualifies as the type of compelling justification that the rational liberty view requires for violating one person, one vote. While judicial exploration of the rationale for a system's enactment is difficult, this inquiry would look for explicit defenses of the measure, not for any underlying legislative motives. Hence the task is one that courts routinely undertake in construing both legislative and constitutional provisions.

Since the requirement to conform to existing political subdivisions can limit the possibilities for gerrymandering more effectively than the one person, one vote rule, departures from that rule to ensure subdivision conformity might also be claimed as necessary for rational liberty goals. Yet the conformity demand alone would not be much more effective in preventing gerrymanders that violate the rights to rational self-governance of some. The only really powerful means to challenge gerrymanders is judicial inquiry into the nature of the apportioners' intentions and motives. The difficulty of proving invidious purposes suggests only that the problem is too intractable for reliable judicial resolution. At any rate, there is no point in abandoning one person, one vote out of concern for this sort of malapportionment. Some justices have occasionally suggested that departures from the rule might also be justified to promote the stability of the two-party system or to protect incumbents with seniority. It is doubtful, however, that these ends always further the goal of rational self-governance. Such concerns can also be accommodated much more easily than geographic concerns without violating the one person, one vote requirement.[38]

Consequently, a rational liberty construction of the Constitution's political equality requirements can consistently reject absolute social and political egalitarianism and accept those undemocratic institutions that are established in the document itself, and it can justify any further inequalities that survive strict scrutiny. For the most part, however, the theory would probably uphold the *Reynolds* ruling and its more demanding progeny. The theory also supports legislative and executive actions establishing even more fully egalitarian forms of representation. It can also provide grounds for challenging systems that meet one person, one vote but still deny effective opportunities for self-governance to discernible segments of the population, such as the at-large city commission system sustained in *Mobile* v. *Bolden*.[39] Overall, the rational liberty view produces a standard for adjudicating political inequalities that does more justice to the enhanced popular and constitutional commitment to democracy than the current Court's increasingly deferential approach, even while it provides principled grounds for stopping short of egalitarian absolutism. The theory thus gives coherent articulation to the consensus that appears implicit in the diverse values and aspirations expressed in the Court's evolving treatment of the apportionment cases.

Probably no general question troubles liberalism more than the relationship of economic systems to the liberties it wishes to secure, and the specific issue of the national government's constitutional responsibilities for individual and social economic welfare is just as intractable. As in the area of political equality, the American constitutional tradition's liberal assumptions about the sorts of economies that are conducive to personal freedom are now in dispute. The long-standing acceptance of liberal economic principles means at a minimum, however, that the Constitution must be held to permit policies based on the belief that a market economy with significant private ownership is not only consistent with but also conducive to the realization of universal rational liberty. The Constitution can equally be read to permit, though not to require, different views.

The rational liberty theory does require that liberty, not property rights or even economic prosperity per se, be the ultimate standard for economic as well as all other liberal institutions. Thus, if particular property rights on balance jeopardize the attainment of this goal, or if further economic prosperity is simply not important to the rational self-direction of the bulk of a liberal community at a given time, economic concerns need not be shown special solicitude by either legislatures or courts. But in practice the legitimate plans of most citizens will require their personal employment of a range of material resources and also a generally prosperous and technically current national economy. Hence, if the government created by the Constitution aims to promote rational liberty for all, it must be vitally concerned with both national economic welfare and the resources of each individual.

The implications of these economic responsibilities for the functions of the national government are debatable, for the policies conducive to economic prosperity and individual well-being are intensely controversial.

Early English liberals contemplated some governmental intervention in the economy to protect new and fragile industries, balance trade, and help create an infrastructure, and they acknowledged public responsibility on the local level for those unable to work. While Americans in the early nineteenth century accepted similar beliefs about local charity, republican concerns about the dangers of a powerful central government deeply involved with financial interests prevented national agencies from playing much of an economic role, apart from curbing protectionist state policies, acquiring land, setting tariffs, and trying to stabilize the currency. In later years the rise of laissez-faire economic theories, which saw antibusiness interventions as inefficient and unjust, also limited the growth and nature of the federal role.

In the twentieth century the national government has increasingly accepted broad responsibilities for both general prosperity and individual welfare, but extensive reliance on private forces and state and local aid remains. The new national posture has also not been formally constitutionalized through amendment, and recently proposed changes, notably the balanced budget amendment, reflect a renewed conviction that the government's welfare role is in the long run counterproductive. In light of this history, neither the constitutional text nor current doctrines and practices articulate any consensus on the sorts of economic arrangements that best provide the material conditions required for the rational pursuits of most citizens. Consequently, the Constitution must be read as permitting extensive discretion to the political branches to choose the economic and social welfare policies that seem appropriate for these goals.

The rational liberty theory, however, does not view economic and social welfare matters with the same deference as did the utilitarian, relativistic post-1937 Court. The theory in principle supports judicial recognition of constitutional rights to welfare assistance and meaningful work, but only for those who are unable to provide for themselves, and only within the limits of economic feasibility, as decided chiefly by the political branches. Meeting basic subsistence needs can obviously be assumed to be central to the liberty of all, and as Robert Lane notes, virtually nothing is more essential than gainful employment to the sense of self-respect that is equally vital to everyone.[40] Consequently, insofar as meeting subsistence and employment needs does not produce even greater infringements on the just liberties of the remainder of the community, the goal of advancing each citizen's capacities for rational self-direction requires these forms of governmental economic assistance.

Obviously, however, the qualification swallows up most of the substantive implications of this conclusion. Since people are never entitled to burden others simply because they are unwilling to provide for themselves, the rational liberty view would permit denials of welfare to those who refuse work. Furthermore, most types of guaranteed benefits and employment could be held to jeopardize the ability of the economy to meet the basic needs of all in the long run. That is a sufficient reason in rational liberty terms to justify legislative refusals to provide such services, particularly since courts are ill-suited to challenge all but the most patently arbitrary legislative judgments of necessity in such matters. This approach implies, however, that administrative denials of welfare and employment opportunities that appear warranted by existing legislation merit strict judicial scrutiny, for these are infringements of vital rational liberty interests that cannot claim clear support from legislative decisions.

Even legislative actions would be subject to strict scrutiny on the rational liberty approach if they deny to some the opportunity to pursue their preferred occupations. Troubling as governmental refusals to provide resources for the exercise of basic rights may be, governmental refusals even to permit the exercise of such rights are still more dubious. Although both sorts of action can strike deeply at a citizen's effective capacities for self-direction, there are practical limits to the aid that government can provide, while complete bans on conduct integral to rational liberty are required, if ever, only in extraordinary circumstances. Hence more deference is appropriate when the legislature limits welfare than when it forbids certain employments. Mere regulation of occupations to ensure competence and safety or to provide incentives for the efficient allocation of human resources is a lesser infringement, justifiable on a showing of reasonable competing interests. If a certain business could be proven to pose clear and imminent dangers to the self-directive capacities of some, these dangers would count as a sufficiently compelling reason for its restraint to withstand strict scrutiny. But since the denial of all opportunity to pursue one's trade is an absolute deprivation of something ordinarily integral to rational self-direction, regulations that amount to such a denial merit the closest judicial attention.[41]

Thus, due process cases such as *Williamson* v. *Lee Optical Company,* where a state prevented opticians from replacing lenses in frames without a prescription from an optometrist or ophthalmologist, and equal protection cases such as *Kotch* v. *Board of River Pilot Commissioners,* where a state board granted pilot licenses only to friends and relatives, would be judicially reviewed under the higher tier of scrutiny in the rational liberty view. Since the reasons provided for each of these laws were largely invented by the justices and were less than overwhelming, the decisions in these cases would probably be different.[42] Again, this consequence is more consistent with contemporary concerns for personal liberties than with the excessively deferential post-1937 approach that arose in response to the abuses of the *Lochner* years.

Due process and equal protection adjudication also raise questions about the rational liberty prescription for governmental actions that burden or benefit citizens differently according to their economic status. Ordinarily the courts must regard the inequalities of a liberal market society as legitimate if they are widely believed to promote material welfare for all. There are also practical limits to governmental capacities to reduce those inequalities via redistribution, and these limits must largely be matters for legislative judgment. But the rational liberty position suggests that governmental actions which prohibit the exercise of fundamental freedoms are suspect, and hence if a public measure exacerbates the significance of economic differences in ways that endanger the basic liberties of some, strict scrutiny is demanded.

The fact that some people are relatively deprived in terms of the resources needed to take opportunities or avoid burdens provided by the government is not in itself sufficient to subject official actions to strict scrutiny. The rational liberty view assumes that the relative deprivation of economic goods need not endanger any basic liberty interest. The crucial sense of self-respect, in particular, is held to derive instead from meeting the minimal standards of moral character.[43] But if governmental measures render some people so unable to exercise their vital liberties as to make those freedoms meaningless, this treatment is a sufficient deprivation to trigger strict scrutiny.

The liberties deemed vital would essentially be those previously discussed as fundamental substantive due process rights. Hence, governmental incarceration of a citizen, when part of a criminal process in which the ability to obtain an effective appeal depends on the capacity to pay certain fees, denies liberty to the indigent in ways that require compelling justification. In contrast to typical welfare situations, where persons denied benefits are simply left to fend for themselves, here the state denial of aid results in continual confinement and thus deprives indigents of much opportunity to regain the freedoms that the state is taking from them. Hence the element of active governmental prohibition of what may be legitimate liberties is more inarguably present. While legislative withdrawal of previously guaranteed welfare services may be equally burdensome on the capacities of some to exercise their freedoms and should require compelling justifications, again the courts would usually have to accede to documented legislative claims that economic necessities constitute such justifications.

The rational liberty view applies to education in the same way as to welfare. It suggests that modern American governments are in principle required to promote the universal education that today is essential to the development of capacities for rational self-guidance. But again, those recipients unwilling to respect the educational rights of others could be expelled, and the extent of the services provided would be left largely to legislative judgments of feasibility. In situations such as *San Antonio School District* v. *Rodriguez,* where the state financing system produced inequalities in the capacities of districts to fund education, this analysis of the constitutional significance of relative economic deprivation suggests the appropriate standards. If, by adopting a system, the state endangers the capacities of some school districts to provide the minimum education necessary to prepare citizens for free adult lives, this unequal treatment merits strict scrutiny. In contrast to Powell's approach, the deprivation need not be absolute, only extensive enough to endanger significantly future capacities for self-direction; and those deprived need not be a definable class of "poor" people, since the deprivation by itself triggers strict scrutiny. If, however, the funding system allows adequate training for all, despite the relative deprivation in educational resources of certain districts, it needs only minimal scrutiny. Strict scrutiny might, however, still be appropriate if the evidence shows relative deprivation to be so extensive as to render insufficent what would otherwise be adequate training. Since the enhancement of capacities for rational liberty is ultimately largely a personal achievement, the state can be required to do no more than make the training needed for basic competencies equally available to all.

In the particular circumstances in *Rodriguez,* it is not clear whether the state system produced a universally adequate minimum training. All districts appeared to believe that funds in addition to those provided by the state were required, and some felt that they could not raise the necessary additional amounts. Furthermore, it is not clear that the financing system should have withstood even minimal scrutiny, since it seemed only distantly related to the professed goal of local control, involving as it did a ceiling on the extent to which districts could tax themselves. Finally, arguments might have been made that the discrepancies in education were sufficiently great so as to endanger seriously the comparative cognitive capacities of those in the more poorly funded areas. Many of these issues, especially questions of the adequacy of educational services, are complex enough to make competent judicial resolution difficult. It is also debatable whether either local control or education are served by extensive court interventions in school financing. *Rodriguez* might consequently have been a case where the courts could usefully have engaged in the sort of colloquy with the political branches urged by

Alexander Bickel. The judges might have defined constitutional limits on permissible financing schemes and then given the state further opportunities to establish alternate systems against which difficult questions of minimal or relative adequacy could not be so credibly raised.[44]

A rational liberty construction of the Constitution also could define appropriate limits to the national commerce power more clearly, without jeopardizing governmental authority to meet economic and moral objectives that are essential to securing basic freedoms for all. As under the prevailing approaches, federal commercial regulations would be expected to respect all rights guaranteed elsewhere in the Constitution, and the fuller elaboration of those rights provided by the rational liberty view should make it more possible for the Court to check insufficiently justified infringements of integral constitutional freedoms. More important, the commerce power could be construed by interpreting its intended functions in light of rational liberty goals. It would be seen as an instrument to ensure that interstate commerce operates to provide economic conditions facilitating the exercise of freedom by all, not as a mandate for legislation for any end that can somehow be said to involve commerce. This interpretation is consonant with the clause's historic purposes and also with its basic concern to ensure that the government has no powers that are not limited by its ultimate legitimate ends. The application of the clause's power against forms of discrimination in interstate commerce that deny necessary resources to some, such as the activities forbidden by the 1964 Civil Rights Act, could therefore be deemed legitimate. But the use of the clause for moral or other regulations having no connection with providing for the economic well-being of all would be invalid. A similar rational liberty construction of the purposes of other powers should still permit any necessary authority for such ends to be found elsewhere in the Constitution. For example, some noneconomic forms of private discrimination might be reachable under the Fourteenth Amendment, if a state is held to have abdicated its responsibility to protect the legitimate liberties of some citizens; and the Thirteenth Amendment is also available for many such purposes. Except, perhaps, for some essentially criminal legislation, most existing commerce laws would probably survive this test. But the test would make it more difficult to turn the commerce clause from a broad power for fostering economic development into an illiberal blank check for virtually any governmental action.

Finally, according to the rational liberty view, underlying all the specific issues concerning national authority for economic welfare is a more general concern. So long as material prosperity is valued and pursued largely through personal efforts, and so long as a liberal market system ensures that unequal economic statuses result, the risk remains of the halo effect, where wealth becomes the ultimate standard by which all are evaluated and hence the overriding goal of the community's members. No specific governmental action is likely to combat this tendency effectively in liberal societies. It can at best be attenuated, not eradicated. But the various rational liberty positions discussed here express a consistent strategy for discouraging such inferences. In regard to welfare and vocational rights, as well as to differential economic effects and commerce regulation, the approach evaluates economic activities in terms of their contribution to the capacities for self-direction of all, and it never equates the achievement of this goal simply with the attainment of enhanced wealth. If a society's constitutional principles express this moral standard, and if governmental policies in regard to spending and taxing priorities, welfare and regulatory measures, education, criminal justice, and myriad other matters not only remain within the limits of the rational liberty standard but explicitly strive to promote its goals, this ideal of human worth will probably come to be more widely accepted in society. If so, it may alleviate some of the most invidious psychic consequences of liberal economies.

Clearly, these basic principles of the rational liberty view have to be elaborated further in particular constitutional contexts in order to develop full legal doctrines in each area. But the general theory, by responding to the fundamental theoretical dilemmas of liberal constitutionalism, produces useful arguments on contemporary constitutional issues that collectively articulate a consistent understanding of the government's purposes. This fact indicates the value of recognizing that constitutional problems have roots in the ongoing difficulties of liberalism's first principles, and of explicitly and systematically addressing those basic difficulties. While neither the rational liberty view in particular, nor such efforts in general, can promise an end to the failings of American constitutional governance, they may move it closer to the Constitution's basic aspiration of establishing a consciously self-governing and free human community.

· Notes

Introduction

1. Louis Hartz, *The Liberal Tradition in America* (New York: Harcourt Brace Jovanovich, 1955), pp. 9–10, 259–276, 284–286; Martin Shapiro, *Freedom of Speech: The Supreme Court and Judicial Review* (Englewood Cliffs, N.J.: Prentice-Hall, 1966), p. 47.

2. See e.g. Richard Parker, "The Jurisprudential Uses of John Rawls," in *Nomos XX: Constitutionalism,* ed. Roland Pennock and John Chapman (New York: New York University Press, 1979); Michael Walzer, "Philosophy and Democracy," *Political Theory* 9 (August 1981): 379–399; Martin Shapiro, "Father and Sons: The Court, the Commentators, and the Search for Values," in *The Burger Court,* ed. Vincent Blasi (New Haven: Yale University Press, 1983); Bruce Ackerman, *Reconstructing American Law* (Cambridge: Harvard University Press, 1984); Chaim Waxman, ed., *The End of Ideology Debate* (New York: Simon and Schuster, 1968). Hartz did anticipate some difficulties caused by America's "irrational Lockianism," but he chiefly feared American parochialism in foreign affairs. Hartz, *Liberal Tradition,* p. 308.

3. See e.g. Paul Brest, "The Fundamental Rights Controversy: The Essential Contradictions of Normative Constitutional Scholarship," *Yale Law Journal* 90 (April 1981): 1063–1109; Roberto Mangabeira Unger, "The Critical Legal Studies Movement," *Harvard Law Review* 96 (January 1983): 561–675; Ackerman, *Reconstructing American Law;* Ackerman, *Private Property and the Constitution* (New Haven: Yale University Press, 1977).

4. See Hartz, *The Liberal Tradition,* pp. 6, 10–11, 14, 31–32, 284–309; Bernard Bailyn, *The Ideological Origins of the American Revolution* (Cambridge: Harvard University Press, 1967); J. G. A. Pocock, *The Machiavellian Moment* (Princeton: Princeton University Press, 1975); Edmund S. Morgan, ed., *Puritan Political Ideas* (Indianapolis: Bobbs-Merrill, 1965); Henry F. May, *The Enlightenment in America* (Oxford: Oxford University Press, 1976); Lawrence Goodwyn, *The Democratic Promise* (New York: Oxford University Press, 1976); M. J. C. Vile, *Constitutionalism and the Separation of Powers* (Oxford: Clar-

endon Press, 1967), pp. 347–349; Edward Purcell, *The Crisis of Democratic Theory* (Lexington: University Press of Kentucky, 1973).

5. May, *Enlightenment*, pp. 88–101.

6. See e.g. Paul Brest, *Processes of Constitutional Decisionmaking* (Boston: Little, Brown, 1975), p. 2.

7. See Glendon Schubert, "Academic Ideology and the Study of Adjudication," *American Political Science Review* 61 (March 1967): 107; Ronald Dworkin, *Taking Rights Seriously* (Cambridge: Harvard University Press), p. 149.

8. See e.g. Elizabeth Mensch, "The History of Mainstream Legal Thought," in *The Politics of Law*, ed. David Kairys (New York: Pantheon Books, 1982). Her analysis of "classical legal consciousness" in the late nineteenth and early twentieth century, when such "grandly integrated" "liberal legalism" is said to have reached its apogee (p. 23), derives largely from Duncan Kennedy's influential but unpublished "Rise and Fall of Classical Legal Thought" (1975).

9. See e.g. Duncan Kennedy, "The Structure of Blackstone's Commentaries," *Buffalo Law Review* 28 (Spring 1979): 213; Brest, "The Fundamental Rights Controversy," p. 1108; Unger, "Critical Legal Studies Movement," pp. 650–651, 662.

10. See e.g. Robert Dahl, *Democracy in the United States*, 4th ed. (U.S.A.: Rand McNally, 1981), pp. 160–163.

11. This characterization holds through 1982. The Court, of course, is still evolving. For accounts of the Burger Court in this era as "ad hoc," "pragmatic," "inconsistent," without a coherent "theme" or jurisprudence, see e.g. A. E. Dick Howard, "The Burger Court: A Judicial Nonet Plays the Enigma Variations," *Law & Contemporary Problems* 43 (Summer 1980): 7, 25; Martin Shapiro, "Judicial Activism," in *The Third Century*, ed. Seymour Martin Lipset (Stanford: Hoover Institution, 1979), pp. 109, 119–120; Thomas Emerson, "First Amendment Doctrine and the Burger Court," *California Law Review* 68 (May 1980): 440; Archibald Cox, *Freedom of Expression* (Cambridge: Harvard University Press, 1980), pp. 19, 88; John Hart Ely, *Democracy and Distrust* (Cambridge: Harvard University Press, 1980), p. 248; Blasi, ed., *The Burger Court*.

Introduction to Part I

1. See Bernard Bailyn, *The Ideological Origins of the American Revolution* (Cambridge: Harvard University Press, 1967); Gordon S. Wood, *The Creation of the American Republic* (Chapel Hill: University of North Carolina Press, 1968); J. G. A. Pocock, *The Machiavellian Moment* (Princeton: Princeton University Press, 1975); Garry Wills, *Inventing America* (New York: Vintage Books, 1978); Clinton Rossiter, *Seedtime of the Republic* (New York: Harcourt Brace Jovanovich, 1953); Henry F. May, *The Enlightenment in America* (Oxford: Oxford University Press, 1976); Morton White, *The Philosophy of the American Revolution* (New York: Oxford University Press, 1978); Edmund S. Morgan, ed., *Puritan Political Ideas* (Indianapolis: Bobbs-Merrill, 1965).

2. May, *Enlightenment*, Chs. 1, 5, esp. pp. 88–90; Gordon S. Wood, "Heroics," *The New York Review of Books* 28 (April 2, 1981): 16; Bailyn, *Origins*,

pp. 45, 46; Wood, *American Republic,* pp. 16, 17; White, *American Revolution,* Ch. 6; Donald H. Meyer, *The Democratic Enlightenment* (G. P. Putnam's Sons, 1976), chs. 7, 12; Herbert Storing, *What the Anti-Federalists Were For* (Chicago: University of Chicago Press, 1981), p. 83n7. Garry Wills has argued that the Scottish theorists departed significantly from Locke's politics. Wills, *Inventing,* pp. 233, 236, 250. It is true that they stressed the universality of moral capacities and duties of benevolence. This did not, however, make their politics much more egalitarian, communitarian, or less property-oriented than Locke's. Wills exaggerates Locke's individualism, misrepresents Locke's very similar doctrine of property, and underplays the Scots' own political inegalitarianism. See also White, *American Revolution,* pp. 37, 99–100, 111–112, 210; Storing, *What the Anti-Federalists Were For,* p. 83n7.

3. See M. J. C. Vile, *Constitutionalism and the Separation of Powers* (Oxford: Clarendon Press, 1967); Ray Forrest Harvey, *Jean Jacques Burlamaqui* (Chapel Hill: University of North Carolina Press, 1937); Wills, *Inventing;* Garry Wills, *Explaining America* (Garden City, N.Y.: Doubleday, 1981); Gordon S. Wood, "The Tradition of American Freedom," in Norman Graebner, ed., *Freedom in America* (University Park: Pennsylvania State University Press, 1977), pp. 52–53; Pocock, *Machiavellian Moment,* pp. 421, 424, 441, 474, 492–493; Bailyn, *Origins,* pp. 30, 59, 77–79.

4. Wills, *Inventing,* pp. 170–172, 174, 176; John Dunn, "The Politics of Locke in England and America in the Eighteenth Century," in *John Locke: Problems and Perspectives,* ed. John W. Yolton (Cambridge, Eng.: Cambridge University Press, 1969), p. 78; Bailyn, *Origins,* p. 30; Pocock, *Machiavellian Moment,* p. 424; Neal Wood, *The Politics of Locke's Philosophy* (Berkeley: University of Chicago Press, 1983); Jay Fliegelman, *Prodigals and Pilgrims* (Cambridge, Eng.: Cambridge University Press, 1982). Significantly, Locke himself distinguished the *Second Treatise's* statement of governmental "rights and principles" from practical considerations on the "art of governing." James Axtell, *The Educational Writings of John Locke* (Cambridge, Eng.: Cambridge University Press, 1968), p. 400. All this is not to deny, however, that Americans with common ends have often disagreed on the institutions and devices for realizing them. And for many structural issues, including, for example, the separation of powers, the organization of the legislature, executive power and administrative discretion, and federal-state spheres of responsibility, Pocock's tradition of republican institutional discourse is often an appropriate historic starting point.

1. Principles of Early Liberalism

1. These four goals were to be pursued for all, since all free and rational human beings were held equal in their basic rights. Lockean liberalism was thus more egalitarian than the traditions it opposed, but it guaranteed only legal, not political, economic, or social equality. Laws were to be applied as written, not varied due to the nature of the parties to a dispute, but those laws could reflect and reinforce any inequalities in status that were thought to be consistent with recognition of the natural rights of all. Given the limits of this objective, full

equality was not a central goal of early liberalism. Scottish Enlightenment thought may appear more egalitarian, since it does not stress rational self-direction so much as guidance by a universally possessed "moral sense." But the "moral sense" was never seen as superseding the necessity for moral education and rational self-regulation. And many Americans, including the early Jefferson, accepted some synthesis of the moral sense and rationalist positions. See Garry Wills, *Inventing America* (New York: Vintage Books, 1978), pp. 181–192, 198, 201; Morton White, *The Philosophy of the American Revolution* (New York: Oxford University Press, 1978), ch. 3.

2. John Locke, *The Second Treatise of Government,* ed. Thomas Peardon (Indianapolis: Bobbs-Merrill, 1952), p. viii; Locke, *Two Treatises of Government,* ed. Peter Laslett (New York: New American Library, 1965), p. 312; Thomas Hobbes, *Leviathan,* ed. C. B. Macpherson (Baltimore: Pelican Books, 1968), pp. 189, 713, 728; Locke, *A Letter Concerning Toleration* (Indianapolis: Bobbs-Merrill, 1955), p. 57; Locke, *An Essay Concerning Human Understanding,* ed. Peter Nidditch (Oxford: Clarendon Press, 1975), pp. 702–703.

3. Locke, *Letter,* pp. 16–19, 29, 52.

4. Hobbes, *Leviathan,* pp. 200, 231; Locke, *Letter,* pp. 52, 54.

5. Ibid., pp. 27, 46, 50, 51.

6. Locke, *Essay,* pp. 43, 45, 688–696; Maurice Cranston, *John Locke* (London: Longmans, Green, 1957), p. 200.

7. Locke, *Essay,* pp. 516–518, 548–552, 643.

8. Locke, *Two Treatises,* pp. 311, 313, 315.

9. Locke, *Essay,* pp. 6, 229, 232, 237, 250, 252.

10. Hobbes, *Leviathan,* pp. 297, 298, 300, 376; Locke, *Letter,* pp. 17, 48.

11. Locke, *Two Treatises,* pp. 331–333, 337, 339–341, 344, 395; Hobbes, *Leviathan,* pp. 296–297.

12. Locke, *Two Treatises,* pp. 344, 406–407. Thus, while Locke does not believe civil society is necessary for men to have property rights, he also does not think of property as wholly "inalienable" or beyond regulation. And since Locke justifies property rights because they "benefit Life" by furthering prosperity, his position is not hostile to regulation on behalf of the general welfare. See James Tully, *A Discourse on Property* (Cambridge, Eng.: Cambridge University Press, 1980).

13. Locke, *Two Treatises,* pp. 460–461.

14. Ibid., pp. 339–340. While Locke mentions increasing lands, his real stress is on their "right (productive) imploying," for he notes that, due to the value-generating quality of labor, "numbers of men are to be preferd to largenesse of dominions."

15. Hobbes, *Leviathan,* pp. 116, 682, 688.

16. Ibid., pp. 683, 703.

17. Locke, *Essay,* pp. 6, 271.

18. Ibid., pp. 644–645, 720.

19. Ibid., pp. 646, 647, 720.

20. Ibid., pp. 641–642, 646; Locke, *Letter,* pp. 45–46.

21. Locke, *Two Treatises,* pp. 347–352; Locke, *Essay,* pp. 45–46, 646.

22. Ibid., pp. 9–10.
23. Locke, *Two Treatises,* pp. 325, 371–372.
24. Ibid., pp. 406–407.
25. Locke, *Letter,* p. 54; Locke, *Essay,* p. 251.
26. Ibid., pp. 237, 241.
27. Ibid., pp. 263–265.
28. Ibid., pp. 43, 267, 268; John Locke, *The Conduct of the Understanding,* ed. Frances Garforth (New York: Teacher's College Press, 1960).
29. Cranston, *Locke,* p. 225.
30. Most of the American founders, like Locke, understand political liberty, self-government, as essentially a means to preserve personal liberty, not an end in itself. They nonetheless recognize and approve with qualifications the human desire for glory through participation in public affairs. See e.g. Jean Yarbrough, "Republicanism Reconsidered," *Review of Politics* 41 (January 1979): 61–95.
31. Locke, *Essay,* pp. 252–254.
32. Thomas Paine, *The Rights of Man,* ed. Henry Collins (Baltimore: Penguin Books, 1969), pp. 185–187; William Godwin, *Enquiry Concerning Political Justice,* ed. Isaac Kramnick (Baltimore: Penguin Books, 1976).
33. See Francis Wormuth, *The Origins of Modern Constitutionalism* (Cambridge: Harvard University Press, 1944), pp. 163, 214; Donald W. Hanson, *From Kingdom to Commonwealth* (Cambridge: Harvard University Press, 1970), p. 34. Cf. Charles Howard McIlwain, *Constitutionalism: Ancient and Modern,* rev. ed. (Ithaca: Cornell University Press, 1947); Locke, *Two Treatises,* pp. 309, 376; Hobbes, *Leviathan,* ch. 13.
34. Locke, *Letter,* pp. 47–48; Locke, *Two Treatises,* pp. 395, 402.
35. Ibid., pp. 446–449.
36. Ibid., pp. 374–375, 392; Hobbes, *Leviathan,* pp. 207–208, 232.
37. Locke, *Two Treatises,* pp. 367, 373–374, 399.
38. Ibid., p. 409.
39. Ibid., pp. 422, 448.
40. Edward S. Corwin, *The Higher Law Background of American Constitutional Law* (Ithaca: Cornell University Press, 1955), pp. 61–89; Marvin Meyers, ed., *The Mind of the Founder* (Indianapolis: Bobbs-Merrill, 1973); Merrill D. Peterson, ed. *The Portable Thomas Jefferson* (New York: Penguin Books, 1977); Samuel McKee and J. Harvie Williams, eds., *Papers on Public Credit, Commerce, and Finance* (Indianapolis: Bobbs-Merrill, 1934); George A. Peek, ed., *The Political Writings of John Adams* (Indianapolis: Bobbs-Merrill, 1954).

2. Problems and Criticisms

1. John Locke, *An Essay concerning Human Understanding,* ed. Peter Nidditch (Oxford: Clarendon Press, 1975), pp. 129–130, 229, 231; Thomas Hobbes, *Leviathan,* ed. C. B. Macpherson (Baltimore: Penguin Books, 1968), pp. 120, 189–192, 215–217, 270–272, 718–719; Locke, *Two Treatises on Government,* ed. Peter Laslett (New York: New American Library, 1965), p. 311.
2. Locke, *Two Treatises,* pp. 315, 396–397; Locke, *Essay,* pp. 53–54.

3. See e.g. John Locke, *The Reasonableness of Christianity* (Stanford: Stanford University Press, 1958), p. 67; Locke, *Essay,* pp. 691–695.

4. Locke, *Essay,* p. 352; Locke, *Two Treatises,* p. 313.

5. See e.g. Francis Hutcheson, *A Short Introduction to Moral Philosophy,* 3rd ed. (Glasgow, 1764), pp. 1–41.

6. David Hume, *A Treatise of Human Nature,* ed. L. A. Selby-Bigge (Oxford: Clarendon Press, 1968), pp. xx, 465–466, 471, 491, 493, 542–543, 549; Charles Hendel, ed., *David Hume's Political Essays* (Indianapolis: Bobbs-Merrill, 1953), p. 44.

7. Jeremy Bentham, "Anarchical Fallacies," in *The Works of Jeremy Bentham* (Edinburgh, 1843), II, 501; Bentham, "An Introduction to the Principles of Morals and Legislation," in Jeremy Bentham and John Stuart Mill, *The Utilitarians* (Garden City, N.Y.: Anchor Press, 1973), pp. 17, 300, 386; Hume, *Treatise,* p. 489; John Austin, *The Province of Jurisprudence Determined,* 2d ed. (London, 1861); Edgar Bodenheimer, *Jurisprudence,* rev. ed. (Cambridge: Harvard University Press, 1974), p. 43.

8. See Hutcheson, *Introduction;* Francis Hutcheson, *A System of Moral Philosophy* (New York: A. M. Kelley, 1968); Thomas Reid, *Essays on the Active Powers of Man* (New York: Garland Publications, 1977).

9. Hume, *Treatise,* p. 550; Hendel, *Essays,* pp. 16, 20, 45, 86, 117, 138.

10. Charles Everett, ed., *Jeremy Bentham* (Great Britain: Weidenfeld and Nicholson, 1969), pp. 234, 239, 243; Bentham and Mill, *The Utilitarians,* pp. 281–282, 301, 395.

11. Hobbes, *Leviathan,* pp. 192, 268.

12. Ibid., p. 232.

13. Ibid., p. 269.

14. Ibid., p. 231; Locke, *Two Treatises,* pp. 374–375, 392.

15. Ibid., pp. 392, 394, 402.

16. Ibid., pp. 400, 463.

17. Of course, it is now well-established that there are many ways in which even well-intentioned democratic electoral systems can produce results that do not accurately reflect popular preferences. See e.g. Kenneth Arrow, *Social Choice and Individual Values,* 2d ed. (New York: Wiley, 1963); A. K. Sen, *Collective Choice and Social Welfare* (San Francisco: Holden-Day, 1970); Dennis C. Mueller, *Public Choice* (New York: Cambridge University Press, 1979).

18. Locke, *Two Treatises,* pp. 375, 399–400.

19. Ibid., pp. 406–407, 418–420.

20. The classic analysis of this trend is, of course, Alexis de Tocqueville, *Democracy in America,* ed. J. P. Mayer (Garden City, N.Y.: Anchor Books, 1969).

21. Hobbes, *Leviathan,* p. 26; pt. 1, pp. 85–188.

22. Locke, *Essay,* pp. 259, 272.

23. Locke, *Two Treatises,* pp. 313, 374; Hobbes, *Leviathan,* p. 190.

24. See Hutcheson, *Introduction,* bk. 2, ch. 4; Jean-Jacques Burlamaqui, *Principles of Natural and Politic Law,* 2d ed. (London, 1763), I, 37, 42–43; William Blackstone, *Commentaries on the Laws of England* (Chicago: University

of Chicago Press, 1979), I, 43, 47; Baron de Montesquieu, *The Spirit of the Laws* (New York: Hafner Publishing, 1949), pp. 3–4; Edmund Burke, *Reflections on the Revolution in France* (Great Britain: Penguin, 1969), pp. 193–195, 300; Robert C. Tucker, ed., *The Marx-Engels Reader* (New York: W. W. Norton, 1972), pp. 40, 44, 72, 347.

25. Ernest Barker, ed., *The Politics of Aristotle* (Oxford: Oxford University Press, 1968), pp. 4–6.

26. Locke, *Two Treatises,* pp. 380–388; Hutcheson, *Introduction,* bk. 3, chs. 4–5; Burlamaqui, *Principles,* vol. II, pt. 1, chs. 2–4; Blackstone, *Commentaries,* pp. 47–48; Hume, *Treatise,* bk. 3, secs. 7–10.

27. I will not discuss further the criticism of the later empiricists and utilitarians, since this was a critique from "within" liberalism, meant to advance further the essentially liberal ends of intellectual progress, prosperity, security, and freedom. Nor will I examine another "internal" revision of liberalism, the moral idealism of Kant, which did maintain that the early liberals had not provided an adequately elevated moral vision; for despite this, Kant's practical political views were also much like Locke's. Immanuel Kant, "Idea for a Universal History from a Cosmopolitan Point of View," in *Kant on History,* ed. Lewis White Beck (Indianapolis: Bobbs-Merrill, 1963), p. 11; Kant, *Critique of Practical Reason* (Indianapolis: Bobbs-Merrill, 1956); Kant, *The Metaphysical Elements of Justice* (Indianapolis: Bobbs-Merrill, 1965). I will later consider a modern descendant of Kant's position, the contemporary "right to equal respect view." None of the critiques, moreover, represents the precise position of any individual theorist or philosophical school. Rather they distill from the wealth of attacks made on early liberalism basic criticisms that are common to otherwise diverse positions. Nonetheless, these admittedly abstracted critiques indicate intellectual trends across a wide range of political movements that arose in the aftermath of early liberalism. A number of actual political positions can be understood as particular combinations of the values that these critiques represent. The critiques thus describe not specific theories but rather basic, crosscutting intellectual movements that have affected American constitutionalism.

28. See Burke, *Reflections,* pp. 194–195; Jean-Jacques Rousseau, *The Social Contract* (Great Britain: Penguin Books, 1968).

29. Jean-Jacques Rousseau, *The First and Second Discourses,* ed. Roger Masters (New York: St. Martin's Press, 1964), pp. 48–51.

30. Ibid., pp. 52, 55–56, 58–59, 64.

31. Burke, *Reflections,* p. 194.

32. Rousseau, *Social Contract,* pp. 180, 185; Burke, *Reflections,* pp. 189–191.

33. Burke, *Reflections,* p. 373.

34. See e.g. John H. Schaar, *Legitimacy in the Modern State* (New Brunswick: Transaction Books, 1981); Richard Viguerie, *The New Right: We're Ready to Lead* (Falls Church, Va.: Viguerie, 1981).

35. Ralph Waldo Emerson, *Representative Men* (Boston, 1850), pp. 12–14; Emerson, *Essays,* 1st series (Boston, 1841), pp. 35–36, 45, 47, 52; *The Portable Emerson,* ed. Mark Van Doren (Kingsport, Tenn.: Viking Press, 1977), p. 35;

Henry David Thoreau, *Thoreau*, ed. Joseph Krutch (U.S.A.: Bantam Books, 1962), p. 97.

36. Van Doren, *Emerson*, pp. 625–626; Krutch, *Thoreau*, pp. 5, 356, 115.

37. Emerson, *Essays*, p. 71; Emerson, *Representative Men*, p. 32; Van Doren, *Emerson*, p. 112; Krutch, *Thoreau*, p. 260.

38. Emerson, *Essays*, p. 42; Van Doren, *Emerson*, pp. 195, 198; Krutch, *Thoreau* pp. 86, 104; Even Stanley Cavell, who lays unusual stress on Thoreau's sense of community membership and on *Walden* as a "tract of political education," agrees that Thoreau see the state as "not to be obeyed but, at best, to be abided," because "it is a great evil to make a stir about it." Stanley Cavell, *The Senses of Walden* (New York: Viking Press, 1972), pp. 84, 86.

39. Emerson, *Representative Men*, pp. 24–29; Van Doren, *Emerson*, pp. 40, 108.

40. Emerson, *Representative Men*, p. 36; Van Doren, *Emerson*, pp. 130, 199, 41; Krutch, *Thoreau*, p. 372.

41. H. S. Reiss, ed., *The Political Thought of the German Romantics* (Oxford: Basil Blackwell, 1955), pp. 3–4, 6–7, 9–10, 27; Siegbert Prawer, ed., *The Romantic Period in Germany* (New York: Schocken Books, 1970), pp. 5–6, 11; Peter Viereck, *Metapolitics: From the Romantics to Hitler* (New York: Alfred Knopf, 1941), pp. 18–19, 32–33.

42. Locke, *Two Treatises*, pp. 342–343.

43. Ibid., pp. 342–343, 387.

44. Ibid., pp. 339, 344; John Locke, "Some Considerations of the Consequences of the Lowering of Interest and Raising the Value of Money," *Works*, 12th ed. (London, 1824), IV, 11, 24–25.

45. Tucker, *Reader*, pp. 63, 336–337, 348–349; Robert Dahl, *After the Revolution* (New Haven: Yale University Press, 1970), pp. 114, 106.

46. Tucker, *Reader*, pp. 63, 336–337, 348–349.

47. John H. Schaar, "Equality of Opportunity, and Beyond," in *Nomox IX: Equality*, ed. J. R. Pennock and John Chapman (New York: Atherton Press, 1967), pp. 229, 235, 241, 245, 246, 248; J. R. Pennock, *Democratic Political Theory* (Princeton: Princeton University Press, 1979), pp. 442–443; Carole Pateman, *Participation and Democratic Theory* (Cambridge, Eng.: Cambridge University Press, 1970), pp. 20–21, ch. 2.

48. Ibid.; William Kelso, *American Democratic Theory* (Westport, Conn.: Greenwood Press, 1978), pp. 175–177; C. B. Macpherson, *The Life and Times of Liberal Democracy* (Oxford: Oxford University Press, 1973), p. 93; Herman Belz, "New Left Perspectives in the Academy," *Review of Politics* 36 (April 1974): 275.

Introduction to Part II

1. See pp. 48–49, 51, 54–55.

2. *Lochner* v. *New York*, 198 U.S. 45 (1905). This case is the conventional symbol for referring to the period, roughly 1890–1937, when the Supreme Court periodically struck down state and national regulatory and social welfare legis-

lation as violations of essential economic liberties and other constitutional guarantees.

3. Due Process and Concepts of Law

1. See e.g. Martin Shapiro, "Judicial Activism," in *The Third Century: America as a Post-Industrial Society,* ed. Seymour Martin Lipset (Stanford: Hoover Institution, 1979), p. 111; H. L. A. Hart, *The Concept of Law* (Oxford: Clarendon Press, 1961), pp. 156–157, 127; Ronald Dworkin, *Taking Rights Seriously* (Cambridge: Harvard University Press, 1978), pp. 14–45; Edward S. Corwin, *The "Higher Law" Background of American Constitutional Law* (Ithaca: Cornell University Press, 1955); Robert McCloskey, *The American Supreme Court* (Chicago: University of Chicago Press, 1961); Archibald Cox, *The Role of the Supreme Court in American Government* (New York: Oxford University Press, 1976), p. 113.

2. John Locke, *An Essay Concerning Human Understanding,* ed. Peter Nidditch (Oxford: Clarendon Press, 1975), pp. 263–264.

3. Corwin, *"Higher Law,"* pp. 75, 89; Thomas Grey, "Do We Have an Unwritten Constitution," *Stanford Law Review* 27 (February 1975): 703–718; Clinton Rossiter, ed., *The Federalist Papers* (New York: New American Library, 1961), pp. 317, 432, 469–470; Gary Jacobsohn, "Hamilton, Positivism, & the Constitution," *Polity* 14 (Fall 1981): 86–87.

4. Sir William Blackstone, *Commentaries on the Laws of England* (Chicago: University of Chicago Press, 1979), I, 41, 61, 118, 121–125; Duncan Kennedy, "The Structure of Blackstone's Commentaries," *Buffalo Law Review* 29 (Spring 1979): 217, 234–236; G. Edward White, *The American Judicial Tradition* (Oxford: Oxford University Press, 1976), pp. 8, 11, 13–16; Robert Faulkner, *The Jurisprudence of John Marshall* (Princeton: Princeton University Press, 1968); Robert Cover, *Justice Accused* (New Haven: Yale University Press, 1975), pp. 34, 125, 221. Justice Story argued explicitly that constitutional ambiguities should be resolved in ways "most consonant with the apparent objects" of the document, derived from its "spirit . . . not less than its letter," and indicated he understood these to be the "preservation" of individual "rights, and property, and liberty." Joseph Story, *Commentaries on the Constitution of the United States* (New York: Du Capo Press, 1970), I, 383, 396, 404, 406–407. A few judges suggested that legislative acts were void even if they violated no express provision but only the constitution's general spirit of natural rights. Those who so desired could often reach the same results through interpretation of uncertain statutory and constitutional purposes in light of natural law principles. See e.g. *Calder v. Bull,* 3 Dall. 386 (1798); *Fletcher v. Peck,* 6 Cranch 87 (1810).

5. Roberto Mangabeira Unger, *Knowledge and Politics* (New York: Free Press, 1975), p. 95. Unger's discussion of Locke is brief because, like many scholars, he views Locke and liberalism through the prism of Hobbes' more egoistic and anti-Christian psychology, thereby distorting, I think, liberalism's moral purposes. Taking the opposite extreme, John Dunn argues forcibly that Locke's attempt to provide standards ultimately had to rely on his religious faith.

See John Dunn, *The Political Thought of John Locke* (Cambridge, Eng.: Cambridge University Press, 1969).

6. Charles A. Miller, "The Forest of Due Process of Law: The American Constitutional Tradition," in *Nomos XVIII: Due Process,* ed. Roland Pennock and John Chapman (New York: New York University Press, 1977), pp. 4–7; Keith Jurow, "Untimely Thoughts: A Reconsideration of the Origins of Due Process," *American Journal of Legal History* 19 (October 1975); Corwin, *"Higher Law,"* pp. 30–32, 43–51, 54–55.

7. Blackstone, *Commentaries,* pp. 125–134. See also Miller, "Forest," pp. 6–11.

8. Miller, "Forest," pp. 3, 12–14.

9. *Murray's Lessee* v. *Hoboken Land and Improvement Co.,* 18 How. 272, 277 (1856). See also Miller, "Forest," pp. 12–16.

10. *Scott* v. *Sandford,* 19 How. 393, 450 (1857); Miller, "Forest," pp. 13–15.

11. *Slaughter-House Cases,* 16 Wall. 36 (1873); Field dissent at 96, 110, Bradley dissent at 118, 122. The privileges and immunities clause was used once for a majority's invalidation of state law, in *Colgate* v. *Harvey,* 296 U.S. 404 (1935). That decision, however, was overruled in *Madden* v. *Kentucky,* 309 U.S. 83 (1940).

12. *Davidson* v. *New Orleans,* 96 U.S. 97, 102, 104 (1878).

13. *Hurtado* v. *California,* 110 U.S. 516, 521, 532, 537 (1884); J. Harlan dissent at 547–548, 550.

14. See Benjamin Wright, *The Growth of American Constitutional Law* (Chicago: University of Chicago Press, 1967), pp. 102–105, 155–179; *Lochner* v. *New York,* 198 U.S. 45, 53, 57 (1905); *Coppage* v. *Kansas,* 236 U.S. 1, 17 (1915) (on permissible ends); *Weaver* v. *Palmer Brothers Co.,* 270 U.S. 402, 414 (1926) (on permissible means).

15. See e.g. Richard Hofstadter, *Social Darwinism in American Thought,* rev. ed. (Boston: Beacon Press, 1955); Robert McCloskey, *American Conservatism in the Age of Enterprise* (Cambridge: Harvard University Press, 1951); Miller, "Forest," p. 22; Loren Beth, *The Development of the American Constitution, 1877–1901* (New York: Harper Torchbooks, 1971).

16. See *Chicago, Burlington & Quincy Railroad* v. *Chicago,* 166 U.S. 226 (1897) at 234–236. Cf. *Maxwell* v. *Dow,* 176 U.S. 581 (1900); Richard Cortner, *The Supreme Court and the Second Bill of Rights* (Madison: University of Wisconsin Press, 1981), pp. 24–37.

17. *Twining* v. *New Jersey,* 211 U.S. 78, 98–99 (1908).

18. *Powell* v. *Alabama,* 287 U.S. 45, 73 (1932). The incorporation of free speech rights came in *Gitlow* v. *New York,* 268 U.S. 652, 666 (1925).

19. See e.g. Harlan's opinions in *Malloy* v. *Hogan,* 378 U.S. 1 (1964) at 27–28; *Duncan* v. *Louisiana,* 391 U.S. 145 (1968) at 171; *Palko* v. *Connecticut,* 302 U.S. 319, 321, 324–326 (1937).

20. See Wilfred Rumble, *American Legal Realism* (Ithaca: Cornell University Press, 1968); William Twining, *Karl Llewellyn and the Realist Movement* (Lon-

don: Weidenfeld and Nicolson, 1973); Felix Cohen, "Transcendental Nonsense and the Functional Approach," *Columbia Law Review* 35 (June 1935): 809–849; Mark DeWolfe Howe, *Justice Oliver Wendell Holmes: The Shaping Years* (Cambridge: Harvard University Press, 1957), p. 69; Paul Rosen, *The Supreme Court and Social Science* (Urbana: University of Illinois Press, 1972), pp. 156–157; Roscoe Pound, "Liberty of Contract," *Yale Law Journal* 18 (May 1909): 464; Pound, "Mechanical Jurisprudence," *Columbia Law Review* 8 (December 1908): 609; Karl Llewellyn, "The Constitution as an Institution," *Columbia Law Review* 34 (January 1934): 7–10.

21. O. W. Holmes, "The Path of the Law," *Harvard Law Review* 10 (March 25, 1897): 470; Pound, "Liberty of Contract," p. 470; Pound, "Mechanical Jurisprudence," pp. 606–607; Llewellyn, "Constitution as an Institution," pp. 31–35; John Dewey, *Reconstruction in Philosophy*, rev. ed. (Boston: Beacon Press, 1957), pp. 180–183; Grant Gilmore, "Legal Realism: Its Cause and Cure," *Yale Law Journal* 70 (June 1961): 1037–1038; Holmes, "Path of the Law," p. 468.

22. See Cohen, "Transcendental Nonsense"; Morton White, *Social Thought in America: The Revolt Against Formalism* (Boston: Beacon Press, 1957); Edward Purcell, *The Crisis of Democratic Theory* (Lexington: University of Kentucky Press, 1973), pp. 206–210; White, *Judicial Tradition*, p. 159; Pound, "Liberty of Contract"; *Whitney v. California*, 274 U.S. 357, 375 (1927); James Bradley Thayer, "The Origin and Scope of the American Doctrine of Constitutional Law," *Harvard Law Review* 7 (October 25, 1893): 129; Holmes, "Path of the Law," p. 468; Nancy Rosenblum, *Bentham's Theory of the Modern State* (Cambridge: Harvard University Press, 1978), pp. 146, 150; John Austin, *The Province of Jurisprudence Determined*, 2d ed. (London: J. Murray, 1861), p. 222.

23. See *Nebbia v. New York*, 291 U.S. 502 (1934); *West Coast Hotel v. Parrish*, 300 U.S. 379, 399 (1937); *United States v. Carolene Products Co.*, 304 U.S. 144 (1938); *Williamson v. Lee Optical Co.*, 348 U.S. 483 (1955).

24. Purcell, *Crisis*, pp. 267–268.

25. See e.g. *Dennis v. United States*, 341 U.S. 494 (1951) at 524, 525; *Kovacs v. Cooper*, 336 U.S. 77 (1945) at 95–96.

26. See Alfred Kelly, "Clio and the Court: An Illicit Love Affair," *The Supreme Court Review, 1965* (Chicago: University of Chicago Press, 1966), p. 129; Morton Horwitz, "The Jurisprudence of Brown and the Dilemmas of Liberalism," *Harvard Civil Rights–Civil Liberties Law Review* 14 (Fall 1979): 600–601; *U.S. v. Carolene Products* at 152–153n4.

27. See e.g. *Powell v. Alabama; Brown v. Mississippi*, 297 U.S. 278 (1936); *Spano v. New York*, 360 U.S. 315 (1959).

28. *Adamson v. California*, 332 U.S. 46 (1947) at 58–59, 68–70.

29. Ibid.

30. Ibid. at 63, 65.

31. Ibid. at 67, 124.

32. *Wolf v. Colorado*, 338 U.S. 25 (1949); *Rochin v. California*, 342 U.S. 165 (1952); *Irvine v. California*, 347 U.S. 128 (1954) at 132, 133, 145.

33. *Mapp* v. *Ohio,* 367 U.S. 643, 656, 684 (1961).

34. *Duncan* v. *Louisiana,* 391 U.S. 145, 148–149 (1968); *In Re Winship,* 397 U.S. 358 (1970).

35. For Brennan's "slow strangulation" characterizations, see *United States* v. *Peltier,* 422 U.S. 531 (1975) at 561; *United States* v. *Janis,* 428 U.S. 433 (1976) at 460. For Powell's opposition to full incorporation, see e.g. his concurrence in both *Johnson* v. *Louisiana,* 406 U.S. 356 (1972), and *Apodaca* v. *Oregon,* 406 U.S. 404 (1977) at 369–370, 375. Since the late 1960s, the Court has increasingly engaged in a further sort of procedural due process adjudication, deciding when special procedures (usually hearings) are required before governmental agencies execute various administrative actions, such as terminating employment or welfare benefits or altering the conditions of confinement for prisoners or mental patients. To avoid imposing too many procedural requirements on governmental bodies, the Burger Court began in *Board of Regents* v. *Roth,* 408 U.S. 564 (1972), to undertake largely novel inquiries into whether litigants in particular cases actually possessed due process "liberty" or "property" interests that the governmental action would adversely affect. These inquiries have reproduced the clash between higher and positive law approaches in a different form. Justice Rehnquist has urged the Court to define liberty and property interests, and the procedures they require, entirely by reference to statutory provisions and explicit guarantees in the Bill of Rights. *Arnett* v. *Kennedy,* 416 U.S. 134 (1974); *Paul* v. *Davis,* 424 U.S. 693 (1976). But as in the fundamental fairness due process cases, here too the Court prefers to include basic but nontextual ideals contained in American legal and social traditions as sources of due process liberty and property claims. See e.g. *Bell* v. *Wolfish,* 441 U.S. 520 (1979); *Vitek* v. *Jones,* 445 U.S. 480 (1980); *Logan* v. *Zimmerman Brush Co.,* 455 U.S. 422, 433–437 (1982).

36. The Supreme Court, especially in the later Warren years, gave more weight to egalitarian claims under the equal protection clause while pursuing First Amendment protection more unequivocally. Its increased concern for criminal rights was part of its new egalitarianism. See e.g. Archibald Cox, *The Warren Court* (Cambridge: Harvard University Press, 1968). But romantic concerns for personal autonomy also motivated the Warren Court's jurisprudence. See Smith, "Autonomy," pp. 175–205. These autonomy concerns were evident in its procedural due process decisions. For example, the Court explicitly reinterpreted the Fourth Amendment's ban on unreasonable searches and seizures to replace an inherited emphasis on protecting property rights with Brandeis's view that the amendment was concerned with personal privacy. *Warden* v. *Hayden,* 387 U.S. 294 (1967); *Katz* v. *United States,* 389 U.S. 347 (1967). The Court similarly indicated that the Fifth Amendment's protection against self-incrimination was aimed at protecting the individual's "right to be let alone." *Tehan* v. *United States ex rel. Shott,* 382 U.S. 406, 416 (1966). Furthermore, following the nineteenth century pattern, this theme in the Court's procedural activism came only after the Court had overtly revived substantive due process in 1965 in order to provide more wide-ranging protection for its new constitutional "right of privacy." Hence, both egalitarian and romantic values characterized the expansion of due process rights following *Mapp.*

37. See Eugene Rostow, *The Sovereign Prerogative* (New Haven: Yale University Press, 1962), pp. 124–126; McCloskey, *American Supreme Court*, p. 182; Richard Kluger, *Simple Justice* (New York: Vintage Books, 1978), pp. 226–228, 239; Michael Walzer, *Radical Principles: Reflections of an Unreconstructed Democrat* (New York: Basic Books, 1980), ch. 1.

38. See e.g. *Dennis v. United States,* 341 U.S. 494 (1951); Grant Gilmore, *The Ages of American Law* (New Haven: Yale University Press, 1972), pp. 105, 146; Jerold Auerbach, *Unequal Justice* (New York: Oxford University Press, 1976), p. 261; Leonard Levy, ed., *Judicial Review and the Supreme Court* (New York: Harper Torchbooks, 1967).

39. Alexander Bickel, *The Least Dangerous Branch* (Indianapolis: Bobbs-Merrill, 1962), p. 24.

40. *Sweezy v. New Hampshire,* 354 U.S. 234 (1957) at 255–267; Bickel, *Least Dangerous Branch,* pp. 111–198, 236–237; *Poe v. Ullmann,* 367 U.S. 497 (1961) at 551–552; *Gray v. Sanders,* 372 U.S. 368 (1963) at 381; *Griswold v. Connecticut,* 381 U.S. 479 (1965) at 493–495; Kelly, "Clio and the Court," pp. 134–135; Charles Miller, *The Supreme Court and the Uses of History* (Cambridge: Harvard University Press, 1969), pp. 141–142; Rogers M. Smith, "Constitutional Interpretation and Political Theory," *Polity* 15 (Summer 1983): 492–505.

41. Harlan thus gave fundamental fairness a substantive significance Frankfurter was unwilling to embrace. Bickel strove for a middle ground: he agreed with Harlan that such substantive rights sometimes had to be defended under due process, but he thought, with Frankfurter, that the activism Harlan urged in *Poe v. Ullmann* was premature. Bickel, *Least Dangerous Branch,* pp. 42, 143–156. *Griswold v. Connecticut,* 381 U.S. 479 (1965) at 500, 501, 508, 519, 522.

42. See *Roe v. Wade,* 410 U.S. 113, 164, 165 (1973); *Moore v. City of East Cleveland,* 431 U.S. 494, 501–503 (1977); *Youngberg v. Romeo,* 73 L. Ed. 2d (1982). Despite the Burger Court's general reliance on an historical "fundamental values" approach, some overt appeals to higher law still appear. Thus the maverick Justice Stevens invoked "cardinal inalienable" rights with which "all men are endowed by their creator." *Meachum v. Fano,* 427 U.S. 215 (1976) at 230.

43. See e.g. *Moore v. City of E. Cleveland,* 431 U.S. 494 (1977) (upholding rights of extended families to live together despite contrary zoning ordinances); *Village of Belle Terra v. Boraas,* 416 U.S. 1 (1974) (ruling against unrelated students faced by similar zoning restrictions, adopted to further "family values"); *Zablocki v. Redhail,* 434 U.S. 374 (1978) (deeming the right to marry "fundamental" at 384); *Hollenbaugh v. Carnegie Free Library,* 439 U.S. 1052 (1978) (sustaining dismissal of adulterous library employees). See also *Doe v. Commonwealth's Attorney,* 425 U.S. 901 (1976) (affirming dismissal of homosexual challenge to Virginia sodomy law); *Warden v. Hayden,* 387 U.S. at 325; *Katz* at 360–361; *Smith v. Maryland,* 442 U.S. 735, 740–741, 750–751 (1979); *Rawlings v. Kentucky,* 448 U.S. 98 (1980); *Rakas v. Illinois,* 439 U.S. 128, 156 (1978).

44. Dworkin, *Taking Rights Seriously,* pp. 56–57, 8–13, 149. See also David

Richards, "Human Rights and the Moral Foundations of the Substantive Criminal Law," *Georgia Law Review* 13 (Summer 1979): 1395–1446.

45. Rostow, *Sovereign Prerogative,* pp. 78, 117, 122–123, 151–152, 160–161, 168, 173; Charles Black, *The People and the Court* (New York: Macmillan, 1960), pp. 52–55, 94–95, 103, 106, 146, 178, 183, 219.

46. John Hart Ely, *Democracy and Distrust* (Cambridge: Harvard University Press, 1980), pp. 21, 73, 96, 97, 172–173, 221; Ely, "The Wages of Crying Wolf," *Yale Law Journal* 82 (April 1973): 920.

47. Ely, *Democracy and Distrust,* pp. 76–77, 82; Ely, "Constitutional Interpretivism: Its Allure and Impossibility," *Indiana Law Journal* 53 (Spring 1978): 399, 405–408. See also Ely, "Democracy and the Right to Be Different" and "Commentary," in "Symposium: Constitutional Adjudication and Democratic Theory," *New York University Law Review* 56 (May–June 1981): 399, 401, 540.

48. Alexander Bickel, *The Supreme Court and the Idea of Progress* (New York: Harper and Row, 1970), pp. 99, 108, 138, 174; Bickel, *The Morality of Consent* (New Haven: Yale University Press, 1975), pp. 4–5, 18, 123.

49. Bickel, *Morality of Consent,* pp. 18, 24, 77.

4. Freedom of Speech

1. See John Milton, *Areopagitica,* ed. John Hales (Oxford: Oxford University Press, 1961), esp. pp. 51–52; Benedict de Spinoza, *A Theologico-Political Treatise and A Political Treatise,* trans. R. H. M. Elwes (New York: Dorr Publications, 1951), esp. pp. 5–6, 190–199, 257–266; John Locke, *A Letter Concerning Toleration* (Indianapolis: Bobbs-Merrill, 1955), pp. 45–46; Locke, *An Essay Concerning Human Understanding,* ed. Peter Nidditch (Oxford: Clarendon Press, 1975), pp. 642, 646–647; Leonard Levy, *Legacy of Suppression* (Cambridge: Harvard University Press, 1960), pp. 100–102.

2. Locke, *Essay,* p. 45.

3. Locke, *Essay,* pp. 268, 279–282.

4. Spinoza, *Treatise,* pp. 259, 261, 263; Milton, *Areopagitica,* p. 54; Levy, *Legacy,* p. 97.

5. Merrill Peterson, ed., *The Portable Thomas Jefferson* (New York: Penguin Books, 1977), pp. 253, 211–212; Marvin Meyers, ed., *The Mind of the Founder* (Indianapolis: Bobbs-Merrill, 1973), pp. 10, 14.

6. See Bernard Bailyn, *The Ideological Origins of the American Revolution* (Cambridge: Harvard University Press, 1967), pp. 35–36; David Jacobson, ed., *The English Libertarian Heritage* (Indianapolis: Bobbs-Merrill, 1965), pp. 31, 38–42, 130, 131, 133, 172; Levy, *Legacy,* pp. 116–121.

7. Ibid., pp. 176–177, 258–283, 297–309; Clinton Rossiter, ed., *The Federalist Papers* (New York: New American Library, 1961), pp. 81–82; Walter Berns, "Freedom of the Press and the Alien and Sedition Acts," *The Supreme Court Review, 1970* (Chicago: University of Chicago Press, 1971).

8. For example, obscenity restraints, a relatively late eighteenth century development in English law, were not much enforced in America until the early

nineteenth century. Then, however, the English common law offense, state legislation, and federal actions restraining the importation and mailing of obscenity were adopted. Alec Craig, *Suppressed Books* (Cleveland: World Publishing, 1963), pp. 22–23, 26, 127–128; David Rabban, "The First Amendment in Its Forgotten Years," *Yale Law Journal* 90 (January 1981): 524, 527; *Robertson v. Baldwin,* 165 U.S. 275 (1897) at 281.

9. Rabban, "Forgotten Years," pp. 543–549, 562–563; Zechariah Chafee, *Free Speech in the United States,* rev. ed. (New York: Atheneum Press, 1969), pp. 24–28, 49–51; Laurence Tribe, *American Constitutional Law* (Mineola, N.Y.: Foundation Press, 1978), p. 688. Even the leading opponent of obscenity suppression at the time, Theodore Schroeder, shared the liberal concern that the emotional nature of such materials would prevent rational deliberation on their permissibility. Theodore Schroeder, *"Obscene" Literature and Constitutional Law* (New York: Da Capo Press, 1972), pp. 24–32.

10. John Stuart Mill, *Three Essays* (London: Oxford University Press, 1975), pp. 9, 16, 134–139.

11. Ibid., pp. 26, 30, 36–37.

12. Ibid., pp. 28, 42, 141.

13. Ibid., pp. 18, 71, 73.

14. Ibid., pp. 77, 79, 84.

15. Geraint Williams, ed., *J. S. Mill on Politics and Society* (Glasgow: Fontana Press, 1976), p. 121; John Dewey, *Liberalism and Social Action* (New York: Capricorn Books, 1963), p. 23; Robert Paul Wolff, *The Poverty of Liberalism* (Boston: Beacon Press, 1968), p. 38; Mill, *Essays,* pp. 77, 82.

16. *Schenck v. United States,* 249 U.S. 47 (1919).

17. *Schenck* at 52; *Frohwerk v. United States,* 249 U.S. 204 (1919); *Debs v. United States,* 249 U.S. 211 (1919).

18. *Abrams v. United States,* 250 U.S. 616 (1919) at 620, 624.

19. Ibid. at 627; *Patterson v. Colorado,* 205 U.S. 454 (1907); Gerald Gunther, "Learned Hand and the Origins of Modern First Amendment Doctrine: Some Fragments of History," *Stanford Law Review* 27 (Fall 1975): 719; G. Edward White, *The American Judicial Tradition* (Oxford: Oxford University Press, 1976), pp. 150–177.

20. *Abrams* at 630; Chafee, *Free Speech,* p. 86.

21. *Gitlow v. New York,* 268 U.S. 652 (1925) at 673, 669.

22. *Whitney v. California,* 274 U.S. 357 (1927) at 374, 375; Max Lerner, "The Social Thought of Mr. Justice Brandeis," in *Mr. Justice Brandeis,* ed. Felix Frankfurter (New Haven: Yale University Press, 1932), pp. 11, 24, 41–42: Alpheus T. Mason, *Brandeis—A Free Man's Life* (New York: Viking Press, 1946), p. 39; Samuel Warren and Louis Brandeis, "The Right to Privacy," *Harvard Law Review* 4 (December 15, 1890): 193–220; *Olmstead v. United States,* 277 U.S. 438 (1928) at 478.

23. *Whitney* at 376–378.

24. *Herndon v. Lowry,* 301 U.S. 242 (1937); *Cantwell v. Connecticut,* 310 U.S. 296 (1940) at 311. For examples of symbolic speech cases during this period, see *Stromberg v. California,* 283 U.S. 359 (1931); *Minersville School District v.*

Gobitis, 310 U.S. 596 (1940); *W. Virginia Bd. of Education* v. *Barnette,* 319 U.S. 624 (1941). For national security cases, see *Fiske* v. *Kansas,* 294 U.S. 380 (1927); *DeJonge* v. *Oregon,* 299 U.S. 353 (1937); *Herndon* v. *Lowry,* 301 U.S. 242 (1937). For fair trial cases, see *Bridges* v. *California,* 314 U.S. 152 (1941); *Pennekamp* v. *Florida,* 328 U.S. 331 (1946); *Craig* v. *Harney,* 331 U.S. 367 (1947). On picketing, see *Thornhill* v. *Alabama,* 310 U.S. 88 (1940); *Giboney* v. *Empire Storage and Ice Co.,* 336 U.S. 490 (1949). On commercial speech, see *Valentine* v. *Chrestensen,* 316 U.S. 52 (1942). For public order cases, see *Lovell* v. *Griffin,* 303 U.S. 444 (1938); *Cox* v. *New Hampshire,* 312 U.S. 569 (1941); *Prince* v. *Massachusetts,* 321 U.S. 158 (1944); *Saia* v. *New York,* 334 U.S. 558 (1948); *Kovacs* v. *Cooper,* 336 U.S. 77 (1949); *Kunz* v. *New York,* 340 U.S. 290 (1951); *Feiner* v. *New York,* 340 U.S. 315 (1951).

25. See Frank Strong, "Fifty Years of 'Clear and Present Danger,' " *The Supreme Court Review, 1969* (Chicago: University of Chicago Press, 1970); *Cox* v. *New Hampshire; Chaplinsky* v. *New Hampshire,* 315 U.S. 568 (1942); *Valentine* v. *Chrestensen,* 316 U.S. 52 (1942).

26. See *Dennis* v. *United States,* 341 U.S. 494 (1951); *Slochower* v. *Bd. of Higher Education,* 350 U.S. 551 (1956); *Lerner* v. *Casey,* 357 U.S. 468 (1958); *Watkins* v. *U.S.,* 354 U.S. 178 (1957); *Sweezy* v. *New Hampshire,* 354 U.S. 234 (1957); *Uphaus* v. *Wyman,* 360 U.S. 72 (1959); *Barenblatt* v. *United States,* 360 U.S. 109 (1959).

27. *Yates* v. *United States,* 354 U.S. 298 (1957); *Scales* v. *United States,* 367 U.S. 203 (1961); *Noto* v. *United States,* 367 U.S. 290 (1961).

28. *Dennis* v. *United States* at 524–525, 552.

29. Ibid. at 508–509; John Locke, *Two Treatises of Government,* ed. Peter Laslett (New York: New American Library), pp. 467–468, 476–477.

30. *Dennis* at 501; Locke, *Two Treatises,* p. 448; Declaration of Independence, para. 2 (1776).

31. Alexander Meiklejohn, *Political Freedom* (New York: Harper Bros., 1960), pp. 79, 102–104; Henry Abraham, *Freedom and the Court,* 3d ed. (Oxford: Oxford University Press, 1977), pp. 240–242.

32. *Scales* v. *United States,* 367 U.S. 203 (1961); *Noto* v. *United States,* 367 U.S. 290 (1961); *Aptheker* v. *Secretary of State,* 378 U.S. 500 (1964); *U.S.* v. *Robel,* 898 U.S. 258 (1967); *Cramp* v. *Bd. of Public Education,* 368 U.S. 278 (1961); *Keyishan* v. *Bd. of Regents,* 385 U.S. 589 (1967); *Gibson* v. *Florida Legislative Investigating Committee,* 372 U.S. 539 (1963); *DeGregory* v. *New Hampshire,* 383 U.S. 825 (1966); *NAACP* v. *Alabama,* 357 U.S. 449 (1958) at 460.

33. *Roth* v. *United States,* 354 U.S. 476 (1957) at 481, 484, 487, 489, 508.

34. *New York Times* v. *Sullivan,* 376 U.S. 254 (1964) at 273, 279–280, 293; *Curtis Publishing Co.* v. *Butts* and *Associated Press* v. *Walker,* 388 U.S. 130 (1967); Abraham, *Freedom and the Court,* p. 242.

35. Thomas Emerson, *The System of Freedom of Expression* (New York: Random House, 1970), pp. 6–7; Emerson, *Towards a General Theory of the First Amendment* (New York: Random House, 1970, p. 1); Emerson, "First Amendment Doctrine and the Burger Court," *California Law Review* 68 (May

1980): 443; Emerson, "Colonial Intentions and Current Realities of the First Amendment," *University of Pennsylvania Law Review* 125 (April 1977): 738, 749. Emerson still maintains there that the founders' views were "essentially the same" as those of Brandeis.

36. *Memoirs* v. *Massachusetts*, 383 U.S. 413, 418 (1966); *Redrup* v. *New York*, 386 U.S. 767 (1967).

37. *Stanley* v. *Georgia*, 394 U.S. 557 (1969) at 564–565.

38. *United States* v. *Reidel*, 402 U.S. 351 (1971); Marshall Berman, *The Politics of Authenticity* (New York: Atheneum Press, 1970), pp. x, 312–317; *Cohen* v. *California*, 403 U.S. 15 (1971) at 16, 26.

39. See *Gooding* v. *Wilson*, 405 U.S. 518 (1972); *Rosenfeld* v. *New Jersey*, 408 U.S. 901 (1972); *Lewis* v. *New Orleans*, 408 U.S. 913 (1972); *Brown* v. *Oklahoma*, 408 U.S. 914 (1972).

40. *Miller* v. *California*, 413 U.S. 15 (1973) at 24; *Paris Adult Theatre I* v. *Slaton*, 413 U.S. 49 (1973) at 73, 83.

41. *Paris Adult Theatre* at 59–61, 63, 67.

42. Ibid. at 59–60, 69; *Jenkins* v. *Georgia*, 418 U.S. 153 (1974); *Schad* v. *Boro of Mt. Ephraim*, 452 U.S. 61 (1981).

43. In 1982, the Court defined an important further exception to this insistence on content neutrality when it designated visual child pornography a form of expression that governments could restrict even if the materials could not be judged obscene under the *Miller* standard. The Court stressed, however, that the *Miller* approach was not being abandoned. It was simply too restrictive of the state's compelling interest in preventing the use of children to produce pornographic materials. (Only films, photographs, or live visual displays of sexual conduct by children were forbidden by the law, not fictional literary accounts.) The Court accepted that this aim could practically be achieved only by curbing the distribution of the materials thus produced. Although Justice White's opinion for the Court cited *Chaplinsky* and Justice Stevens on the permissibility of content-based restrictions, only the close connection between this form of expression and the performance of acts deemed harmful to children permitted this content to be restrained. Hence this decision did not represent a major departure from the general stance of content neutrality. See *New York* v. *Ferber*, 458 U.S. 747 (1982).

44. *Young* v. *American Mini Theatres*, 427 U.S. 50 (1976); *FCC* v. *Pacifica Foundation*, 438 U.S. 726 (1978). In each case Justice Stevens' opinion had a majority only for its holding, not for his two-tiered reasoning; four justices dissented each time, and Justice Powell wrote concurring opinions dissociating himself from Stevens' content-conscious approach.

45. *Virginia State Board of Pharmacy* v. *Virginia Citizens Consumer Council*, 425 U.S. 748 (1976).

46. Ibid. at 771; *Linmark Associates, Inc.* v. *Willingboro*, 431 U.S. 85 (1977); *Ohralik* v. *Ohio State Bar Association*, 437 U.S. 447 (1978) at 456; *Friedman* v. *Rogers*, 440 U.S. 1 (1979); *Central Hudson Gas* v. *Public Service Commission*, 447 U.S. 557 (1980); *Metromedia, Inc.* v. *San Diego*, 453 U.S. 490 (1981); *Bolger* v. *Youngs Drug Products Corp.*, 77 L. Ed. 2d 469 (1983); T. H. Jackson,

and J. C. Jeffries, Jr., "Commerical Speech: Economic Due Process and the First Amendment," *Virginia Law Review* 65 (Fall 1979): 1–41; Archibald Cox, *Freedom of Expression* (Cambridge: Harvard University Press, 1981), pp. 32–48.

47. *First National Bank of Boston* v. *Bellotti,* 435 U.S. 765 (1978) at 776–777, 804–805, 809–810.

48. See e.g. *Buckley* v. *Valeo,* 424 U.S. 1 (1976); *Citizens Against Rent Control* v. *Berkeley,* 454 U.S. 290 (1981); *Gertz* v. *Robert Welch, Inc.,* 418 U.S. 323 (1974); *Hutchinson* v. *Proxmire,* 443 U.S. 111 (1979); *Branzburg* v. *Hayes,* 408 U.S. 665 (1972); *Zurcher* v. *Stanford Daily,* 436 U.S. 547 (1978); *Houchins* v. *KQED, INC.,* 438 U.S. 1 (1978).

49. Cox, *Freedom of Expression,* pp. 19, 88; Emerson, "First Amendment Doctrine and the Burger Court," p. 440.

50. See Cox, *Freedom of Expression,* p. 34; Norman Dorsen and Joel Gora, "The Burger Court and Freedom of Speech," in *The Burger Court,* ed. Vincent Blasi (New Haven: Yale University Press, 1983), pp. 30–41.

51. For a democratic relativism that takes the tack of protecting only narrowly political speech to avoid unbounded First Amendment claims, see Robert Bork, "Neutral Principles and Some First Amendment Problems," *Indiana Law Journal* 47 (Fall 1971): 20, 25.

52. Ralph Waldo Emerson, "Self-Reliance," *Essays,* first series (Boston, 1841), p. 42; Emerson, "First Amendment Doctrine," p. 426; Edwin C. Baker, "Scope of the First Amendment Freedom of Speech," *U.C.L.A. Law Review* 25 (June 1978): 974, 986, 991, 997–1005; Mill, "On Liberty," pp. 15–16, 77; Emerson, *System,* pp. 17–18; Tribe, *American Constitutional Law,* pp. 576–588, 598–601.

53. See Alexander Bickel, *The Morality of Consent* (New Haven: Yale University Press, 1975), esp. ch. 1.

54. See e.g. Baker, "Scope of the First Amendment," p. 985.

5. Voting Apportionment

1. See e.g. *Reynolds* v. *Sims,* 377 U.S. 533 (1964) at 554.

2. See, e.g., Robert McKay, *Reapportionment: The Law and Politics of Equal Representation* (New York: The Twentieth Century Fund, 1965), p. 21; Robert G. Dixon, *Democratic Representation: Reapportionment in Law and Practice* (New York: Oxford University Press, 1968), p. 44 (ascribing to Locke an "untrammelled majoritarianism"), cf. p. 30 (the partial recognition of Locke's distance from this position); John Locke, *Two Treatises of Government,* ed. Peter Laslett (New York: New American Library, 1965), pp. 419–420. If one largely abandons geographical considerations, it might be possible to create districts equal both in population and wealth; but it seems likely that Locke would have been satisfied with representation assigned to reflect both the wealth and numbers of traditional geographical districts.

3. See *Wesberry* v. *Sanders,* 376 U.S. 1 (1964); Clinton Rossiter, ed., *The Federalist Papers* (New York: New American Library, 1961), pp. 326, 336, 340, 355, 377; McKay, *Reapportionment,* pp. 92–93.

4. Rossiter, ed., *Federalist Papers,* pp. 339, 355.

5. Ibid., pp. 81, 317, 432.

6. Rossiter, ed., *Federalist Papers*, pp. 79, 81, 85, 89–90, 211–216, 324, 342, 412–413, 423–424, 432, 469–471; *Gray v. Saunders*, 372 U.S. 368 (1963) at 377. For different characterizations of the *Federalist's* view of representation, see e.g. Robert Dahl, *A Preface to Democratic Theory* (Chicago: University of Chicago Press, 1956), pp. 4–33; Garry Wills, *Explaining America* (Garden City, N.Y.: Doubleday, 1981), pp. 179–264. For a view that stresses the *Federalist's* effort to create a religiously tolerant commercial nation with consequent restraints on the nature of the diverse interests represented, see Martin Diamond, "Democracy and the *Federalist*," *American Political Science Review* 53 (March 1959): 52–68.

7. On Jacksonian reforms, see Dixon, *Democratic Representation*, pp. 42–43. On later developments, see Fernando Padilla and Bruce Gross, "Judicial Power and Reapportionment," *Idaho Law Review* 15 (Spring 1979): 279; J. R. Pole, *The Pursuit of Equality in American History* (Berkeley: University of California Press, 1978), pp. 89, 144–146, 209, 215–216; Ward Elliott, *The Rise of Guardian Democracy* (Cambridge: Harvard University Press, 1974), pp. 38–43, 90–96, 330. The framers of the Fourteenth Amendment did not consciously intend application of the equal protection clause to reapportionment. See William Van Alstyne, "The Fourteenth Amendment, the 'Right' to Vote, and the Understanding of the Thirty-Ninth Congress," *The Supreme Court Review, 1965* (Chicago: University of Chicago Press, 1966); Raoul Berger, *Government by Judiciary* (Cambridge: Harvard University Press, 1977), chs. 2, 3. While the Amendment's framers clearly countenanced unequal apportionments, they would surely have subscribed, at least in principle, to a political egalitarianism as extensive as that of their leader, Abraham Lincoln. Lincoln stood in principle for a truly equal voice for all the governed, defending the "moral claim to political equality" that Harry Jaffa sees embedded in the Fourteenth and Fifteenth Amendments. This moral claim could be limited for a time if full equality endangered the rights of all, but legitimate policy had to pursue its realization. Harry Jaffa, *Crisis of the House Divided* (Garden City, N.Y.: Doubleday, 1959), esp. p. 375.

8. Dixon, *Democratic Representation*, pp. 60–78, 82. The extent to which congressional districts were actually equal in population remains unclear. The chief concern of congressional apportioners was traditionally the number of representatives assigned to each state; intrastate district equality was a secondary concern. The issue of interstate assignments of representatives has not been adjudicated, and I will not pursue it here, for no approach to interstate representation can fulfill one person, one vote unless intrastate district equality is also required. See Michael Balinski and H. Peyton Young, *Fair Representation* (New Haven: Yale University Press, 1982), pp. 1, 17–18, 32, 37–40, 51, 56–57, 76–77, 85.

9. See Dixon, *Democratic Representation*, pp. 83, 91; Elliott, *Guardian Democracy*, pp. 91–93, 95–96; McKay, *Reapportionment*, pp. 27, 29; *Wood v. Broom*, 287 U.S. 1 (1932).

10. *Colegrove v. Green*, 328 U.S. 549 (1946) at 554–556; *Baker v. Carr*, 369 U.S. 186 (1962) at 300.

11. See Elliott, *Guardian Democracy*, pp. 77–81; *Colegrove* at 566. In *Cole-*

grove the Court was temporarily understaffed because Chief Justice Stone had recently died and Justice Robert Jackson was serving as Chief Prosecutor at the Nuremberg Trials.

12. See e.g. Gordon E. Baker, *Rural Versus Urban Political Power* (New York: Random House, 1963); Anthony Lewis, "Legislative Reapportionment and the Federal Courts," *Harvard Law Review* 71 (April 1958): 1057–1098; Elliott, *Guardian Democracy*, pp. 13–14, 109–111, 218; *Gomillion* v. *Lightfoot,* 364 U.S. 339 (1960).

13. *Baker* v. *Carr* at 198, 217, 226.

14. Ibid. at 244–245, 254, 258–259; Dixon, *Democratic Representation,* pp. 250–255. Douglas would soon advance instead the more absolutist approach of *Gray* v. *Sanders.*

15. *Baker* at 268, 269, 300.

16. *Gray* v. *Sanders* at 379–381.

17. The broad implications of this holding have been well captured in Jonathan Still, "Political Equality and Election Systems," *Ethics* 91 (April 1981): 388–390.

18. *Wesberry* at 15–17; Alfred Kelly, "Clio and the Court: An Illicit Love Affair," *The Supreme Court Review, 1965* (Chicago: University of Chicago Press, 1966), p. 119; Dixon, *Democratic Representation*, pp. 182–195.

19. *Reynolds* v. *Sims* at 533, 560–561.

20. Ibid. at 565, 573.

21. Ibid., pp. 579–581.

22. *Lucas* v. *Forty-Fourth General Assembly of Colorado,* 377 U.S. 713 (1964) at 750. This point has been affirmed, often enthusiastically, by subsequent more formal analyses of political equality. See Still, "Political Equality," p. 386; Ronald Rogowski, "Representation in Political Theory and in Law," *Ethics* 91 (April 1981): 411, 420, 428–430.

23. Andrew Hacker, *Congressional Districting: The Issue of Equal Representation* (Washington, D.C.: Brookings Institution, 1963), p. 120.

24. *Lucas* v. *Forty-Fourth General Assembly* at 736. It may be argued on utilitarian grounds that without a one person, one vote rule, there is no assurance that everyone's interests will be equally considered. But utilitarians have traditionally accepted that a people can decide where to allocate the authority for calculating the public interest, to experts if need be. Hence, to rule out a federal analogy system, especially where initiative and referendum are available, is to demand a more stringent egalitarian requirement than utilitarianism demands on its own terms. Thus the efforts of both Dworkin and Ely, for example, to oppose systems in which majorities can undervalue some interests of others rest on a nonutilitarian, absolutist principle of equality. Ronald Dworkin, *Taking Rights Seriously* (Cambridge: Harvard University Press, 1978), pp. 232–238, 272–278; John Hart Ely, *Democracy and Distrust,* (Cambridge: Harvard University Press, 1980), pp. 76–77, 135–136. While the at least quasi-utilitarian John Stuart Mill advocated proportional representation to ensure that all interests were counted in calculations of public welfare, he also recommended giving extra votes to the well-educated to ensure that this welfare was properly understood and sought.

While "every man ought to have a voice, that every one should have an equal voice is a totally different proposition." And "only a fool of a peculiar description, feels offended by the acknowledgement that there are others whose opinion, and even whose wish, is entitled to a greater amount of consideration than his." Mill favored such plural voting even if proportional representation should achieve his "best hopes" for it. John Stuart Mill, *Three Essays* (London: Oxford University Press, 1975), pp. 254, 282–283, 288; Dennis F. Thompson, *John Stuart Mill and Representative Government* (Princeton: Princeton University Press, 1976), pp. 99–107.

25. Alexander Bickel, *The Morality of Consent* (New Haven: Yale University Press, 1975), p. 121. The Court struck down the poll tax in *Harper v. Virginia Board of Elections,* 383 U.S. 663 (1966); the requirement that one be either subject to the relevant taxes or a parent to participate in a school district election in *Kramer v. Union Free School District No. 15,* 395 U.S. 621 (1969); and lengthy residence requirements in *Dunn v. Blumstein,* 405 U.S. 330 (1972). It extended the one person, one vote rule to local governmental units exercising "general governmental powers over the entire geographic area served by the body" and even to bodies exercising specific "governmental functions" in *Avery v. Midland County,* 390 U.S. 474 (1968); *Hadley v. Junior College District,* 397 U.S. 50 (1970). *Kirkpatrick v. Preisler,* 394 U.S. 526 (1969) at 531–534, 549; Rogowoski, "Representation," p. 419. The broad readings of *Reynolds* led analysts to develop measures of the actual voting power afforded by different districting schemes, calculated generally in terms of the chance of voters to elect legislators positioned to cast pivotal votes in minimal winning coalitions. See e.g. John F. Banzhaff, "Multimember Electoral Districts—Do They Violate the 'One Man, One Vote' Principle," *Yale Law Journal* 75 (July 1966): 1309. Population equality did not prove to guarantee this sort of equality in actual influence, especially in multimember districts. But White, writing for the Court, dismissed the "real-life impact" of these inequalities as insufficiently demonstrated in *Whitcomb v. Chavis,* 403 U.S. 124 (1971) at 146–147.

26. Hans Linde, "Judges, Critics and the Realist Tradition," *Yale Law Journal* 82 (December 1972): 232.

27. *Gordon v. Lance,* 403 U.S. 1 (1971) at 4, 7, 8. This approach was continued in *Lockport v. Citizens for Community Action,* 430 U.S. 264 (1977) at 266, and extended in *Ball v. James,* 451 U.S. 355 (1981).

28. See *Abate v. Mundt,* 403 U.S. 182 (1971); *Mahan v. Howell,* 410 U.S. 315 (1973) at 321, 325–326, 328; *Gaffney v. Cummings,* 412 U.S. 735 (1973) at 752–754; *White v. Regester,* 412 U.S. 755 (1973); *Chapman v. Meier,* 420 U.S. 1 (1975) at 26–27.

29. *Conrad v. Finch,* 431 U.S. 407 (1977) at 429–430; *Brown v. Thomson,* 77 L. Ed. 2d 214 (1983). In another case, *United Jewish Organization v. Carey,* 430 U.S. 144 (1977), an otherwise fragmented Court similarly agreed that while the Voting Rights Act authorizes apportionments protective of racial equality, there is no constitutional right to equal representation of all ethnic groups as groups. It upheld a state apportionment plan that split a Hasidic community into several districts.

30. See *White* v. *Weiser*, 412 U.S. 783 (1973) at 791; *Karcher* v. *Daggett*, 77 L. Ed. 2d 133 (1983).

31. *Mobile* v. *Bolden*, 446 U.S. 55, 75, 76, 80 (1980). The Court subsequently decided, apparently against Stewart's *Mobile* opinion, that circumstantial evidence, such as historical patterns of other discriminatory practices and ongoing discriminatory effects, was sufficient to allow an inference of intent. *Rogers* v. *Lodge*, 458 U.S. 613 (1982). Standards for proving intent thus remain strongly contested. But these complexities aside, the Burger Court, like all modern Courts and even Frankfurter, has been quick to strike down infringements on voting rights shown to result from racial discrimination. *Whitcomb* v. *Chavis*, 403 U.S. 124 (1971); *White* v. *Regester*, 412 U.S. 755 (1973).

32. Ibid. at 116.

33. Ibid. at 111, 123. In *Holt Civic Club* v. *Tuscaloosa*, 439 U.S. 60, 69 (1978), Rehnquist's opinion for the Court explicitly rejected the egalitarian view that all those significantly affected by a city's decisions should receive its franchise and thus permitted Tuscaloosa to exercise certain policy, sanitation, and licensing powers over an adjacent suburb.

34. This pattern is confirmed by *Buckley* v. *Valeo*, 424 U.S. 1, 48 (1976), where the Court rejected expenditure limits partly aimed at "equalizing the relative ability of all voters to affect electoral outcomes" on free expression grounds. One need not push the fundamental principle stated in *Reynolds* very far to conclude that this is constitutionally legitimate, if not constitutionally demanded, to promote the goal of equally effective participation. Still, "Political Equality," pp. 386–390; Rogowski, "Representation," pp. 411, 419–420, 428–430; Dixon, *Democratic Representation*, pp. 267–273.

35. Ely, *Democracy and Distrust*, pp. 98–99.

36. Dixon, *Democratic Representation*, pp. 56–57, 525–527; Douglas Rae, *The Political Consequences of Electoral Laws*, rev. ed. (New Haven: Yale University Press, 1971), pp. 96–99, 149, 173–174.

37. See Jean-Jacques Rousseau, *The Social Contract* (Great Britain: Penguin Books, 1968), pp. 140–142; Thomas Carlyle, *Sartor Resartus and Selected Prose* (New York: Holt, Rinehart and Winston, 1970), pp. 225–233; Carlyle, *On Heroes, Hero-Worship, and the Heroic in History* (Boston: Ginn, 1902), pp. 225–282 (arguing that the rule of the "Ablest Man" is superior to "ballot box . . . machinery," and evaluating Cromwell and Napoleon in terms of their "sincerity" out of a belief that "the first law of our existence" is to "unfold your *self*"); G. F. W. Hegel, *The Philosophy of History* (New York: Dover Press, 1956), pp. 29–32 (also describing political "Heroes" who are held to represent the true will of their people).

38. See e.g. Ely, *Democracy and Distrust*, p. 121; Alpheus T. Mason, *The Supreme Court from Taft to Burger* (Baton Rouge: Louisiana State University Press, 1979), p. 301. The organized efforts in the 1960s to overturn the one man, one vote rule do not belie the fact that it has become part of the conventional wisdom of American opinion. A stringent insistence on one person, one vote also seems practical because, with computers to canvass the possibilities, most districting objectives can be achieved without having to violate the one person, one

vote rule. But respect for existing geographical and political subdivisions can greatly limit redistricting options, and therefore also the possibilities for gerrymandering, so the problem remains of how much weight should be given to these subdivisions. Dixon, *Democratic Representation*, pp. 457, 537–543.

39. Jan Deutsch's well-known argument that the Warren Court adopted one person, one vote precisely to avoid these apparently unmanageable complexities is no doubt correct. Jan Deutsch, "Neutrality, Legitimacy, and the Supreme Court: Some Intersections Between Law and Political Science," *Stanford Law Review* 20 (January 1968): 247. But since the Court still permitted some deviations, these complexities were not wholly avoided; so it is still worthwhile to seek more substantive solutions.

6. Economic Welfare

1. See e.g. Joyce Oldham Appleby, *Economic Thought and Ideology in Seventeenth-Century England* (Princeton: Princeton University Press, 1978), pp. 28–30, 42–47, 100.

2. Ibid., pp. 31–33, 62–63, 78, 103–108; J. G. A. Pocock, *The Machiavellian Moment* (Princeton: Princeton University Press, 1975), pp. 426–432.

3. Appleby, *Economic Thought*, pp. 114, 118–122, 250–251, 265; Pocock, *Machiavellian Moment*, pp. 422–431; Gerald Stourzh, *Alexander Hamilton and the Idea of Republican Government* (Stanford: Stanford University Press, 1970), pp. 85–86.

4. Appleby, *Economic Thought*, pp. 183–184, 193, 271–275, 277; Pocock, *Machiavellian Moment*, pp. 441, 469–470, 474, 492–493.

5. This attention culminated, of course, in the work of Adam Smith and the other political economists of the Scottish Enlightenment.

6. John Locke, "Some Considerations of the Consequences of the Lowering of Interest and Raising the Value of Money," in *Works*, vol. 4, 12th ed. (London, 1824), pp. 13–14, 21, 24, 62; Karen Iverson Vaughn, *John Locke: Economist and Social Scientist* (Chicago: University of Chicago Press, 1980), p. 121; Appleby, *Economic Thought*, p. 254.

7. Locke, "Some Considerations," pp. 11–13. Locke did not address the attendant problems of how the abundance that property creates comes to be distributed and how economic gain can corrupt human motives. See Locke, *Two Treatises of Government*, ed. Peter Laslett (New York: New American Library, 1960), pp. 333, 407.

8. Locke, *Two Treatises*, pp. 337, 339; Locke, "Some Considerations," pp. 13–14, 28–29.

9. Ibid., pp. 22, 50–51, 63–64.

10. Ibid., pp. 11, 24–25; John Locke, "Venditio," published in John Dunn, "Justice and the Interpretation of Locke's Political Theory," *Political Studies* 17 (February 1968): 68–87; Vaughn, *John Locke*, pp. 121, 128.

11. Lawrence M. Friedman, *A History of American Law* (New York: Simon and Schuster, 1973), pp. 55, 65–67, 70–71, 77; Walter Trattner, *From Poor Law to Welfare State*, 2d ed. (New York: Free Press, 1979), pp. 16–25, 29–30.

In the eighteenth century, some colonial governments did begin to provide funds to local communities for the care of certain classes of nonresidents, and private charitable groups grew.

12. See Oscar Handlin and Mary Flug Handlin, *Commonwealth,* rev. ed. (Cambridge: Harvard University Press, 1969), pp. 51, 56, 134–136; Gordon S. Wood, *The Creation of the American Republic* (Chapel Hill: University of North Carolina, 1969), pp. 63–68; Friedman, *American Law,* pp. 157–158; Morton J. Horwitz, *The Transformation of American Law* (Cambridge: Harvard University Press, 1977), pp. xv, xxi, 2, 7–9; Stourzh, *Hamilton,* p. 167; Clinton Rossiter, ed., *The Federalist Papers* (New York: New American Library, 1961), pp. 143–144, 292–293; Martin Diamond, "Democracy and *The Federalist,*" *American Political Science Review* 53 (March 1959): 59–68; Pocock, *Machiavellian Moment,* pp. 488–498.

13. Wood, *American Republic,* pp. 484, 499–500, 516–517, 523–526, 536–537; Bernard H. Siegan, *Economic Liberties and the Constitution* (Chicago: University of Chicago Press, 1980), pp. 100–104; Pocock, *Machiavellian Moment,* pp. 528–542; Herbert J. Storing, *What the Anti-Federalists Were For* (Chicago: University of Chicago Press, 1981), pp. 20–21, 30–32; Arthur M. Schlesinger, Jr., *The Age of Jackson* (Boston: Little, Brown, 1945), pp. 8–29, 76–82, 334–349; Marvin Meyers, *The Jacksonian Persuasion* (Stanford: Stanford University Press, 1960), pp. 10–32, 101–162.

14. See Merrill D. Peterson, ed., *The Portable Thomas Jefferson* (New York: Penguin Books, 1977), pp. 216–217, 549; Pocock, *Machiavellian Moment,* pp. 535–542; Friedman, *American Law,* pp. 157–158, 203, 365; Stourzh, *Hamilton,* pp. 191–192, 201–202; Schlesinger, *Jackson,* pp. 344–349.

15. Friedman, *American Law,* pp. 100, 157–166; Handlin, *Commonwealth,* pp. 62–67, 106, 127. The states lacked the financial base and administrative structure to make their regulations fully effective and to service the growing demands for economic infrastructure, although they contributed to this economic growth.

16. Friedman, *American Law,* pp. 187–191; Trattner, *Welfare State,* pp. 47–53.

17. Horwitz, *Transformation,* pp. 31, 32, 77.

18. G. Edward White, *The American Judicial Tradition* (New York: Oxford University Press, 1976), p. 16; *Gibbons* v. *Ogden,* 9 Wheat. 1 (1824) at 6, 189, 194, 196.

19. Marshall never answered the question of whether the commerce power of its own force precluded all state regulation of interstate trade, but in *Willson* v. *Black Bird Creek Marsh Co.,* 2 Peters 245 (1829), he appeared to indicate that in the absence of contrary congressional action the states could undertake some regulation as an exercise of their police powers. Marshall's aversion to state restraints on commerce is exemplified in *Brown* v. *Maryland,* 12 Wheat. 419 (1827), which struck down a state license fee imposed on wholesalers of imported goods as contrary to the commerce clause with its free trade aims and to a congressional act authorizing importation.

20. Friedman, *American Law,* p. 244; Benjamin F. Wright, *The Growth of*

American Constitutional Law (Chicago: University of Chicago Press, 1967), p. 41.

21. *Fletcher* v. *Peck*, 6 Cranch 87, 139 (1810); Wright, *American Constitutional Law*, pp. 42–43; White, *Judicial Tradition*, p. 22; Robert Faulkner, *The Jurisprudence of John Marshall* (Princeton: Princeton University Press, 1968).

22. *Sturges* v. *Crowninshield*, 4 Wheat. 122 (1819); *Dartmouth College* v. *Woodward*, 4 Wheat. 518 (1819). As the advantages bestowed by the states in the early nineteenth century came to be seen as outmoded privileges that produced wealth for a few at the expense of economic progress for all, Marshall became more concerned to tip the balance constitutionally in favor of vested rights. In *Ogden* v. *Saunders*, 12 Wheat. 213 (1827), he voted to give the contract clause prospective application, ruling out relief to the bankrupt, even in the future, though the Court refused to go along, holding that prospective legislation created implied conditions in all future contracts. Marshall's willingness to protect existing property rights was still limited, however. In *Barron* v. *Baltimore*, 7 Peters 243 (1833), he refused to apply the "just compensation" guarantee in the Bill of Rights against the states, rejecting the argument of a wharf owner whose property had been made worthless by the diversion of streams during the construction of city roads. The historical record weighed against any reference of the Bill of Rights to the states, and Marshall chose not to appeal to general principles on Barron's behalf, perhaps because he was more willing to accept state infringements resulting from the promotion of commercial development.

23. Marshall was fortunate that Congress did not choose in this era to use the commerce power for extensive regulation. As a result, the Court never had to decide the limits set on national actions by property rights. Since the late nineteenth century, however, this issue has been inescapable.

24. *Charles River Bridge* v. *Warren Bridge*, 11 Peters 420 (1837) at 547–548, 553. For Marshall decisions, see *Providence Bank* v. *Billings*, 4 Peters 514 (1830); *Beaty* v. *Lessee of Knowler*, 4 Peters 152 (1830); *U.S.* v. *Arredondo*, 6 Peters 691 (1832). For Taney cases enforcing the contract clause, see *Bronson* v. *Kinzie*, 1 Howard 311 (1843); *McCracken* v. *Hayward*, 2 Howard 608 (1844); *Lessee of Gantley* v. *Ewing*, 3 Howard 707 (1845); *Howard* v. *Bugbee*, 24 Howard 461 (1861). See also Wright, *American Constitutional Law*, pp. 61–65.

25. Morton Horwitz stresses the developmental goals of Jacksonian jurisprudence, seeing it as favoring "emergent entrepreneurial and commercial groups," while the Handlins instead emphasized the concern to set "the balance against privilege." Horwitz, *Transformation*, pp. 132–139; Handlin, *Commonwealth*, pp. 89–190, 194–198. On neither ground, however, did the Court question, as Story had, the priority of the slaveowning rights favored by the rural South.

26. *Mayor of New York* v. *Miln*, 11 Peters 102 (1837); *Cooley* v. *Board of Wardens of the Port of Philadelphia*, 12 Howard 299 (1851); *License Cases*, 5 Howard 504 (1847); *Passenger Cases*, 7 Howard 283 (1849); *U.S.* v. *Coombs*, 12 Peters 72 (1838); *U.S.* v. *Marigold*, 9 Howard 560 (1838).

27. See Joseph Blau, ed., *Social Theories of Jacksonian Democracy* (Indianapolis: Bobbs-Merrill, 1954), esp. pp. 1–37; Schlesinger, *Jackson*, pp. 322–

349; Friedman, *American Law*, pp. 107–108, 264, 428–429; Trattner, *Welfare State*, pp. 58–59.

28. See esp. *Slaughter-House Cases*, 16 Wallace 36 (1873).

29. See e.g. William Graham Sumner, *What the Social Classes Owe to Each Other*, (Caldwell, Id.: Caxton, 1982), p. 114. "A drunkard in the gutter is just where he ought to be, according to the fitness and tendency of things." See also Richard Hofstadter, *Social Darwinism in American Thought* (Boston: Beacon Press, 1955), pp. 39, 41, 46–47.

30. Wright, *American Constitutional Law*, p. 89, lists fourteen such cases between 1877 and the *Wabash* case of 1886.

31. *United States* v. *DeWitt*, 9 Wallace 41 (1870); *Wabash, St. Louis, & Pacific Ry. Co.* v. *Illinois*, 118 U.S. 557 (1886); *Cincinnati, New Orleans and Texas Pacific Railway Company* v. *Interstate Commerce Commission*, 162 U.S. 184 (1896) (the *I.C.C. Case*); *I.C.C.* v. *Illinois Central R.R. Co.*, 215 U.S. 452 (1910); Sheldon Goldman, *Constitutional Law and Supreme Court Decision-Making* (New York: Harper and Row, 1982), p. 165.

32. *United States* v. *E. C. Knight Co.*, 156 U.S. 1, 14, 16 (1895); *Loewe* v. *Lawlor*, 208 U.S. 274 (1908); *Duplex Print Press Co.* v. *Deering*, 254 U.S. 443 (1921); *Bedford Cut Stone* v. *Journeymen Stone Cutters' Association*, 274 U.S. 37 (1927); *Employer's Liability Cases*, 207 U.S. 463 (1908).

33. *U.S.* v. *Trans-Missouri Freight Association*, 166 U.S. 290 (1897); *Addyston Pipe & Steel Co.* v. *United States*, 175 U.S. 211 (1899).

34. *Swift & Co.* v. *United States*, 196 U.S. 375, 399 (1905); *Stafford* v. *Wallace*, 258 U.S. 495, 516 (1922).

35. *Houston E. & W. Texas Railway Co.* v. *United States*, 234 U.S. 342, 355 (1914); *Champion* v. *Ames*, 188 U.S. 321 (1903).

36. *Standard Oil Co.* v. *United States*, 221 U.S. 1 (1910); *United States* v. *American Tobacco Co.*, 221 U.S. 106 (1911); *United States* v. *Winslow*, 227 U.S. 202 (1913); *United States* v. *U.S. Steel Corp.*, 251 U.S. 417 (1920).

37. *Hammer* v. *Dagenhart*, 247 U.S. 251 (1918); *Brooks* v. *United States*, 267 U.S. 432 (1925).

38. Raymond Mohl, "Three Centuries of American Public Welfare: 1600–1932," *Current History* 65 (July 1973): 7; Theda Skocpol and John Ikenberry, "The Political Formation of the American Welfare State," paper presented at annual meeting of American Sociological Association, San Francisco, September 7, 1982, pp. 13–17, 23–56; Friedman, *American Law*, pp. 429–431; Trattner, *Welfare State*, pp. 72–73, 137, 151, 179–184.

39. See Howard Zinn, ed., *New Deal Thought* (Indianapolis: Bobbs-Merrill, 1966), pp. xv–xxxvi; Richard Hofstadter, *The Age of Reform* (New York: Vintage Books, 1955), pp. 302–328; Arthur M. Schlesinger, Jr., *The Coming of the New Deal* (Boston: Houghton Mifflin, 1959), pp. 179–194, 315; Schlesinger, *The Politics of Upheaval* (Boston: Houghton Mifflin, 1960), pp. 385–408; William E. Leuchtenberg, *Franklin D. Roosevelt and the New Deal* (New York: Harper & Row, 1963), pp. 326–348; Roberto Mangabeira Unger, *Law in Modern Society* (New York: Free Press, 1976), pp. 192–194; Robert Stern, "The Commerce Clause and the National Economy, 1933–1946," *Harvard Law Re-*

view 59 (May, 1946): 947; Paul Murphy, *The Constitution in Crisis Times* (New York: Harper and Row, 1972), p. 168.

40. The National Industrial Recovery Act of 1933, the cornerstone of the "first New Deal," has often been characterized as "corporatist" because it delegated quasi-legislative power to associations representing major industrial and labor sectors, the "estates" of an advanced industrial economy. But for Roosevelt and most other New Dealers these measures represented means of aggregating interests efficiently, not acquiescence in Rexford Tugwell's organic view of society. Furthermore, the failures of the NRA and the Supreme Court's opposition soon led the New Dealers to adopt less corporatist, more decentralized and regulatory programs. Schlesinger, *New Deal,* pp. 179–194; Schlesinger, *Upheaval,* pp. 385–408, 649–653; Leuchtenberg, *Roosevelt,* pp. 34, 148–150, 162–164, 341, 344; Nancy Rosenblum, *Bentham's Theory of the Modern State* (Cambridge: Harvard University Press, 1978), pp. 29, 37, 47–50; Edward A. Purcell, Jr., *The Crisis of Democratic Theory* (Lexington: University Press of Kentucky, 1973), pp. 239, 265–266; Leuchtenberg, *Roosevelt,* pp. 34, 341, 344; John Dewey, *Liberalism and Social Action* (New York: Capricorn Books, 1963), pp. 54–55, 62–63.

41. Rosenblum, *Bentham's Theory,* pp. 47–50; John Maynard Keynes, "Am I a Liberal?" in *The Liberal Tradition from Fox to Keynes,* ed. Alan Bullock and Maurice Shock (London: Adam & Charles Block, 1956); L. T. Hobhouse, *Liberalism* (Oxford: Oxford University Press, 1911), pp. 146, 160, 186, 210; John Dewey, *Social Action,* pp. 19, 26–27, 54–55; Schlesinger, *New Deal,* p. 194; Leuchtenberg, *Roosevelt,* pp. 264, 338–339; Zinn, *New Deal Thought,* pp. xxxi–xxxiv; Murphy, *Crisis Times,* pp. 128, 459; Dewey, *Individualism Old and New* (New York: Capricorn Books, 1962), pp. 168–171 (evoking Emerson's ideal of individuality); Dewey, *Reconstruction in Philosophy* (Boston: Beacon Press, 1957), pp. 182–186 (criticizing utilitarian preoccupations with economic materialism instead of with "all-around growth").

42. Zinn, *New Deal Thought,* p. xxi; Murphy, *Crisis Times,* pp. 249, 458–459; Arthur Selwyn Miller, *The Supreme Court and American Capitalism* (New York: Free Press, 1968), p. 74; Leuchtenberg, *Roosevelt,* p. 335.

43. Schlesinger, *New Deal,* p. 309; Leuchtenberg, *Roosevelt,* pp. 132–133; Martha Derthick, *Policymaking for Social Security* (Washington, D.C.: Brookings Institution, 1979), pp. 199–201, 224–287, 289–292.

44. Schlesinger, *New Deal,* pp. 179–194; Schlesinger, *Upheaval,* pp. 212–215, 220–231; Leuchtenberg, *Roosevelt,* pp. 34–36, 148–154; Zinn, *New Deal Thought,* pp. xiii, xvi, xxvii, xxxii–xxxiii; Friedman, *American Law,* pp. 569–571; H. N. Hirsch, *The Enigma of Felix Frankfurter* (New York: Basic Books, 1981), pp. 104–119; Bruce Allen Murphy, *The Brandeis-Frankfurter Connection* (New York: Oxford University Press, 1982).

45. Hofstadter, *Age of Reform,* p. 319; *Railroad Retirement Board v. Alton Railroad Co.,* 295 U.S. 330 (1935); *Schechter Poultry Corp. v. United States,* 295 U.S. 495, 543, 549 (1935). The contract clause was unavailable against the federal government, and the Court was at any rate no longer inclined to read it restrictively. In *Home Building and Loan Ass'n v. Blaisdell,* 290 U.S. 398 (1934),

the Court sustained a Minnesota law forbidding foreclosures on farms and homes for up to three years. Although it could be argued that the contract clause forbade this sort of debtor relief in emergencies, Hughes held that since the measure was only a temporary one, required by the economic crisis, it was consistent with the intent of the framers. In *Louisville Joint Stock Bank* v. *Radford*, 295 U.S. 555 (1935), a similar congressional effort to provide relief for mortgagors was struck down under the Fifth Amendment due process clause, indicating both that the Court's attitude toward welfare legislation was again hardening and that the reach of the inexplicit due process liberty of contract was more extensive than that of the actual contract clause.

46. *Carter* v. *Carter Coal Co.*, 298 U.S. 238, 303–304, 307–309 (1936).

47. *National Labor Relations Board* v. *Jones & Laughlin Steel Corp.*, 301 U.S. 1, 41 (1937) (Hughes did make some effort to distinguish *Carter* by asserting that no similar affect on interstate commerce had been shown there, but the records made this claim implausible); *Santa Cruz Fruit Packing* v. *National Labor Relations Board*, 303 U.S. 453 (1938); *Consolidated Edison Co.* v. *National Labor Relations Board*, 305 U.S. 197 (1938); *National Labor Relations Board* v. *Fainblatt*, 306 U.S. 601 (1939).

48. *Steward Machine Co.* v. *Davis*, 301 U.S. 548 (1937) at 580, 586–587, 590, 603; *Helvering* v. *Davis*, 301 U.S. 619 (1937) at 641, 644–645.

49. *United States* v. *Darby*, 312 U.S. 100, 115–117 (1941). In *Mulford* v. *Smith*, 307 U.S. 38, 47 (1939), the Court upheld agricultural marketing quotas while emphasizing that these did not affect production as such but only affected sales to the marketing warehouse, the "throat" of the stream of commerce. It thereby maintained continuity with Holmes's reading of Marshall's limitation.

50. *Wickard* v. *Filburn*, 317 U.S. 111, 118–119, 125 (1942).

51. *Griffin* v. *Illinois*, 351 U.S. 12, 19, 34 (1956). For the Court's deferential equal protection posture, see e.g. *Kotch* v. *Board of River Pilots*, 330 U.S. 552, 563, 564 (1947); *Railway Express* v. *New York*, 336 U.S. 106, 111 (1949).

52. *Douglas* v. *California*, 372 U.S. 353, 357, 361–362 (1963).

53. *Harper* v. *Virginia Board of Elections*, 383 U.S. 663 (1966), 668–669, 674, 686.

54. See Charles Reich, "The New Property," *Yale Law Journal* 73 (April 1964): 733, 771, 785–787; Frank Michelman, "Foreword: On Protecting the Poor Through the Fourteenth Amendment," *Harvard Law Review* 83 (November 1969): 9, 29–30; *Goldberg* v. *Kelly*, 397 U.S. 254 (1970).

55. Theodore Lowi, *The End of Liberalism*, 2d ed. (New York: W. W. Norton, 1979), pp. 200, 210–215, 274–281.

56. See *Heart of Atlanta Motel* v. *United States*, 379 U.S. 241 (1964); *Katzenbach* v. *McClung*, 379 U.S. 275, 294 (1964); *Daniel* v. *Paul*, 395 U.S. 298, 305 (1969); Laurence Tribe, *American Constitutional Law* (Mineola, N.Y.: Foundation Press, 1978), p. 241.

57. *Rodriguez* culminated a movement away from constitutional welfare rights that was visible in such cases as *Dandridge* v. *Williams*, 397 U.S. 471 (1970), rejecting a challenge to Maryland's limits on Aid to Families with Dependent Children assistance; *James* v. *Valtierra*, 402 U.S. 137 (1971), denying a challenge

to California's constitutional requirement of local referendum approval for low-rent housing projects; and *Lindsey* v. *Normet,* 405 U.S. 56 (1972), upholding judicial procedures for eviction of nonpaying tenants. Although the Court struck down a state law requiring a $60 filing fee for a divorce petition in *Boddie* v. *Connecticut,* 401 U.S. 371 (1971), it stressed that here the state had a monopoly of the basic service required, foreshadowing the demand in *Rodriguez* for an absolute deprivation of a fundamental interest.

58. *San Antonio School District* v. *Rodriguez,* 411 U.S. 1, 19, 22–23 (1973).

59. Ibid. at 70. For example, the Court has refused to find any obligation to pay for abortions, even when medically necessary services had previously been guaranteed. *Maher* v. *Roe,* 432 U.S. 464 (1977); *Harris* v. *McRae,* 448 U.S. 297 (1980). The Court has, on the other hand, struck down residency requirements for welfare and medical assistance, held to infringe on the fundamental right to interstate travel. *Shapiro* v. *Thompson,* 394 U.S. 618 (1969), followed in *Memorial Hospital* v. *Maricopa County,* 415 U.S. 250 (1974), though not in *Sosna* v. *Iowa,* 419 U.S. 393 (1975). It has also overturned, allegedly under minimal scrutiny, denials both of food stamps to households of unrelated individuals and of disability benefits to classes of illegitimate children born after the wage earner's disability. *U.S. Dept. of Agriculture* v. *Moreno,* 413 U.S. 528 (1973); *Jimenez* v. *Weinberger,* 417 U.S. 628 (1974). Scholarly efforts to find social egalitarian duties in the equal protection clause and elsewhere in the Constitution remain vigorous, if increasingly unconventional. See e.g. Kenneth Karst, "Foreword: Equal Citizenship under the Fourteenth Amendment," *Harvard Law Review* 91 (November 1977): 1–71; Roberto Mangabeira Unger, "The Critical Legal Studies Movement," *Harvard Law Review* 96 (January 1983): 611–615. But without the presence of the *Rodriguez* criteria the Court still insists on minimal scrutiny of a law's economic consequences.

60. *United States Trust Co.* v. *New Jersey,* 431 U.S. 1 (1977); *Allied Structural Steel Co.* v. *Spannaus,* 438 U.S. 234 (1978).

61. See e.g. *Raymond Motor Transportation Inc.* v. *Rice,* 434 U.S. 429 (1978); *City of Philadelphia* v. *New Jersey,* 437 U.S. 617 (1978); *Lewis* v. *BT Investment Managers,* 447 U.S. 27 (1980); *NLRB* v. *Catholic Bishop of Chicago,* 440 U.S. 490 (1979); *NLRB* v. *Yeshiva University,* 444 U.S. 672 (1980).

62. For later cases that read *National League of Cities* so narrowly as almost to overturn it, see *United Transportation Union* v. *Long Island R. Co.,* 455 U.S. 678 (1982); *FERC* v. *Mississippi,* 456 U.S. 742 (1982); *Equal Employment Opportunity Commission* v. *Wyoming,* 460 U.S. 226 (1983). See also *First National Bank of Boston* v. *Bellotti,* 435 U.S. 765 (1978).

63. But cf. Siegan, *Economic Liberties.* The Reagan Administration has also tried to reduce national responsibility for individual welfare on the ground that it has proven unworkable.

64. The romantic thrust of Reich's argument is evident in his claim that property rights should be understood as social creations that from "the very foundation of individuality" and his conclusion that making governmental largesse matters of right would create zones of privacy permitting unconstrained individual fulfillment. Reich, "New Property," pp. 771, 773, 785–787. For the

manner in which claims to unbridled personal expression can support inequalities, see e.g. *Buckley v. Valeo*, 424 U.S. 1 (1979).

65. See Reich, "New Property," p. 787; Michelman, "Protecting the Poor," pp. 9, 29–30; Karst, "Equal Citizenship," pp. 11, 63.

Introduction to Part III

1. For an argument that the basic "American Creed" remains essentially unchanged, see Samuel P. Huntington, *American Politics: The Promise of Disharmony* (Cambridge: Harvard University Press, 1981). For an argument that Huntington exaggerates this continuity, see Rogers M. Smith, "The 'American Creed' and Constitutional Theory," *Harvard Law Review* 95 (May 1982): 1691–1702.

2. See Guido Calebresi, *The Cost of Accidents* (New Haven: Yale University Press, 1970); Richard A. Posner, *Economic Analysis of Law*, 2d ed. (Boston: Little, Brown, 1977); Posner, *The Economics of Justice* (Cambridge: Harvard University Press, 1981); J. Roland Pennock and John W. Chapman, eds., *Nomos XXIII: Ethics, Economics and the Law* (New York: New York University Press, 1982).

7. Alternative Constitutional Theories

1. John Hart Ely, *Democracy and Distrust* (Cambridge: Harvard University Press, 1980), pp. 87, 73–179.

2. Ibid., pp. 75, 100–102.

3. The concern for minority rights no doubt explains why the original footnote contained not only paragraph two, the democratic process argument, but also paragraphs one and three, suggesting activism on behalf of explicit constitutional rights and discrete and insular minorities. But neither of these aspects can be fully squared with the purely democratic theory its authors (like Ely) wished to accommodate.

4. Ely, *Democracy and Distrust*, pp. 146–148, 152–155, 157.

5. Ibid., pp. 243, 256.

6. Alexander Bickel, *The Least Dangerous Branch* (Indianapolis: Bobbs-Merrill, 1962), p. 24.

7. Ibid., pp. 24–25, 51, 64, 79, 235, 238.

8. Ibid., pp. 236–239.

9. Ibid., p. 239.

10. Alexander Bickel, *The Supreme Court and the Idea of Progress* (New York: Harper & Row, 1970), pp. 99, 108, 110, 116, 138–139, 173–175.

11. Ibid., pp. 177–178, 113; Alexander Bickel, *The Morality of Consent* (New Haven: Yale University Press, 1975), p. 4.

12. Bickel, *Morality of Consent*, pp. 12, 19.

13. Ibid., pp. 6, 17–19, 21, 24, 77. It is a measure of how much Bickel's views had hardened that, while in *The Least Dangerous Branch* he had said that "the real question" for a judge might be whether a law is "good," he now

castigated the Warren Court for its pride in asking litigants, "Is it *right?* Is it *good?*" Bickel, *Least Dangerous Branch*, p. 39; Bickel, *Morality of Consent*, p. 120. I am grateful to John Satalic for calling my attention to this contrast.

14. Ibid., pp. 5, 15, 23–24, 77, 123, 129.

15. Ibid., p. 116. Bickel thus went further than Jackson, who accepted that expediency might drive the military beyond the bounds of the Constitution but nonetheless opposed judicial ratification of such expedient acts.

16. It is logically possible, and it may be more common, to base a relativistic democratic political position on a much less thoroughgoing skepticism by holding that discernible ultimate values exist but are best pursued in private groups, not through public life directly. But as long as this view is defended in terms of the practical difficulties of deciding publicly on ultimate values, it comes down to the same skeptical position that there are no universally self-evident values. And any effort to establish publicly that the nature of those values requires them to be sought privately would involve the sort of assertion of fixed moral principles undertaken by the other possible versions of liberal constitutionalism I will consider.

17. One partial exception to the general neglect of America's higher law traditions is Michael Perry's theory of constitutional interpretation, which claims to be religious because it permits the Supreme Court to appeal to the beliefs in transcendental moral standards that are widespread in American society. But with modern relativism, Perry understands these moral ideals to evolve over time, and he attributes to them a content that is much closer to the morality of contemporary neo-Kantian liberals than to the older religious and natural law traditions. Michael J. Perry, *The Constitution, the Courts and Human Rights* (New Haven: Yale University Press, 1982), esp. pp. 97–119. Recent Locke scholarship, on the other hand, lays renewed emphasis on his religious assumptions, suggesting the prevalence of these views among even those founders oriented toward the Enlightenment. See John Dunn, *The Political Thought of John Locke* (Cambridge: Cambridge University Press, 1969); James Tully, *A Discourse on Property* (Cambridge: Cambridge University Press, 1980). Cf. James Madison, "Memorial and Remonstrance," in *The Mind of the Founder*, ed. Marvin Meyers (Indianapolis: Bobbs-Merrill, 1973), p. 9. For an example of modern conservative, religious political activism, see Richard A. Viguerie, *The New Right: We're Ready to Lead* (Falls Church, Va.: Viguerie, 1981), pp. 123–136, 151–162.

18. Edward A. Purcell, Jr., *The Crisis of Democratic Theory* (Lexington: University Press of Kentucky, 1973), pp. 139–178.

19. Alexis de Tocqueville, *Democracy in America* (Garden City, N.Y.: Doubleday, 1969), pp. 295, 443–444, 530, 543.

20. John Courtney Murray, *We Hold These Truths* (Garden City, N.Y.: Doubleday, 1960), pp. 28, 36–37, 39.

21. Ibid., pp. 69, 78, 109, 296–298.

22. Walter Berns, *Freedom, Virtue, and the First Amendment* (Baton Rouge: Louisiana State University Press, 1957), pp. 188, 197; Berns, *The First Amendment and the Future of American Democracy* (New York: Basic Books, 1976), p. 228; Berns, "Judicial Review and the Rights and Laws of Nature," *The Su-*

preme Court Review, 1982, ed. Philip B. Kurland, Gerhard Casper, and Dennis J. Hutchinson (Chicago: University of Chicago Press, 1983), pp. 66, 80.

23. Berns, *Freedom,* pp. 171–172, 175–176, 244–245.

24. Ibid., pp. 222, 225–226, 244, 250; Murray, *Truths,* p. 37. Berns does agree with Murray that America's Lockean founders tried to end the debate over ultimate ends by creating a commercial society in which virtually all would be preoccupied with "making money." Berns, "Judicial Review," p. 65.

25. Murray, *Truths,* pp. 37, 69, 78; Berns, *Freedom,* pp. 162, 190, 224.

26. See Dino Bigongiari, ed., *The Political Ideas of St. Thomas Aquinas* (New York: Hafner Press, 1953), pp. 46, 93, 180, 190; Aristotle, *Nicomachean Ethics* (Indianapolis: Bobbs-Merrill, 1962), pp. 93–99, 288–292; Purcell, *Crisis,* pp. 230, 268. This failure is exacerbated by the fact that, claiming to follow Aristotle, some advocates of these views evade the problem by holding that "to demonstrate virtue to the virtuous is redundant and it is impossible to demonstrate virtue to the unvirtuous." Richard Loss, "Alexander Hamilton and the Modern Presidency," *Presidential Studies Quarterly* 12 (Winter, 1982): 9. Cf. Aristotle, *Ethics,* pp. 34–35, 168.

27. Berns, *Freedom,* pp. 198, 219–225, 251, 257. Murray's resistance to full separation of church and state indicates that his views have similar potential, though he stresses even more heavily the limitations of censorship. Murray, *Truths,* esp. pp. 154–171.

28. Berns, *Freedom,* pp. 220–221; Michael Walzer, "Civility and Civic Virtue in Contemporary America," *Social Research* 41 (Winter, 1974): 607, 609.

29. See e.g. Robert Paul Wolff, "Violence and the Law," in *The Rule of Law,* ed. Robert Paul Wolff (New York: Simon and Schuster, 1971), defending violent civil disobedience.

30. See e.g. Thomas Emerson, *The System of Freedom of Expression* (New York: Random House, 1970); Kenneth Karst, "Equality as a Central Principle of the First Amendment," *University of Chicago Law Review* 43 (Fall 1975): 20; Laurence Tribe, *American Constitutional Law* (Mineola, N.Y.: The Foundation Press, 1978), esp. pp. 576–608, 991–1011.

31. John Rawls, *A Theory of Justice* (Oxford: Oxford University Press, 1971); Ronald Dworkin, *Taking Rights Seriously* (Cambridge: Harvard University Press, 1978). The notion that the most viable conception of equality is one of a basic duty to respect others was popularized by Bernard Williams, "The Idea of Equality," in *Philosophy, Politics, and Society,* ed. Peter Laslett and W. G. Runciman (Oxford: Basil Blackwell, 1962). See also Rawls, "A Kantian Conception of Equality," *Cambridge Review* 76 (February 1975): 94–99. For a general analysis of Rawls's constitutional relevance, see Richard Parker, "The Jurisprudential Uses of John Rawls," *Nomos XX: Constitutionalism,* ed. J. Roland Pennock and John L. Chapman (New York: New York University Press, 1979).

32. Dworkin, *Taking Rights Seriously,* p. 357; Williams, "Idea of Equality," p. 117; Rawls, *Theory,* pp. 181–182, 505, 509.

33. Dworkin, *Rights,* pp. 158, 177; Rawls, *Theory,* pp. 20–21, 48–51.

34. Dworkin, *Rights,* pp. 158–159; Rawls, *Theory,* pp. 445, 529; Rawls,

"Kantian Constructivism in Moral Theory: Rational and Full Autonomy," *Journal of Philosophy* 77 (September 1980): 526–527.

35. Rawls, *Theory*, p. 396; Ronald Dworkin, "Liberalism," in *Public & Private Morality*, ed. Stuart Hampshire (Cambridge: Cambridge University Press, 1978). Cf. Michael J. Sandel, *Liberalism and the Limits of Justice* (New York: Cambridge University Press, 1983), esp. pp. 15–103.

36. Rawls, *Theory*, pp. 62, 260, 396, 440, 505–506, 534, 544; Frank Michelman, "In Pursuit of Constitutional Welfare Rights," *University of Pennsylvania Law Review* 121 (May 1973): 990; Karst, "Equality," pp. 28–29; David Richards, "Free Speech and Obscenity Law: Towards a Moral Theory of the First Amendment," *University of Pennsylvania Law Review* 123 (November 1974): 45. Self-respect also has a special status because Rawls prefers not to include it in the index of primary goods when applying his "difference principle." It complicates the calculus of benefits to the least advantaged, and so it is assumed that progress in terms of the other goods does promote self-respect. Rawls, *Theory*, pp. 543, 546.

37. Rawls, *Theory*, p. 442; Rawls, "Kantian Conception," p. 96; Michelman, "Welfare Rights"; Richards, "Free Speech"; Kenneth Karst, "Foreword: Equal Citizenship under the Fourteenth Amendment," *Harvard Law Review* 91 (November, 1977): 1–71; Morris Rosenberg, "Rawls' 'Unwelcome Complication': Social Status and Self-Esteem," paper presented at annual meeting of International Society of Political Psychology, Boston, Mass., June 6, 1980.

38. Rawls, *Theory*, pp. 441–442, 450, 536, 544; Rawls, "Kantian Conception," p. 95.

39. Rawls, *Theory*, pp. 260, 350–391, 396, 506; Rawls, "Kantian Conception," p. 95; Rawls, "Fairness to Goodness," *The Philosophical Review* 84 (October 1975): 539; Dworkin, *Rights*, pp. 206–222.

40. Rawls, "Fairness," pp. 547, 549, 554; Rawls, *Theory*, p. 529.

41. See Sandel, *Limits of Justice*.

42. Dworkin, *Rights*, p. 357; Richards, "Free Speech"; Rawls, *Theory*, p. 107.

43. See Douglas Rae, "Maximin Justice and an Alternative Principle of General Advantage," *American Political Science Review* 69 (June 1975): 637–641; Rae et al., *Equalities* (Cambridge: Harvard University Press, 1981), pp. 110–123; Robert Paul Wolff, *Understanding Rawls* (Princeton: Princeton University Press, 1977), pp. 75–78, 107, 200–201, 228–234, 536, 546; Dworkin, "Liberalism," p. 133; Michelman, "Welfare Rights," p. 990; Frank Michelman, "Foreword: On Protecting the Poor Through the Fourteenth Amendment," *Harvard Law Review* 83 (November, 1969): 13; Richards, "Free Speech," pp. 73, 82; Karst, "Equal Citizenship," pp. 11, 29.

44. Dworkin, *Rights*, p. 143; Rawls, *Theory*, p. 501.

45. Robert Lane, "Government and Self-Esteem," *Political Theory* 10 (February 1982): 8, 12, 26–27.

46. Rawls, *Theory*, pp. 441–442, 450; Lane, "Self-Esteem," p. 17; Jean-Jacques Rousseau, "Discourse on the Origins and Foundations of Inequality

among Men," in *The First and Second Discourses,* ed. Roger Masters (New York: St. Martin's Press, 1964), p. 227; Rosenberg, "Unwelcome Complication," pp. 12–13, 17. See also Nathan Glazer and Daniel Patrick Moynihan, eds., *Ethnicity: Theory and Experience* (Cambridge: Harvard University Press, 1975), pp. 12, 14.

47. Rosenberg, "Unwelcome Complication," p. 21; Lane, "Self-Esteem," p. 16; M. Rosenberg and L. I. Pearlin, "Social Class and Self-Esteem among Children and Adults," *American Journal of Sociology* 84 (July 1978): 71.

48. Rawls, *Theory,* pp. 106, 311, 536.

49. Rosenberg, "Unwelcome Complication," pp. 5–9; Robert Nozick, *Anarchy, State and Utopia* (New York: Basic Books, 1974), pp. 242–243.

50. Rawls, *Theory,* pp. 543, 546. This is also the approach that Rosenberg ultimately favors. He does call for society to value "human uniqueness and diversity" positively and to specialize labor, but as he recognizes, Rawls does the same. Since valuing "diversity" still amounts to valuing everything, this stance still does not provide the necessary baseline for senses of worth, and so it still induces reliance on society's tacit, inegalitarian standards, and on groups. Hence Rosenberg too ends up hoping that affirmation by associations functioning as "mutual admiration societies" will overcome the problems he has raised with Rawls's analysis. Rosenberg, "Unwelcome Complication," pp. 15, 20–22. The following points also challenge the realism of his reliance on such societies.

51. Cf. Leon Festinger, "A Theory of Social Comparison Processes," *Human Relations* 7 (May 1954): 136; Morris Rosenberg, *Conceiving the Self* (New York: Basic Books, 1979), pp. 156, 164.

52. See Rosenberg and Pearlin, "Social Class and Self-Esteem," pp. 53, 57, 61, 71. Much of Rosenberg's own analysis relies on his extensive 1968 survey of Baltimore school children. Some studies also deal with unusually isolated groups, who are less likely to look beyond those immediately around them in self-evaluation. See e.g. L. G. Reeder, G. A. Donohue, and A. Biblarz, "Conceptions of Self and Others," *American Journal of Sociology* 66 (September 1960), pp. 153–159 (surveying military personnel on an isolated base). On the influence of social standards, see Rosenberg, *Conceiving the Self,* pp. 161, 171, 173. Rosenberg even indicates that in 1968 black children still implicitly tended to view lighter skin color as more attractive. See also M. Rosenberg and R. Simmons, *Black and White Self-Esteem* (Washington, D.C.: American Sociological Association, 1971).

53. Ralph Alan Rovner, "Ethnocultural Identity and Self-Esteem," *Human Relations* 34 (May 1981): 431. Somewhat like Rawls, Rovner points to the "de facto ethnocultural segregation" prevalent in our society to conclude that this fact is not of great concern. But our society, again, is pockmarked by the scars of prejudice. Surely on a strong egalitarian view, this "solution" must be unsatisfactory.

54. Rosenberg, *Conceiving the Self,* pp. 101–102, 168–169, 171–172; J. R. Pole, *The Pursuit of Equality in American History* (Berkeley: University of California Press, 1978), pp. 140, 339.

55. Roberto Unger elaborates this point as a dilemma of "communitarian

politics" in *Knowledge and Politics* (New York: Free Press, 1975), p. 287. See also Theodore Lowi, *The End of Liberalism,* 2d ed. (New York: W. W. Norton, 1979), pp. 280–281, 290–291.

56. Milton Gordon, *Assimilation in American Life* (New York: Oxford University Press, 1964), pp. 231–239; Gordon, *Human Nature, Class and Ethnicity* (New York: Oxford University Press, 1978), pp. 89–90, 151–152; Michael Walzer, "Pluralism: A Political Perspective," in *The Harvard Enclyclopedia of American Ethnic Groups,* ed. Stephan Thernstrom (Cambridge: Harvard University Press, 1980), p. 786.

57. Rawls, *Theory,* p. 516; Rawls, "Fairness," p. 549; Unger, *Knowledge and Politics,* p. 287. Moreover, it is unclear that the "destruction of homogeneous and relatively self-contained subcommunities through the subtle corrosion of liberal society or the direct assault of liberal social policy" is always to be welcomed, for those ways of life that do not easily "flourish in the midst of social heterogeneity" are not always worthless or repressive. William Galston, "Defending Liberalism," *American Political Science Review* 76 (September 1982): 627.

58. Rosenberg, *Conceiving the Self,* p. 188; Rosenberg, "Unwelcome Complication," pp. 16–17, 23.

8. A Liberal Theory of Political Purpose

1. For broadly similar views of liberalism's substantive values, see Sotirios A. Barber, *On What the Constitution Means* (Baltimore: Johns Hopkins University Press, 1984); William Galston, "Defending Liberalism," *American Political Science Review* 76 (September 1982): 621–629; Nathan Tarcov, *Locke's Education for Liberty* (Chicago: University of Chicago Press, 1984); Neal Wood, *The Politics of Locke's Philosophy* (Berkeley: University of California Press, 1983).

2. Robert Nozick, *Anarchy, State, and Utopia* (New York: Basic Books, 1974), p. 243.

3. Morris Rosenberg, "'Rawls' 'Unwelcome Complication': Social Status and Self Esteem," paper presented at annual meeting of International Society of Political Psychology, June 6, 1980, Boston, Mass., p. 19; David Sachs, "How to Distinguish Self-Respect from Self-Esteem," *Philosophy and Public Affairs* 10 (Fall 1981): 346–360; Michael Walzer, *Spheres of Justice* (New York: Basic Books, 1983), pp. 272–280. Cf. Stephen Darwall, "Two Kinds of Respect," *Ethics* 88 (October 1977): 36–49; Laurence Thomas, "Morality and Our Self-Concept," *The Journal of Value Inquiry* 12 (Winter 1978): 258–268.

4. Steven Lukes, *Individualism* (Oxford: Basil Blackwell, 1973), pp. 131–133, 151–152, provides a view resembling the one described here. The extent of the similarity is uncertain, however, because Lukes gives no clear argument as to why we should value human capacities for conscious self-direction, and he suggests a doctrine of "intrinsically" admirable human "excellences" that remains largely undefined.

5. Under the conditions of contemporary advanced societies, few persons

are likely to develop adequate capacities for self-guidance without public education, but under different social circumstances private training or even self-education might suffice.

6. This emphasis on preserving our capacities for critical reflection, rather than any denial that moral personality begins with inherited commitments, is what makes this view different from, and more liberal than, the renewed stress on our constitutive social identities advanced by recent critics of liberalism on the right and left. See e.g. Alasdair MacIntyre, *After Virtue* (Notre Dame: University of Notre Dame Press, 1981), pp. 204–207; Michael J. Sandel, *Liberalism and the Limits of Justice* (Cambridge, Eng.: Cambridge University Press, 1982), pp. 172, 179.

7. See C. B. Macpherson, *The Political Theory of Possessive Individualism* (New York: Oxford University Press, 1962); Roberto Mangabeira Unger, *Knowledge and Politics* (New York: Free Press, 1975); Brian Barry, *The Liberal Theory of Justice* (Oxford: Clarendon Press, 1973), p. 126; Leo Strauss, *Natural Right and History* (Chicago: University of Chicago Press, 1953); John Rawls, "Kantian Constructivism in Moral Theory: Rational and Full Autonomy," *Journal of Philosophy* 77 (September 1980): 517–518; Sandel, *Limits of Justice*, pp. 13–14.

8. Locke's position is thus defensible against Richard Rorty's charge that it conflates psychological accounts of how our ideas arise with their justification. Since Locke concedes that we cannot settle the issue of our essences, he holds that it is chiefly for purposes of moral and political philosophy that we need to treat ourselves as capable of moral agency. Different assumptions for different purposes are not irrational. This position is not far from Rorty's pragmatic endorsement of the existentialist distinction between people as empirical selves and as moral agents, an endorsement that Rorty believes supports a commitment to "Enlightenment values." For moral and political theorizing, Rorty also views it as perfectly appropriate to begin with a notion of ourselves as moral agents and to give weight to our apparent capacities for understanding, reflection, discussion, and choice. Richard Rorty, *Philosophy and the Mirror of Nature* (Princeton: Princeton University Press, 1979), pp. 139–148, 335–336, 365–366, 382.

9. Geraint Parry, *John Locke* (London: George Allen and Unwin, 1978), pp. 24, 33, 41–42; John Locke, *An Essay Concerning Human Understanding*, ed. Peter Nidditch (Oxford: Clarendon Press, 1975), pp. 6, 43, 146–148, 266, 269, 279–282.

10. See Wood, *Locke's Philosophy*, pp. 30, 94–95, 143–148, 154–161, 178–179.

11. Locke, *Essay*, pp. 43, 267, 444, 453–454, 517, 538.

12. See e.g. Andrew Milner, *John Milton and the English Revolution* (New York: Macmillan, 1981); Locke, *Essay*, pp. 264–266; John Locke, *The Conduct of the Understanding*, ed. Francis Garforth (New York: Teacher's College Press, 1966), pp. 129–130.

13. Locke, *Essay*, pp. 259–260, 264–265.

14. Ibid., p. 6; Charles Taylor, *Hegel* (Cambridge, Eng.: Cambridge University Press, 1975), p. 9; Locke, *Conduct*, pp. 129–130.

15. Locke, *Essay*, pp. 115, 335, 343, 346, 516–517.

16. Ibid., pp. 335, 341. John Dunn finds this sense of "essential unease" present from early on in Locke's writings. John Dunn, *The Political Thought of John Locke* (Cambridge, Eng.: Cambridge University Press, 1969), p. 23.

17. See Wood, *Politics*, pp. 5–7, 81–82, 94–96, 137–140, 147, 158–161; Locke, *Essay*, pp. 70–71, 349, 353–357. It remains true, however, that Locke's focus is on enabling persons to achieve a critical distance from the moral "outrages" their societies often embrace, and that he devotes little attention to the forms of social life appropriate to a liberal polity.

18. Ibid., p. 264; John Locke, *Second Treatise*, in *Two Treatises on Government*, ed. Peter Laslett (New York: New American Library, 1965), pp. 314–315, 350.

19. John Dunn, *Western Political Theory in the Face of the Future* (New York: Cambridge University Press, 1979), p. 40; Locke, *Second Treatise*, pp. 311–315; Locke, *Essay*, p. 549. Cf. Parry, *Locke*, pp. 27–28; Wood, *Politics*, pp. 145–146, 160–161.

20. Locke, *Second Treatise*, pp. 313–315; Dunn, *Western Political Theory*, p. 40. Dunn notes that Locke once speculated that if man were not divinely created, he "could have no law but his own will, no end but himself. He would be a god to himself and the satisfaction of his own will the sole measure and end of all his actions." It has been amply shown that Locke did not wish people to believe they had such absolute moral discretion.

21. Madison similarly argued that the protection of property included assuring citizens "the free use of their faculties" and that conscience "is the most sacred of all property." James Madison, *The Mind of the Founder*, ed. Marvin Meyers (Indianapolis: Bobbs-Merrill, 1973), pp. 243–245. See also Jean-Jacques Burlamaqui, *The Principles of Natural and Politic Law*, 2d ed. (London, 1763), p. 43; William Blackstone, *Commentaries on the Laws of England*, vol. I (Chicago: University of Chicago Press, 1979), p. 39; James Madison, *Notes on Debates in the Federal Convention of 1787* (New York: W. W. Norton, 1966), p. 287.

22. Michael Walzer, *The Revolution of the Saints* (New York: Atheneum Press, 1966), pp. 302–303; Donald Hanson, *From Kingdom to Commonwealth* (Cambridge: Harvard University Press, 1970), pp. 11, 31–32, 346, 372; Cecelia Kenyon, "Constitutionalism in Revolutionary America," in *Nomos XX: Constitutionalism*, ed. J. Roland Pennock and John W. Chapman (New York: New York University Press, 1979), pp. 118–119; Jean Yarbrough, "Republicanism Reconsidered," *Review of Politics* 41 (January 1979): 88, 92; Eugene F. Miller, "On the American Founders' Defense of Liberal Education in a Republic," *Review of Politics* 46 (January 1984): 65–90; Merrill D. Peterson, ed., *The Portable Thomas Jefferson* (New York: Penguin Books, 1975), pp. 198, 335; Leonard W. Levy, *Jefferson and Civil Liberties: The Darker Side* (New York: Quadrangle, 1973), pp. 9–15.

23. Ely Moore, "On Labor Unions," and Stephen Simpson, "Political Economy," in *Social Theories of Jacksonian Democracy*, ed. Joseph L. Blau (Indianapolis: Bobbs-Merrill, 1954), pp. 137, 291; Robert Faulkner, "Bickel's Constitution: The Problem of Moderate Liberalism," *American Political Science*

Review 72 (September 1978): 33; John Stuart Mill, *Three Essays* (London: Oxford University Press, 1975), pp. 42, 141; L. T. Hobhouse, *The Rational Good* (New York: Henry Holt, 1921); John Dewey, *Reconstruction in Philosophy* (Boston: Beacon Press, 1957), pp. 96–97, 162–165; John Rawls, *A Theory of Justice* (Oxford: Oxford University Press, 1971), pp. 505–506. See also Bruce Ackerman, *Social Justice in the Liberal State* (New Haven: Yale University Press, 1980), pp. 139–167, 359–371, 375. Ackerman's very insistence on giving reasons for all one's moral rules is reminiscent of Locke, and his discussion of education aims at enhancing the capacity for "independent moral judgment" that is at the heart of liberal moral character. Ackerman insists that while one can reach his position on the basis of the sort of the normative commitment described here, more skeptical grounds will equally suffice. But he acknowledges that he has not shown this convergence in detail, and the problems of neutralist positions to provide for the self-respect of all apply with particular force to his approach. Ackerman agrees that in a society bound only by neutral liberal dialogue, "overwhelming numbers" might opt for lives that seem "mean and narrow," and responds that if so, "we should at last learn what human freedom amounts to." The rational liberty view instead proposes a substantive conception of freedom that, if pursued, provides a reason for belief in human dignity.

24. Douglas R. Hofstadter, and Daniel C. Dennett, eds., *The Mind's I* (New York: Basic Books, 1981), "Introduction," pp. 10–15.

25. Rorty, *Mirror*, pp. 213–214; Milton M. Gordon, *Human Nature, Class, and Ethnicity* (New York: Oxford University Press 1978), p. 41.

26. Thomas Nagel, "What Is It Like to Be a Bat?" in Hofstadter and Dennett, *Mind's I*, pp. 392–393; Rorty, *Mirror*, pp. 382–383.

27. Even the determinist behavioral psychologist B. F. Skinner acknowledges that, as a practical imperative, we must strive to make people feel as if they are engaged in deliberative self-direction. B. F. Skinner, *Walden Two* (New York: Macmillan, 1948), pp. 257–258, 263–264.

28. Roberto Unger nevertheless terms his version of this radical position "superliberalism." Roberto Mangabeira Unger, "The Critical Legal Studies Movement," *Harvard Law Review* 96 (January 1983): 602.

29. Locke, *Essay*, p. 10; Jefferson, "Letter to David Rittenhouse," in Peterson, *Portable Jefferson*, p. 362. John Dunn also described Locke's moral "self-reproach for the independent single-mindedness of his own past intellectual activity." Dunn, *John Locke*, p. 232.

30. Dunn, *John Locke*, pp. 231–232. Dunn concluded (p. 260) that Locke "*did* continue to take seriously the problem of preserving rationality for the lives of all men." Neal Wood has objected that Locke did not really think of the poor and laboring classes as part of the "people," but as a "breed apart," less capable of rationality. Yet he undermines this assertion by conceding that Locke thought that rationality "cut across class lines," that the propertied gentry might realize their rational potential less fully than craftsmen, and that differences in rationality "stem largely from environment and education." Wood, *Politics*, pp. 35, 115–118, 194.

31. Aristotle, *The Politics*, ed. Ernest Barker (Oxford: Oxford University Press, 1958), pp. 5–6.

32. For example, David Richards, the most prolific exponent of neo-Kantian constitutionalism, supports a right to suicide and virtually unlimited rights to pornography and refuses to adopt any special presumptions in favor of family relationships. These positions emphasize unbridled personal autonomy more than does the rational liberty view, which esteems human capacities for reflective self-direction, and the human relationships that are ordinarily most conducive to their flourishing, too much to regard conduct destructive of those capacities and relationships as presumptively equally legitimate. David A. J. Richards, "The Individual, the Family and the Constitution: A Jurisprudential Perspective," *New York University Law Review* 55 (April 1980): 1–62; Richards, "Free Speech and Obscenity Law: Toward a Moral Theory of the First Amendment," *University of Pennsylvania Law Review* 123 (November 1974): 45–91; Richards, *The Moral Criticism of Law* (Encino, Cal.: Dickerson, 1977).

33. See e.g. H. L. A. Hart, "Between the Utility and Rights," *Columbia Law Review* 79 (June 1979): 839, 841, 844; Bruce Ackerman, *Private Property and the Constitution* (New Haven: Yale University Press, 1977), pp. 279–280.

34. Peter Gabel, "Book Review, 'Taking Rights Seriously,'" *Harvard Law Review* 91 (November 1977): 312–315.

35. Ronald Dworkin, for example, argues that we can restrict pornography only when it can be shown to harm others directly, because the state cannot express the judgment "that those who do enjoy pornography have worse character on that account." Ronald Dworkin, "Is There a Right to Pornography?" *Oxford Journal of Legal Studies* 1 (Summer, 1981): 195–196. Rawls does describe evaluations of moral character that his position makes possible, but these evaluations are all in terms of why a person has violated his principles of justice, and they do not alter his insistence that we must not evaluate those who have not committed overtly unjust acts. Rawls, *A Theory of Justice*, pp. 437, 442, 510.

36. Ibid., pp. 20–21, 49; Barry, *Liberal Theory*, p. 126.

37. Admittedly, the rational liberty theory would provide no legal protection either for views that a society's legislatures, executive agencies, courts, and political parties all deem to be not just wrong but dangerously antirational or for subgroups that are overwhelmingly considered incapable of rational thought. However, no preestablished principles are likely to oppose such a consensus effectively, and recognition and respect for human deliberative capacities seem as likely as any moral view to unmask unjustifiable biases and corrode them over time.

38. Contemporary American education is predominantly devoted either to the development of skills needed by the economy or to the "progressive" aim of unleashing student "creativity." Christopher Hurn, *The Limits and Possibilities of Schooling* (Boston: Allyn and Bacon, 1978), pp. 31–33. The rational liberty view suggests a more Jeffersonian goal. Education should not simply inculcate the knowledge and abilities necessary to function in society but should also include a moral component. Students should be required to reflect systematically on the

possible modes of life, values and ideals, and forms of satisfaction open to them, and this reflection should be presented as morally estimable.

39. There are also problems concerning resident and temporary aliens. If native birth confers citizenship, as in the United States, it may be argued that the only aliens are those who have chosen to come, knowing the restrictions that will be placed upon them. Hence these restrictions may seem legitimate. But on a rational liberty view, even voluntarily accepted restraints can never amount to a denial of respect for the basic liberties of the aliens—a principle that American law honors in theory but does not adequately realize in practice. See e.g. Peter H. Schuck, "The Transformation of Immigration Law," *Columbia Law Review* 84 (January 1984): 1–90.

9. Rational Liberty and Constitutional Problems

1. Jerome Frank, *Law and the Modern Mind* (Garden City, N.Y.: Anchor Books, 1963); Frank, "Are Judges Human?" *University of Pennsylvania Law Review* 80 (November 1931): 17; Ronald Dworkin, *Taking Rights Seriously* (Cambridge: Harvard University Press, 1978), pp. 1–149, 340, 342; Dworkin, "The Forum of Principle," *New York University Law Review* 56 (May–June 1981): 469–518; Stanley Fish, *Is There a Text in This Class?* (Cambridge: Harvard University Press, 1980), pp. 303–321; H. L. A. Hart, *The Concept of Law* (Oxford: Clarendon Press, 1961), p. 86; William F. Harris, II, "Bonding Word and Polity," *American Political Science Review* 76 (March 1982): 34–45.

2. See e.g. Sanford Levinson, "Law as Literature," Ronald Dworkin, "Law as Interpretation," and Stanley Fish, "Working on the Chain Gang: Interpretation in Law and Literature," *Texas Law Review* 60 (March 1982): 373–403, 527–567.

3. Bruce Ackerman, *Private Property and the Constitution* (New Haven: Yale University Press, 1977), pp. 11–13, 24. Cf. Laurence Tribe, *American Constitutional Law* (Mineola, N.Y.: Foundation Press, 1978), pp. iii, 1137, 1139, suggesting we avoid "generalization" about constitutional roles and purposes and instead seek "particular decision structures for particular sustantive purposes in particular contexts."

4. See Rogers M. Smith, "Constitutional Interpretation and Political Theory," *Polity* 15 (Summer 1983): 492–514.

5. Stanley Fish and Ronald Dworkin agree that legal interpretation is ultimately political, involving reliance on the judges' views of the proper nature of the political system. They disagree on what this fact means for interpretive practices. Dworkin is worried lest anyone think this view means that judges may simply follow their own subjective values, and he insists they are constrained by a requirement to provide a theory of the legal enterprise that largely accounts for its past decisions and institutional principles. Fish maintains there is no way to constrain judicial subjectivity, understood as reliance on the judges' own notions about what past decisions and principles permit, and no need to constrain judicial subjectivity, understood as absolute arbitrariness or idiosyncrasy. Any constraints on interpretation must themselves be interpreted by judges; their

discretion is therefore inescapable. But their own understanding as judges is shaped in innumerable intangible ways by the prevailing assumptions, norms, and expectations of the legal community that socialized them. They are unlikely to be able to depart radically from its conventions, and if they did so, their action would by definition be unrecognizable as a legal decision within the conventions of that community. Dworkin, "Law as Interpretation," pp. 544–550; Fish, "Chain Gang," pp. 552–559, 562.

By describing constitutional adjudication as a means of achieving agreement, or choosing among, distinct but overlapping political visions, the account here may aid this dispute. Fish seems right that imaginative interpreters can overcome most constraints conventional ones see in precedents. But Dworkin fears the possibility that the shared assumptions and enterprises of an interpretive community may break down over time, bringing an end to that enterprise and community as forms of social life. In particular, if the legal community's sense of shared assumptions and standards becomes eroded because of the prevalence of arguments that only a part of the community regards as valid legal discourse, for good reasons or bad, then it becomes more difficult to sustain the enterprise of law. For better or worse, American law is not about to go away. But it is not unthinkable that the legal enterprise will be carried on with increasing cynicism and attendant self-seeking, rendering it less satisfactory to all concerned. Some leading academic lawyers believe we are tending in this direction. See e.g. Levinson, "Law as Literature"; Paul Brest, "The Fundamental Rights Controversy: The Essential Contradictions of Normative Constitutional Scholarship," *Yale Law Journal* 90 (April 1981): 1063–1109; Roberto Mangabeira Unger, "The Critical Legal Studies Movement," *Harvard Law Review* 96 (January 1983): 561–675.

But if we accept that legal interpretations rely on contrasting political visions, and if we then strive to identify their areas of agreement and to clarify what is being lost when we are compelled to choose one over another, the processes of persuasion in the legal community may be more widely understood, open, and honest. Such processes seem more likely than any alternative to limit cynicism and distrust of opponents, to produce more stable compromises, and to sustain a sense of shared understandings. Positions that deny or limit the political nature of interpretation, and even Dworkin's efforts to limit this aspect, fly in the face of common experience today. Fish's assurance that genuinely illegitimate arguments are not a danger equally fails to take seriously the sense of lack of common standards that practitioners of legal persuasion currently report.

6. Herbert Packer, *The Limits of the Criminal Sanction* (Stanford: Stanford University Press, 1968), pp. 149–173; Edward Chase, "The Burger Court, the Individual, and the Criminal Process," *New York University Law Review* 52 (June 1977): 518–597; Yale Kamisar, "The Warren Court (Was It Really So Defense-Minded?), the Burger Court (Is It Really So Prosecution-Oriented?), and Police Investigatory Practices," in Vincent Blasi, ed., *The Burger Court* (New Haven: Yale University Press, 1983).

7. See Charles E. Silberman, *Criminal Violence, Criminal Justice* (New York: Vintage Books, 1978), pp. 410–415.

8. Leonard Levy, *Origins of the Fifth Amendment* (New York: Oxford University Press, 1968); Robert Justin Goldstein, *Political Repression in Modern America* (Cambridge: Schenkman, 1978), pp. 285–574. Even Kent Greenawalt, who opposes any broad right against self-incrimination, admits that the case for the guarantee has great strength in the two cases cited, when an innocent person legitimately fears political or simply erroneous prosecution. He believes these instances are too few to justify the "fearful price" the liberty exacts on the system's ability to convict the guilty. Kent Greenawalt, "The Right to Silence," *William and Mary Law Review* 23 (Fall 1981): 37, 45, 47. But there is little solid evidence that the right involves such a price. And the McCarthy era of governmental witch hunts is not so remote as to render Fifth Amendment protections obsolete.

9. *Miranda v. Arizona*, 384 U.S. 436 (1966). Cooperation with the police or a court may also raise the threat of criminal prosecution of persons close to us, and this can be claimed to endanger our own rational self-direction. But we can rarely know the innocence or guilt of others as we do our own. We are, moreover, limited in our rights to try to govern their lives. Given the danger of using the right to remain silent to protect the guilty, the language properly states that the right can be invoked only when one is being required to witness against oneself.

10. This similarity is unfortunate, since the reasonable expectations of privacy test has proven so ambiguous as to be of dubious worth. See e.g. Rogers M. Smith, "The Constitution and Autonomy," *Texas Law Review* 60 (February 1982): 198, 201–203. But the ambiguity is traceable to the Fourth Amendment's stricture against only unreasonable searches and seizures, and the rational liberty approach is at least true to the concern to preserve the boundaries of rational conduct that language suggests. Less ambiguous tests probably have less affinity with the historic philosophy underlying the clause, and they might well fit less naturally into an interpretation that can be applied consistently to all the Constitution's clauses.

11. See Silberman, *Criminal Justice*, pp. 4, 271, 344, 354–357; *Report to the Nation on Crime and Justice: The Data* (Washington, D.C.: Bureau of Justice Statistics), esp. pp. 6–9; David Rudovsky, "The Criminal Justice System and the Role of the Police," in David Kairys, ed., *The Politics of Law* (New York: Pantheon Books, 1982), p. 247; James Q. Wilson, *Thinking about Crime*, rev. ed. (New York: Basic Books, 1983), p. 14; Jerome H. Skolnick, *Justice Without Trial*, 2d ed. (New York: John Wiley & Sons, 1975), pp. 227–245. The rational liberty theory does not support denying legitimate liberties to some simply so that others can exercise and enjoy their liberties more fully, but it does justify infringements in cases where some liberties must be denied to preserve the basic capacities of others for rational self-direction—where, for example, a wave of terrorist murders cannot be stilled without greater discretion to search individuals.

12. See Wilson, *Thinking about Crime*, pp. 117–144, 156–177; Silberman, *Criminal Justice*, pp. 247–248, 254, 256–259. Those who believe the American criminal justice system enforces property and personal rights that constitute an exploitative and repressive economic and political order will reject these defenses of punishment. But in contemporary America judges cannot plausibly claim that

the bulk of the criminal law punishes conduct which society believes to be integral to the rational self-direction of some and consistent with respect for the liberties of others. Most law would therefore have to be found within the bounds of permissible legislative choice, with the exception of archaic, badly designed, or politically repressive criminal laws. Cf. Mark Kelman, "The Origins of Crime and Criminal Violence," and William J. Chambliss, "Toward a Radical Criminology," in Kairys, *Politics of Law*, pp. 220–221, 233–235.

13. Silberman, *Criminal Justice*, pp. 258, 404–409; Wilson, *Thinking about Crime*, pp. 4–5, 131–137; *Time*, Sept. 13, 1982, pp. 40–41; Michael E. Sherman and Gordon Hawkins, *Imprisonment in America: Choosing the Future* (Chicago: University of Chicago Press, 1981).

14. Smith, "Autonomy," pp. 183–184, 189–198; Wilson, *Thinking about Crime*, pp. 237–238, 247–249.

15. John Hart Ely, *Democracy and Distrust* (Cambridge: Harvard University Press, 1980), pp. 28–29, 196–197.

16. My comments here will be aimed at defining these interests for purposes of substantive due process. Since *Board of Regents* v. *Roth*, 408 U.S. 564 (1972), much procedural due process has been devoted to defining not only what procedures are required but when they are necessary, through largely novel inquiries into whether liberty or property interests exist in particular cases. These inquiries represent a partial reaction to cases such as *Goldberg* v. *Kelly*, 397 U.S. 254 (1970), and *Bell* v. *Burson*, 402 U.S. 535 (1971), which held that a due process hearing was required before termination of various governmental benefits, viewed as statutory entitlements and hence forms of property. It would take us too far afield to explore these cases here, but I should note that the rational liberty approach repudiates the positivistic definition of basic liberty or property interests, and the procedures they entail, wholly in terms of statutory provisions and explicit Bill of Rights guarantees, as urged by Justice Rehnquist. *Arnett* v. *Kennedy*, 416 U.S. 134 (1974); *Paul* v. *Davis*, 424 U.S. 693 (1976). Instead, it demands protection for any interest falling within the scope of social standards for behavior that is rationally self-directed and consistent with concern for the similar liberties for others. It thus is closer to the Court majority's usual reference to social conceptions of liberty and property. *Bell* v. *Wolfish*, 441 U.S. 520 (1979); *Vitek* v. *Jones*, 445 U.S. 480 (1980).

17. Ronald Dworkin has argued that there is no general right to liberty because it does not make sense to think of all liberties as parts of one commodity, to be maximized in whatever form it appears. Yet to distinguish qualitatively among liberties, Dworkin thinks we need a standard beyond liberty itself, which he takes to be equal concern and respect. Dworkin, *Taking Rights Seriously*, pp. 266–278. The necessary distinctions among liberties can be obtained, however, by differentiating reflective self-direction, or liberty, from merely following one's impulses; and by differentiating conduct integral to reflective self-direction from conduct consistent with but not essential to it. These distinctions allow us to say what Dworkin thinks a view based on a right to liberty cannot, that denial of freedoms of political expression is a more fundamental violation of liberty than denial of freedom to drive the wrong way on one-way streets.

18. Intermediate scrutiny, adopted by the Court more or less explicitly in *Craig* v. *Boren,* 429 U.S. 190 (1977), calls for determining whether gender classifications serve "important governmental objectives" by means that are "substantially related" to the achievement of those goals. It thus falls between the minimal scrutiny test's requirement that classifications be reasonably related to legitimate objectives and the strict scrutiny test's demand that classifications be necessary for compelling state interests. Marshall has called for abandoning this structure in favor of an explicit "sliding scale," with scrutiny varying according to constitutional weight of the interests involved. *San Antonio Ind. School Dist.* v. *Rodriguez,* 411 U.S. 1 (1973) at 70. Because the Court's scrutiny of due process interests parallels the fundamental interests strand of equal protection analysis, adoption of Marshall's approach would probably presage a similar due process jurisprudence. On the comparative democratic merits of judicial activism, see e.g. Jesse H. Choper, *Judicial Review and the National Political Process* (Chicago: University of Chicago Press, 1980), pp. 4–59.

19. While these constitute due process liberties that a liberal state should not infringe without compelling reasons, the state can also be held to have duties to protect such rights against others and to provide the conditions for their meaningful exercise. If, under the rational liberty view, the Fourteenth Amendment is held to create state obligations to protect such basic liberties against private infringement, the theory also provides a basis for finding state inactions to be action reachable under the Fourteenth and Fifteenth Amendments. See Tribe, *American Constitutional Law,* pp. 1147–1174.

20. While determining if a certain activity is significant to someone else may seem difficult, this inquiry does not differ greatly from the Court's examination of the sincerity of religious claims in free exercise cases. See e.g. *U.S.* v. *Ballard,* 322 U.S. 78 (1944); *Wisconsin* v. *Yoder,* 406 U.S. 205 (1972). The inquiry would not ordinarily parallel the inquiry that the Court refuses to undertake into how vital a precept is to a litigant's religious belief system, because it would focus rather on how far people's conduct and ways of life show the importance of the claimed liberty to them, not on analysis of their articulated philosophies.

21. *Shapiro* v. *Thompson,* 394 U.S. 618 (1969); *Pierce* v. *Society of Sisters,* 268 U.S. 510 (1925); *Moore* v. *East Cleveland,* 431 U.S. 494 (1977); *Zablocki* v. *Redhail,* 434 U.S. 374 (1978); Robert McCloskey, "Economic Due Process and the Supreme Court: An Exhumation and Reburial," *Supreme Court Review, 1962* (Chicago: University of Chicago Press, 1963): pp. 34, 46; Tribe, *American Constitutional Law,* pp. 948–953. The Court (arguably) recognized a freedom to pursue one's vocation as fundamental. *Hampton* v. *Mow Sun Wong,* 426 U.S. 88 (1976) at 102.

22. *Kelley* v. *Johnson,* 425 U.S. 238 (1976); *Hollenbaugh* v. *Carnegie Free Library,* 439 U.S. 1052 (1978). The view also might support giving only minimal protection to the claim of unrelated college students to reside together temporarily in *Village of Belle Terre* v. *Boraas,* 416 U.S. 1 (1974), although the ordinance in question seems overbroad. My students assure me, however, that strict scrutiny is required; and if student litigants could show that living together in a particular neighborhood was vital to them, perhaps due to a paucity of housing alternatives,

a compelling justification for the restraint would be necessary. The gay rights claimed in *Doe* v. *Commonwealth's Attorney*, 425 U.S. 901 (1976) pose an even more difficult issue. It seems certain that at times in the past the overwhelming judgment of American society has been that homosexual conduct was beyond the range of rational self-direction and corrosive of essential moral values. Some state laws still reflect such beliefs, but today there is much wider acceptance of the rationality of accepting homosexual inclinations and incorporating them into a reflectively guided pattern of life. The success of state and local drives for legislative reform, the removal of homosexuality from the category of mental illness by American psychiatrists, and the election of gays to public office in some localities are proof of this change. Hence homosexuality can no longer be placed outside the bounds of rationally adopted conduct; and since it is integral to the self-direction of many persons, the issue now is whether the restraints upon it serve compelling state interests. Many would still argue that they do, and while I do not share this opinion, for the present a "rational liberty" judge might still decide that the issue must be left to the evolving deliberations of the community for clarification. Despite the existence of organizations working to alter current laws, nothing like the same ambiguity exists in American attitudes on the harmfulness of other forms of sexual conduct, such as intercourse with children and incest.

23. While the rational liberty view thus accords fundamental status to freedom for most expression, it treats this freedom as an aspect of the basic aim of promoting rational liberty, not as an independently justified right. Cf. Frederick Schauer, *Free Speech: A Philosophical Enquiry* (New York: Cambridge University Press, 1982).

24. As John Hart Ely has pointed out, the standard formula for such restrictions, "time, place and manner," invites abuse due to the vagueness of the term "manner." He and Laurence Tribe therefore try to achieve the goals of such restraints by distinguishing between regulations aimed at the communicative and noncommunicative aspects of expression and permitting more regulation of the noncommunicative. This distinction presents practical difficulties of its own, however, so it seems sufficient to make the manner element more specific and to emphasize that other forums for the expression must be available if speech is constrained on these grounds. Ely, *Democracy and Distrust*, pp. 111–116, 231–232; Tribe, *American Constitutional Law*, pp. 580–584, 682–688.

25. Again this test relies on community standards of what is consistent with preserving personal capacities for rational self-direction. It is thus distinct from T. M. Scanlon's original formulation of his "Millian principle" for freedom of expression, which allowed an individual to apply "his own canons of rationality" in his self-guidance. T. M. Scanlon, "A Theory of Freedom of Expression," in Ronald Dworkin, ed., *The Philosophy of Law* (New York: Oxford University Press, 1977), p. 162. Subsequently, Scanlon appears to have moved closer to the position described here, finding his original formulation too restrictive of "justified paternalism," and defending "autonomy understood as a good to be promoted." But he suggests this conception of autonomy is "vague, somewhat grandiloquent, and perhaps misleading"; so while we agree on some points, I

hesitate to judge how close Scanlon actually is to the concept of rational liberty. Scanlon, "Freedom of Expression and Categories of Expression," *University of Pittsburgh Law Review* 40 (Summer 1979): 532–533.

26. The distinction proposed here, between cognitive communication that can aid reflective deliberation and communication that is noncognitive in form and substance, appears more precise than Frederick Schauer's related but somewhat tenuous distinction between "communication," which has "intended intellectual appeal," and the "communicative potential of physical acts." He would deem the latter "action," not "communication" for purposes of free speech protection. But it is not "action with communicative potential" that is unrelated to the purposes of the First Amendment. It is, as he partly recognizes, communication that does not assist the processes of cognitive deliberation. Hence his categories seem improperly drawn. Schauer, *Free Speech*, pp. 182–184.

27. See e.g. Alec Craig, *Suppressed Books* (Cleveland: World, 1963, pp. 36–37); *The Report to the Task Force on Pornography and Obscenity* (New York: Stein and Day, 1970), p. 51; David A. J. Richards, "Free Speech and Obscenity Law: Toward a Moral Theory of the First Amendment," *University of Pennsylvania Law Review* 123 (November 1974): 62, 68; Kenneth Karst, "Equality as a Central Principle of the First Amendment," *University of Chicago Law Review* 43 (Fall 1975): 20.

28. See Scanlon, "Categories of Expression," p. 548.

29. Even David Richards, who praises obscenity for conveying a vision of a "pornotopia," admits that some sadistic obscenity, at least, portrays improper acts and so may have a "deleterious effect on some fundamental democratic virtue." Richards, "Obscenity Law," pp. 68, 81, 88.

30. The position would thus confirm the result in *New York v. Ferber*, 458 U.S. 747 (1982), where the Court sustained a state ban on the sale of visual child pornography, accepting it as the only effective means to prevent the use of children in the production of such materials. Because the rational liberty definition focuses on threats to capacities for rational self-direction, not on explicit sexual portrayals per se, the approach would include more of this material under its obscenity exception to full First Amendment protection than the Court was able to do. Thus, unlike the Court, the theory need not significantly expand its exceptions to full First Amendment coverage to reach this result. The position would, however, face the difficulty, which produced dispute in *Ferber*, of whether depictions of sexual activity by children in works that are not obscene under its standards, such as medical textbooks, can be deemed sufficiently harmful to basic constitutional values to warrant restraint. My surmise, like the Court's, is that the harm to the capacities for rational liberty of the children involved in the making of such materials should usually qualify as a compelling interest that could survive even strict scrutiny of bans on such nonobscene publications. For a summary of the Skokie controversy, see Gerald Gunther, *Cases and Materials on Constitutional Law*, 10th ed. (Mineola, N.Y.: Foundation Press, 1980), pp. 1275–1278.

31. On the value of a "buffer zone," see Schauer, *Free Speech*, p. 187.

32. While many artistic works also may be aimed at affecting emotional attitudes rather than informing, they usually do not do so chiefly to further an

economic enterprise; and although some works, such as popular novels, might be so aimed, their harmlessness from a rational liberty standpoint, combined with the practical difficulties of distinguishing them from works with artistic aspirations, indicate that as a class they should be accorded full First Amendment protection.

33. *Gray v. Sanders*, 372 U.S. 368 (1963); Douglas Rae, *The Political Consequences of Electoral Laws*, rev. ed. (New Haven: Yale University Press, 1971), pp. 96–99.

34. See Paul T. David and James W. Ceaser et al., *Proportional Representation in Presidential Nominating Politics* (Charlottesville: University Press of Virginia, 1980), pp. 64–71. Cf. Enid Lakeman, *How Democracies Vote*, 3d ed. (London: Faber and Faber, 1970).

35. The view therefore supports the revival of judicial attention to the excessive delegation of legislative power that Theodore Lowi, especially, has forcefully advocated. It differs from his espousal of "juridical democracy" primarily because it not only advocates processes that lead to the legislative and administrative adoption of clear standards and purposes but also sets forth a sense of what those purposes should be. Theodore Lowi, *The End of Liberalism*, 2d ed. (New York: W. W. Norton, 1979), pp. 92–126, 298–313.

36. For an unpersuasive example of the first claim, see *Karcher v. Daggett*, 77 L. Ed. 2d 133 (1983). For a somewhat more convincing instance of the second claim, see *Abate v. Mundt*, 403 U.S. 182 (1971).

37. *Lucas v. Forty-Fourth General Assembly of Colorado*, 377 U.S. 713 (1964).

38. See *Gaffney v. Cummings*, 412 U.S. 735 (1973), esp. at 752–754; *Karcher v. Daggett*, 77 L. Ed. 2d 133 (1983); *White v. Weiser*, 412 U.S. 783 (1973); Robert G. Dixon, *Democratic Representation* (New York: Oxford University Press, 1968), pp. 457–458, 537–543.

39. *Mobile v. Bolden*, 446 U.S. 55 (1980).

40. Robert Lane, "Government and Self-Esteem," *Political Theory* 10 (February 1982): 13, 26–27.

41. Although it can be difficult to tell when regulation of a trade amounts to a denial of opportunities to enter it, this problem seems no greater than the issue of when a regulation becomes a taking within the scope of the just compensation clause. See Ackerman, *Private Property*.

42. *Williamson v. Lee Optical Co.*, 348 U.S. 483 (1955); *Kotch v. Board of River Pilots Commissioners*, 330 U.S. 552 (1947).

43. Cf. Kenneth Karst, "Foreword: Equal Citizenship under the Fourteenth Amendment," *Harvard Law Review* 91 (November 1977): 6, 40–41, 61–63.

44. *San Antonio School District v. Rodriguez*, 411 U.S. 1 (1973), esp. at 70; Alexander Bickel, *The Least Dangerous Branch* (Indianapolis: Bobbs-Merrill, 1962), pp. 143, 240.

· Index of Cases

· General Index